# *Chan Rhetoric of Uncertainty* *in the* Blue Cliff Record

# Chan Rhetoric of Uncertainty in the *Blue Cliff Record*

*Sharpening a Sword at the Dragon Gate*

STEVEN HEINE

OXFORD
UNIVERSITY PRESS

# OXFORD
UNIVERSITY PRESS

Oxford University Press is a department of the University of Oxford. It furthers
the University's objective of excellence in research, scholarship, and education
by publishing worldwide. Oxford is a registered trade mark of Oxford University
Press in the UK and certain other countries.

Published in the United States of America by Oxford University Press
198 Madison Avenue, New York, NY 10016, United States of America.

© Oxford University Press 2016

Cataloging-in-Publication data is on file at the Library of Congress
ISBN 978–0–19–939776–1 (hbk); 978–0–19–939777–8 (pbk)

1 3 5 7 9 8 6 4 2
Printed by Webcom, Canada

# *Contents*

# *Preface*

IN THE SUMMER of 2015 I had the opportunity to visit Mount Jiashan, the Buddhist temple located in a relatively remote spot of northwestern Hunan province that was the main site where the original lectures commenting on Chan gongan (J. kōan) cases with verses by Xuedou were delivered by master Yuanwu in the early 1100s and were published more than a decade later as the *Blue Cliff Record*. The text had a rocky early history in that, following considerable initial fanfare, it was apparently lost or destroyed within two decades after publication, but then it was recovered and brought a century and a half later to Japan, where it has ever since been celebrated and cherished. There are also legends that, in the intervening years, Japanese pilgrims to the mainland, including Dōgen, were shown copies of the collection during a long phase in which, to the best of our understanding based mainly on a lack of citations, it was otherwise kept out of mainstream circulation. In recent years the text is once again being studied and appreciated in China even as we must still grapple with the complex legacy of the collection.

The main goal of my trip was to gain a better sense of the significance of some of these mysterious developments. The visit at once confirmed and overturned many of my assumptions and expectations. It was intriguing to learn that with the ongoing revival of traditional Buddhist sites in China today, the temple is now promoting the heritage of its "three treasures," about which some legends and rumors were no doubt being mixed or conflated. One of the treasures is the text of the classic gongan commentary, recently printed in a new edition that includes a rendering in modern Chinese and is sold in a shop there. Another treasure is the Blue Cliff Spring, as shown in Figure 0.1, which is situated down the hill from the temple buildings and supposedly inspired the lectures and also helped create the third treasure of tea.

**FIGURE O.I** Author visiting Blue Cliff Spring in Hunan province. Jiashan Temple, courtesy of the author.

Because of the supposedly perfect balance in the water (hard to believe in smog-ridden China), this purity helped lead to the famous saying, "Chan and Tea Have One Taste," which was written on a scroll attributed to Yuanwu, although the practice of linking the beverage with meditation preceded his tenure as abbot. Meanwhile I was not surprised to find that near the spring a man-made lake was built for boating and a new "ancient street" for entertaining tourists with old-fashioned cultural attractions including tea was under construction. As in many well-traveled places in China these days, when something is called ancient this can mean it is actually a year or two old.

It struck me that the most important feature being promoted was not religious but political. Based on another legend that is highly contested the temple claims that Li Zicheng, a late Ming rebel who was able to declare himself King Dashun in Beijing for forty-eight days before being vanquished by Qing invaders, retired after his battles to these grounds where he lived in retreat for nearly thirty years. A colossal mausoleum along with a museum dedicated to memorializing the warrior, who also wrote dozens of poems about plum blossoms, is the largest structure on the compound. Another political aspect is that the only temple building that is older than thirty years is a hall that was once used by soldiers in the Long March, who scrawled, "Death to wealthy landlords," on the rear wall, which ensured that it was preserved during the Cultural Revolution; otherwise the temple was entirely rebuilt over the past decades, especially since the time of a visit by Jiang Zemin in the mid-1990s, and now it is designated a four-star tourist site (out of five).

One experience that amused me was a sign hung over the urinal in the men's room that cautioned, "Lean forward a step so you won't drip urine" 向前一步靠.滴水不外漏. This headline was accompanied by an explanation of a passage from Yuanwu's recorded sayings suggesting, "The Barrier of Jiashan means stepping back three hundred paces." Another Chan paradox, I thought, while pondering that after my nearly fifty years of studies of Chan it had all come down to that one drop of pee! Meanwhile a friend pointed out that similar signs are common in China as part of a campaign since the 2008 Olympics to encourage "civilized behavior" (*wenming*), but this may be the only example featuring a Buddhist interpretation.

On a more serious note, I was interested to find a stele near the spring inscribed with a poem titled, "From Above Jiashan Temple," by Li Qunyu 李群玉 (813–860), a famous Tang dynasty poet:

> *The cloister is filled with the sound of the spring, and the temple halls*
> *    feel refreshed,*
> *Through an opening in the curtain, the light rain carries the scent of*
> *    forested pines.*
> *Gazing to the south from the eastern peak, the moon appears through*
> *    the raindrops,*
> *And is smiling, while its golden light gently touches the cool*
> *    waters below.*

夾山寺上方. 滿院泉聲山殿涼. 疏簾微雨野松香. 東峰下視南溟月. 笑踏金波看海光.

Note that the last character in the first line is typically used in poetry to mean a qualitative sense of what is "cool," much the way we say today "that feels cool," but it is also tinged with a poignant quality. Also "moon appears" is not quite literal but emphasizes the personality of nature as expressed in the next line, and since this site is nowhere near the ocean or a large body of water (other than a man-made lake) the literal reference to "sea" 海 in the last phrase is taken to refer to the spring itself that appeared grander than what it is (or maybe it was different then).

During the visit I was most deeply influenced by the retelling by representatives of the temple of their version of the story of how the *Blue Cliff Record* came to Japan—a historical puzzle that had become my scholarly kōan. According to this account, which I feel rings true despite its indebtedness to hagiography, during increasingly difficult times for Chan under shifting political circumstances in its native land there was an impetus on the part of various temple leaders to transfer important documents for safekeeping to another country that was newly interested and eager to learn the intricacies of this religious philosophy and practice. Eventually, one way or another, this effort was successful.

The people I spoke with at Jiashan were also happy to acknowledge that following the Cultural Revolution it was the Japanese who, after keeping alive the legacy of the temple for centuries, came to China and taught them the history of gongan/kōan training as well as the role of tea ceremony. They enthusiastically told the story, illustrated in Figure 0.2 as part of a series of drawings on the history of the temple, of a tea master who came from Kyoto in the early 1990s to taste the water from Blue Cliff Spring. He declared that it was perfectly suited to preparing the beverage. A temple website also states that in 1998 Professor Ishii Shūdō of Komazawa University, who has mentored me and numerous Western scholars, led a delegation of authorities who gave instruction on the history of the *Blue Cliff Record* and its impact on Japanese Zen.

Meanwhile back in Hangzhou, I was pleased to see the inscription on a new stele composed by a mayor of Gifu city in Japan, which sent a

**FIGURE 0.2** Japanese tea master at Blue Cliff Spring in the early 1990s. Jiashan temple, courtesy of the author.

regiment to the Nanjing area including Shanghai and Hangzhou in the 1930s, that helps today inspire the spirit of transnational cooperation to which interactions fostered by Buddhism and Buddhist studies contribute. The saying in Figure 0.3 proclaims, "No more war between Japan and China." This motivated me to begin writing my next book, which is a study of transition and transformation of Chinese Chan to Japanese Zen in the thirteenth and fourteenth centuries.

There are many people I wish to thank for their ongoing help and support, especially Ishii Seijun, Ishii Shūdō, and Matsumoto Shirō, all from Komazawa University in Tokyo, in addition to my good friend and colleague Mali (Li Ma), who accompanied me on the trip to Jiashan. I am particularly grateful to Kazuaki Tanahashi for providing the cover calligraphy and two more pieces in the main body of the book. I appreciate the many useful ideas that came out of a seminar on the *Blue Cliff Record* I gave in the fall semester of 2014; and I also thank participants and former FIU

**FIGURE 0.3** "No More War Between Japan and China." Hangzhou Park, courtesy of the author.

Asian Studies MA students Greg Bryant and Ian Verhine, who both continued to discuss and assist me with some of the technical materials in the
manuscript. Maria Sol Echarren and Rebecca Richko also helped with the
editing process in addition to polishing the images.

Some of the materials in the book appeared in two articles of a special
issue of *Frontiers of History of China* that I edited: "Introduction: Fourth-
Wave Studies of Chan/Zen Buddhist Discourse," *Frontiers of History of
China* 8/3 (2013), 309–315; and "Unintended Baggage? Rethinking Yuanwu
Keqin's View of the Role of Language in Chan Gongan Discourse," *Frontiers*

**FIGURE 0.4** Sites related to *Blue Cliff Record*, courtesy of the author.

*of History of China* 8/3 (2013), 316–341. This topic, for which research was supported in part by Japan Foundation funding, was presented in several venues, especially the 2012 annual meeting of the Association for Asian Studies held in Toronto and a retreat at the Upaya Zen Center in Santa Fe in July 2015. Unless otherwise noted, translations are mine. The map in Figure 0.4 shows sites in China related to the formation of the *Blue Cliff Record.*

# Chan Rhetoric of Uncertainty
## in the Blue Cliff Record

# *I*

# *Prolegomenon to a New Hermeneutic*

## ON BEING UNCERTAIN ABOUT UNCERTAINTY

## *Certain of Uncertainty?*

My aim in this book is to provide a critical textual and innovative discursive analysis in light of Song dynasty (960–1279) Chinese cultural and intellectual historical trends of the inventive rhetorical style and its intimate relation to the fundamental religious message of the *Blue Cliff Record* 碧巖錄 (C. *Biyanlu*, J. *Hekiganroku*). This collection, in which Yuanwu Keqin (1063–1135, aka Foguo Yuanwu) provides various kinds of prose remarks regarding one hundred gongan/kōan 公案 cases that were originally selected and given poetic comments by Xuedou Chongxian (980–1052, aka Mingjue), is recognized as the seminal Chan Buddhist commentary. It has long been celebrated for its use of intricate and articulate interpretative devices as the masterpiece or "premier work of the Chan school" 禪門第一書 (or 宗門第一書) that has greatly influenced the development of the tradition for nearly a thousand years.

The spiritual vision expressed in the *Blue Cliff Record*, apparently originally known as the *Blue Cliff Collection* 碧巖集 (C. *Biyanji*, J. *Hekiganshū*), with the title undergoing a change in the Edo period in Japan,[1] is based on what I refer to as the principle of "uncertainty," which indicates a resourceful approach to discourse that is characterized by fundamental ambiguity and purposeful inconclusiveness. This approach places full responsibility for attaining self-realization on the individual trainee, who through engaging multiple rhetorical perspectives without fixation or limitation gains spontaneous liberation from intellectual fetters and emotional attachments. What the authors try to reveal are not definitive explications or solutions for enigmatic gongan cases, but a way of exploring and making an assessment of various viewpoints that serve as a model for self-reliance and self-awareness. In numerous examples throughout the work, highly stylized remarks seek to upend dramatically or reverse radically staid and stereotypical opinions via a Chan adept's symbolic ability to "overturn a trainee's meditation seat and chase the great assembly" 掀倒禪床.喝散大眾,[2] or more expansively to "reverse the flow of the great seas, topple Mount Sumeru [the mythical cosmic Buddhist summit], and scatter the white clouds" 掀翻大海.踢倒須彌.喝散白雲.[3]

The text's method begins by identifying problematic stances derived from conceptually or volitionally based explanations of gongan that are generally either too literal or overly abstract. For example, Yuanwu complains in case 3 that in his day people were often saying of a famous phrase attributed to master Mazu (782–865), though without any firm basis, that the "Sun-faced Buddha represents the left eye, whereas the Moon-faced Buddha is the right eye 左眼是日面.右眼是月面.[4] Yuanwu similarly grumbles in his comments on case 56 that when a teacher once hit a disciple seven times, learners spent their time wondering unproductively why it was not eight times or six times, as if determining the "correct" number might make a difference.

Xuedou's verses consistently demonstrate that the poet-monk functions as an active and inspired interpreter, rather than as a passive observer or distant reflective voice, by suggesting in dramatic fashion the merit of his own approach, the aim of which is to challenge any and all opinions, including those of masters portrayed in gongan sources. Examples of Xuedou's facility with paradox appear in cases 28 and 50 when he refers to seeing the Big Dipper in the north by looking to the south, yet indicates that while its handle hangs down below and is available to be grasped it remains ever elusive and out of reach. In case 30, in which Zhaozhou (778–897) answers a monk's query with the non sequitur, "Zhen province produces big radishes," Xuedou follows up his four-line ode with the exclamatory, "Thief! Thief!" 賊賊.

To show that Xuedou's expressions must not be either taken at face value or placed on a pedestal but are, like all other sayings and doings cited in the text, subject to criticism, Yuanwu adds to case 30, "Well! It's none other than Xuedou himself who is the one being held in stocks, thus giving evidence of his crime." 咄更不是別.自是擔枷過狀.[5] In many instances, such as cases 4, 19, and 24, Yuanwu offers great praise for Xuedou's literary composition, which he says is "consummately accomplished" and "the best of its kind," since only Xuedou truly understands gongan in an appropriately effective manner. Yet Yuanwu's approval is almost always peppered with disclaimers. In case 78 when Xuedou tells his followers, "Although you've washed in fragrant water I'll spit right in your face" 香水洗來驀面唾, Yuanwu notes, "Too bad! He adds a layer of mud on dirt and should know better than to defecate on pure soil." 咄.土上加泥又一重.莫來淨地上屙.[6] Yuanwu's testing and contesting with alternative attitudes and outlooks does not stop there. In case 56 he takes Xuedou to task for attributing a Chan saying cited in the verse to the wrong teacher, while in case 79 in which Touzi (1032–1083) strikes an unwary monk, Yuanwu demands with irony, "[The inquirer] deserved to be hit, but why did Touzi stop before his staff was broken?" 好打.拄杖未到折.[7]

In numerous examples in the *Blue Cliff Record* and other writings included in their respective recorded sayings collections Xuedou and Yuanwu strike disciples or feign doing so for rhetorical effect to impart a sense of immediacy and urgency to the quest for understanding. Looking at their commentaries overall, there are instances in which the authors either greatly admire or harshly denigrate a participant in the gongan exchange under consideration, and examples in which the encounter partners are both praised, such as case 24, and others in which they are considered to fall equally short of the mark, including case 23. At times Xuedou's and Yuanwu's views of a case are in accord, but on other occasions a disagreement flares up, which gives evidence of the latter's independent evaluative approach toward his predecessor.

An interesting instance of the interaction of the respective standpoints of Xuedou and Yuanwu occurs in case 84 on a dialogue that layman Vimalakirti held with Manjusri and other bodhisattvas, which in traditional accounts ends with the former one-upping his interlocutor by remaining silent. In the gongan as cited the *Blue Cliff Record* Xuedou interjects, "What did Vimalakirti say?" 維摩道什麼 and also adds, "I've seen through him!" (or "Completely exposed!") 勘破了也. But Yuanwu remarks, "Xuedou draws his bow after the thief has already fled. Although he uses all his strength to help the assembly the result is that misfortune leaks out from his own gate. . . . Since he hasn't known the truth even in a dream how can he say that this dialogue has been seen through? Watch out! Even the golden-haired lion is unable to find it." 雪竇也是賊過後張弓.雖然為眾竭力.爭奈禍出私門. . . . 夢也未夢見.說什麼勘破.嶮.金毛獅子也摸索不著.[8] Yet Yuanwu then praises Xuedou's verse, which gives evidence of possessing the "Diamond King's jewel sword" that cuts through ignorance. As Sonja Arntzen remarks, "What we see functioning in this kind of Zen rhetoric is an endlessly circling dialectic. When something is asserted, one must tear it down, cancel it out. The cancelling out will represent another assertion, so it too must be torn down and cancelled out. A perpetual iconoclasm is the order of the school."[9]

Yet for all the appreciation and acclaim the *Blue Cliff Record* has received because of its open-ended and flexible approach to uncertainty, this compilation has also been the single most controversial and perhaps least understood text from the voluminous canon of Chan's classical era. This is a result of the complexity of its multilayered construction, in addition to the persistence of a couple of powerful legends that tend to cloud or mystify the legacy of this remarkable two-author text. As noted by Sueki Fumihiko, a prominent Japanese scholar who has published extensively on the collection, "Although the Chan or Zen tradition in China, Korea and Japan has attached great importance to the *Biyanlu*, it has not been studied well because of its difficulty. It is difficult to understand partly because of the ironical and complex thought of Chan Buddhism and partly because of the difficulty of the language which is both colloquial and full of particular terms of Chan Buddhism."[10]

Probably as a consequence of this almost intimidatingly demanding quality the *Blue Cliff Record* is perhaps best known today for having apparently been destroyed shortly after its original publication in 1128. This was the result of discord between Yuanwu and his foremost disciple about the significance of the collection for teaching because of its putative overreliance on literary effect in a religious tradition that favors mystical reticence and rhetorical simplicity. Although few facts are clear about the controversy, it seems that the text was lost around 1140 and remained out of circulation for nearly two centuries, as there was little discussion or commentary on it despite voluminous citations of other texts by Xuedou and Yuanwu. Then the collection was reconstituted around 1300 and shortly after this was transmitted to Japan, where it gained a strong new following as Zen practice was spreading rapidly with the support of the shogunate for teachers who became well versed in Chinese literature.

The matter of the text's fate during this period remains unclear, but it must not have disappeared altogether since there are occasional references to it in writings from the intervening period, including the *Record of Serenity* (*Congronglu*), another major gongan collection from 1224 that cites the *Blue Cliff Record* over a dozen times. Also a Southern Song verse anonymously inscribed on Xuedou's stupa that alludes in its first half to a couple of lines from the ode to case 3 expresses regret that the *Blue Cliff Record* (or perhaps it refers only to the *One Hundred Odes*) was not then a part of the published Buddhist canon: "The Three Sovereigns and Five Emperors, what were they like?/ [Xuedou's] suffering lasted twenty long hard years./ Still not included in the Great Treasury,/ Even today, cast about, the words struggle to find their proper place." 三皇五帝是何物.辛苦曾經二十年.一大蔵中收不得.至今狼藉乳峰前.[11]

Given that there was an ongoing and pervasive ambivalence about the ultimate value of the work, my main goal is to develop a hermeneutic approach that helps illumine the accomplishments of the creators' ingenious rhetorical techniques while also coming to terms with some of the various factors and, at times, rather questionable judgments that lie at the root of the *Blue Cliff Record*'s contentious history. My standpoint is informed by textual historical and discursive studies from both sides of the Pacific, including recent scholarly developments in China and Japan, yet acknowledges the innate limitations of any contemporary method used to assess the full impact and legacy of the collection.[12]

## *Historical Issues and Hermeneutic Aims*

The text of the *Blue Cliff Record* is based on a series of sermons delivered in the Dharma hall that were first given by Yuanwu in 1111–1112 when he resided in the Blue Cliff Cloister (Biyan Yuan) of Lingquan temple on Mount Jiashan, which was the location of Tang dynasty (618906) master Jiashan Shanhui (805–881) that is situated in a remote but beautiful corner of the northwestern section of Hunan province near the city of Shimen. The cloister is adjacent to the Blue Cliff Springs (Biyan Quan), which is famous for the production of tea because of the pure waters.[13] However the production of the text has a complicated history that covers much more than these two years of lectures.

Yuanwu hailed from and spent the early days in addition to the end of his career at Zhaojue temple in Chengdu, the capital city of Sichuan province. Sichuan was long known as a hotbed of literary activity, both Buddhist and secular, despite being located far from the national center of Song culture including Chan temple activities in Zhejiang province on the eastern seaboard.[14] It is clear that at least some of the lectures and much of the editing of the *Blue Cliff Record* took place at Zhaojue, which thereby played a highly significant role in the historical development of the compilation; another Sichuan monastery, Daolin temple where Yuanwu stayed for a time after his days at Jiashan, also contributed to the textual production.

Produced over the course of two decades—rather than two years, as is sometimes presumed—in the later stages of the Northern Song (960–1126) dynasty but not officially published until the dawn of the Southern Song (1127–1279), the *Blue Cliff Record* consists of several distinctive types of prose and poetic remarks interwoven across multiple commentarial layers on cases that were derived from an extensive corpus of precedent encounter dialogues 機緣問答 (*jiyuan wenda*). This body of dynamic and provocative exchanges reflects the challenging spiritual interactions and sometimes explosive exploits of Tang Chan ancestors often referred to as "former masters" 古人 (*guren*, literally "old men"),[15] who communicated in strange and deliberately disconcerting verbal and nonverbal ways. The dialogues helped form the basis of gongan collections and ritual techniques for testing disciples linked to this literary genre that was part of the instruction for monks, who studied these texts as a central component of their monastic training. Encounter dialogues appealed to scholar-officials (*shidafu*), who were intrigued by the Chan philosophy of self-realization and often attended the sermons or interacted in various ways with renowned teachers.

All the cases cited by Yuanwu were chosen nearly a century before and were appended with verse remarks 頌古 (*songgu*), or appreciatory odes, by Xuedou, who was referred to posthumously as Mingjue. An important reviver of the lineage founded by Yunmen Wenyan (864–949), Xuedou completed the *One Hundred Odes* (*Baize Songgu*), or *Verse Comments on One Hundred Old Cases*, in 1026 (variously dated 1038) when he was at a temple in Zhejiang province, but some of the composition may have taken place earlier at a temple in Suzhou in Jiangsu province—both locations were in the prestigious Jiangnan region. He composed other kinds of gongan commentary that are contained in his recorded sayings.[16] Xuedou cited cases culled from hagiographical anecdotes covering the encounter dialogues of Tang teachers that were mainly based on the *Jingde Transmission of the Lamp Record* (*Jingde Chuandenglu*), one of the first major compilations of Chan hagiographical narratives composed in 1004.

The *Jingde Record*, probably influenced by the *Records from the Ancestors' Hall* (*Zutangji*) of 952, is the basis for forty-two cases, and eighteen cases were extracted from the recorded sayings of the founder of Xuedou's lineage contained in the *Yunmen Record* (*Yunmen Yulu*). Twenty of the cases probably came from the gongan collection of Fenyang Shanzhao (947–1024), and the remaining twenty were from the records of Zhaozhou, Zhimen, Fengxue, and other masters.[17] In addition to having the greatest number of gongan attributed to him in the *Blue Cliff Record*—Zhaozhou Congshen (778–897) is next with twelve cases, followed by his teacher Nanquan Puyuan (749–835) with five—Yunmen's sayings are frequently cited in Yuanwu's prose remarks.

Xuedou and many other Song Chan leaders regarded Yunmen as the single major role model for the prototypical Chan adept 作家 (literally, "one accomplished in the ways of a house or school"), who responds swiftly and skillfully by seizing an opportune moment 機 (*ji*) to demonstrate his openness and flexibility in order to address and instruct trainees at their level of understanding. Yuanwu says that, "Yunmen all of a sudden breaks up emotional barriers and intellectual ideation or any sense of gain versus loss, or affirmation versus negation." He cites Xuedou on two occasions (cases 6 and 62) for declaring, "I greatly admire the remarkably vibrant, lively, and decisive teaching devices [used by Yunmen], who spent his entire life removing fixations and obstacles for people ... with a sharp sword constantly cutting away ignorance." 雲門與爾一時.打破情識意想得失是非了也雪竇道.我愛韶陽新定機.一生與人抽釘拔楔 ... 利刃剪卻.[18]

The ability to be "responsive as suited to the occasion" 對機, which is suggested in the title of the first section of Yunmen's recorded sayings, is the primary ingredient of a spiritual truth expressed in the *Blue Cliff Record* that bridges any apparent gaps or lines of division among Chan factions based on a universal vision of how authentic masters are able to exert an eminently agile pedagogical approach that adapts quickly to the needs of disciples.[19] This ability can be referred to as "turnabout Chan" 轉身禪, in that the true adept demonstrates a perpetual knack for finding a way to stay unstuck and free from attachment so as to change direction instantaneously as required by circumstances. Xuedou says, "Patch-robed [Chan] monks have this special skill and if a prominent teacher [literally, "person and a half"] demonstrates it for you clearly, the ancient sages did not come forward even a single time in vain." 衲僧有此奇特事.若一人半个互相平展.古聖也不虛出來一回.[20] As Yuanwu writes in the introduction to case 1, "Being shown one corner and finding the other three, or with the glance of an eye sizing up all the fine grains and ounces—these are nothing more than the everyday tea and rice imbibed by patch-robed monks." 舉一明三.目機銖兩.是衲僧家尋常茶飯.[21]

Xuedou and Yuanwu both hailed from Sichuan, but neither regional nor lineal loyalties (or divisions) need be overemphasized in appraising the *Blue Cliff Record*, since the influences on the literary production of its authors were many and varied. Their combined work created during an era that embraced evenhandedly multiple branches and styles of Chan theory and practice continues to have broad implications that transcend provincial or sectarian affiliations. Xuedou left Sichuan while still young to study Buddhism in the south before becoming abbot of Cuifeng temple located beside Lake Dongting near the town of Suzhou in Jiangsu province. That is where he started his teaching career and first delivered sermons using verses to comment on representative gongan, although he rarely referred to dialogues by using the term "gongan," which was subsequently developed in its full nuance by Yuanwu.[22] Xuedou later served as the long-standing abbot, for thirty-one years beginning in 1021, at the prestigious Zisheng monastery on Mount Xuedou in Zhejiang province, a short distance from Hangzhou, which later became the capital city of the Southern Song.[23] This temple, which happens to be located across the road from the hometown of Chiang Kai-shek (Jiang Jieshi) and served as a summer retreat during his youth, has been revived since the Cultural Revolution but today has a focus on community outreach that for better or worse does not regard studying Xuedou's texts as an important feature of contemporary Chan practice.[24]

Both Xuedou and Yuanwu were extraordinary literary talents as seen in their voluminous prose and poetic writings. According to his funerary inscription, Xuedou's disciples compiled seven texts containing his prose and poetic comments on cases plus sermons, epistles, and records of conversations testing disciples through questions and answers. These texts include (1) the *Dongting Record* (*Dongting Yulu*), (2) *Xuedou's Opening the Hall Record* (*Xuedou Kaitanglu*), (3) the *Waterfalls Collection* (*Puquanji*), (4) the *Ancestral Luminaries* (*Zuyingji*), (5) *Odes on Old Cases* (*Songguji*, aka *Baize Songgu*, or *One Hundred Odes*), (6) *Prose Comments on One Hundred Old Cases* (*Nianguji*), and (7) *Xuedou's Late Record* (*Xuedou Houlu*).[25] According to the traditional account the seven works were circulating individually and with independent titles by 1065, just thirteen years after Xuedou's death. Also in 1032 Xuedou's disciples compiled another independent text titled *Master Xuedou's Prose Comments on Old Cases* 雪竇和尚拈古集 (*Xuedou Heshang Nianguji*), which is a different version of item (6) above, and this became the basis for another gongan collection created by Yuanwu as a second-level commentator.

However Xuedou did not write many examples of some of the literary styles that became de rigueur for Southern Song poet-monks a century later, including memorial poems at funerals, encomia for the portraits of deceased masters, or parting poems for visitors and travelers. Moreover, since his main goal was gentle persuasion rather than producing poetic composition 詩 as either an end in itself or as a form of persuasion to convert others, his lyricism demonstrates a distinctively religious rather than aesthetic function yet without a reliance on doctrine. It features the kind of self-deprecating humor and disingenuous blasphemy that has characterized so many styles of Chan discourse since the Tang dynasty.

The only complete collection of Xuedou's seven works is found in the Japanese Gozan version printed in 1289, which includes the *One Hundred Odes*, and is preserved in the Tōyō Bunko collection that was republished in the second volume of the series *Zengaku Tenseki Sōkan* that contains all seven of Xuedou's original texts. However the current mainstream version of the Buddhist canon published in the *Taishō Shinshū Daizōkyō* (and duplicated electronically on the CBETA.org website that is cited here) contains just six of these writings. This edition is missing the *One Hundred Odes* as an independent text, so that it is primarily accessed today by virtue of its inclusion in the *Blue Cliff Record*, which is historically ironic in that the *One Hundred Odes* was likely available during the thirteenth century when the *Blue Cliff Record* was not.

In addition to the *Blue Cliff Record*, other major collections by Yuanwu include the twenty-volume *Yuanwu Record* 圓悟佛果禪師語錄 (*Yuanwu Foguo Chanshi Yulu*) produced by disciples during his lifetime, which contains verse and prose comments on scores of gongan; *Essentials of Mind* 圓悟心要 (*Yuanwu Xinyao*), which contains 145 letters composed at various stages of his career for both monks and lay followers that also frequently comment on gongan cases and related practices; and the undated *Record of Keeping the Beat* 擊節錄 (*Jijielu*), which offers additional prose comments (*niangu*) to *Master Xuedou's Prose Comments on Old Cases* that consists of one hundred cases with concise remarks. Many of the cases cited throughout these writings are common, but the diversity of examples, as well as the variety of interpretative approaches, is exceptionally extensive in demonstrating Yuanwu's prowess as the principal commentator in the gongan tradition. While some observers claim that Yuanwu preferred prose to verse, or vice versa, the full textual evidence makes it abundantly clear that he considered both commentarial styles suitable and appropriate depending on circumstances for excavating the multiples levels of meaning of sources in ways that vary with the instructional needs and literary styles called for by particular situations.[26]

In supplementing Xuedou's remarks in the *Blue Cliff Record*, Yuanwu, a leader of the Yangqi stream of the Linji school, creatively uses a variety of rhetorical techniques to comment on the main cases 本則 (*benze*). These include introductory declarations 垂示 (*chuishi*) to exhort the reader and elaborate prose remarks 評唱 (*pingchang*)—note that this is a multifaceted term discussed in more detail below—that examine the background and assess other thinkers' views of each gongan. The prose commentary combines explanations containing biographical elements and attempts to track down citations and allusions and to clarify semantic and syntactical structures with at times drastic and far-reaching interpretations that question and reverse conventional views.

In addition Yuanwu inserts into each and every line of both the cases and verses interlinear capping phrase 着語 (*zhuoyu*) annotations that offer a pithy and ironic adjudication about which of the interlocutors in the source dialogue appears to be winning the Dharma battle that is played out through the interaction.[27] This rhetorical effort combines literary Chinese and Buddhist-hybrid Chinese with vernacular Chinese expressions, including local as well as era-specific locutions.[28] These elaborate discursive devices enable Yuanwu to comment in a complex and sometimes purposefully contradictory fashion in that he frequently changes course or reverses opinion by combining appreciation with deprecation for participants in the encounters, which are invariably puzzling and perplexing, and for Xuedou's seemingly impenetrable poetic interpretations.

The *Blue Cliff Record* thereby pioneers or refines ways of interpreting the main cases derived from established or paradigmatic accounts of encounter dialogues as initiated at the beginning of the eleventh century by Linji school monk Fenyang. The first formal commentator on cases whose sayings often evoke the image of striking with his staff, a rhetorical conceit that inspired his successors, Fenyang produced three gongan collections all contained in the middle section of his 3-volume recorded sayings known as the *Fenyang Wude Chanshi Songgu Daibei*: one subsection features verse comments 頌古 (*songgu*) on one hundred established cases; another uses replacement or substitute words 代語 (*daiyu*) to resolve similar kinds of cases; and the third subsection offers separate or alternate words 別語 (*bieyu*) for cases that Fenyang himself devised.[29]

Fenyang's first set of gongan comments became the model for the poetry of Xuedou, who is considered more of an expert in literary skill in

Chinese-regulated verse composition than his precursor, and Fenyang is also respected for initiating a style of brief prose remarks 拈古 (*niangu*) on cases. The latter two categories used by Fenyang of substitute and alternate words were a crucial influence on the formation of the capping-phrase technique pioneered in the *Blue Cliff Record*. Yuanwu's approach takes Fenyang's style of making informal comments that either replace previous remarks or create new interpretations of an encounter dialogue a step further by interjecting brief annotations in between the lines of case and verse. Many of the capping phrases that cite or allude to prior commentaries demonstrate a whimsical outlook and poetic flair evoking everyday aphorisms and idioms in remarking sardonically on the intricacy of what transpires within the exchanges.

In addition to citing Xuedou in every case and Yunmen extensively throughout the collection, Yuanwu frequently mentions his mentor, Wuzu Fayan (1024–1104), another Sichuan native who was known along with his teacher, Baiyun Shouduan (1023–1072), as an eleventh-century advocate of using gongan studies as a crucial vehicle for attaining awakening. Yuanwu also cites a former colleague during his period of training under the auspices of Wuzu known as Librarian Qing (n.d.), whose remarks are quoted in eight cases. While Wuzu and Yuanwu were part of the Linji-Yangqi stream, it is also noteworthy that prominent Caodong school monks Touzi Yiqing (1032–1083) and Danxia Zichun (1064–1117) were very much involved in commenting on dialogues. Like many of their Linji school colleagues, the monks received training in Chan monasteries and meditation retreats located in the Longmian Mountains of southwestern Anhui province, a major Northern Song incubator for advancing gongan theory and practice across partisan lines. These masters produced early examples of gongan collections in the second half of the eleventh century that had an enduring significance in the history of the tradition and no doubt greatly influenced Yuanwu's creativity.[30]

The perspectives of Xuedou and Yuanwu are complementary and reinforcing yet also at times purposefully conflicting and undermining of one another. In nearly every case Xuedou praises but challenges or disparages one or more interlocutors, and then Yuanwu makes comments that express admiration yet at the same time call into question or try to overturn much of what Xuedou has articulated. The combined effect of their rhetorical efforts is to provide probing assessments of the significance of Chan encounters in a way that explores all possible standpoints and stimulates the audience to remain unattached to any particular view.

Instead of adhering to clichés or stereotypes that may satisfy the "fools" and "phonies" who had infiltrated Chan temples by showing the head of a dragon while revealing they have the tail of a snake, readers of the *Blue Cliff Record* are encouraged or even required to reach their own independent conclusion. This is based on thoughtful reflection and emulation of the original inspirational experience that motivated the ancestors' quixotic utterances and gestures.

Danxia's student Hongzhi Zhengjue (1091–1157) apparently met Yuanwu briefly in the mid-1120s, and by the middle of the twelfth century he had become the main rival to Dahui Zonggao (1089–1163) for supposedly endorsing the approach of silent-illumination (*mozhao Chan*) in contrast to keyword meditation (*huatou Chan*).[31] Hongzhi's collection of verse remarks on one hundred cases served as the basis for another illustrious gongan collection titled the *Record of Serenity* (*Congronglu*). This was compiled in 1224 by Wansong Xingxiu (1166–1246), who was located at a temple in Beijing that functioned, first, under the sway of the Jurchen Jin empire that conquered northern China and, then, under the new and even more imposing dominance of Mongol rule, which had in its own way a receptive attitude toward the role of religions, including support for Chan Buddhism. The *Record of Serenity* was one of several commentaries produced by the Caodong school in the thirteenth century, including two by Wansong's main disciple Linquan Conglun (n.d.) that are based on compilations by Touzi and Danxia. Both Wansong and Linquan apparently had a relationship with advisors to Genghis Khan and Kublai Khan, respectively, and compiled impressive works that were received favorably by these rulers during a tumultuous era in which the Chan school competed with other Buddhist, as well as Daoist, Confucian, and Christian movements, for the attention of the Mongol leaders.

The notion of uncertainty as an innovative interpretative tool for deconstructing each and every standpoint put forth is elucidated here as part of my hermeneutic approach that seeks to unpack the distinctive method of thought and manner of discourse of the *Blue Cliff Record*, which endorses indeterminacy on literary and experiential levels as the key to undergoing spiritual realization. Uncertainty indicates that the primary aim of Chan awakening is to acknowledge constructive ambiguity in coming to terms with perennial issues that are crucial elements in the quest for spiritual realization. There is no attempt on the part of either Xuedou or Yuanwu—in fact such an effort is deliberately avoided and disputed—to reach a firm or clear-cut conclusion that may become the source of a preoccupation or attachment involving such Buddhist topics as the role of language (whether it is considered a vehicle or obstacle to truth), the function of doubt (as either debilitating or exhilarating along the spiritual pathway), suspicions about perception (as either detrimental or conducive to self-awareness), and the meaning of time (whether a hindrance or entry point to enlightenment).

The emphasis on uncertainty is not intended to indicate a form of nihilism or pessimism that gives up and abandons the quest for awakening in pursuit of primarily literary rather than religious goals, which is the way the *Blue Cliff Record* has frequently been (mis)understood. The collection is especially buoyant and optimistic about the possibility that each and every person has the potential to develop the skill or knack for attaining and expressing insight and is thereby able to become an adept in his or her own way. As Yunmen declares in case 6, "Every day is a good day," and in case 89 he says, "All people have a light," regardless of extenuating circumstances or divisions and distinctions made in ordinary life. Therefore uncertainty can be referred to more positively as the expressive activity (*hyōgen sayō*), borrowing a Nishida Kitarō philosophical notion, of "sharpening a (critical discursive) sword" 機鋒 (*jifeng*; literally, a "crossbow arrow" hitting its mark or any "razor-like device" that cuts through obstacles). This term implies a quick-witted talent for answering effectively no matter the situation and breaking any impasse that emerges in Chan's combative spiritual encounters. As conveyed by the verse and capping phrases on case 75, which declares, "Observe carefully the interaction of action points [between interlocutors]! (One entry, one exit. Two adepts are both parrying with the same staff, but which one is really holding it?)" 互換機鋒子細看 (一出一入.二俱作家.一條拄杖兩人扶.且道在阿誰邊),[32] *jifeng* suggests a vivid, alert, and timely elicitation of words and gestures. Expressions are deployed either sparingly but with precision and great effect or with parsimony yet a generosity of spirit by nimbly communicating clever retorts that at first disarm the adversary, but in the end disclose deeper wisdom that is available to all parties.

Chan encounters are said to take place at the proverbial "Dragon Gate" (*longmen*). This mythical barrier is where diligent and determined fish swimming upstream in a waterfall during a raging spring thunderstorm are said to be able leap past the peak once and for all and thereby transform into dragons that fly away on clouds toward heaven while peach blossoms of the third lunar month fall and float calmly in the choppy waters below.[33] This image symbolizing the attainment of transcendental awareness was a traditional analogy for those select few competitors who passed strict imperial examinations based on their dedicated effort. In a related use of the metaphor of exams, at the end of case 46, master Jingqing comments, "Overcoming the body [or, everyday success] is easy to achieve but the path of full detachment is difficult" 出身猶可易.脫體道應難.[34] The first phrase used in secular discourse is an idiom for performing well on an entrance test that would normally be considered quite difficult to attain, but here it is contrasted with realizing enlightenment that represents the real challenge.

Building on the innovations of predecessors, what the *Blue Cliff Record* achieves that has fascinated and inspired readers for centuries is an uncanny knack for keeping alive a timeless sense of participating in the immediacy of the original Chan encounters that supposedly transpired long before the text's comments were composed. The remarks of Xuedou and Yuanwu frequently intrude on the source dialogues or make asides or let out haughty chuckles in order to express disdain for others or to confess humbly the commentator's own sense of insecurity or indecision. As John McRae points out, gongan "stories were clearly passed around and subjected to repeated reevaluations and modification ... [that] occurred in a complex environment of both oral and written transmission," Yet "Yuanwu's commentary on ... Xuedou's verse and the case itself impart the sense that he was attempting to use the medium of writing to ... enter into the dialogue, to live within the idealized Tang-dynasty realm of spontaneous interaction." McRae suggests that this "feeling of 'being there' is a literary effect contrived through literally centuries of combined effort."[35]

I further argue that recognizing this rhetorical construction does not diminish the impact of the conceit but rather heightens an understanding and appreciation for how effective it can be in communicating the text's religious vision. The source dialogues feature many verbal irruptions and nonverbal interruptions, including slaps, shouts, and strikes, and we do not know if these reflect accurate reporting of the original event or an editor's retrospective exaggeration. These occurrences are at once enhanced and evaluated through the frequent recorded cries by Xuedou and Yuanwu of "Bah!" and "Hah!," as well as their refrains of "I strike!," "He deserves thirty blows of the stick!," or "He falls back three thousand miles!" We can only guess or speculate on the influence this performative element may have generated on the part of the audience of monks in the assembly who heard the sermons' delivery, but if read properly it serves as a crucial discursive component underscoring the meaning of uncertainty.

Even though there are about one-and-a-half fascicles containing verse comments on gongan in his twenty-volume recorded sayings in addition to a collection of miscellaneous poems for various occasions in the last volume, Yuanwu does not contribute his own odes to the *Blue Cliff Record*. The lone exception is a single poem included in the commentary on the final case. In playful fashion the text's concluding verse expresses Yuanwu's equivocation in regard to the role of language and his mixed feelings about the efficacy of the overall commentarial project as a response to the religious aspirations of his readers:

> *Filled with countless bushels a boat effortlessly pulls away,*
> *Holding just one grain of rice a jar entraps a snake;*
> *When offering comments on one hundred transformative old cases*
> *(gongan),*
> *Just how many people will end up with sand tossed in their eyes?*

萬斛盈舟信手拏. 却因一粒甕吞蛇. 拈提百轉舊公案. 撒却時人幾眼沙.[36]

This poem recalls Xuedou's self-deprecating saying, "Raising the ancient [masters] and raising the present [masters] is like tossing sand and sprinkling mud. There is in fact nothing!" 舉古舉今拋沙撒土.直下無事.[37]

Xuedou also says in his *Record*, "For all my life I deeply regret that I have relied too much on words [to explicate Chan teachings]. Next time I would simply use my staff, sandals, robe, and bowl." 吾平生患語之多矣.翌日出杖屨衣盂.[38] In a capping phrase on the verse on case 50, in which Xuedou deploys one of his favorite discursive techniques by citing the key phrase from the main case ("Rice in the bowl, water in the bucket" 鉢裏飯桶裏水) as the opening line, Yuanwu remarks, "Truth is apparent. Why scatter sand and dirt? You must wash your mouth out for three years before you'll get the point" 露也.撒沙撒土作什麼.漱口三年始得.[39] Also in case 41 Yuanwu caps Xuedou's final line, "I don't know who explains by scattering sand and dust" 不知誰解撒塵沙 with the phrase, "There is quite a bit of this taking place right now. Whether open or closed it still gets in the eyes" 即今也不.開眼也著.合眼也著.[40] While not primarily a poet himself, although he was known to use romantic poetic imagery from Chinese love stories as symbolic of the pathway to attaining enlightenment, should Yuanwu's remarks on verses by Xuedou, who also composed prose commentary, be seen as supporting and clarifying or denigrating and diminishing the religious significance of Chan poetics?[41] Or is this question a red herring?

An example of complex interactions involving their respective forms of rhetoric occurs when Yuanwu cites the first four lines of Xuedou's ten-line verse on case 1, "Sacred truths are empty,/ What do you discriminate?/ Who stands before the Emperor?/ And [Bodhidharma] said, I don't know" 聖諦廓然.何當辨的.對朕者誰.還云不識.[42] Yuanwu then comments, "This is like skillfully doing a sword dance while, graceful in midair, [Xuedou] naturally dodges the sharp point" 一似善舞太阿劍相似.向虛空中盤礴.自然不犯鋒鋩.[43] In considering another line in the poem, "How could [Bodhidharma] avoid the growth of a thicket of brambles?" 豈免生荊棘,[44] it seems for Yuanwu that Xuedou is fully consistent with and greatly advances the spirit of the gongan since, "Bodhidharma originally came to this country to dissolve the sticking points, untie the bonds, pull out the nails and draw out the pegs, and cut down brambles for people" 達磨本來茲土.與人解粘去縛.抽釘拔楔.鏟除荊棘. But, he also asks, "Why then [does Xuedou] say that [Bodhidharma] gave rise to a thicket of brambles? This is not confined to the old days because today the brambles under everyone's feet are several yards deep" 因何卻道生荊棘.非止當時.諸人即今腳跟下.已深數丈.[45]

By emphasizing the inevitability of brambles lying underfoot, Yuanwu recognizes, and probably feels Xuedou knows this, that any form of expression including poetry and prose can at any time become a mixed blessing or even an impediment to understanding. Yuanwu sometimes takes Xuedou to task for saying too much or not enough. For instance in commenting on the verse in case 1 he suggests that the poet is overly kind: "Xuedou asks, 'How will all you patch-robed monks be able to discriminate?' 'Who stands before the Emperor?' He adds the line, 'Again [Bodhidharma] said, I don't know.' Xuedou has such grandmotherly kindness that he repeats the line to make the meaning clear to people" 雪竇道.爾天下衲僧.何當辨的.對朕者誰.著箇還云不識.此是雪竇忒殺老婆.重重為人處.[46] The implication is that the simple repetition of the line from the original dialogue may represent a doting granny's saying that is a distraction from, rather than conducive to, the attainment of realization.

Furthermore Yuanwu comments on the first of two verses on case 20, "Longya's Meaning of Bodhidharma Coming from the West" 龍牙祖師西來意, in which Xuedou starts with an ironic wordplay on the literal meaning of Longya's name, "On Dragon Tusk Mountain the dragon has no eyes/ When has dead water ever displayed the ancient style?" 龍牙山裏龍無眼.死水何曾振古風.[47] According to Yuanwu's questioning of the verse in a way that throws the responsibility for understanding back on the reader, "Xuedou earnestly wraps up the case. Although his verse explains it this way the meaning of what he said is still a concern. Why does the dragon lack eyes? Why is he in dead water? If you realize this point, surely you must have attained an inner transformation in order to initiate the understanding" 雪竇據欵結案.他雖恁麼頌.且道意在什麼處.甚處是無眼.甚處是死水裏.到這裏須是有變通始得.[48] Self-realization is the key to true awareness, rather than accepting any established interpretation in a way that quickly becomes stale and an impediment to knowledge. As Yuanwu also proclaims, "All the Buddha's teachings were expounded to liberate minds. In me there is no trace of mind—what use have I for any teachings?"[49]

Renowned for its elaborate multilayered structure showcasing Yuanwu's inter- and extralinear comments on Xuedou's puzzling verse remarks on perplexing cases, the *Blue Cliff Record* represents the pinnacle of Chan's distinctive approach to highlighting the resourceful role of language when used inventively to disclose various stages of the existential quest for religious fulfillment.[50] The collection epitomizes an emphasis on evoking the discourse of indirection, allusiveness, irony, paradox, and wordplay that characterized the approach of literary or lettered 文字 (*wenzi*) Chan. This method of discourse dominated the intellectual landscape of the school during the Northern Song dynasty, when Chan masters regularly interacted with the mannered elite class of scholar-officials, who in turn were inspired by the Buddhist striving to gain liberation from the fetters of ordinary life. In their roles both as official bureaucrats, who either sought respite from official duties or, instead, tried to improve their status by cultivating connections to the church, and as individual seekers interested in self-discovery, literati engaged with priests in mutually beneficial symbiotic relationships that enhanced the prosperity of their respective domains.[51] Therefore "it is undeniably the case that during the Song dynasty Chan attained an unprecedented plateau of ascendancy throughout Chinese and eventually all East Asian culture."[52]

The Northern Song Chan focus on the priority of letters was part of an extensive governmental campaign to reverse and replace an emphasis on gaining expertise in the martial arts that was prevalent in previous stages of Chinese society. It was felt that this represented an aggressive trend that had resulted in a centuries-long period of disunity and chaos, so the new key to the success of civilization would come about through establishing a unified public order based on "valuing literary learning and deemphasizing military force" 重文輕武 (zhongwen qingwu). This pervasive societal campaign based in large part on the Confucian notion of cultivating arts of peace led to the prolific production of various kinds of writings by Chan monks. This was a spontaneous yet sustained response to the court's public literary 文 (wen) policy that was enthusiastically supported by the first three Northern Song emperors, Taizu (r. 960–975), Taizong (r. 976–997), and Zhenzong (r. 998–1022).

Each of these rulers took steps to expand the civil service examination system as a major means of recruiting government officials while also sponsoring many large-scale printing projects. However the last emperor, Huizong (r. 1110–1126), was politically weak and ineffective, in large part because of an overindulgence in literary arts that helped precipitate the demise of the Northern Song by leaving the country vulnerable to attacks from northern invaders. Although he generally favored other religious traditions and often discriminated against Buddhism, Huizong traveled to visit Yuanwu when he was at the Daolin temple in Sichuan province in 1114 and offered him the purple robe with the honorary name Foguo Chanshi, or Fruition of Buddha Chan Teacher, a moniker often used in the titles of Yuanwu's works, including the full title of the Blue Cliff Record.[53] The first Southern Song emperor, Gaozong (r. 1127–1162), bestowed the designation of Yuanwu Chanshi, or Perfectly Enlightened Chan Master.

Many Chan priests of the era, often referred to as poet-monks, were expected just like their secular counterparts to demonstrate compositional skills in order to advance in the monastic institutional system. In addition to absorbing the influences of the luminary poet and public servant Su Shi (1037–1101, aka Su Dongpo), who was greatly involved with Buddhist meditative practice, and the close friend with whom he had a famed spiritual and artistic exchange poet-monk Foyin Liaoyuan (1032–1098),[54] Yuanwu apparently greatly benefited from his close personal associations with several key figures among other notable literary luminaries and supporters. These included Chan chronicler Juefan Huihong (1071–1128), known in part for recording the Su Shi-Foyin exchange; Buddhist scholar and politician Zhang Shangying (1043–1121), who befriended a number of important clerics during a turbulent public life; and Yuanwu's Dharma-brother under Wuzu, Foyan Qingyuan (1067–1120).[55]

One of the main tropes that emerged from the mutual influence of poet-monks and literati pertains to the view that any given expression should encompass the connection (not strictly a progression) of four interrelated but unstable and ever shifting—or uncertain—standpoints 起承轉結(合). These include the opening 起 imagery of the first line of a four-line, trun-cated verse (*jueju*), which is regulated by rhyme, tonal patterns, and other discursive markers, followed by further development 承 of this symbol-ism, a turnabout 轉 leading to a standpoint of contradiction toward the views previously articulated, and a conclusion 結 (or harmonization 合 of perspectives).[56] The last line provides final reflections by wrapping up with a sardonic grin the whole situation as depicted in the ostensible conflict of outlooks embodied in the first three segments of the poem.

Although not necessarily strictly followed in every instance in the *One Hundred Odes* an intriguing example from among Xuedou's comments is a four-line verse on case 54, in which Yunmen outsmarts a monk who utilizes words too literally in response to the master's query and ends up first slapping and then striking the trainee. Starting off by signaling approval of the teaching method of Yuanwu, Xuedou says, "In one act he takes the tiger's head and the tiger's tail,/ His imposing majesty extends throughout the four hundred realms./ But I inquire [of Yunmen], 'Didn't you realize how impregnable the position was?'/ [Xuedou] says, 'I leave out the last part'" 虎頭虎尾一時收/ 凜凜威風四百州/ 卻問不知何太嶮/ 師云放過一著.[57]

While the third line reverses the theme of admiration by calling into question Yunmen's approach, the final line is deliberately irregular in terms of the number of characters (six, with the first two meaning, "the teacher says") as Xuedou confesses he has nothing more to add in this context. The syntax further indicates that the final phrase was probably originally uttered as an impromptu remark made to inconclusively con-clude an oral delivery of the poem. Given that the capping phrase provided by Yuanwu says he hits the meditation seat one time—although this part is left out of an alternative version of the *Blue Cliff Record*—perhaps the meaning of Xuedou's last line is, "I don't strike a blow," instead of refer-ring to a lack of words.[58]

Does Xuedou's silence at the end suggest esteem for or criticism of Yunmen? Meanwhile Yuanwu's comments playfully challenge both Yunmen, who he says deserved to be hit for wrongfully punishing an advanced disciple, and Xuedou, who was left speechless because he was unable to defend his ancestor's apparent mistake. Yuanwu concludes by suggesting that he will not be one to leave off hitting, so that "everyone in the world will have to take a beating." Through prose and capping-phrase comments Yuanwu thereby creates a nonpoetic way of capturing and conveying the poetic progression that leads to the final line by Xuedou, and this is carried out in order to at once support and subvert the predecessor's standpoint. While later commentators, as the tradition continued to unfold, have offered different readings of Xuedou's verse, which is deliberately ambiguous and open-ended, and Yuanwu's reproach, the latter's view is usually referred to directly or indirectly as an interpretative anchor.

## Expressions of Approval and Disapproval

With its complex literary structure and eloquent use of language in crafting compelling accounts replete with different sorts of inversions, extensions of verbal meanings, and ingenious neologisms, among other rhetorical techniques, the *Blue Cliff Record* is the first main and still the single most prominent example of the massive number of collections of gongan interpretations composed in China, Korea, and Japan.[59] The phrase "Premier Chan Writing," as shown in Figure 1.1, has consistently appeared for centuries on the cover of nearly every edition of the text that has been published. The collection is also rightfully regarded as a classic in the history of the remarkable tradition of East Asian literature for creatively integrating prose with verse and hybrid or capping-phrase interpretations of enigmatic cases through employing a variety of discursive devices culled from both formal and vernacular Chinese literary sources and styles.

In a preface that was provided for the original edition of the *Blue Cliff Record* the monk Puzhao, a self-proclaimed "clumsy oaf reporting on the roots and branches [of the text]" 鄙拙敘其本末,[60] speaks of how he had the privilege of sitting near Yuanwu's chair during the course of his delivery of sermons at Mount Jiashan.[61] Puzhao says, "Only master Xuedou had the true eye that transcends any sectarian division and goes beyond particular styles of teaching." 其惟雪竇禪師.具超宗越格正眼.提掇正令. Furthermore, "When ancestor Foguo was dwelling at Blue Cliff students were confused [by Xuedou's text] and asked him to probe further. The ancestor took pity on them and therefore extended his compassion to uncover the profound source and explicate its underlying principles." 粤有佛果老人. 住碧巖日.學者迷而請益.老人愍以垂慈.剔抉淵源.剖析底理. Through listening to clear and compelling explanations of the gongan along with Xuedou's verse, Puzhao and his equally enthusiastic colleagues "were able to

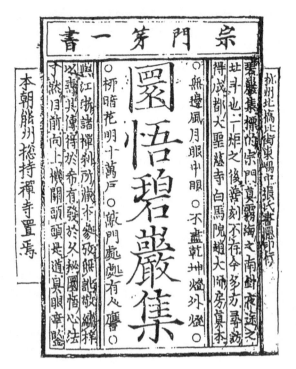

FIGURE 1.1 Medieval edition referring to "Premier Chan Work" (upper left). Komazawa University Library, courtesy of the author.

hear what was never heard before" 得聞未聞, and the monk helped compile the collection as part of a collaborative effort. Using a legal image of dispensing sentences for transgressors that is often evoked playfully in Yuanwu's rhetoric, Puzhao says that "one hundred gongan cases are strung together on a single thread in which the whole crew of old masters is judged, each one of them in his turn." 百則公案.從頭一串穿來.一隊老漢.次第總將按過.[62] Yet Puzhao is also cautious in regard to literary effect, "The ultimate way is in reality wordless but masters of our school extend compassion to rescue the fallen." 至道實乎無言.宗師垂慈救弊.

According to an informative and inspiring afterword written in 1317 by Xi Ling, a monk from the Mount Jingshan temple near Hangzhou, which was one of the leading Chan monastic institutions in China long dominated by followers of Yuanwu's lineage, the *Blue Cliff Record* is an astonishing work because in its pages (the full passage is cited in chapter 4):

Wondrous knowledge is disclosed and transmitted through a spiritual process that seeks to bring illumination to a dusky cave, like a small toad lifting up and shining light on the recesses of a darkened room. . . . Based on just a single perusal of this book, people with great wisdom suddenly awaken their original mind and quickly reach the stage of thoroughly removing all doubts.

Similar acclaim has continued unabated in regard to the exhilaration that ensues through learning from this compilation, which is greatly appreciated and admired today by researchers and aficionados alike in that a global audience has been avidly reading and responding to the significance of this and related texts.

Modern commentators are in accord regarding the value of the complex interpretative quality of the *Blue Cliff Record*, which "as a rich compendium of Ch'an teachings, lore, poetry, and wit . . . reflecting Yüan-wu's exuberant and colloquial style (however inscrutable it may appear initially), represents a peak in the literature of Ch'an."[63] Heinrich Dumoulin refers to the text as "one of the foremost examples of religious world literature,"[64] although he also notes that this work is intricately composed and "not easy" to decipher. A. V. Grimstone remarks in his introduction to a partial translation with commentary by Katsuki Sekida, "Full of paradoxical expressions and all manner of allusions, [the *Blue Cliff Record*] employs a condensed, often involved style, while treating of matters of great subtlety and difficulty."[65] Moreover in the introduction to their 1977 translation of the text, Thomas Cleary and J. C. Cleary suggest that the "literary expressiveness is so rich that it can hardly fail to make an impression."[66] They emphasize that Edo reformer Hakuin Ekaku (1686–1768)—otherwise known as a fierce Rinzai critic of the elaborate discursive style used in the *Blue Cliff Record* and strong supporter of a rival standpoint based on minimalist uses of language—lectured on the collection at least fourteen times over more than thirty years (from the late 1720s until near the end of his life) and said that he continually gained new insights from reading it.

As instrumental and influential as it is regarded, the *Blue Cliff Record* has long been shrouded in contention in regard to the value of its approach to the role of language in relation to the pursuit of Chan enlightenment and also clouded by controversy because of legends often accepted uncritically that obscure the origins and significance of the text. In short it is still very much a contested work in ways that tend to overshadow the meaning of its religious message, and it is often recognized more for the criticism it receives or for myths about its legacy than for gaining appreciation based on historiographically based research. All of these trends contribute to a situation of confusion and instability so that the current state of scholarship seems somewhat mired in stagnation. For various reasons, based primarily on challenges posed by the sheer complexity of the writing, the impact of a legacy of bitter disputes and dislocations surrounding the composition, and the temporary loss and transmission of the text to Japan, the *Blue Cliff Record* has not as yet received the scholarly attention in the modern West that it richly deserves. The unfortunate result is that the collection seems to remain undervalued and is relatively little studied, especially when compared with a host of other classic Chan/Zen texts that have been translated and examined in depth a dozen times or more in some instances.

This collection is probably most widely known today for having apparently been destroyed in 1140 by Dahui, Yuanwu's main disciple yet harshest critic, and it was left out of circulation before being revived and partially reconstructed in the early 1300s. Dahui was no less a literary achiever than his teacher or Xuedou in having produced a significant corpus of nearly a dozen major works including voluminous gongan commentary. But soon after publication of the *Blue Cliff Record*, he supposedly led a harsh critique of any reliance on rhetoric that was seen as a violation of the basic Chan principle of holding to a "special transmission outside the scriptures" (*jiaowai biezhuan*). The notion of antiliterary Chan 無字 (*wuzi Chan*) was revived in the Southern Song, when aesthetic pursuits were considered a mere indulgence to be discarded rather than a refinement to be cultivated in that too much rhetoric had led to the loss of the northern part of the empire. This standpoint, which quickly became dominant among most Chan factions, is mainly attributed to Dahui, who was supposedly responsible for burning the xylographs and all available copies of the *Blue Cliff Record* and was thought to dismiss the collection's rhetoric as a counterproductive contrivance while endorsing instead the minimalism of meditation based on the keyword method. The keyword technique extracts a catchphrase from one of the gongan, such as "No! (*Wu/Mu*)," "Three pounds of flax," or "Cypress tree standing in the courtyard," which constitutes a shortcut path for the practitioner to gain a sudden breakthrough to enlightenment without the need for the embellishments and flourishes of extended literary conceits.

The historicity of the account of what Dahui may or may not have done is and will likely remain undetermined, but it is clear that one way or another the text of the *Blue Cliff Record* was lost for a long time before being retrieved and partially reconstructed by the combined efforts of monastic and lay supporters. The collection was transmitted to Japan shortly after this effort—the date of and circumstances under which the transfer occurred is yet another problematic area of inquiry—where it met with a complex round of fanfare, and it influenced figures such as Daitō Kokushi (1277–1366) and Musō Sōseki (1275–1351). In addition, there were periods of critique and neglect throughout medieval and early modern Japanese history, particularly by Bankei (1622–1693), who advocated the notion of the Unborn (mushō) or the transcendence of subjectivity and objectivity.

The Dahui legend may be looked at from the standpoint of demythologization in that, regardless of the question of historiography, it symbolizes an ideological conflict between two visions of Chan awakening. But does this reductionism really clarify, or does it further obfuscate, the relationship between master and disciple? Another set of myths concerns how the *Blue Cliff Record* was eventually revived and transmitted to Japan. Reports may be unfounded that the Sōtō sect's founder, Dōgen (1200–1253), was the first to bring the collection based on a copy he supposedly made in a single night on the eve of his departure in 1227 from a four-year trip to China that is commonly known as the *One Night Blue Cliff* (*Ichiya Hekigan*). Would Dōgen have had access to a text that was otherwise unavailable in China for another seventy-five years? In fact modern scholars have shown that Dōgen cites Yuanwu frequently but never directly from the *Blue Cliff Record*, and also that the *One Night* legend probably was not formed until a couple of hundred years after his death.[67] Demythologization suggests that the significance of this folklore is to highlight that Dōgen's impressive use of commentarial techniques altering the wording and content of cases was greatly influenced by the interpretative style of the *Blue Cliff Record*. However a failure to investigate fully the origins and implications of the myth may be detrimental to understanding the rhetoric of Xuedou and Yuanwu in relation to Dahui.

The *Blue Cliff Record* has been cast in some circles as a niche collection that was unique to its social historical setting so that, since it can hardly be grasped out of this original context, its overall significance throughout East Asia was relatively short-lived. The collection was, in a sense, a victim of its own success by standing squarely in the crossfire of profound and pervasive underlying counter-tendencies in that the same factors that generated a tremendous sense of approval of its literary qualities also resulted in its destruction or, conversely, a misleading sense of promotion. Therefore the assertions of detractors cannot help but affect the rehabilitative efforts of devotees, who while praising the collection often acknowledge some element of justification in the claims of its opponents.

Instead of losing sight of his distinctive approach by blurring or conflating it with that of his predecessors or successors, here are the central questions I consider: Where does Yuanwu's rhetoric stand in relation to that of his colleagues in terms of the religious vision expressed in the *Blue Cliff Record*? What is Yuanwu's view of Xuedou's poetry in light of the fact that he bases his comments on a source text produced by a follower of a different lineage? Moreover would Yuanwu oppose or might he acquiesce to the standpoint of the minimalist faction? In addition, how do legendary accounts regarding Dahui's act of devastation and Dōgen's efforts at rehabilitation have an impact, for better or worse, on an understanding of the formation and transmission of the *Blue Cliff Record* and its styles of rhetoric that was once seemingly irretrievably lost but then was successfully revived with long-lasting impact?

According to the conventional narrative the emphasis on intricate interpretation in the *Blue Cliff Record* was eclipsed by the debate regarding the viewing-the-phrase (*kanhua*) method associated with the keyword as advocated by Dahui's followers versus the silent-illumination meditation (*mozhao*) method mainly supported by Caodong school leaders, especially the renowned poet-monk Hongzhi, Dahui's rival and primary target of criticism yet also a respected friend. Hongzhi was the long-time abbot of the prestigious Tiantong temple in Zhejiang province, a role he bequeathed to Dahui at the time of his death.

The minimalist approach to language emphasizing the transformative function of the existential sensation of doubt (*yiqing*) as a stepping-stone to the attainment of awakening culminated in the production in 1229 of the streamlined *Wumen's Barrier* (*Wumenguan*, aka *Gateless Gate*), a collection of forty-eight cases that was further propagated in the Yuan dynasty by the writings of Gaofeng Yuanmiao (1238–1295) and his main disciple, Zhongfeng Mingben (1263–1323). After this, gongan were still being studied and used in various kinds of practice, perhaps more so than before, but for the most part in a very different fashion from what Yuanwu envisioned. Meanwhile stereotypes about the main figures based on sectarian biases tend to blur the relation between Yuanwu and Xuedou and also obscure the (dis)connection between Yuanwu and Dahui. In one problematic theory, Yuanwu is seen as a reluctant rather than exuberant commentator, who disputed Xuedou's use of poetics and not only foreshadowed Dahui but would likely have also approved of his burning the text's xylographs as a necessary step leading inevitably to the path of minimalism.

What is the basis for the controversy, and how can the significance of the *Blue Cliff Record* be reconciled with the severe attacks it endured? In many instances of scholarship these questions are dealt with from the standpoint of an ideological commitment to a particular view of Chan that sets Yuanwu and Dahui in opposition or, contrariwise, sees Yuanwu as a precursor of Dahui who perhaps would have supported his act of destruction. What does the topic concerning the aftermath of the text's publication based on Dahui's reaction indicate about the forces leading to the construction of the collection and its overall legacy following its temporary elimination? Did the approach toward Chan language evident in the *Blue Cliff Record* simply fade away? Attempting to answer these questions requires coming to terms with and evaluating systematically the rhetorical style and conceptual content expressed in the collection and related works by Yuanwu and Xuedou.

Probably as a consequence of the classic disputes in addition to the sheer density of the text, and despite its overwhelming importance for understanding the foundation and development of the gongan tradition, the *Blue Cliff Record* has received surprisingly little scholarly attention in the West. Notwithstanding many valuable materials available, this lack is especially evident when compared with other major Chan works from the period, such as the *Record of Linji* (*Linjilu*) and *Wumen's Barrier*, both of which have been translated multiple times and are the subject of several book-length studies. Prominent fascicles of the *Treasury of the True Dharma-Eye* (*Shōbōgenzō*) by Dōgen, who comments in both Japanese vernacular (*kana*) and in Sino-Japanese (*kanbun*) on many of the dialogues included in the *Blue Cliff Record*, have been translated more than a dozen times with at least four complete renderings now in circulation. Some of the translations and studies of these works are produced by scholars while others are by prominent contemporary teachers who address an audience of practitioners.

In the case of the *Blue Cliff Record* there is only one reliable complete translation, and no major scholarly monographs have been published in English explicating the meaning of the text.[68] A few notable articles have appeared but their coverage tends to be highly specialized and either limited in scope or reflective of a particular ideological bent regarding the quality of the collection.[69] An open-ended analysis is needed that examines the diverse ways the text is indebted to, yet influenced, the Song Chinese focus on literary ramifications and shows that it continues, despite the trials it has suffered, to endure in significance and impact the Chan/Zen/ Seon tradition throughout East Asia in ways that are sometimes not recognized or remain little noted at this stage of Western scholarship.

For example there has been no in-depth rhetorical study of the main kinds of interpretative styles Yuanwu presents in the *Blue Cliff Record*'s multilayered structure, including the use of an introduction (*chuishi*) for seventy-nine of the main cases with interlinear capping phrases (*zhuoyu*, also known as *zhujiao*) on all cases plus Xuedou's verses, and prose commentary on case and verse known as an evaluative reaction (*pingchang*). The latter term, sometimes referred to by the more generic sense of prose commentary (*niangu*), literally means a "critical responsive (*ping*) calling out or singing (*chang*)," and thus evokes schools of music criticism that greatly influenced Song Chan poetry, which is based in part on performing traditional odes and chants also stemming from traditional Buddhist *gatha*.[70]

It is important to note that while the title generally used for the compilation is *Chan Master Fuguo Yuanwu's Blue Cliff Record* 佛果圜悟禪師碧巖錄, according to the edition in the Taishō compendium there is a lengthy alternative title that highlights the term *pingchang: Essential Sayings on Priest Xuedou Chongxian's Odes with Evaluative Reactions Created While the Master Stayed at Lingquan Temple on Mount Jiashan in Li State [in Hunan Province]* 師住澧州夾山靈泉禪院評唱雪竇顯和尚頌古語要.[71] *Pingchang* thus has a double meaning. It refers specifically to the two sections of prose remarks in each case included in the *Blue Cliff Record*, and more generally the term suggests the overall commentarial outlook of the entire collection, including all the remarks of Xuedou and Yuanwu, as reflective of the text's spiritual message of self-realization. The *Blue Cliff Record* thereby develops a distinctive discursive style that is particularly conducive to expressing its religious vision of the variability and adaptability of the Chan adept by expanding the horizons of the audience through the method of commentary based on evaluative reactions. The *pingchang* approach is crucial for the subsequent development of nearly all gongan commentarial styles, whether or not they adhere strictly to the form of the *Blue Cliff Record*.

While the introductions for gongan in the *Blue Cliff Record* "raise (an old case)" and verse remarks "praise an old case," to evoke the literal meanings of *chuishi* and *songgu*, respectively, *pingchang* remarks serve to "appraise (an old case)," and in many ways to "re-phrase" its syntax and significance as a crucial part of Yuanwu's assessment. Rather than functioning as a form of literary criticism in the conventional sense of offering a neutral analysis, *pingchang* represents the standpoint of gauging through judgments made, yet regularly modified or overturned, how and to what extent the rhetoric of a case linked with various kinds of comments provides transformational expressions or "turning words" 轉語 (*chuanyu*). These sayings featuring creative uses of language unimpeded by the constraints of logic and rationality are supposed to succinctly and immediately break through obstacles and untie the bonds of ignorance to reveal the experience of awakening to readers who are eager, yet too often blocked in their capacity, to learn and engage existentially with the source dialogues.

In modern Western scholarship there has not yet been a full discussion of the overall meaning and significance of various literary devices used in the *Blue Cliff Record*'s approach to Chan enlightenment vis-à-vis other Song views of the efficacy of discourse, or of Yuanwu's multifaceted relations to his predecessors and successors as well as supporters and opponents, who are frequently of mixed mind or conflicted in their outlook toward the merit of the collection. Instead we are often left by contemporary studies with general impressions derived from traditional sectarian stereotypes. However, significant advances in recent research produced in Japan and China, including extensively annotated modern translations in addition to other kinds of interpretative materials, point the way to a more thoroughgoing hermeneutic examination of the text.[72]

The groundbreaking historical studies of classical Chan discourse by Yanagida Seizan and the detailed analysis of Chinese linguistics by Iriya Yoshitaka, resulting in such works as the *Dictionary of Zen Expressions* (*Zengo Jiten*), examine the use and meaning of Chan phrases, including the role of vernacular locutions that reveal the vibrancy of source materials. Prior to these examples of modern scholarship on the rhetorical structure of the school's sayings, the elusive nature of Chan language was primarily interpreted for transcendental qualities by scholar-practitioners rather than examined in terms of the sociohistorical context of the compositions. Iriya and Yanagida along with Kajitani Sōnin produced a modern translation of the *One Hundred Odes* in 1981 that is one of several important textual studies directly related to the *Blue Cliff Record*, in addition to Itō Yuten's 1963 critical edition of the *One Night Blue Cliff* edition.[73] Some of the many examples of relevant contemporary East Asian research include detailed theoretical studies of the discursive style of the *Blue Cliff Record* by Sueki Fumihiko,

Ogawa Takashi, and Nishimura Eshin in Japan, biographical studies of Yuanwu by Shi Yafan and literary reflections on Chan by Zhou Yukai in China, plus a meticulous examination of related texts from the era by Taiwanese scholar Yi-hsun Huang. These works are further highlighted by an entire course on the collection offered recently at National Taiwan University.[74]

My goal is to explore a number of thorny hermeneutic issues by capturing Yuanwu's distinctive rhetorical voice in order to discuss diverse ideological connections and disconnections from a flexible and unrestricted perspective. This avoids sectarian stereotypes that tend to either blur or exaggerate the significance of conceptual relationships between Yuanwu and the main figures whose teachings he absorbed or influenced.

Yuanwu's creative approach to the use of rhetoric, sometimes characterized as lettered Chan, is reinforced by the remarks of several key poets or monks from the period. For example Su Shi, a Chan sympathizer who also served for nearly twenty years as mayor of Hangzhou in the years before it became the Southern Song capital, remarked that he could determine a man's character and not just the degree of learning from what was expressed in his verse.[75] Also Juefan Huihong, a prolific chronicler of Chan ancestors who probably first coined the term *wenzi Chan*, was known to say, "The subtleties of the mind cannot be transmitted in words, but can be seen in verbal expressions," and in further support of this notion the Yunmen scholar Dajue Huailian (1009–1090) once remarked, "If jade is not polished, it cannot be fashioned into a vessel. If people do not study, then they will not know the path."[76] Furthermore, according to Linquan Conglun, a late thirteenth-century Caodong compiler of gongan commentaries, "Principle is manifested through language, and without language the ultimate truth would become unattainable. Language does not go beyond principle, but without principle language cannot fulfill its proper end."[77]

In light of these reflections by representatives of a literary approach, where does Yuanwu and his relation to Dahui stand between his links with Xuedou at the beginning of the gongan tradition and contrast with Wumen Huikai (1183–1260), compiler of *Wumen's Barrier* at the end of the initial historical arc lasting for about two centuries of composing poetic and prose commentaries on cases? Table 1.1 highlights key transitions for understanding Yuanwu's own point of view separated from the way he interprets Xuedou and succeeds Wuzu or is appropriated by Dahui, whose keyword approach was culminated by Wumen.

Table 1.1 Yuanwu at Conceptual-Historical Crossroads

| Xuedou Verses 1026 | Wuzu Gongan Mentor late 11th c. | Yuanwu Commentator 1128 | Dahui Keyword Method mid 12th c. | Wumen Concise Style 1229 |
|---|---|---|---|---|

A nuanced textual-literary analysis must take into account the broader context of Song culture evident in religious and secular writings, including the diverse styles of Yuanwu's other texts and different works by Xuedou and Dahui, who are complex thinkers, in addition to a wide variety of subsequent materials greatly influenced by the *Blue Cliff Record*'s commentarial styles. Rather than seeing a simple trajectory moving away from Yuanwu's use of rhetoric and toward the minimalism of Dahui and *Wumen's Barrier*, my approach takes into account numerous collections, commentaries, and translations produced in China, Japan, Korea, and the contemporary West. This helps reveal the broad range of developments of gongan/kōan literature in the formative period of the eleventh through thirteenth centuries and well beyond, including the multitude of Chan and Zen texts composed for hundreds of years that reflect the vast and ongoing impact of Yuanwu's work. For example, even though *Wumen's Barrier* does not use the techniques of capping phrase and fully evaluative reaction in prose, its ironic style is derivative of and should not simply be contrasted with the rhetoric of the *Blue Cliff Record*.

In regard to Yuanwu's role as a second-level commentator on Xuedou who at once praises and critiques his predecessor, a preface to the *Blue Cliff Record* from 1300 by Fanghui Wanli refers to the "grandmotherly kindness" 老婆心切 of both figures along with that of Zhanghui Mingyuan (n.d.), who it was said, revived the dead ashes and reprinted the text 燃死灰復板行.[78] This preface also discusses Yuanwu's relation to Dahui in terms of whether he stands in basic opposition or in some degree of sympathy with his one-time trainee, who he helped lead to an experience of enlightenment as part of their set of intricate interactions.[79] Some interpreters claim that Yuanwu actually disclosed the keyword to Dahui at this intimate spiritual moment. Although I will show that a close look at the relevant passages tends to dispute that suggestion, there clearly was a complicated retrospective set of mutual or crosscurrent appropriations of the significance of their respective teachings by later generations of defenders and critics alike. In any event the rhetorical style of the *Blue Cliff Record* was by no means simply eclipsed by the keyword method as it clearly was kept very much alive through the efforts of a multitude of commentators.

## Hermeneutic Reflexivity

My reading of Yuanwu stands in contrast to that of some researchers, who maintain that his approach is more instructive than Xuedou's rather vague and obscure poetry and thus not at all indecisive,[80] and it also is different than interpreters who argue that Yuanwu was an advocate of doubt as an experience that can catapult a trainee to realization in a way that anticipated yet did not go as far in emphasizing this state of mind as what Dahui and his followers proposed.[81] Uncertainty, I suggest, encompasses the notion of Chan doubt that many keyword proponents support, but it represents a more basic and freewheeling interpretative awareness by avoiding the view that this sensation is an inevitable stepping-stone to the attainment of certainty through mastering the keyword. For Yuanwu the only thing that is certain is that uncertainty prevails, but that is not a form of certainty at all since creative tension is purposefully left to stand unresolved.

According to the notion of uncertainty, whatever standpoint is provisionally upheld at any given juncture in interpreting a gongan case, which is already designed to create distrust by challenging commonly accepted notions of reality or expectations about the capacity of thought, is invariably disputed and refuted or confirmed in ironic or deliberately disingenuous fashion. At the same time embracing uncertainty must not be posited as an end in itself, as this perspective also needs to be continually overthrown from its pedestal by Yuanwu, who comments several times on the perpetual deconstructive process by citing an old Chinese saying, "The correct question is situated within the answer, and the answer is situated within the question" 問在答處.答在問處.[82] As Yuanwu remarks of the provisional quality of discourse in the introduction to case 8, in a passage that influenced Dōgen's "Being-Time" (*Uji*) fascicle, "Sometimes a single phrase is like a lion crouching on the ground; sometimes a phrase is like the Diamond King's jewel sword; sometimes a phrase cuts off the tongues of everyone on earth; and sometimes a phrase follows the waves and pursues the currents" 有時一句.如踞地獅子.有時一句/如金剛王寶劍.有時一句.坐斷天下人舌頭.有時一句.隨波逐浪.[83] These images refer to the variability of teaching that must be continually redesigned and refashioned to correspond 對 to the learning requirements of disciples.

The only conclusion Yuanwu offers, which in many ways does resemble Dahui's teaching, is that a trainee or reader cannot rely on doctrine, interpretation, or instruction alone, even as these elements cannot be fully discarded, but must turn inward to reach a realm of self-discovery in order to ascertain the multiple levels of meaning of whatever matter is at hand. Truth is not independent of a given situation or free-floating timelessly above the moment of a Dharma battle. Rather it uncertainly becomes apparent through immediacy, yet remains cloaked so that reading between the lines of the verbiage is necessary to ascertain a perspective of relativism and indeterminacy functioning within the context of continual change.

As Tang master Donghan Liangjie (807–869), founder of the Caodong school, suggests in the *Jewel Mirror Samadhi* (*Baojing Sanmei*), "Meaning does not abide in words but a pivotal moment of change brings forth truth" 意不在言.来機亦赴 (alternatively: "Because intention is not evident in speaking truth appears when one reaches the point of change").[84] According to this standpoint, a particular instance of verbal exchange must be comprehended in terms of a broader sense of expressiveness that encompasses nonverbal demonstrations, such as examples of masters striking and slapping disciples during an encounter, as well as more passive gestures like shaking one's sleeve or raising the ceremonial flywhisk to indicate a comeback or rebuttal or to cast a dismissive tone. In Dongshan's saying, the character 機 (*ji*)—also the first syllable in the compound *jifeng* used extensively by Yunmen and Yuanwu—indicates a transformative opportunity realized by summoning one's utmost proficiency in smashing through all barriers.

The *Blue Cliff Record*'s creative interpretative approach based on the appraisals of the *pingchang* method is revealed in the verse and prose comments to case 1, which involves first patriarch Bodhidharma's fateful conversation in which he tells the emperor there is "nothing holy" and he does "not know his own name," and then departs the territory to return to his homeland, a loss the ruler deeply regrets. Xuedou begins the poem in an evaluative fashion through upending expectations by reversing stereotypes and demanding members of the audience make their own assessment by saying, "The holy truths are empty/ How do you understand this?" 聖諦廓然.何當辨的.[85] He then addresses the emperor with, "Stop your vain yearning!" 休相憶.[86] At the end of his remarks, Xuedou turns to the assembly and, by adding to the verse after "looking around to the right and to the left," he asks boldly, 'Is there any patriarch here?' while answering himself with, 'There is. Call him over so he can wash my feet!'" 師顧視左右云.這裏還有祖師麼.自云有.喚來與老僧洗腳.[87] Yuanwu reacts by suggesting that Xuedou is the one who "deserves a beating of thirty blows of the staff" 三十棒. Yet Yuanwu further comments that "by his acting in this [deliberately eccentric] way, still [Xuedou] has made an accomplishment" 作這去就.猶較些子.[88]

The outlook of *pingchang*, which appears in the title of several prominent collections produced in the thirteenth and later centuries, is crucial for understanding the subsequent development of nearly all gongan/kōan commentarial styles, especially the practice of presenting oral sermons on the meaning of cases that are generally known today by the Japanese term *teishō* 提唱 (C. *tichang*). That term combines the second character *chang/shō* with *ti/tei* (literally "to pick up," as in Sakyamuni holding a flower). However these kinds of sermons or Dharma talks, in which a Chan/Zen teacher addresses various levels of significance of a selected passage such as a dialogue, anecdote, or saying attributed to one of the classic masters, tend to be more homiletic in promoting an exhortative viewpoint based on interpreting the implications of a gongan case. The *pingchang* approach in the *Blue Cliff Record* and other collections, which is at once an appreciation and an interpretative analysis of the sources, tends to represent a more open-ended approach to using critical hermeneutics to examine the import of cases from different angles without attempting to reach a firm conclusion and, indeed, by trying to defeat any standpoint that is reified in being set on a pedestal.

My view that the *Blue Cliff Record* is founded on expressing the rhetoric of uncertainty is intended to encompass but not be limited to the Chan emphasis on undergoing a profound experience of existential doubt, which destabilizes and undermines all assumptions and presuppositions that otherwise obstruct the journey toward religious awakening that consists of freedom from such fetters. According to the commentary on case 51, an unenlightened person is one whose "eyes go blurry and sightless, so they only know how to answer a question by raising a question or react to an answer by giving an answer but without realizing how much they are being swayed by the views of others" 若忽眼目迷黎麻羅.到處逢問便問.逢答便答.殊不知鼻孔在別人手裏.[89] The passage reflects the negative meaning of uncertainty in the sense of one who is unsure and unstable while wavering aimlessly among attitudes that are influenced by external factors. Yet this condition functions as a stage on the path in that it causes the need for everyday awareness to be tossed upside down and cast topsy-turvy by a worthy teacher's elusive instructions that set the stage for a total reorientation of standpoints. According to one of the frequently used capping phrases, such an insecure and apprehensive person "falls back three thousand miles" 倒退三千里 prior to attaining recovery and redemption by being able to overcome all impediments.

Such a reversal represents a bottoming out that ultimately results in the positive meaning of uncertainty, which pertains to the open-ended outlook of the Chan adept who confidently embraces all possible perspectives without clinging to one side or the other while exercising supreme agility along with the ability to adjust to circumstances at the spur of the moment. Yuanwu further writes in case 51, "Whoever upholds Chan teaching is able to discern how to take charge of a situation [or seize an opportunity] by knowing when to advance or retreat, how to distinguish true from false, and understanding whether to kill or give life or to capture or let go [of the disciple]" 大凡扶豎宗教.須是辨箇當機.知進退是非.明殺活擒縱.[90] According to the verse comment on case 52, in which the master's response to a disciple's question uses concrete everyday imagery, the best approach is "not to make a show of transcendence and, in that way, you reveal true loftiness" 孤危不立道方高; that is, by resisting the urge to appear overly clever, crafty, or mannered, an authentic teacher displays his or her wisdom through rhetorical prowess.

Therefore, in contrast to the unenlightened "one who needs to be punished by having their meditation seat overturned" 好與掀倒禪床 since their stereotypes must be shifted upside down, Yuanwu maintains that the enlightened master represents "one who is able to reverse the flow of the great seas to topple Mount Sumeru" 掀翻大海踢倒須彌.[91] In his evaluative reactions Yuanwu uses the same verb 倒 (overturn, topple), which indicates falsity in traditional Buddhist scriptures, to suggest both the negative and positive meanings of the impact of uncertainty.

Whichever consequence the act of capsizing represents depends on whether the state of being uncertain befalls a learner who stands prior to and awaits the experience of awakening or is enacted by an adept existing in the aftermath of said experience. In either instance the term suggests a diversion, inversion, or subversion that epitomizes upending fetters and, thereby, gaining liberation from conventional views by virtue of the Chan master's facility with utilizing diverse sorts of discursive devices. These techniques are apropos to the conditions and circumstances of trainees, who may need to be either symbolically captured and slain if they are incorrigibly stubborn in their fixations or released and given a new lease on life if they are already making good progress in the path toward self-discovery.

The writing style of the *Blue Cliff Record* with its multilayered structure dealing with gongan cases that are by definition opaque and cryptic in their meaning is all the more mysterious and difficult to decipher by virtue of the combined craft of Xuedou and Yuanwu. Based on elaborate levels of evaluation of gongan offered by two authors, whose views are sometimes compatible and reinforcing and at other times conflicting and undermining, the collection imaginatively incorporates varied types of interpretations of enigmatic cases. Apparent contradictions are usually deliberate in that, as a key part of the *pingchang* method, Yuanwu playfully challenges Xuedou's authority. This leaves the overall effect of their remarks incongruously between the extremes of agreement or disagreement, depending on how the comments are interpreted.

The views of Xuedou and Yuanwu consistently demonstrate inconsistency in that as soon as one view is formed in assessing the significance of a case it is deliberately inverted or subverted in order to pull the rug out from under and upend any fixed position that may in the final analysis distract or mislead a seeker. For example, in case 25 during a speech to his assembly while wielding his Chan staff, as a symbol of authenticity, the Hermit of Lotus Blossom Peak seems clearly to have challenged and outsmarted all the disciples with back-to-back queries. There is no response from the group, as everyone in attendance is apparently stunned speechless in an example of unproductive silence. The Hermit then ends up answering both questions himself in a technique that is often used by frustrated Chan teachers. He ends the encounter by tossing his staff across his shoulder and heading off for the hills as a sign of contempt for the ignorance of his followers, while declaring that in his freedom from ignorance he pays heed to no one.

What is the reader to make of this unrestrained show of the Hermit's seemingly impatient haughtiness? Despite the apparent freedom from conventional reins and the exuding of self-assurance that his actions seem to suggest, Yuanwu's capping phrase proclaims, "He still deserves thirty blows for carrying a board across his shoulder" 也好與三十棒.只為他擔板. This phrase suggests that the staff as an object blocking one from seeing in all directions highlights that the Hermit is being narrow-minded or one-sided in his outlook. Yuanwu adds, "When you see a shady character like this (literally, one's whose jowls are so big they can be noticed by

someone looking at the back of his head), do not go chasing after him" 腦
後見腮.莫與往來).⁹² This complication for trying to understand the gist of
the case is further heightened by Xuedou's verse that says in its opening
line, "Dust and sand in his eyes with dirt in his ears" 眼裏塵沙耳裏土.⁹³
This literally means that the Hermit does not see or hear properly in an
apparent attack on his ability. But the saying can also suggest the opposite
of this in that, since the Hermit is transcendent, his activity leaves no trace
of defilement. Xuedou concludes by saying, "Suddenly I raise my eyebrows to look, but where has he gone?" 剔起眉毛何處去,⁹⁴ with the image
of eyebrows symbolizing a master's wisdom and know-how in teaching,
as featured in case 8.

However Yuanwu's remarks take the density of interpretation a step
further in reacting with a scathing critique and feigned assault on Xuedou
by commenting, "[The Hermit] has been right here all along ... I strike!"
元來只在這裏 ... 打.⁹⁵ Moreover in the prose commentary Yuanwu asks,
"Why is it that Xuedou doesn't know where the Hermit has gone? This
would be as if I held up my ceremonial fly-whisk and you could not find
it." The real point of Yuanwu's playful irony becomes clear in the concluding passage in which he addresses the audience with the injunction, "For
all of you who are able to see him, this means you are studying with the
Hermit of Lotus Blossom Peak. But if you do not yet see him, this means
you should go back to square one and start anew to thoroughly investigate
the matter!" 爾諸人若見得.與蓮花峰庵主同參.其或未然.三條椽下.七尺
單.試去參詳看.⁹⁶

In a number of the cases, Xuedou or another interlocutor, such as
Yunmen, interjects his own capping-phrase comments into the case
record, which further complicates the meaning.⁹⁷ Yuanwu's *pingchang*
evaluations of all his predecessors—that is, his interlinear remarks along
with prose comments on case and verse—are homiletic in conveying and
exhorting the reader toward embracing the basic message that one must
study carefully the source materials yet remain altogether detached from
verbal expressions. Yuanwu's work also includes hermeneutical elements
that are exegetical, in providing some of the conceptual and cultural background for understanding the origins and contextual implications of case
and verse by citing sources such as the *Jingde Record* among other texts,
as well eisegetical, in exploring existentially various kinds of Chan as well
as non-Buddhist views that support and augment the complex role of
rhetoric in relation to the goal of attaining spiritual realization.⁹⁸ All the
different types of remarks reflect an outlook based on contradiction and

relativism that results in a refraining from any commitment to embracing a particular standpoint concerning the underlying meaning of the case, which must be left open-ended and variable to an individual's level of religious experience and circumstances of training. This turnaround is accomplished, whether by verbal or nonverbal means, at crucial moments of existential transition and transformation when—to evoke the art of war-based images of competition in combat that often characterized Dharma battles as depicted in gongan exchanges—everything is at stake in a life-or-death struggle whereby all or naught may be won or lost. When push comes to shove there is nothing whatsoever to hide or reveal other than the quality of one's character either demonstrating convincingly or sorely lacking in authenticity and finesse.

Many examinations of the *Blue Cliff Record* tend to emphasize the literary element as key to its greatness that also led to a diminishment of the Chan self-definition as a "special transmission outside the teachings," which is supposedly why the text was destroyed soon after its publication. While acknowledging the importance of the debate between the standpoints of literary and nonliterary Chan and their various offshoots, I suggest that the significance of the dimension of the interiority of self-realization clearly outweighs that of erudition since all the relevant figures, including Xuedou and Yuanwu in addition to Dahui, agree that learning for its own sake is an unedifying goal if pursued as an end justifying the means and that creative expression should not be avoided but must be cultivated as a skillful method. In my reading, Yuanwu, like Dahui, gives ample evidence of maintaining a relentless focus on attaining noncognitive awakening through persistent warnings against depending on verbosity and conceptualization. He constantly labels as fools, phonies, and blind men those who symbolically carry a board across their shoulder or cling to one-sided standpoints by adding frost to snow or mud to dirt, or by placing a head above a head or filling a black lacquer bucket with black ink.

Therefore when the instructional process for overcoming illusion functions well, one "naturally attains insight . . . and with a single stroke of the sword the state of liberation is fully disclosed" 自然見得 . . . 一刀截斷.洒洒落落.[99] If, Yuanwu also points out, "comparative judgments and conceptual fixations" 無計較情塵 continue to get in the way, then in transmitting the Dharma the first patriarch "already is causing brambles to grow several yards deep right under your feet" 諸人即今腳跟下.已深數丈.[100] The outlook of utilizing skillful means to the utmost capacity while remaining cognizant of the inherent shortcomings of language that derive mainly from trainees' incapacities, Yuanwu assures the reader, also holds for all the ancestors of the Chan school for whom he says there is "no other purpose" 其實無他 to their teaching than guiding followers, whether monastic or lay, to realize enlightenment.[101]

The notion of uncertainty, which conveys a spiritual condition of upholding and perpetuating the interior illumination of the ancestors gained through undergoing experiential upheavals and reversals, indicates that the primary aim of the *Blue Cliff Record* is to acknowledge a foundational ambivalence and irreconcilability while trying in utter frustration yet with graceful acceptance to reconcile perennial Chan issues that are crucial elements of the quest for spiritual awakening. The ability to turn the tables 翻倒 by circling around the adversary/partner 交馳 while finding areas of cooperation for mutual benefit enables a crossing of the proverbial checkpoint of the Dragon Gate.

Conventional ways of evaluating the collection tend to get mired in outdated debates about whether it was destroyed, and if so by whom, or whether this should have transpired or was justifiable but without seeking to penetrate the underlying structure of the collection's expansive and imaginative rhetoric free from assumptions of deficiency or duplicity. The main factor for understanding the *Blue Cliff Record* is not so much a matter of discerning its literary prowess or determining whether its use of language is conducive to the quest for awakening. Rhetorical ingenuity is crucial for conveying its message, but the most important hermeneutic factor pertains to the way the text posits a religious goal based on the ability of the enlightened person to seize the opportunity for creative expression as a teaching device appropriate to the needs of the unenlightened. The primary touchstone for grasping the *Blue Cliff Record*'s approach to discourse is not a matter of what is said, or even how or why it is spoken, but the pedagogical context in which wording is uttered for the purpose of liberating trainees from the ignorance and self-imposed impediments that obstruct them from gaining freedom.

The *Blue Cliff Record* is at once a conservative publication in preserving and promoting established cases and masters and a radically creative innovation for consistently breaking the mold in various ways that correspond stylistically to the heart of the message of uncertainty about attaining a spiritual breakthrough by remaining free from the bondage of conceptuality and logic. The collection seeks to disseminate Chan learning faithfully yet critically and tries to capture lightning in a bottle for its audience by developing remarkable new forms of rhetoric demonstrating the ability to reverse any given outcome or verdict 翻案 by presenting different views of prior judgments of a case that have been handed down by tradition or convention.

I put forward the notion of uncertainty in a way that adheres to yet defies the typical Chan mode of discourse by trying to capture in a single word or phrase the achievements of Yuanwu that, I will show, also has a strong resonance with some contemporary Western approaches to knowledge acquisition in relation to spiritual attainment. An emphasis on uncertainty, a term not specifically used in the collection, is not intended to foster one more problematic cliché-ridden label in regard to a religion well known, especially during the Song dynasty when it sought to appeal to a broader audience, for spawning while at the same time repudiating various catchphrases, slogans, monikers, and mottoes that are too often misleading or misunderstood.

The reflexivity of my approach suggests an attempt to formulate a new hermeneutic in light of variant versions and interpretations of the text for understanding how the *Blue Cliff Record* epitomizes Yuanwu's unique rhetorical voice in evoking a theoretical vision of awakening by commenting on Xuedou's enigmatic verse in a way that is conceptually and discursively based on embracing a fundamental level of ambiguity and irresolution. Because the possibility of misrepresenting uncertainty hangs precariously in the air I am ambivalent about using this term in that I remain uncertain about uncertainty. This, I believe, constitutes a constructive initiative for coming to terms with a work whose primary aim is to unsettle and disturb all assumptions and to never let stand any given perspective without making every effort to be sure it has been inverted or subverted by counterarguments or diverted from a fixation with conventional positions. In the upside down, topsy-turvy rhetorical world of the *Blue Cliff Record*, standpoints are undermined or invalidated as soon as they are posited. Paradoxical images like "[s]eeing or not seeing, you can ride backwards on the ox into the Buddha shrine" 見不見.倒騎牛兮入佛殿[102] or "[t]he sword that kills is the sword that gives life" 垂示云.殺人刀活人劍[103]—a phrase used more than a dozen times in the collection and in Yuanwu's other writings—convey through "words that startle the crowd" 語驚群 the essential posture of the inventive and elusive discourse advanced by Xuedou and Yuanwu. The complexity of the text demands the reflexivity of my hermeneutic method.

One way to look at the perpetual pedagogical conundrum regarding knowledge related to language is to consider the observation made by

Ernst Cassirer in *Language and Myth* about how a sense of intellectual frustration and futility becomes a necessary psychological stage that gives way to an undying effort to gain understanding. Cassirer writes, "All the energy devoted to [trying to resolve a basic quandary] seems only to lead us about in a circle and finally leave us at the point from which we started. And yet the very nature of such fundamental problems entails that the mind, though it despairs of ever finally solving them, can never quite let them alone."[104] Cassirer's view is complemented from an opposing angle through a comment in a preface to the *Blue Cliff Record* by Zhou Chi (aka Yucen Xiuxiu) from a 1305 edition that presumes full awareness as a base condition of human experience yet highlights impediments that all too easily obstruct it from being manifested:

> Human mind and the way are one; the way and myriad things are one. This oneness fills cosmic space—is there anywhere that the way is not found? When ordinary people look for it they can only see what they see and not what they do not see. They seek [the way] from others and leave it to others to tell them about it. This is like [Su Shi's] metaphor of the sun. In turning an object of inquiry over and over in their minds to try to figure it out investigators move further away and lose sight of it all the more. That is why Confucius, who gained a personal self-realization of the way, avoided using too many words.
>
> 夫心與道一.道與萬物一.充滿太虛.何適而非道.第常人觀之.能見其所見.而不見其所不見.求之於人.而人語之.如東坡日喻之說.往復推測.愈遠愈失.自吾夫子體道.猶欲無言.[105]

Su Shi's parable of the sun alluded to here is similar to the classic fable of blind men trying to understand an elephant by mistaking each part for the whole (e.g., a leg as a tree). The thoughts of Cassirer and Zhou coincide by suggesting that the more we express about a phenomenon, the greater the distance from the object, but this is exactly the impulse that drives our continuous striving.

Standing aloof and critical of the vicious cycle that invariably emerges in the process of gaining knowledge may be useful to a point but is not sufficient for rectifying the matter. Groucho Marx's career, like that of many comedians, was based on using jabs, putdowns, insults, slams, and zingers that resembles the way Yuanwu's capping phrases savagely critiqued foolishness, even that of Xuedou, by saying nearly twenty times,

"He pulls his arrow after the thief has already fled" 賊過後張弓, or in cases 10 and 65, "The sound of his thunder is great but there is no rain after all" 雷聲浩大, 雨點全無. This is done to offer seriocomic relief in lampooning the temptation either to stay detached or to become bombastic by failing to resort to agile cleverness. Groucho once confessed, "Years ago, I tried to top everybody, but I don't anymore. I realized it was killing conversation. When you're always trying for a topper you aren't really listening. It ruins communication."[106] At some point, one must get down in the brambles or weeds, as Yuanwu characterizes the process, to demonstrate grandmotherly kindness by helping rather than appearing to be snubbing learners along the path.[107]

To show the complexity of uncertainty so that the notion is not reduced to a simplistic interpretation, it is helpful to distinguish between three levels of Chan ambiguity based on using the model of "toward awakening (*satori*, C. *wu*) and from awakening" (*satori e, satori kara* 悟りえ悟りから); that is, by distinguishing whether one is still on the path of striving to achieve self-realization (*satori e*) or one has already attained this goal (*satori kara*) and is endeavoring to teach it persuasively to sometimes stubborn or seemingly incorrigible disciples.[108] As Musō Sōseki writes based on his understanding of a passage from Yuanwu's comments, "For one who has yet to attain realization, it is better to study the intent [or meaning] than to study the words; for one who has attained realization, it is better to study the words than to study the intent."[109]

The first level of uncertainty, or its negative meaning, refers to the pre-*satori* experience that is characterized by feeling a vague sense of underlying doubt or disturbance about unchallenged assumptions so that one clings to meaning while forgetting words as empty containers of intentionality. Feelings of instability and unsettledness persist but are productive in pointing beyond ordinary barriers to the possibility of attaining transcendence. The second level, or the positive meaning of uncertainty, involving the post-*satori* experience reflects the flexibility of the master in trying to determine the most appropriate instructional method that best addresses the pedagogical stage of his trainees. This involves dazzling the reader with elegant language that indulges their current deficient level of understanding by allowing for a gradual process of growth, or puzzling the learner through compelling him to abruptly cast aside misconceptions while spontaneously accepting and adapting to a higher truth.

In addition to pre-*satori* uncertainty about how to gain awakening and post-*satori* uncertainty about how to lead followers, the third level of uncertainty is hermeneutic reflexivity. Objective observers researching the history and ideology of the text continually face indecisiveness about how to read and appreciate the complex quality of the *Blue Cliff Record*, which is attributable to two main factors. One is the text's facility in evoking eloquent prose and poetic rhetoric that is obscurely rooted in Song dynasty locutions so as to craft a vision of the "knack" (another rendering of *ji*) for expressing Chan awakening and how to get it. The other factor is a lack of assuredness in explaining reasons for the enthusiastic approval yet dramatic disavowal the work has received, which cannot help but affect our access and appropriation of the text. To express this ongoing quandary through postulating a faux dialogue: "What about uncertainty? What about it? You tell me. I am uncertain. About? I am uncertain about uncertainty. Are you certain of that? Certainly (not). And that is (not) exactly what I remain uncertain about, and why I am reluctant to assert it with any sense of certainty."

## Chapter Preview

Each of the following five chapters uses the notion of uncertainty as the primary interpretative tool to address and resolve a basic set of hermeneutic issues. These involve the formation of the innovative rhetorical structures and functions of the text based on the complex conceptual relations of Yuanwu with Xuedou and Dahui as well as later commentators. The conventional view for interpreting the *Blue Cliff Record* is described in each instance to open a closer investigation of textual and historical evidence. This examination enables a deconstruction of problematic standpoints derived from misleading assumptions accompanied by a reconstruction of the *Blue Cliff Record*'s distinctive approach to Chan discourse.

The second chapter, "Entering the Dragon Gate: Textual Formation in Historical and Rhetorical Contexts," considers several main areas of influence on how the multilayered organization of the *Blue Cliff Record* was developed. These areas cover the impact of previous masters, including Yunmen and Fenyang among other representatives of the Five Houses (*Wujia*) of Chan (Caodong 曹洞, Fayan 法眼, Guiyang 溈仰, Linji 臨濟, Yunmen 雲門), who created various kinds of impromptu remarks or composed prose and/or verse commentaries on gongan cases; different genres of Chan writings, especially transmission of the lamp texts, which provided much of the descriptive material and mythical background for constructing gongan collections; and the effect of Northern Song literary influences, including such cultural figures as eminent secular poet and Buddhist scholiast Su Shi, Chan poet-monk Juefan Huihong, and Buddhist-based scholar-official Zhang Shangying. Whereas the conventional view assumes that the *Blue Cliff Record* does not transcend its influences, I argue that the notion of uncertainty goes beyond preceding factors in articulating a new religious vision based on the self-confidence of self-realization that has a resonance with modern Western viewpoints to accepting inconclusiveness and chaos as the key to grasping the subjectivity of truth.

The next two chapters examine areas of apparent discrepancy between Yuanwu and Xuedou in addition to the former's ostensible conflict with Dahui in regard to gongan interpretation and practice. This has led to a lingering sense that the *Blue Cliff Record* is overwrought with literary effect and is thereby counterproductive to the single-minded Chan quest for enlightenment.

Chapter 3, "Unintended Baggage? Part I: Yuanwu in His Own Write Vis-à-Vis Xuedou," is a discussion of the main issues concerning Yuanwu's appropriation of Xuedou's poetry through interlinear capping phrases and prose evaluations by looking carefully at examples from selected cases of the way Yuanwu reacts to his predecessor. A crucial passage is Yuanwu's comment in case 1, which deals with Bodhidharma's iconoclastic quip that there is "nothing sacred" in response to the emperor's query about the results of good works. Yuanwu stakes out his distinctive view of language in gongan discourse by valorizing Xuedou's verse comments while also supporting the role of prose commentary. The conventional view is that this passage somehow demonstrates a rejection of Xuedou's verse, but I show that for Yuanwu poetic and prose approaches to gongan commentary are compatible and reinforcing.

The fourth chapter, "Unintended Baggage? Part II: Yuanwu in His Own Write Vis-à-Vis Dahui," provides a critical analysis of two interconnected issues involved in assessing Yuanwu's thought in regard to the efficacy and/or detrimental quality of language compared with Dahui's mature views that seem to be diametrically opposed despite their early mentor-disciple relationship. A key issue is whether the treatment of gongan commentary in the *Blue Cliff Record* somehow foreshadowed the formation of the shortcut-keyword technique, which is suggested in the conventional view, or if it represented a distinct approach. Another issue deals with the role of doubt in Yuanwu's writing about the spiritual experience of working through gongan, especially in case 12 on Dongshan's "Three pounds of flax," and the extent to which this may or may not have influenced or at least strongly resembled Dahui. The topic also involves consideration of whether Yuanwu was really a precursor rather than an antagonist of the keyword method who could or would have approved of the destruction of his own text.

Chapter 5, "Sharpening a Sword: Case Studies of Representative Gongan," gives an explanation of specific rhetorical functions of several *Blue Cliff Record* cases by focusing on several levels of composition. One level includes particularly prominent words or phrasing used by Yuanwu in inventive ways to highlight the significance of Chan thought, such as "activity" or "device" (*ji*) and the compounds "skillful device or knack" (*jifeng*) and "activity-condition" 機境 (*jijing*).[110] Another level of literary construction refers to how Yuanwu's comments on cases with verse selected by Xuedou provide ironic counterpoint remarks regarding the dynamics of the thrust-and-parry competitive style of encounter dialogues. The third level indicates how the various discursive techniques build together to construct the rhetoric of uncertainty, or a studied ambivalence and indeterminacy about the basis for truth-claims regarding perennial issues of language, perception, doubt, and time in relation to awakening and transmission. Special emphasis is given to analyzing the interpretative styles of capping phrases and evaluative reactions used in several key gongan, particularly cases 7, 14, and 15.

Finally chapter 6, "Questions Are in the Answers: Enduring Legacy in Relation to Textual Controversies," provides an epilogue by dealing with the legacy of the *Blue Cliff Record* in light of the twin legends of Dahui incinerating and Dōgen transmitting the collection, which are almost invariably mentioned but rarely examined closely whenever the text is discussed. Behind the mythical quality of these accounts lies a deeper meaning in that Dahui turned gongan meditation in a new direction that was extremely popular throughout East Asia, whereas Dōgen was the first Japanese master to introduce kōan writings into Zen practice in his native country in a trend that soon became and remained dominant in both Sōtō and Rinzai sects. What tends to get overlooked in this kind of sometimes unproductive demythologization are basic questions as to historiography and whether and to what extent the legendary accounts conceal rather than reveal the actual circumstances of the *Blue Cliff Record*'s textual origins and dissemination. In contrast to the conventional view that maintains the impact of the *Blue Cliff Record* rather quickly faded, this chapter gives a brief survey of the aftermath of the legends by investigating the enduring legacy of the collection's interpretative style in two main directions: situating the text in relation to other writings of the classical period including thirteenth- and fourteenth-century gongan/kōan collections, and showing that the discourse of the *Blue Cliff Record* by no means died out—*pingchang*-oriented texts continued to thrive in subsequent periods.

Following the main chapters several tables are provided in the appendices that help contextualize and clarify materials included in the *Blue Cliff Record* and their significance in relation to other Chan works and masters from the Song dynasty as well as earlier and later periods.

## 2

# Entering the Dragon Gate

### TEXTUAL FORMATION IN HISTORICAL
### AND RHETORICAL CONTEXTS

### *Cataloging and Evaluating Chan*
### *Encounter Dialogues*

Through formulating a distinctive discursive style reflecting the notion of uncertainty, the *Blue Cliff Record* articulates a religious vision of self-realization embodied by the instructional activities of such luminaries as Yunmen and Zhaozhou, among a multitude of Tang Chan masters referenced in numerous gongan cases. The conventional view tends to see the collection as an intriguing oddity of the short-lived Northern Song approach to lettered Chan that probably deserved the fate of being burned by Dahui at the dawn of the Southern Song for indulging in literary excess. In contrast to this outlook the key element of my reading steers away from but does not avoid the unresolved debate about the merits or demerits of Dahui's attitude by uncovering the innovative rhetorical structures and methods of Xuedou's and Yuanwu's respective and collective standpoints for expressing Chan discourse.

This chapter examines the origins and implications of Yuanwu's novel commentarial style that constructs multifaceted evaluative responses (*pingchang*) to the views expressed in Xuedou's verses on selected cases. Building on Xuedou's poetic remarks, Yuanwu's interpretative approach creatively yet critically interacts with—at once supporting and disputing—the content of the encounter dialogues in relation to other commentators' comments about them. Discursive practices cultivated by the two masters have helped determine the course of the gongan tradition as the centerpiece of Chan learning; the techniques they developed are still being used widely in one form or another by numerous Chan/Zen teachers.

The intricacy of the open-ended collection accounts for the initial widespread admiration of its compelling commentarial rhetorical qualities yet also led to a sense that it was convoluted and confusing. I argue that the reason the standpoint of uncertainty expressed in the *Blue Cliff Record* has become popular once again with a worldwide following, despite some neglect in scholarly circles, is that it enjoys an undeniable resonance with several recent Western intellectual trends demonstrated in various theories of the origins of knowledge and the power of creative expression. These views are similarly based on coming to terms with ambiguity by adopting a flexibility and agility of spirit that embraces rather than recoils from inconclusiveness. Key examples of such approaches in the West include the literary modernist views of John Keats and James Joyce, whose writings about momentary experiences of insight, or epiphany, are comparable to the teaching of the *Blue Cliff Record* and to the Chan experience of sudden awakening, generally referred to by the Japanese term *satoru* 悟 (C. *wu*, literally, "understanding" or "comprehension"). The Song Chinese and modern Western outlooks appear to have a shared emphasis on attaining spontaneous flashes of an all-encompassing awareness accompanied by an intense sense of clarity by realizing profound levels of spiritual meaning underlying seemingly mundane struggles with disillusionment and disorder.

To understand the roots of its epoch-making rhetorical discursive configurations, it is important to see that the *Blue Cliff Record* represents a culmination in the formation of gongan literature that quickly went through several developmental stages during the eleventh and twelfth centuries. To put in historical perspective the rhetorical acumen of Xuedou and Yuanwu, the initial stage involved transcribing the exploits of Tang masters in transmission of the lamp records or biographies of monks, beginning with the *Ancestors' Hall Collection* of 952 and the *Jingde Record* of 1004. These were among the first specifically Chan school historical sources that supplemented the trans-sectarian *Song Biographies of Eminent Masters* (*Song Kaosengchuan*) of 988. The following—or, rather, accompanying—phase of gongan formation in the early eleventh century involved circulating, assessing, and modifying these accounts by isolating their hagiographical context and commenting ironically on encounter dialogues, especially in the interpretative works of Fenyang and Xuedou. This development springboarded to the third phase, which consisted mainly of the construction of Yuanwu's elaborate evaluative reactions to the *One Hundred Odes* and related texts in the early twelfth century. A fourth stage in the process was Dahui's apparent rejection of intricacy and endorsement of minimalism supported by *Wumen's Barrier*. A fifth phase was marked by the recovery of the *Blue Cliff Record* and restoration of its interpretative methods, leading to coexistence and an ongoing interaction of literary and nonliterary approaches to gongan practice. Additional stages ensued throughout later periods, including sometimes highly specialized, eclectic, or esoteric uses of gongan sources without a single standard of authority for how to appropriate cases.

The formative process of the gongan tradition began with the creation of textual repositories that were established in the Song dynasty to amass and catalog the vast storehouse of established or paradigmatic accounts (*guze*, literally, "old cases") of Dharma battles. These spiritual competitions originated during the pivotal periods of early Chan that transpired in the Tang dynasty (618–907) and its immediate aftermath in the Five Dynasties (907–960).[1] However the earliest beginnings of encounter dialogues can probably be traced to various sources that long preceded the genesis of the Chan school in the sixth century. The rise of Chan was based on absorbing influences from pre-Chinese Indian Buddhist sources, including Sakyamuni's silence on unedifying questions, and volumes of poetry evoking enlightened awareness composed by the elders in works such as the *Therigatha* and *Theragatha*.

In addition, the Chan approach was influenced by pre-Buddhist Chinese religious writings, including records of elusive Confucian aphorisms collected in the *Analects* (*Lunyu*), memoirs of philosophical conversations (*biji*), and compilations of enigmatic metaphysical "pure talks" (*qingtan*) used in Daosim. Chan rhetoric also created nostalgia for the writings of Zhuangzi and Tao Qian, who proclaimed in different ways, as part of a simpler rustic, utopian age, the supreme confidence of attaining the path of free and easy wandering beyond conventional language and thought.

This intellectual atmosphere gave readers a sense that they could avoid religious institutional apparatuses and forgo ritual intermediaries to gain direct access to the images and ideals of spiritual realization through interpreting without attachment literary symbolism instead of doctrinal formulations. Moreover Chan accounts of Dharma battles conjured art of war rhetoric by depicting the strategies of psychological competition between adversaries locked in combat. These writings were also infused with legal imagery associated with the origins of the term gongan as an investigation into the causes and consequences of transgression conducted by an all-knowing magistrate who adjudicates criminal disputes.

All the varied discursive elements contributed to the rise of encounter dialogues that disclosed truth only partially through words and demanded that deeper levels of meaning be revealed by reading between the lines to surmise hidden perspectives expressed via, while remaining unrestricted by, ordinary reason or logic. It is often said that Chan represents a unique amalgam of Mahayana Buddhist views of nonduality communicated through skillfully indirect means that were integrated into Zhuangzi's paradoxical reflections on the provisional utility of language which is considered relevant only to the particular circumstances in which expressions are used. This basic formula helps explain some aspects of the complexity of Chinese literary games that are carried out in the rhetoric of the *Blue Cliff Record* and other major gongan collections.[2] However, a thoroughgoing discussion of the multifarious aspects of the evolution of pre-Chan inspirations lies outside the scope of the present study.

Nearly all the cases cited with verses appended by Xuedou and further comments added by Yuanwu, along with similar kinds of comments made in collections compiled by a host of other Song teachers, are derived from scores, nay thousands, of records of encounter dialogues.[3] The dialogues constitute deliberately disturbing but ultimately mutually beneficial experiential exchanges held between an enlightened master and unenlightened disciple or rival teacher. As opposed to most of the precursors of this literary genre, Chan encounters are almost always cryptic and transformative rather than colloquial and instructional. The anecdotes about momentous interactions in addition to sayings and doings of Tang Chan ancestors were collected and incorporated into a wide variety of voluminous Song writings in which the narratives were significantly enhanced or altered in order to serve as an adroit means for evoking an indirect pathway to the attainment of awakening. Chan literary activity of the eleventh and twelfth centuries was marked by a veritable explosion of texts produced with strong government backing, as well as supervision and oversight with regard to the process of editing and publication. This sometimes greatly affected or skewed the results by leading to a distinctive sectarian outlook or stylistic emphasis based on divisions among the Five Houses of Chan according to their local variations.[4]

In addition to diverse gongan commentaries, the new Song writings included the developing genres of transmission of the lamp records (*chuandenglu*) covering lineal hagiographies, recorded sayings (*yulu*) high-lighting individual masters' lives and teachings conducted both inside and outside the Dharma hall or abbot's quarters of the temple, and monastic rules (*qinggui*) explicating behavioral regulations for monks in training. Rather than featuring encounter dialogues as stand-alone cases ripe for interpretative comments, most Chan works from the period embedded the stories of spiritual contests in accounts of prominent teachers that were included in the triumphal chronicles of the transmission of the lamp records and recorded sayings texts.

The category of gongan collections generally was heavily dependent on these genres for providing the catalogue of cases that served as the basis for inventive prose and poetic comments. The *Jingde Record* contains many of the tales, axioms, and biographical notes that inform so much of the content of the *Blue Cliff Record* by contributing dialogues in addi-tion to historical materials used in the sections of prose commentary. On the other hand, transmission of the lamp texts did not have much impact on the innovative techniques for constructing evaluative interpretations of cases that were formulated in gongan collections beginning with Fenyang and followed by Xuedou and Yuanwu, among others.

Although the developments leading to the flourishing of gongan com-mentary in the Northern Song are quite complex, it seems clear that Fenyang, who penned the initial collection containing 300 cases in the early eleventh century, originated many of the major methods of making remarks on encounter dialogues both in poetry and prose. An emphasis cultivated by Fenyang on coining phrases to replace or substitute stock questions and answers was already anticipated in the records of Yunmen, which were not published until 1054 with reissues in 1076 and 1120 that attracted a wide readership.[5] Xuedou compiled collections that extended some of his predecessor's techniques, and these were further refined yet also challenged and changed by Yuanwu's innovations.

Encounter-dialogues-cum-gongan usually involve brief and deceptively unassuming question-and-answer conversations that begin with unpre-tentious yet disarming queries such as, "What is your name?," "Where are you from?," "What is Buddha?," or "Why did Bodhidharma come from the West?," which are specific probes designed to create freewheeling opportunities that either reveal the wisdom or expose the ignorance of the interlocutor. The queries are replied to with purposefully dense and impenetrable responses, for example, "Three pounds of flax" (case 12), "Seven-pound shirt" (45), or "A flowering hedge" (39). I refer to gongan that use the style of abrupt responses which cut off any further exchange as "puzzlers" and to examples of a more complicated and extended narrative structure for the exchange as "dazzlers."

To clarify this distinction the term dazzler indicates that the core dialogue, while still relatively succinct, is part of a complex and knotty tale usually drawing on events and images that take place in the Chan monastic setting, such as case 4 on "Deshan carrying his bundle," case 46 on "Jingqing's raindrop sounds," or cases 63 and 64 on "Nanquan kills a cat" and "Zhaozhou puts sandals on his head," among many other examples. These complex accounts feature an intensive rapid-fire give-and-take of action-reaction exchanges held between master and disciple. Whereas a puzzler generally consists of a single query and response with a lack of follow-up since the reply cuts off further inquiry, a dazzler is a more involved and drawn-out exchange with multiple levels of conversation.

In both the abrupt style of encounter, or puzzler, and the more complicated narrative, or dazzler, mystifying answers given in response to penetrating inquiries are often punctuated with dramatic gestures, eccentric body language, or unfathomable images. These actions include shaking sleeves to show displeasure or striking incorrigible learners, in addition to the use of symbols representing the religious authority of masters, like wielding staffs or ceremonial fly-whisks, or drawing circles or figures on the ground or in the air to stir the imagination. Whether in a puzzler or a dazzler, Yuanwu's insertion between the lines of the core dialogue of ironic and frequently tongue-in-cheek or disingenuously scathing capping-phrase comments function as a kind of scorecard, since it is not always clear who dominates the exchange and there may be one or more reversals during the interaction which can be variously construed. Yuanwu's commentarial goal is to refuse to let tried and true opinions about the case stand pat, including those proffered by Xuedou, by citing yet quickly undermining and reorienting these stances in a way that opens up multiple perspectives but without pointing to or insisting on a firm conclusion. The primary aim of Yuanwu's comments is to highlight the opportune moment of a turnaround by clarifying the capacity of a true adept to make a pivot at the critical moment.

A survey of dialogues with remarks included in the *Blue Cliff Record* suggests that they sometimes serve another function by offering a panoramic view of the proceedings and procedures of the Chan monastic institution. Case narratives also feature tributes to the triumphs of majestic teachers, who demonstrate insight while undergoing the ups and downs of training

disciples and competing with rivals. Complex interactions also reveal the
religion's foibles and its follies, which are rectifiable by means of an experiential dynamic of change that occurs dramatically within the repartee of
encounter dialogues.

This important thematic trend of the social in addition to spiritual
implications of cases has been noted by R. M. D Shaw, a long-term East
Asian missionary during the pre–WWII period, whose partial translation
of the *Blue Cliff Record* with his own interpolated notes published in 1961
was the earliest such effort in a Western language. Shaw's edition preceded by three years the first of two volumes (a third was not released)
of Wilhelm Gundert's more masterful rendering of the collection into
German. According to Shaw's explanation:

> There are some one hundred and forty names of scholars [priests]
> mentioned in *The Blue Cliff Records,* of whom about one hundred
> and thirty are Chinese and the rest Indian. . . . The book also throws
> light on the social and daily life of Zen temples and monasteries.
> We read of itinerant priests and of the free hospitality given by Zen
> temples to such travellers, and of how that hospitality was often
> abused. We read of the daily chores of the student monks and of the
> Patriarchs themselves. We hear the drums beating to call to meals,
> to services and meditation. We see scholars visiting each other for
> mutual advice. We learn of ten-day retreats and of the various meth-
> ods used by teachers in their desire to instruct and guide their dis-
> ciples. We find women attending the temples of famous Abbots to
> get instruction, and laymen temporarily leaving their homes and
> the world in order to practice meditation. We hear of Zen Patriarchs
> boldly rebuking emperors, or in later times being employed as
> tutors for imperial sons.[6]

In addition to what Shaw observes, and even though the cases and commentaries do not generally address directly particular instances of institutional turmoil in the midst of political upheavals involving Chan's
somewhat tenuous relations with Chinese rulers, including periods of
suppression or persecution that Buddhism underwent during the Tang
dynasty, the collection occasionally includes some informative indicators of such themes. Yuanwu's comments on case 11, for example, refer
to tensions within the imperial family that eventually led to the notorious
temporary proscription of all Buddhist schools by Emperor Wuzong (r.

840–846) in the mid-840s, a ban that was quickly lifted by his successor Xuanzong (r. 846–859) but that had a devastating long-term effect on the Chan institution. Despised and tormented by his elder brother, Xuanzong had studied the Dharma with illustrious master Huangbo Xiyun (d. 850), who was also befriended and written about in glowing terms by prominent government minister Peixiu (787–860). Xuanzong proved to be a strong supporter of Chan, which started to become the major branch a century after the Wuzong persecution in a period that was marked by a significant revival of Buddhist practices, and this trend continued to develop during the Song dynasty.

A powerful example from the records of Tang dynasty masters that greatly influenced the rhetorical quality of the *Blue Cliff Record* involves a monastic anecdote featuring a core dialogue topped by poetic comments and various comebacks and reversals that is included in the account of the enlightenment experience of Xiangyan Zhixian (?–898), who is mentioned in Yuanwu's remarks in cases 2, 12, 16, 82, and 92.[7] Although he is not cited in one of the main gongan of the *Blue Cliff Record*, Xiangyan devised the symbolism of hen and chick that are both pecking at a shell as a symbol of the process of breaking through self-imposed barriers to attain insight, which is highlighted in the commentary on case 16. In that dialogue a monk says to master Jingqing, "I am breaking out and ask the teacher to break in," and in response the master calls the inquirer, "a man in the weeds." Xiangyan is also appreciated for inventing the image suggesting extreme doubt, included as case 5 in *Wumen's Barrier*, of a person hanging desperately from the branch of a tree who is required to express the Dharma even if doing so threatens to cause his demise.

Xiangyan is probably best known for the story of his own enlightenment as chronicled in transmission of the lamp records. Prior to attaining awakening, he was asked by his teacher Guishan to contemplate Huineng's (638–713) saying, "What was your original face before you were born?," as an early example of a monk in training being tested with an important precursor of a gongan case. Xiangyan, who was respected at the time for his erudition, at first scoured his library looking for answers to the query but could not find any. Disappointed, he burned all his books in frustration and was determined to dedicate his meditative practice to answering that single, simple question in a convincing manner. This incineration was one of several notoriously destructive acts in early Chan history, including Huineng ripping the sutras and Deshan destroying his notes on the *Diamond Sutra*, which reinforce reports that followers of Dongshan

Liangjie (807–869) and Yunmen were told they would not be allowed to record their master's sayings so they did so surreptitiously. It turned out these were all harbingers of the fate to which Dahui would subject the *Blue Cliff Record*. As Thornton Wilder once said, "An incinerator is a writer's best friend."

Then one day as he was working in the fields while studying under another teacher, Xiangyan heard the sound of a clay tile breaking suddenly as it struck a bamboo tree and fell to the ground with a "ping." At the moment of hearing this sound, Xiangyan was enlightened and spontaneously composed the verse, "One strike and I forgot all I knew/ No more will I rely on cultivation./ I have been moved by the ancient teaching/ And will no longer fall back on idle devices" 一擊忘所知.更不假修時.動容揚古路.不墮悄然機.[8] Hearing of the story, Guishan's colleague Yangshan went to test Xiangyan, who responded with a poem that was rejected for being exemplary of Tathagata Chan (*rulai Chan* 如来禪), which was considered a deficient standpoint because it was dependent on teachings from the sutras. Thus challenged, Xiangyan delivered another verse, "I have a knack for pivotal activity,/ It is seen in the twinkling of an eye./ If someone is unable to understand,/ I will summon a different practitioner" 我有一機.瞬目視伊.若人不會.別喚沙彌.[9] Yangshan approved this poem in consultation with Guishan since it gave evidence of the true path of Ancestral Chan (*zushi Chan* 祖師禪), which—even though the distinction is not clearly explained in the text—is the preferred method in that enlightenment is based on individual attainment gained through personal experience rather than doctrinal treatises.

One area of affinity with Yuanwu's approach is the way the Xiangyan anecdote affirms that an example of everyday perception can serve as a vehicle to gaining sudden enlightenment. According to Yuanwu's *Record*, "At any time of the day any sensation in the eyes or the ears, or even the sound of a bell or boom of a drum, a mule's whinny or a dog's bark—there are no instances that fail to bring news of this [original endowment]" 二六時中眼裏耳裏.乃至鐘鳴鼓響驢鳴犬吠.無非這箇消息.[10] The matter of perceiving sounds in relation to Chan awakening is explored in the dialogue of case 46, in which Jingqing tells a monk who says that listening to the sound of raindrops is a typical instance of misconstruing a superficial sense of unity since the relationship between subjective perception and objective reality is quite complex.

Another link with the *Blue Cliff Record* involves the term *ji* 機, which is used in a twofold sense of an idle contrivance that distracts from liberation as expressed in Xiangyan's initial enlightenment verse and as a distinctive skill that epitomizes Chan freedom as evoked in the second poem submitted to Yangshan that was acknowledged for successfully conveying Ancestral Chan. One of Yuanwu's rhetorical innovations, with a debt to the recorded sayings of Yunmen, in which the term appears in the title of the first section, was to use *ji* almost always in a positive sense indicating an adept's exceptional knack or ability to make a turnaround by taking advantage of a fulcrum-like opportunity that reflects his own knowledge and also helps cause the awakening of a disciple.

## Heroic Chan Masters

By the end of the Tang dynasty, many of the encounter dialogues that are still well known today had already been created and were circulating widely while being interpreted by leaders of various Chan factions. Although the trend of crafting new dialogues continued into the Song dynasty and beyond (a prime later example is Hakuin's "sound of one hand clapping," which derives from Xuedou's capping remark in case 18 in the *Blue Cliff Record*),[11] the meaning of the early exchanges was being debated during the Five Dynasties by eminent masters whose recorded sayings were compiled by their disciples, although these accounts would generally not be published for a hundred years or more. In the tenth century Yunmen and Fayan Wenyi (885–958) did much to promote the use of precedent dialogues as essential ingredients in the training of disciples. These two exceptionally influential figures were considered the last of the classical teachers, who founded their own schools that were accepted as part of the Five Houses. Even though the movements attributed to Yunmen and Fayan had faded from importance by the end of the eleventh century along with the previously demised Guiyang school, various Song commentators, including Yuanwu, were still enthusiastically citing their teachings in the following years for being exemplary of the heroic spiritual qualities a true Chan adept embodies.

Both Yunmen and Fayan were descendants of master Xuefeng Yuanwu (822–908), a tremendously successful Chan leader who hailed from southeasterly Fujian province. After a lengthy period of itinerancy to sites throughout the country, Xuefeng became abbot of a major temple in Fujian province, where he oversaw a large assembly with 1,500 disciples, as mentioned in the core dialogue of case 49. Yunmen was one of several prominent followers who received direct transmission from Xuefeng, and Fayan was a third-generation descendent in the lineage of Xuansha Shiben (805–908), who helped extend Xuefeng's family tree. Nearly half the gongan in the *Blue Cliff Record* are derived from the three masters and their close associates or disciples. This is notable because all the figures lie outside the mainstream Linji school, which is generally thought to have dominated the era and was the basis of Yuanwu's affiliation within the Yangqi wing even though the direct Linji lineage accounts for a total of only seven cases.

The house established by Fayan was strong in the Five Dynasties period, especially through the evangelical efforts of his main disciple Tiantai Deshao (891–972), who also helped revive Tiantai teachings by reimporting the school's texts from Korea and Japan after a period of dormancy in China, in addition to Tiantai's disciple, the eclectic and prolific Chan writer Yongming Yanshou (904–975).[12] During the Northern Song the Fayan school ultimately gave way to the leading role played by the Yunmen, Linji, and Caodong schools, and eventually the Yunmen school for the most part died out as well, leaving two (or three) main factions (Linji was split into the Huanglong and Yangqi streams) that were competitive and occasionally hypercritical of one another (more vitriol stemmed from Linji-based Dahui attacks on Caodong).

In remarking on the exchange cited in case 7 that took place between Fayan and a little known disciple named Huichao, Yuanwu discusses Deshao's crucial role and, furthermore, says that the main technique adopted by this school is that of "arrowheads meeting point to point" 箭鋒相拄. This is an approach in which the master's response treats in a direct and succinct yet cryptic manner any type of question raised by a novice or challenge presented by a rival without mincing words or indulging in idle conceptualization. Several examples are discussed in case 7 in which Fayan simply echoes the question or answer that was given by the disciple until an experience of awakening is stimulated in the interlocutor.

Yunmen was perhaps the first Chan leader to discuss in novel ways precedent dialogues based on the adventurous and provocative transcendental exploits and interactions of Tang ancestors, who were often referred to in his talks as former masters or, more poetically, "the ancients" (*guren*). Yunmen's new evaluative approach based on discerning what was appropriate to the needs of the disciple led to the formation of gongan collections and ritual practices for testing disciples associated with this rapidly developing literary genre. Because Xuedou was a fourth-generation follower of this lineage, Yunmen is the single most frequently cited master in the *Blue Cliff Record* with fourteen cases that are his own dialogue with a follower or the assembly, in addition to four cases (8, 22, 34, 88) in which he makes comments on the core exchange of predecessors for a total of eighteen gongan in which Yunmen is featured. The next highest total of twelve cases belongs to Zhaozhou, who was in Mazu's Hongzhou school lineage but is generally considered independent because of his unique teaching style that is unaffiliated with any one of the Five Houses.[13]

Yunmen's career path was greatly admired in part because he once served as a close advisor to the king. In 923, at age sixty-four, he gave up that prestigious post to establish a remote monastery located in southern Guangzhou province, where he could be free of secular distraction. This location is still active today and was one of the main sites of twentieth-century master Xu Yun's abbacies. Yunmen was famous for expressing inscrutable one-word barriers that, according to Yuanwu's remarks, each contain multiple levels of meaning based on "three sayings" (*sanju*) that connect the transcendental realm with the practicality of teaching relative to circumstances. Examples of how Yunmen, or perhaps an idealized image of him, played a decisive role as a model of the savvy and heroic Chan adept include his answer, "Cake," in case 77 in reply to a question about what lies beyond buddhas and patriarchs, and "Barrier!" (*guan* 關) used in case 8 as the final example of remarks offered by three Tang masters in response to the opening query about whether the master Cuiyan's eyebrows have fallen off. The term "barrier" in Chan discourse originates from checkpoints that were routinely used in countryside locations to secure travelers while they were trying to cross a frontier pass but symbolizes states of mind in the process of trying to attain enlightenment. The other two comments in case 8 are by Baofu and Changqing; all four monks featured in the case were leading disciples of Xuefeng, whose lineage also gave rise to the Fayan stream.

The *Record of Yunmen* (*Yunmen Yulu*) received considerable acclaim when it was first published in 1054 as perhaps the first widely released example of the recorded sayings genre in giving a full account of an individual master's life and teachings. By demonstrating a consistently effective knack for responding appropriately to the learning needs of his disciples while guiding them through pithy exchanges in order to create a quick turnabout from ignorance to realization, Yunmen was revered by monastics and literati alike for proficient teaching abilities meant to aid practice, spur insight, and foster spontaneous realization. Even though the standing of the lineage founded in his name was somewhat diminished by the time of Yuanwu, Yunmen's status as a Chan hero was enhanced and disseminated to an ever-growing audience through the reissue of his recorded sayings to great fanfare in 1076 (and again in the 1120s), less than thirty years before Yuanwu started giving the lectures that formed the *Blue Cliff Record*.

In commenting in case 87 on the saying, "The whole world is medicine, why have people of past and present been so utterly mistaken?" 盡大地是藥.古今何太錯, Yuanwu notes that "Yunmen's one line threw everyone in the world into a state of bewilderment" 為雲門這一句惑亂天下人他. This was productive in causing an awareness of awakening, but in *pingchang* fashion Yuanwu does not let the supposed hero off the hook as he charges that Xuedou's verse comments "cut off Yunmen just below the knees" 解截雲門腳跟.

At the beginning of the eleventh century, Fenyang's collections represented the first systematic effort to interpret cases, as such, by specifically identifying and providing ingenious remarks on established or paradigmatic encounter dialogues rather than embedding the exchanges in accounts of the life and sayings of teachers. Drawing dialogues mainly from the *Jingde Record*'s hagiographical accounts that were recently completed, Fenyang established the trend of preferring the use of an enigmatic and deliberately disturbing yet thought-provoking and poetic manner of discourse to clear-cut instructions or straightforward enunciations of principle, on the one hand, or to drastic and seemingly impenetrable iconoclasm as expressed in many of the dialogues when left to stand alone unaccompanied by remarks, on the other hand.

Fenyang's verse comments based on allusion, wordplay, and metaphor are designed to uncover and amplify hidden meanings embedded in the originally paradoxical dialogues found in transmission records. Unlike Xuedou's form of poetry, which uses lyrical imagery to draw out the ironic and perplexing ramifications of the particular cases, Fenyang uses verse to express various formulas, such as the three mysteries (*sanxuan*) and three essentials (*sanyao*), derived mainly from the record of Linji Yixuan (d. 866), as well as other Tang Chan teachings in order to address the doctrinal significance reflected in gongan cases.[14] In addition, Fenyang devised his own list of eighteen kinds of questions to sum up different types of inquiries.

The reliance on formulaic Chan teachings evident in Fenyang's poetry is an approach that Yuanwu does not necessarily repudiate but seeks to at once incorporate and surpass in favor of a more intricately crafted style of interlinear interpretation of Xuedou's verse. The *One Hundred Odes* reflects a refined literary approach fully integrated with contemporary genres of Chinese poetry and a firm knowledge and facility with the rules for regulated truncated verse (*jueju*). Yuanwu may have turned to Xuedou as a source of inspiration, despite crossing sectarian boundaries, based on a regional affinity with another Sichuan native's rhetorical prowess, as one scholar suggests.[15] But it is much more likely that Yuanwu cites Xuedou and his ample views on Yunmen's record because both of these works were highly valued at the time and were frequently studied, though probably only poorly understood by monks in various Chan monasteries in addition to secular literati intrigued by Buddhist thought.

The creation of ideological and practical divisions among the Five Houses was becoming an important factor in determining the thought of individual teachers and how their peers received them. In a contrary trend there was a vigorous effort being made to identify universally accepted standpoints underlying diverse factions. That approach is expressed in the *One Hundred Odes*, which cites masters who are representative of every period and stream of Chan, although Xuedou does have his own favorites.

An example from the mid-eleventh century of testing disciples explicitly with gongan involves Baiyun, who also composed verse commentaries on numerous cases. One time while residing in a Longmian area retreat in Anhui province, Baiyun interviewed a supposedly awakened lay official by using cases as a method of examination and was at first greatly impressed, but then he quickly became somewhat disapproving and even disparaging. In a poem about the incident in which he is critical of this follower, Baiyun writes, "I had long since heard that he has stolen [i.e., grasped the essence of] Chan,/ But had not yet had a chance to make a face-to-face judgment./ [So] during a long night sitting in front of the fireplace,/ We coursed through precedent gongan/ And I summoned him to confess his transgressions, case by case" 久聞竊我宗/未得當面斷/一夜燈火前/行過舊公案/所犯一一招.[16]

In referring to cases as a matter of making a spiritual judgment about transgressions committed, Baiyun evokes legal imagery that no doubt had a strong influence on Yuanwu's understanding of the term "gongan." Like Fenyang, Xuedou mainly uses the terms "cases" (*ze*) or "old cases" (*guze*) to refer to dialogues cited as discrete literary units, and in the *One*

*Hundred Odes* he mentions the term gongan in only one instance (case 64's verse). A few decades later, the term had developed into a more specialized meaning involving an assessment that exposes the truth or falsity of a novice's attitude. One of Yuanwu's many rhetorical innovations greatly influenced by the teachings of his mentor Wuzu, with whom he reflected on the significance of Xuedou's text for several years before offering his own commentaries, was to devise a more formal connotation of gongan emphasizing how judicial terminology from the legal tradition amplified the imagery of indictment and punishment as well as redemption.

Yuanwu's commentary draws heavily yet somewhat ironically on the original notion of gongan used in the legal sense of the public (*gong*) records (*an*) of criminal cases taken under consideration by a local magistrate, who functions as a combined detective, prosecutor, judge, and jury—that is how the Chinese magistrate system functioned in the Tang dynasty as portrayed in the celebrated "Cases of Judge Dee" 狄公案—in investigating the truth of alleged wrongdoings and meting out different levels of retribution once the matter is settled. Detective stories, which were also known by the term "gongan" and became a popular style of fiction during the Song dynasty, were written like Chan dialogues in vernacular rather than literary Chinese. In these accounts, the magistrate discovers and exposes the basis of a misdeed by unlocking the mystery behind its perpetrator's transgression, and then assigns the appropriate penalty to the guilty party that often involves corporal punishment like thirty blows.[17]

In the Chan literary context the abbot assumes the role of the law official while the unwary interlocutor who expresses a misunderstanding of the Dharma is given his just deserts in the form of verbal comeuppance or nonverbal humiliation, such as "I give you thirty blows," or contrariwise, "I spare you thirty blows." Rather than penal reform in a legalistic sense these instances of repudiation are designed to trigger an experience of redemption by the ignorant through attaining a spontaneous spiritual insight that ultimately reforms and thus dispenses with their flaws. Extending the analogy of investigative work, Yuanwu frequently praises the ways that Xuedou's verse comments are able to "wrap up a case" 欸結案 or allow its experiential significance to be revealed through poetic evocations that highlight yet seek to overcome the misguided views of the unenlightened. In a capping-phrase comment on a line from a Xuedou verse, Yuanwu remarks, "A double case, he handles all crimes with the same indictment" 兩重公案.一狀領過.依舊一般,[18] and then adds an ironic comment on the

next line, "A triple case, a quadruple case. He puts a head above a head."
三重也有.四重公案.頭上安頭.¹⁹

In considering diverse influences on Yuanwu's discourse it is necessary
to recognize that some recent scholarship has shown that the Song dynasty
production of Chan writings was not limited to the main genres discussed
above, including transmission of the lamp records and recorded sayings
texts, but also spawned a variety of additional sources. Dictionaries, con-
cordances, other kinds of reference works, and collections of aphorisms
or correspondences all had a tremendous impact on the formation of
gongan commentaries. Therefore the construction of the *Blue Cliff Record*
needs to be seen in light of the full context of Song Chan publications
in that some texts that were highly instrumental at the time may have
become lesser known or obscure by now so that their significance should
be recovered and reassessed.

In addition to the *Record of Yunmen* that was published in the mid-
eleventh century and reissued at least a couple times during Yuanwu's
life, a small sample of the many texts that undoubtedly impacted the formation of his approach includes the *Essential Collection of the Chan School*
(*Zongmen Tongyaoji*) of 1093,[20] which compiled over a thousand cases separated from hagiographies and was often distributed to monks along with
the more prominent lineage-based transmission text the *Jingde Record;*
*Shimen's Record of the Monastic Groves* (*Shimen Linjianlu*) published in 1107
by poet-monk Juefan Huihong, who in the 1120s also coined the term "literary Chan" and was a longtime friend to both Yuanwu and Dahui;[21] and
*Lexicon of the Ancestral Garden* (*Zuting Shiyuan*), an encyclopedic reference work, produced in 1108 by Muan Shanqing and reissued in 1154, that
functions as a glossary by offering explanations for technical terms and
obscure names used in Chan works.

The *Lexicon* was an important resource that Yuanwu had at his disposal
to research the background of Xuedou's verse: "The collection includes
over 2,400 items related to Chan pedagogy, culled from Buddhist and secular stories, proverbs, numerological lists, personal names, local dialects,
and so forth. Muan is said to have embarked on this project in response
to the growing number of monks who were unable to understand the rich
content and context of the many [gongan] exchanges found in Chan literature."[22] The text is now included in the supplemental canon.[23]

Although Muan's material is drawn from over twenty important Chan
sources, as shown in Table 2.1, the recorded sayings of Yunmen and Xuedou
are of primary importance, especially the latter's seven texts contained in

his recorded sayings that fill nine, or a plurality, of the total number of sections. The reference work explains the textual and historical significance of particular terms and concepts but, unlike Yuanwu's creative approach, Muan does not attempt a synthetic style of elucidation based on ongoing personal engagement with the sources. Muan produced other important commentarial materials no longer contained in the Buddhist canon, including further comments on the writings of Xuedou.

Additional texts published during the Southern Song but after the death of Yuanwu in 1135 that remain important for understanding the trajectory of Chan gongan writings existing within the orbit of the *Blue Cliff Record* include the following three sources. One is the *Treasury of the True Dharma-Eye* (*Zhengfayanzang*, Jp. *Shōbōgenzō*) of 1147, which contains 661 cases compiled by Dahui that was used as part of his keyword-teaching method yet shows how much he valued the use of gongan in Chan training.[24] Another key text is the *Eyes of Humans and Gods* (*Rentian Yanmu*) of 1188, a collection in six fascicles by Huiyan Zhizhao (n.d.), from three generations after Dahui that summarizes the teachings of Chan's Five Houses by presenting biographies of the founders while citing representative sermons, cases, doctrines, and verses with a final section of miscellaneous records on important events and various other matters relating to

**Table 2.1 Contents of First Four Volumes of the *Lexicon of the Ancestral Garden***

| 第一卷 | VOLUME 1 |
|---|---|
| 雲門錄上 | *Yunmen Yulu* Volume 1 |
| 雲門錄下 | *Yunmen Yulu* Volume 2 |
| 雲門室中錄 | *Yunmen Shizhonglu* (Records Visiting the Abbot's Room) |
| 雪竇洞庭錄 | *Xuedou Dongtinglu* (Xuedou's Dongting Record) |
| 雪竇後錄 | *Xuedou Houlu* (Xuedou's Late Record) |
| 第二卷 | VOLUME 2 |
| 雪竇瀑泉集 | *Xuedou Puquanji* (Xuedou's Waterfalls Collection) |
| 雪竇拈古 | *Xuedou Niangu* (Prose Comments on Old Cases) |
| 雪竇頌古 | *Xuedou Songgu* (One Hundred Odes) |
| 第三卷 | VOLUME 3 |
| 雪竇祖英集上 | *Xuedou Zuyingji* (Xuedou's Ancestral Luminaries) Volume 1 |
| 第四卷 | VOLUME 4 |
| 雪竇祖英集下 | *Xuedou Zuyingji* Volume 2 |
| 雪竇開堂錄 | *Xuedou Kaitanglu* (Xuedou's Opening the Hall Record) |
| 雪竇拾遺 | *Xuedou Shiyi* (Additional Works of Xuedou) |

the study of Chan.[25] The third Southern Song text is *Precious Lessons from the Chan Forest (Chanlin Baoxuan)* from 1189 that was compiled by masters Dahui and Zhuan as a compendium of private dialogues, discussions, and letters. It covers a broad range of topics regarding some of the political, social, and philosophical issues faced by Chan practitioners during the twelfth century, including the burning of the *Blue Cliff Record.*

In addition to these three works, an important Yuan dynasty text that sheds light on Yuanwu's work is the *Classified Anthology of the Chan Forest (Chanlin Leiju)* published with a preface in 1307. It is one of the largest and most comprehensive of the gongan collections that serves as an anthology of old cases and verses grouped into over one hundred miscellaneous categories with comments added by various later masters.[26]

## *Construction of Yuanwu's Interpretative Comments*

To see how the multifaceted yet flexible rhetorical structure devised for the *Blue Cliff Record* facilitates and supports the delivery of its religious message about embracing the meaning of uncertainty it is important to clarify when and where Yuanwu delivered the sermons recorded by his disciples in light of his motivations for commenting on Xuedou's verse remarks. Trying to answer basic questions of how and why the collection came into existence is for the most part a matter of conjecture based on piecing together an understanding of the biographical narrative of Yuanwu (see timeline in Appendix 4) from sparse and inconclusive resources that are not fully reliable from a contemporary historiographical standpoint.

Available materials include indicators within the main text itself about its construction, such as Yuanwu's more than occasional references to the reflections of his teacher Wuzu in addition to citations in eight cases of a former colleague referred to as Librarian Qing.[27] There are also suggestions and hints about the formation of the collection in the various para-texts that accompany the mainstream edition included in the modern Taishō canon; this category refers to four prefaces and six postfaces, or afterwords, plus a note included after case 50 by layman Zhang Mingyuan, who recovered the text in 1300, for a total of eleven items. Many of the para-texts originated at the time of the reconstituted version, and some were written by lay followers; one is from as late as 1859, showing the staying power of the collection, and a couple are by anonymous authors.

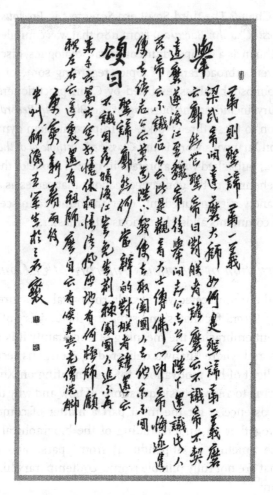

**FIGURE 2.1** Modern calligraphy of a passage from Xuedou's *One Hundred Odes*. Xuedou Temple, courtesy of the author.

It seems that by the late eleventh and early twelfth century the *One Hundred Odes*, a small portion of which is shown in Figure 2.1, was being widely read and appreciated for its depth and complexity at most Chan monasteries and was also studied by a host of lay adherents, but the verse comments were not well understood due to their enigmatic subject matter with obscure allusions and elusive metaphors. Even though Xuedou clearly knew the rules for regulated verse, he did not consistently adhere to these guidelines and deliberately broke some of the typical procedures. He expressed his views in an eclectic fashion peppered with interjections, modifications, interpolations, and other ways, keeping the reader off guard and susceptible to rhetorical surprises. Yuanwu and his teacher Wuzu were among many practitioners in the habit of remarking on Xuedou's verse comments as a de rigeur feature of Northern Song Chan training.

Yuanwu labored for years trying to discern the full background and implications of Xuedou's text. In his commentary on the verse to case 18, which says, "Xuedou is exceedingly compassionate in telling you that, 'A clear pool allows no place for the blue dragon's coils'" 雪竇忒殺慈悲.更向爾道.澄潭不許蒼龍蟠, Yuanwu remarks in tongue-in-cheek fashion, "My late master Wuzu said, 'In Xuedou's whole volume of odes on precedent cases I just like this ... one line'" 五祖先師道.雪竇頌古一冊.我只愛他 ... 一句.[28] Yuanwu concludes with irony that Xuedou's "saying is actually pretty good" 猶較些子.[29]

In his comments on the verse to case 73, in which Mazu says "Zhizang's head is white, Baizhang's head is black" in response to a monk's query about his perplexing interactions with two teachers who were both disciples of Mazu, Yuanwu cites Wuzu's brief interjection, "Master of Roadblocks" 封后先生 (literally, "Teacher of how to cut off any outlet or block any pass-through," thus keeping a seeker trapped in a seemingly inescapable impasse to force him to discover and negotiate another path), before then turning to the citation of Xuedou's verse.[30] It is also interesting to note Yuanwu's view that "[p]eople today who rely on words try to make their living by expressing notions like, 'White indicates merging in brightness, and black indicates merging in darkness,' but these calculations are a far cry from understanding how the ancients could cut off intellectualization at the root with just a single solitary word." 如今人只管去語言上 .作活計云.白是明頭合.黑是暗頭合.只管鑽研計較.殊不知.古人一句截斷 意根.[31]

Yuanwu also sometimes recalls the words of Librarian Qing, an otherwise anonymous colleague while he was still a disciple under Wuzu. In discussing a line in Xuedou's verse remark on case 100 that says, "The jeweled sword is sometimes manifested on the fingertip, and suddenly it appears in the palm" 此寶劍或現在指上, Yuanwu notes, "In the old days when Librarian Qing had reached this point in his explanation he raised his hand and said, 'Do you see?' However the sword is not necessarily in the hand or the finger, as Xuedou takes a shortcut to let you know the intention of the ancients" 昔日慶藏主說.到這裏.竪手云.還見麼 .也不必在手指上也.雪竇借路經過.教爾見古人意.[32] The commentary on case 73 mentions Zhenjue, someone else who Yuanwu knew when he was studying at Zhaojue temple in Chengdu, but he now challenges while also praising his former colleague's assessment of the gongan. Yuanwu also sometimes cites Tang poet-monk Chanyue (832–911) and another Tang master Panshan (n.d.), who he may have talked about with Wuzu, in addition to the famous Hanshan (9th c.), whose poetic writings were creatively appropriated as an ideal literary model by many Song Chan masters.[33] Additionally there are over forty instances throughout in which Yuanwu notes that "an ancient said," and cites a pithy saying or expression of spiritual insight, though in some cases modern research identified the source.

Once he became a temple abbot and saw the enthusiastic level of interest on the part of his followers that was somewhat diminished by the great difficulty they endured in trying to interpret Xuedou's work Yuanwu was motivated to offer for trainees in the assembly a systematic yet provocative set of clarifications, explanations, and annotations of the *One Hundred Odes*. Case 100, for instance, includes a lengthy citation from *Lexicon of the Ancestral Garden*, which may have been inserted by a later editor, on the meaning of a legendary smith named Gan Jiang, who was known for crafting a famous sword that Yuanwu refers to in his capping phrases on Xuedou's verse.[34]

In examining the issue of when and where the collection was produced it must be noted that this was a rather labor-intensive process that took place over the course of two decades involving numerous parties, many of whom are anonymous, and multiple sites, some of which are unclear. The *Blue Cliff Record* is probably primarily based on diverse kinds of interpretative remarks presented as a specific set of sermons delivered while Yuanwu resided at the cloister of the Blue Cliff (Biyan) Spring on the grounds of the Lingquan temple at Mount Jiashan in Hunan province, as shown in Figure 2.2, where he was a head monk (abbacy is not absolutely certain) from 1111 to 1112.

The idea that the collection stems from a specific period is supported by the introduction to case 98 that, as Tenkei Denson points out, probably should be used for case 100 instead because of the sense of finality it expresses with appropriate self-deprecation:[35]

All summer I have been talking endlessly about so many stories (*geteng*; literally, "entangled vines") that have caused monks throughout the land to question their fetters and see matters in a topsy-turvy way. When the diamond-studded sword cut directly I began to realize that explicating all one hundred [cases] persuasively would not

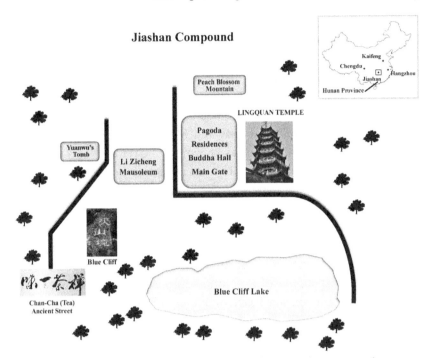

**FIGURE 2.2** Diagram of the current state of Jiashan temple compound, courtesy of the author. The Ancient Street and the Lake are recent constructions.

be feasible. But tell me, what is the diamond-studded sword like? Keep your eyes wide open and I will display the sword's razor-sharp edge for you to see.

垂示云.一夏嘮嘮打葛藤.幾乎絆倒五湖僧.金剛寶劍當頭截.　始覺從來百不能.且道作麼生是金剛寶劍.眨上眉毛.試請露鋒鋩看.[36]

It is highly unlikely that all one hundred cases would have been treated during the course of a ninety-day summer retreat at Lingquan, but in the postface to case 50, compiler Zhang Mingyuan says that around 1300 he found two separate handwritten copies of the *Blue Cliff Record*, with each version containing fifty gongan.[37] This may indicate that two separate retreats were held in successive years with half the total covered during each session, which corresponds to the notion of a two-year stint at Mount Jiashan that is supported by various sources.

This temple—renowned for the growing of tea that prompted the saying, "Tea and Chan are one flavor," which is sometimes misguidedly attributed to Yuanwu and is also conflated with a mysterious scroll that exists in Japan known as the "Floating Yuanwu"[38], was established with the abbacy of Jiashan Shanhui 夾山善會 (805–881), who had his own remarkable path to enlightenment. One of Jiashan's main encounters was with the so-called Boat Monk, Huanting Decheng (or Chuanzi Decheng, 820–858), who was a student of Caodong master Yaoshan Weiyan (745–828).[39] Decheng resided on a boat and ferried people across the river while teaching them Chan. He was known for the verse, "For thirty years I have been floating on this lake/ The fish appearing in clear waters won't take the bait./ Breaking the fishing pole made from cultivated bamboo,/ I relinquish any thought of finding peaceful repose." 三十年來海上遊.水清魚現不吞鉤.釣竿斫盡重栽竹.不計功程得便休.[40]

One day, on the recommendation of his teacher, Shanhui came to ask the Boat Monk for instructions. After an exchange of words, Decheng realized the great potential of Shanhui, so he posed a question but as soon as Shanhui tried to answer Decheng knocked him off the boat into the water and exclaimed, "Speak, speak!" At this point the young monk was enlightened, and Decheng pulled him out and said, "Today I have finally caught a big golden fish!" The two stayed all night floating on the lake, sometimes talking but at other times remaining silent. In the morning Decheng bade farewell to Shanhui and left him on the shore saying, "I studied under Yangshan for thirty years. Today I have repaid his kindness. From now on you need not think of me again." Then he rowed the boat to the middle of the river and tipped it over and disappeared "without a trace."[41]

Sometime later, when asked about the remote "mountain environment (or landscape)" 如何是夾山境 (the last character, *jing*, indicates the Sanskrit term *visaya*, or realm of perception), as shown in Figure 2.3, which is now covered with calligraphy painted in bright red for the purpose of promoting tourism, Jiashan replied with the following verse that probably influenced Yuanwu's sense of lyricism and helped give his text its name: "Monkeys clasping their young withdraw to the green peaks; Birds are dropping flowers before the Blue Cliff" 猿抱子歸青嶂後.鳥銜花落碧巖前.[42] Tradition holds that Fayan once remarked, "For thirty years I mistook this to be a picture of the world around Mount Jiashan," until he realized it was to be understood not as just a description of a quiet secluded place in the hills because it was reflective of a state of mind.[43] A later commentator, Linquan Conglin, in a major late thirteenth-century gongan collection added this remark on the first line, "Spring brings the opening of flowers

FIGURE 2.3 "Jiashan Jing" with Shanhui at Jiashan. Jiashan temple, courtesy of the author.

and during autumn leaves are falling" 春日花開秋時葉落. To the second line he appended the cautionary note, "Don't try to grasp [meaning] in words as our school maintains that truth is perceived directly, outside of phrases" 莫向言中取則.直須句外明宗.[44]

In considering the construction of the *Blue Cliff Record*, while the focus is usually on what Yuanwu accomplished while residing at Mount Jiashan, it is mistaken to link the literary activity that resulted in the collection to that site alone. Rather, this was one of three or possibly four periods and locations during which Yuanwu lectured on the *One Hundred Odes* while leading several assemblies at temples he occupied over a period of "more than twenty years," according to an afterword written prior to publication by Guanyu Wudeng on a spring evening in 1125.[45] That was the same year Yuanwu first met his most famous disciple Dahui, who after the teacher's death proved to be the harshest critic of the collection. This postface may have been composed before the last of the phases of Yuanwu giving lectures on the *One Hundred Odes* (or continuing to edit his previous work) when he returned to Chengdu in 1130.

Following the death of Wuzu, Yuanwu probably gave his first informal lectures while instructing disciples on the significance of Xuedou's enigmatic text in the first decade of the 1100s when he held forth at Zhaojue temple. After leaving Jiashan, as part of the third phase of composition of the *Blue Cliff Record*, Yuanwu may have continued to give lectures on Xuedou's text from 1113 until 1116 at the next temple where he resided, Daolin, located in the southeastern sector of Sichuan province. It seems clear that he and/or his disciples were continuing to work on editing the collection. There then ensued an extended period during which Yuanwu traveled frequently between various temple locations, but meanwhile some of his followers who remained at Jiashan were polishing the sermons. Eventually the text was given a preface by Puzhao and published in 1128. In his postface from three years earlier, Guanyu suggests there may have been some reluctance about making a permanent document of Yuanwu's oral comments, but this concern was outweighed by the perceived need to preserve this precious resource for posterity.

To summarize, the *Blue Cliff Record* reflects at least two decades of lectures that Yuanwu delivered at several temples he led, including Zhaojue temple in his native town of Chengdu in western Sichuan province where the master preached from 1105 to 1111 and Daolin temple on Mount Shizi in Sichuan after he left Jiashan. Additional manuscripts were later found at Zhaojue, to which Yuanwu had returned after he retired in 1130 and resided as abbot until the time of his death five years later. Yuanwu's final years after returning to Zhaojue may represent a fourth period of sermonizing, a notion that is suggested by the Zhang Mingyuan postface to case 50; this comment is not included in the Guanyu postface since that was written five years prior to Yuanwu's retirement. The *One Night Blue Cliff* edition that is attributed to Dōgen and linked by some modern Japanese scholars, especially Itō Yuten, with the version produced at Daolin temple further complicates any attempt to evaluate multiple versions of the text.

No doubt aided in large part by the editing of the manuscript by disciples, which may have contributed to the text's current complex rhetorical structure as much as Yuanwu's own input, the *Blue Cliff Record* features a baroque seven-layer style of commentary. As shown in Table 2.2, in the standard Taishō edition Yuanwu's remarks add to each (2) main case (*benze*) and (5) verse (*songgu*)—in several instances multiple or additional poems by Xuedou are cited from one of his other records—the following rhetorical elements: (1) introduction (*chushi*), or brief, opening observations usually indirectly related to the gongan dialogue that are available for 79 cases, as apparently others were lost over time due to the reconstitution process; capping phrases (*zhuoyu*), or pithy, ironic interlinear remarks inserted into each and every line of the (3) case and (6) verse; and evaluative remarks (*pingchang*), or prose explanations further elaborating and reacting to (4) case and (7) verse by including illustrative or exegetical materials in addition to interpretative comments. The sequence for these

## Table 2.2 *Blue Cliff Record* Textual Structure

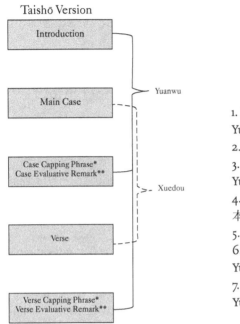

Taishō Version

Introduction

Main Case

Case Capping Phrase*
Case Evaluative Remark**

Verse

Verse Capping Phrase*
Verse Evaluative Remark**

Yuanwu

Xuedou

1. Introduction 垂示 (79 cases),
Yuanwu
2. Main Case 本則, Xuedou
3. Case-capping Phrases 着語,
Yuanwu
4. Case Evaluative Remark
本則評唱, Yuanwu
5. Verse 頌, Xuedou
6. Case-capping Phrases 着語,
Yuanwu
7. Verse Evaluative Remark 頌評唱,
Yuanwu

*Notes Embedded in Text
**Reference Materials and Interpretation

sections is somewhat different in the *One Night Blue Cliff* associated with the Daolin temple text in that the case and verse appear in succession uninterrupted by the two sections of prose commentary, which come at the end.

These seven commentarial layers reflect three historical levels of the development of gongan commentary. These include (a) Tang dialogues cited in the main case and prose remarks that give examples of related cases; (b) Xuedou's eleventh-century views about the dialogues in his verse and related remarks (in fifteen cases Xuedou interjects his own capping phrases in the dialogue—we can imagine other instances got lost in later editions);[46] and (c) Yuanwu's twelfth-century evaluative responses to the previous levels. As discussed in chapter 1, the various rhetorical components evoke four conceptual approaches to undertaking an assessment of the case and Xuedou's verse by raising the main case (*benze*) with Yuanwu's introduction; praising (the literal meaning of the term *song* in *songgu*) the case with Xuedou's ode or eulogistic verse; rephrasing both case and verse by means of Yuanwu's capping phrases; and appraising (*pingchang*) of both case and verse through Yuanwu's evaluative remarks.

## *Examples of Evaluative Reactions* (Pingchang)

Particularly significant in the *Blue Cliff Record*'s rhetoric of uncertainty is the function of *pingchang*-based remarks. The term is used in the title of several later gongan collections, most notably the *Record of Serenity* from 1224 in which Wansong comments on his Caodong predecessor Hongzhi Zhengjue's (1091–1157) verses on 100 cases composed over a half century before, but it also covers many offshoot or derivative approaches that include some degree of capping phrase and/or prose remarks. *Pingchang* in the narrow sense is more or less a synonym for *niangu*, which indicates prose as opposed to poetic remarks. But in a more general and significant sense that marks one of the main contributions of the *Blue Cliff Record* to overall Chan discourse, the term suggests the entire inventive commentarial style of Yuanwu, which builds on Xuedou's precedent. This interpretative approach is interactive with source materials and imaginative. It at once encourages intimacy with and keeps a distance from the various standpoints sources express, while also evoking an atmosphere of a live situation in which the same doubts, tensions, and breakthroughs that characterize the early dialogues are carried out by the commentator.

The second character in the compound, *chang*, literally means singing or chanting, and in this context suggests a kind of instruction based on formal rhetoric, such as Xuedou's verses that follow the rules of Chinese poetry. In a number of cases, including 37, 39, 51, 62, 64, 65, 69, and 92, among others, Xuedou or Yuanwu use the terms "song" or "tune" 曲 to refer to the "long tongue of Buddha" reciting the Dharma through Chan teachings that few can understand because one must be a connoisseur to appreciate fully the resonances of harmony. In his verse comment on case 88, which deals with three disabled people (blind, deaf, and mute), Xuedou declares that even a mythical music teacher who is known for perfect pitch and a prescient knowledge based on making or perceiving subtle sounds could not imagine the Chan tune since it is beyond ordinary sound, no matter how elegant. Thus it is preferable to sit alone next to a window and watch the leaves fall and flowers bloom, each in its own time.

The first character in the compound, *ping*, suggests a freestyle appraisal of the meanings of a source and various ways it has heretofore been appropriated. The full term therefore implies the critical remarks that are made throughout the *Blue Cliff Record* and the comprehensive religious-philosophical outlook they convey. Reflecting the imagery of musicality to convey a sense of harmonization while also subtly critiquing or resourcefully altering the cases, *pingchang* can be understood as a kind of "harmoneutics," whereby an interpreter standing at a critical distance takes part in or becomes integral to the thought processes of the original dialogue partners and also of Xuedou's poetic comments. This represents contrapuntal harmony in which competing and sometimes conflicting rhythms coexist and play off one another. In case 157 cited in Dōgen's *Mana Shōbōgenzō* collection it is said of Guishan (771–853) that, "We can say he's right from head to tail. He just hasn't met someone who 'knows the music.'" 溈山可謂.頭正尾正.只是不遇知音.[47]

In another example of the imagery of music representing creative literary-philosophical criticism, the term *jijie* 擊節, the style used in works by Yuanwu and others for interpreting with prose commentary the original prose remarks regarding gongan of the previous commentator (for Yuanwu this is, again, Xuedou), is derived from the term 擊節嘆賞, or showing appreciation for a melodically based piece of music or writing by beating time with one's hand 嘆賞. This image evokes the rhythmic quality of commentary in relation to the metrical components of the rhetoric in the source passages.[48]

This *pingchang* approach also recalls the brief prose introduction by Guoan to the sixth image in the series of *Ten Oxherding Pictures*, "The battle is already over, and gain and loss are also empty. He sings a woodcutter's rustic song (*chang*) and whistles a child's tune. Straddled on the ox's back he gazes at the clouds. Though you call him he will not return; though you try to catch and hold him he will not stay." 干戈已罷.得失還無.唱樵子之村歌.吹兒童之野曲.橫身牛上.目視雲霄.呼喚不回.撈籠不住.[49] However this innocent, unadorned singing based on establishing self-discipline and self-control symbolized by riding effortlessly on top of the ox that no longer needs to have its nose pierced with a ring—in some versions the rider has the luxury of sitting while facing backward—is quite different than the sometimes confrontationally critical spirit of the *pingchang* method, which continually challenges and changes its sources.

A modern scholar notes that *pingchang* "became a format in which Chan masters could rework older poems and pay homage to their predecessors, very similar to the *he* 和 ("harmonizing" or "matching") poems in secular poetic tradition. In these writings Chan masters evoked the philosophy embedded in Chan poems of the Tang and Five Dynasties."[50] While this observation has much merit, its emphasis on harmony may fall short of clarifying that by using this commentarial technique Yuanwu fulfills yet extends the gongan tradition by conveying a degree of uncertainty about Xuedou, who receives both praise and criticism that are intricately yet ironically interwoven. This interpretative interaction allows fundamental ambiguity to resound and reverberate on multiple levels of awareness and reflection. Through this inventive discursive method, Yuanwu accomplishes—to paraphrase what has been said about Mozart's reworking of a Handel score—the transformation of a two-dimensional black-and-white landscape provided by Xuedou into the Technicolor Cinerama of the seven-layer construction of the *Blue Cliff Record*.

An important feature shared by Xuedou and Yuanwu along with a multitude of Song Chan abbots is the fundamentally oral or ritual performance aspect of sermonizing. The deliveries of Xuedou's verse and later of Yuanwu's *pingchang* lectures were live events that were recorded or were perhaps originally given based on written notes as a kind of script and were subsequently edited. The presentations tried to capture and recreate the initial spontaneity and impromptu quality of source dialogues. By virtue of what was a live process, their remarks seek to disturb and disrupt as well as to persuade and transform the then-current audience in addition to subsequent readers by creating a collaborative, participatory environment. As noted of case 88 Xuedou ends his verse with simple eloquence: "Leaves fall and flowers bloom, each in its own time" 葉落花開自有時 and Yuanwu comments in his capping phrase on the progression of temporality. Xuedou exclaims, "Do you understand or not? An iron hammerhead with no hole," and Yuanwu reacts with, "It's a shame he let go, so I strike!" 可惜放過.便打.[51] In case 97 the text indicates that after his verse Xuedou adds the remark, "I've thoroughly seen through" 勘破了也, as an exhortative aside made to the assembly. This phrase is included in two of the capping phrases added by Yuanwu, who then says sardonically of Xuedou's final remark, "Each blow of the staff leaves a welt."[52]

In case 60, another example evoking the Chan stick as an imple-
ment of instruction based on a dialogue in which Yunmen has told
his assembly that his "staff has changed into a dragon and swallowed
the whole universe," Xuedou remarks, "I have picked up [the staff]/
Hearing or not hearing/ One must simply be free/ Stop any further
mixed-up confusion/ With seventy-two blows I am still letting you off
easy/ Even after one hundred and fifty it will be hard to forgive you."
拈了也.聞不聞.直須灑灑落落.休更紛紛紜紜.七十二棒且輕恕.一百五十
難放君.[53] The text notes that "Xuedou then suddenly grabbed his staff
and descended from the dais," apparently waving it wildly in a mock
threatening way, "while all at once the great assembly scattered and
fled" 師驀拈拄杖下座.大眾一時走散. Yuanwu adds with quasi-approval
to the first line of the verse, "He is being compassionate like an old
granny" 謝慈悲.老婆心切; with skepticism to the fifth line about dishing
out seventy-two blows he says, "I strike and say, 'Letting go [releasing
the disciple from the teacher's grasp] does no good" 打云放過則不可;
and with faux contempt to the last note on Xuedou wielding his staff
he adds, "Why does Xuedou have the head of dragon but the tail of a
snake?" 雪竇龍頭蛇尾作什麼.

Other instances in which the living situation of the verse delivery
becomes apparent from reading the transcribed text according to the modern typography of the Taishō edition, which contains line breaks but minimal punctuation, include case 20, in which Xuedou appends a second
verse since he says the first poem in which he demanded that the meditation bench and cushion possessed by Longya be handed over did not complete his thoughts; and case 45, in which Xuedou says he has thrown down
or discarded Zhaozhou's "seven-pound shirt" into the West Lake, which
was near the location of his first temple in Suzhou before he occupied the
monastery in Zhejiang province.

Another example of the use of the *pingchang* approach is case 11 in
which Yuanwu asks rhetorically, "But tell me, where does [Huangbo's]
meaning lie?" 且道意在什麼處. After describing the teaching of the Chan
school, Yuanwu says to the assembly, "I dare to ask all of you, who could
be a teacher of Chan? But as soon as I speak this way I've already lost my
mind. People, where are your nostrils [to be put in tow with a ring]?" 作
麼生是禪中師.山僧恁麼道.已是和頭沒卻了也.諸人鼻孔在什麼處. Then,
"after a pause" 良久 that is recorded in the text (unusual in this collection
though not in related texts from the era that are more clearly records of

oral sermons) to indicate that during the hiatus the assembly may have asked questions or made comments, Yuanwu concludes, "Their nostrils have been pierced through!" 穿卻了也,[54] which means, somewhat sardonically, that he has the members of his group under his control.

John McRae says there is a "feeling of 'being there'" created by *Blue Cliff Record* rhetoric. In that vein it is helpful to recall the saying of John Knox, one of the early great Protestant sermonizers, "It is possible to preach a quite unbiblical sermon on a biblical text. It is also possible to preach a biblical sermon on no text at all." If "Chan" were substituted for "biblical" and "unbiblical" in the three places where Knox uses the words as both adjective and noun the same would hold true for the lectures of Xuedou and Yuanwu, who explored every possible topic, theme, saying, or image as a vehicle for expounding the significance of Chan insight but resisted turning clichés and catchphrases into prized expressions.

Part of Yuanwu's goal is to unpack and clarify Xuedou's sources of inspiration in their appropriate context by annotating critically many of their mysterious citations and allusions. In addition to providing these kinds of reference materials Yuanwu consistently goes beyond exegesis to eisegesis by offering his own creative evaluations of Xuedou as well as the encounter dialogue partners. This is done sometimes by offering praise but at other times through harsh criticism, and also covers reversals and inversions of standpoints and perspectives in an ongoing process that is referred to in one of the collection's prefaces as "reviewing and reversing gongan case judgments" 翻案法. The goal of this interpretative effort is to direct the audience to not take for granted facile conclusions or idealized interpretations and to think for themselves to reach an understanding of the dialogues. Yuanwu exposes readers to various views but discourages accepting any particular interpretation at face value since it easily becomes the basis of a fixation or attachment.

Yuanwu adds various kinds of commentary that at once explicate through exposition and problematize by challenging many of the assumptions and conclusions indicated in the *One Hundred Odes*. He shows that understanding the verse in case 37, for example, requires a broad knowledge of various Chan and Chinese literary sources that inspired Xuedou. But he also boldly proclaims that the verse should not be interpreted as an instance of "singing out from within nothingness" 無中唱出, which apparently was a common reading that needed to be dispelled (although elsewhere Yuanwu indicates he admires that view). Yuanwu suggests it takes the ear of an aficionado to appreciate the harmony expressed by the tune of Xuedou's elegant poetry, yet he also comments ironically that "listening makes you go deaf" 聽則聾.[55]

In building on the innovations of predecessors the *Blue Cliff Record* achieves a style of writing that has fascinated and inspired readers for centuries with an uncanny knack for keeping alive a timeless sense of participating in the immediacy of the dynamics of the original Chan encounters that supposedly transpired long before. Through developing a variety of inventive linguistic devices culled in large part from both classic and vernacular Chinese literary sources and methods in what was initially delivered as oral sermons, which as soon as they were recorded became textual materials, the collection creates an atmosphere reflecting the urgency of uncertainty, in which the encounters play out their drama and intrigue in disparate yet integrated ways.

Table 2.3 shows the underlying connection at different stages of the developmental progression of the gongan tradition linking the interpretative methods of Xuedou, who develops ways of using cases as the basis for spiritual renewal based on the precedents set by Yunmen and Fenyang, with the approach of Yuanwu, who emphasizes the impromptu effect of ritually delivered sermonizing as key to the *pingchang* method.

**Table 2.3 Role of Xuedou and Yuanwu Rhetorical Styles in Gongan Tradition**

| Stage | Style | Impact | Text | Content | When |
|---|---|---|---|---|---|
| Formative | Dialogues | impromptu | Ascribe | quasi-fictive stories | 7–9th c. |
| Informative | *Jingde Rec* | lineage | Scribe | chronicles | 10th–11th c. |
| Transformative | Xuedou | comments | Inscribe | prose/verse remarks | 11th c. |
| Conformative | Muan, Juefan | standards | Scripture | reference | 1108 |
| Performative | Yuanwu | individualism | Script | *pingchang* | 1125 |
| Reformative | Dahui | Keyword | Prescribe | contemplation | 1134 |
| Deformative | Rinzai/Sōtō | apply | De-scribe | esoteric remarks | Muromachi |
| Restorative I | Hakuin | rehabilitate | Subscribe | textual studies | Edo |
| Restorative II | Square/Beat | reinvent | Scribbles | eclectic interests | Current |

Xuedou's primary aim in verses delivered orally is to be transformative by engaging in intimate fashion with the source dialogues, whereas Yuanwu's main goal in live lectures is to be performative, not as an idle or imitative ceremonial pursuit but to enhance an atmosphere of participatory drama that motivates the audience to attain self-realization.

## Uncertainty as a Model of Self-Realization

The key to my hermeneutic method for explicating the *Blue Cliff Record* is to invert without altogether abandoning the customary nearly exclusive focus on the question of the role of literary prowess by seeing the religious goal as paramount and, thereby, to retrieve and reconsider the collection's discursive techniques in terms of how they serve rather than eclipse its fundamental spiritual message. I argue that resolving the perpetual predicament about utilizing or abandoning language, advocating literary (*wenzi*) or nonliterary (*wuzi*) standpoints, or using words versus no words, comes not through taking one side or another of the debate about the relative value of eloquent phrasing representing either a meaningful communication or idle distraction. Instead, it is crucial to see that at its core the text's main concern lies in promoting a lifestyle rooted in awakening, which is based on breakthrough instances that create a radical turnabout at the spur of the moment. This approach is exemplified by the activities of numerous teachers like Yunmen and Zhaozhou, whose sayings and doings are appropriated and appreciated by the collection's commentaries for their poise and suppleness in reacting to challenges while teaching.

Remarks offered by Xuedou and Yuanwu evaluate the interpersonal relational patterns underlying scores of dialogues by using verbal and nonverbal expressions as instances of Dharma battles. The exchange partners engaged in a process of "continuously circling" 交馳 in order to first unsettle, then judge, and finally enlighten one another are at once adversarial, by challenging and contesting in the spirit of competition or combat, and collaborative, by changing and converting the partner with an attitude of cooperation and enhancement. Despite—or perhaps by virtue of—the charming artlessness and simplicity of the query used in most dialogues about a monk's name or place of study, or about the meaning of Buddha or Bodhidharma, the encounter situation taken as a whole provides a distinctive opportunity for a radical spiritual upheaval. This refers to the unenlightened, who has the proverbial rug signifying ignorance pulled out from under them, and the enlightened, who display a rousting rejoinder when their position is confronted as they manage to turn the tables in order to set a proper example of imperturbability for those seeking attainment.

The interlocutor who prevails in this complicated interplay is the one who most convincingly demonstrates the flexibility and versatility to be able to counter, come back, and recover from any temporary setback with quick-witted repartee revealing his inner acumen and self-assurance that anticipates, adjusts, and adapts without hesitation or deliberation in the face of any obstacle or interference. The ability to turn around a deficit situation by gaining leverage and revealing prowess is indicated by the terms 転機 (turning skill) and 転身 (a place to turn). Like a number of phrasings used inventively by Yuanwu, "turn" can in a certain context indicate a counterproductive situation, as when it is used as part of a compound with the character for "backward" in a Japanese version of the maxim, "Don't put the cart before the horse" 本末を転倒するな. However those who are able to make an adjustment quickly and effectively also know how to distinguish between the "sword that kills" 殺人刀, or cuts off illusions at the root, and the "blade that gives life" 活人劍, or indulges the trainee at their level while leading them gradually to a higher stage of awareness.

The appraisals that Xuedou and Yuanwu contribute to the dialogical competitions are variable and open-ended, and often intentionally inconsistent and contrary or subject to reversal or indeterminacy. Sometimes these two commentators highlight an unadorned and undisguised truth reflected in a dialogue, and at other times they point indirectly to a complex web of associations or relationships nearly impossible to decipher without a manual, which is what Yuanwu provides in part through his remarks. These crossover and inconstant tendencies are presented in a way that ultimately puts the onus and/or credit on the audience/reader to determine the outcome for him- or herself as a stimulant for taking action that emulates in one's own daily life the flexible and resourceful behavior of prototypical masters represented in source dialogues. Yuanwu frequently concludes the discussion of a case by saying, in effect, that everyone else including Xuedou had it wrong or at least no better than partially right, so here is what he has to offer. But, he emphasizes, do not be satisfied with this, as you must go on and say what it is that you think about the matter and, furthermore, how you demonstrate your own awakening.

An example of the significance of uncertainty for envisioning Chan awakening is Yuanwu's remarks on case 69, in which Nanquan challenges three colleagues who accompany him on a journey to speak about a circle he has drawn on the ground and finds they respond in typically baffling nonverbal ways. According to Yuanwu's commentary, "The true eye of a patch-robed monk contemplating elusive responses sees they are only a matter of the playfulness of the spirit; but just when you call it the 'playfulness of the spirit,' then it is no longer the playfulness of the spirit." 若是衲僧正眼覷著.只是弄精魂.若喚作弄精魂.卻不是弄精魂.[56] Following this Zhuangzi-inspired disclaimer, Yuanwu defies the audience/reader to gauge where they are at while figuratively climbing the proverbial pathway to reach the ultimate spiritual destination: "Each of you should observe closely your own footsteps." 各自看腳下.[57]

Both Xuedou and Yuanwu are ecumenical in finding a way to express approval and admiration, along with occasional criticisms or preferences, in regard to each of the various instructional devices representative of the houses of Chan as reflected in the dialogues. According to the commentary on case 2, Zhaozhou is considered an exemplary adept whose agility in responding in compelling and unflappable ways to challenging questions posed by disciples reveals the rhetoric of uncertainty by means of a dynamic approach to teaching that is singularly unbound by the need to resort to any particular technique, such as the extreme methods that were typical of Linji and Deshan, who frequently struck and screamed:

It is generally not recognized that while Zhaozhou ordinarily never used beating or shouting to deal with people and only evoked everyday speech, but there was no one in the world who could manage to get the best of him. This was all because he never made typical kinds of calculating judgments. Instead, on the basis of having attained a great self-liberation, he could take up the matter at hand from a sideways standpoint or use an inverted (upside-down) perspective by either going against or going along [with the needs of a student] to help them attain great freedom.

殊不知.這老漢.平生不以棒喝接人.只以平常言語.只是天下人不奈何.蓋為他平生無許多計較.所以橫拈倒用.逆行順行.得大自在.[58]

While discussing in case 45 the way Zhaozhou responds to a challenge by dodging with dexterity a monk's bullet-like probing inquiry, Yuanwu comments, "See how at the ultimate point where it seems impossible to make a turn 轉 he does find a place to turn, and this act spontaneously covers the whole universe. If you are able to make such a turn then you will not get stuck wherever you set foot on the path." 看他恁麼向極則轉不得處轉得.自然蓋天蓋地.若轉不得.觸途成滯.[59] This passage sums up the full import of Yuanwu's teaching based on asserting that knowing one case thoroughly unlocks the mystery to every other case.[60]

The components of the turnabout experience expressed in the *Blue Cliff Record* include in a more or less sequential pattern:

1. Transmission of truth takes place by virtue of engaging with examples of untruth, or communication that uses various sorts of indirection ranging from metaphor and parable to obscure allusions or obtuse references, and to non sequitur or absurdity, silence, nonverbal gestures or symbols, or natural or innocuous sounds; illumination occurs by disclosing a level of insight that has always been available in everyday experience but was long hidden by ignorance and attachment.

2. Tendentious tendencies on the part of the exchange contestants are exposed at each and every turn as seemingly impenetrable obstacles and obstructions, so that a dramatic reversal is needed to force change to occur by ending the gridlock derived from stubborn insistence in regard to any and all one-sided or partial views.

3. Topsy-turvy sayings and doings create a profound sense of doubt, or generate what is often referred to as the Zen malady (comparable to Kierkegaard's "sickness unto death" as the cause of anxiety and dread); it is necessary for one to have their fixations drastically confronted and overturned so that barriers or checkpoints are transformed from an impediment, whether conceptual or practical, into a vehicle for realization.[61]

4. Tension between dialogue partners is dialectical, as reflected in the teacher's ability to mix censure, reprimand, dismissal, and rejection with acceptance, tolerance, admiration, and praise by virtue of a compassionate lowering oneself to the "in-the-mud (or weeds)" level of the trainee's ignorant standpoint in order to help ripen and polish their understanding.

5. Turnabouts occurring in a dialogue reveal the adept's knack for maneuvering, so that in case 10, involving master Muzhou Chenzun (n.d.), a disciple of Huangbo (and Dharma brother of Linji) an inquiring "monk is speechless and at a loss: he is no longer able to turn the circumstance freely. On the other side, Muzhou is neither scared nor stuck. He waits in confidence for the opportune moment. When the moment comes, he recognizes it immediately and turns it around."[62]

6. Transformational experiences are continuously deepened in the aftermath of awakening as the master seeks ways to describe the mystery

by evoking serene natural imagery or to apply the acupuncture needle exactly where it hurts most but without wounding healthy tissue; this effort culminates in his ability to criticize all those who have gone before by uttering the equivalent of the German saying, "Others think this, but I (*Aber Ich*) think ..." and then taking the challenge to the audience/reader by demanding, "What do you think?"

This teaching results in a trainee transitioning from the desperation of "fishing for a whale but coming up with a frog" to the triumph of "buying iron but getting gold." Xuedou says in the verse comment on case 10, "Adepts know how to seize the opportunity for change" 作者知機變,[63] while also implying that Muzhou, the apparent victor in the dialogue, is just as blind as the anonymous disciple. This stands in contrast to case 9 in which he suggests that both Zhaozhou and his monk-adversary are winners for "showing their ability in direct encounter" 句裏呈機劈面來.[64] However blindness, which can symbolize delusion, also has virtue in representing transcendent wisdom as in the nonpreferential sense that "Justice is blind."[65]

As Yuanwu's comments on case 45 indicate, the opposite of Zhaozhou's turnabout approach, which is eminently capable of moving in different directions depending on pedagogical demands, and thus the bane of Chan practitioners everywhere who are seeking to overcome their own limitations, is the fixed and obstructive standpoint of calculation that derives from what the text calls the inauthentic mentality of "being unconcerned" 無事 (*wuji*). This refers to a passive and inactive state of expecting enlightenment to occur automatically rather than being vigilant and vigorous in actualizing attainment. The *Blue Cliff Record* commentary mockingly says, "These days everyone makes unconcern the basis of understanding. Some suggest, 'Since there is neither delusion nor enlightenment it is not necessary to go on seeking Buddha.'" 如今人盡作無事會.有底道.無迷無悟不要更求.只如佛未出世時.[66]

Throughout their commentaries Xuedou and Yuanwu show no mercy in attacking such hopeless scoundrels as fools, phonies, thieves, or blind men who carry a board on their shoulder (symbolizing narrowmindedness) or who shoot their arrow vainly at an intruder after the bandit has already fled and allowed the thief to occupy their domain and rob them mercilessly. However, like a number of such terms that are used in the collection in radically different, even opposite, ways depending on context, in several instances the compound 無事 can also indicate the positive meaning of transcendence in the sense of authentic detachment that is manifest

by Zhaozhou and others as in cases 30 and 33. Being authentically unconcerned, however, only occurs after true awakening is experienced.

Whereas the unenlightened are uncertain about intent or meaning, and
the enlightened are sure about this but remain inconclusive about which
words to use depending on the teaching circumstances, in case 11 an adept,
Huangbo, employs his "active edge" (*jifeng*) to show that "the key element of
the school that has been handed down from ancient times is to determine
whether to express oneself in a way that kills or gives life, holds on and con-
trols or lets go and releases, or rolls up or rolls out the trainee" 他從上宗
旨.有時擒.有時縱.有時殺.有時活.有時放.有時收.敢問諸人.[67] According to
Yuanwu, Huangbo's greatness is marked by the fact that he "is not contesting
others or asserting himself, displaying himself or boasting of himself. If you
understand what he has done, you are free in all directions: sometimes you
stand alone on a solitary peak and sometimes you reach out in the bustling
marketplace." Furthermore Yuanwu praises a line by Huangbo that may at
first seem mundane but actually shows, "Right here in his own words there's
a place for him to make his turnaround" 他底句下.便有出身處.[68]

Although there is general agreement about the ample capacity of eminent masters like Huangbo as well as many other pre-Song luminaries,
because of the fundamental indirection and ambiguity of the dialogues,
the perspectives expressed in comments about who are the winners versus
the losers of any given Dharma battle can vary significantly. What looks like
a stunning maneuver to one interpreter may be cast as a partial or disas-
trous response by another explainer, so we find that Xuedou and Yuanwu
are not always in accord, and the friction that arises from the interaction
of their standpoints is quite thought-provoking but also perplexing. While
Yuanwu happily dishes out lavish praise, he also rarely lets Xuedou off the
hook. In case 65 in a capping phrase on the predecessor's verse evoking
the image of "snapping my fingers three times to call back a good horse
that has run off," Yuanwu comments, "He neither reaches the village nor
gets to the shop. With your staff broken where will you go? The sound of
Xuedou's thunder is great, but there is no rain at all." 喚得回鳴指三下前
不搆村.後不迭店.拗折拄杖子.向什麼處去.雪竇雷聲甚大.雨點全無.[69]

## *Song Dynasty and Contemporary Resonances*

The notion of uncertainty encompasses, but is not limited to, the traditional view of Ancestral (or Patriarchal) Chan, which indicates that

enlightenment is based on personal experience rather than doctrinal teachings as in the approach of Tathagata Chan. The latter method is sometimes compared by detractors to reading a geography book while the former, according to proponents, is like actually navigating the highways and byways with a map. An illustration of Ancestral Chan is found in the use, in a couple dozen cases usually as a final remark on the case or verse, of the declaration, "I strike" 便打, which represents Yuanwu's entering or intruding directly into the topic raised by the dialogical encounter in his own inimitable way but without indicating a firm conclusion. His aim is not to persuade the audience to adopt a particular viewpoint that may become the source of fixation or attachment but, rather, to encourage and demand that they think through the answer for themselves.

The need for readers to understand gongan in their own fashion is addressed in case 20 when Yuanwu lists six different masters before his day who had responded to the quixotic exchange cited as the main case, and then makes it clear he does not agree with any of these but instead offers his own alternative interpretation of the topic. While Xuedou's verse is highly commended as superior to other versions, Yuanwu also prods the reader to question its meaning. At the end of the section of his prose commentary on the poem, he follows up several rhetorical queries with the exhortation, "When you reach the pathway, who else is there to point to the matter at hand?" 到此且道是什麼人分上事.[70]

An understanding of the significance of uncertainty as it was developed and designed in the *Blue Cliff Record* in the context of Song Chinese intellectual history is enhanced by seeking out resonances with contemporary Western worldviews that are often at least indirectly influenced by the influx of East Asian writings and ideas beginning in the nineteenth century. The Song dynasty, an era when the creative impulse evident in religion was expressed through literary, fine, and performing arts, featured meritocracy reached through the educational exam system and some indicators of the arising of democracy. These conditions fostered a focus on erudition enhanced through leisure activities spent, not as a mindless passing or killing of time for the sake of entertainment, but in order to heighten self-awareness through intense personal reflections on selfhood in communion with nature.

This state of aesthetic spirituality was accompanied by an admiration and appreciation for those talented individuals who could bridge sacred pursuits with secular accomplishments, while fearing the possible consequences of social upheaval or political turmoil. Possible exile or imprisonment could be a consequence of imminent dangers of invasion from the north or through coming in conflict with current Chinese leadership, which often reacted strongly to domestic turmoil if linked to the kind of foreign threats that led to the fall of the Northern Song. This caused a sense of melancholy and world-weariness based on sensitivity to the fleetingness of opportunities for gaining spontaneous flashes of insight through an instantiation of mystical insight. Analyzing the Song worldview that informed the composition of Chan gongan commentaries suggests the following main elements:

1. The main goal was to gain self-knowledge 自知 realized by means of creative self-expression, sometimes free from and sometimes adhering to literary rules and regulations in a way that can be likened to harmonizing with a song, chant, ode, or recitation, or listening to a tune played with a wind, percussion, or string instrument.
2. This involved undergoing a profound experience of doubt 疑 and anxiety, leading to physical and psychological symptoms associated with the Chan illness, which could be intense and prolonged, and could make one feel that he or she puts their life at stake in the pursuit of knowledge that sometimes had "real world" implications since Yuanwu and, especially, Dahui and their associates underwent extensive periods of persecution and exile.
3. The goal was reached by seizing opportune moments 機緣 during the course of verbal and nonverbal exchanges or testing situations in order to develop an intensely intimate yet forbearing mentor-mentee relationship that fostered spiritual growth through spontaneous awakening, rather than the gradual accumulation of evidence or data lacking intuitive awareness.
4. There was no destination, as realization requires that one continues to probe further 請益 by looking into a matter from all sides and every angle (upside down, inside out, sideways, and backward), whereby a single word or phrase, or sound or gesture, becomes an entryway for demonstrating what can be compared to the knack of a card player finding his way out of losing hand by knowing "when to hold 'em, and when to fold 'em."
5. The result was an inconclusive and ambiguous state of mind based on making one's own personal judgment through an assessment in accord with circumstances 對機 by accepting, sometimes reluctantly, alternative views while also severely criticizing those who fall into the trap of

conceptualization and cliché or use idle contrivances. Adepts were expected to be able to persuade others by example while admitting that, ultimately, literary and artistic expression is the scattering of sand into the eyes 撒眼沙 of the reader; yet this could not be helped as teachers hoped to inspire without predetermining their trainees' power of observation and insight.

One caveat in my approach is that there is no term used in *Blue Cliff Record* that can be translated as "uncertainty." The modern construction *buqueding* 不確定 (J. *fukakutei*) comes close in implying what is not to be relied on or what cannot be known in a definitive way, while the traditional Japanese term *hakanai* 儚い(はかない) suggests a sorrowful acceptance of what is invariably absent, lost, missing, or inconclusive. Part of the impetus for using the term is that uncertainty corresponds to or evokes some contemporary Western attitudes about accepting chaos and finding purpose through abandoning the pursuit of certitude, ranging from scientific investigation in theoretical physics to literary modernism and philosophical existentialism. These outlooks stress awareness of the limits of human knowledge and the incapacity of speech acts in conveying information or achieving articulation. Such an outlook reflects a different state of mind than mere inaccuracy or indecision in the ordinary sense because it represents a state of confidence and prescience while recognizing indeterminacy.

The term uncertainty is perhaps best known today from Werner Heisenberg's principle as part of quantum mechanics, which argues that only probabilities can be calculated. Unlike Isaac Newton's clockwork universe, where everything follows clear-cut laws on how to move and prediction is fairly easy if you know the starting conditions, the uncertainty principle enshrines a level of ambiguity and indecision into the theory of physics. Calculation of either position or momentum will be inaccurate in that the act of observation itself affects the situation by skewing the particle being detected, thus limiting the possibility of exactitude.[71]

Perhaps more pertinent to the meaning of Chan rhetoric are various cultural notions that emphasize the role of uncertainty in terms of personal growth in seeking spiritual realization. For example, a professor of leadership studies, Richard Schell, in an unorthodox recent approach to self-attainment celebrates the "power of uncertainty" and says of the viewpoint of his book *Springboard: Launching Your Personal Search for Success*, "You don't need to avoid uncertainty. ... The truth of the matter is that nobody is certain."[72] A sophisticated philosophical outlook was developed by nineteenth-century poet John Keats in the theory of negative capability that links the indeterminacy of finding a single fixed truth, which Keats felt was being pursued in futility by some of his colleagues, to the inexhaustible richness and aptitude of an individual to perceive, think, and function beyond any presupposition. Keats's notion further captures the rejection of the constraints of any particular context and the ability to experience phenomena free from the bonds of conventional epistemology, or the assertion of one's own will and individuality upon their activity.[73]

In that vein, though not necessarily through direct influence, American author Stephen Crane once told an editor of his struggles with creative writing, "I cannot help vanishing and disappearing and dissolving. It is my foremost trait."[74] Similarly in *On Late Style* Edward Said examines the production of great modern Western writers, artists, and musicians at the end of their lives and shows that, rather than the resolution of a lifetime's artistic endeavor, most of the late works are rife with unresolved contradiction and almost impenetrable complexity.[75] Their artistic genius was evident through the foreshadowing in their world of future developments in respective disciplines, even if this stood in contrast to general tastes and expectations.

Perhaps the main example of a Western resonance with Chan rhetoric of uncertainty involves novelist James Joyce, who epitomized the movement known as literary modernism with his early collection of short stories, *Dubliners*, published in 1914, and his massive tome *Ulysses*, published in 1922. The was around the same time as comparable literary developments with fusing form and function to capture and convey interiority in the literature of T.S. Eliot, William Faulkner, Eugene O'Neill, Virginia Woolf, and others who innovated expressionism or stream of consciousness. Like his peers Joyce experimented with style and typography including the use of discontinuity, the juxtaposition of contradictory or ironic narrative elements such as the uninterrupted depiction of feelings and an unreliable or perspective-bound narrator, and intertextuality through the use of classical allusions as well as borrowings with wordplays from other languages, cultures, and texts. Critic L. J. Morrissey notes that the narration in the first story in *Dubliners* first reveals but then withdraws judgments and confidences just when the reader needs the most help in building to the denouement so that "the method of telling itself forces us to judge, to interpret, to participate in the text."[76]

Joyce's primary contribution to modernist discourse that touches base with classical Chan experience is his formation of the notion of epiphany, which is comparable to *satori* and represents an idea he almost single-handedly transformed from an obscure medieval theological term to a vital aspect of contemporary spirituality attained through literary refinement and aesthetic sensibility. Each of the fifteen stories of *Dubliners* is composed to crescendo in the revelatory experience of an epiphany. In these writings, to at least one of the characters based on the fine details of conversation or observation and in an altogether unexpected and unintended way through a sudden awareness of quiddity, or what Joyce calls the "whatness," of a single common object that has become radiant, in a moment suddenly and open-endedly the meaning of all things emerges in a way that is crystal clear in its uncertain and ephemeral nature. The theme is perhaps best summed up by a passage in *Ulysses*, which was originally conceived as the sixteenth story of *Dubliners*. This occurs in Episode 3, *Proteus*: "remember your epiphanies on green oval leaves, deeply deep, copies to be sent if you died to all the great libraries of the world."[77] A commentator further notes:

> By the time he scrawled those words, James Joyce had long been working to claim the term "epiphany" on behalf of secular literature. Hitherto, the word had an ancient, and predominantly religious, history. It has its genesis in ancient Greece (ἐπιφάνεια), where it was used beautifully to refer to the first glimmer of dawn, the first sight of the enemy in battle, or the first vision of a god. It became Judaised in 2 Maccabees, when it was used to describe the God of Israel, and was Christianised in 2 Timothy, where it mainly referred to the Second Coming; thereafter it came to describe the personal realisation that Christ was the Son of God.[78]

An interesting Chan connection with the early Greek meaning of the term as the first glimmer of a truth that is about to unfold, whether in the human or natural realm, is expressed in case 41 of the *Blue Cliff Record*, in which Zhaozhou asks about "one who has died the great death and returns to life" and Touzi says, "He must not go by night; he must get there in daylight." 投子云.不許夜行.投明須到.[79] A modern Chinese scholar suggests this rendering (emphasis added): "He is not permitted to walk in the night, but must get there *as soon as the day starts to become bright*." 不許夜里行走.但要天一明就要赶到.[80]

The main link with Song Chan gongan literature is that Joyce rejected his Catholic upbringing to apply the term epiphany to the humanist context of self-awareness as "a sudden spiritual manifestation, whether in the vulgarity of speech or of gesture or in a memorable phase of the mind itself. [Joyce] believed that it was for the man of letters to record these epiphanies with extreme care, seeing that they themselves are the most delicate and evanescent of moments."[81] For Joyce, as for Xuedou and Yuanwu, revelation occurs in the context of a brief, cryptic exchange in which the delivery of truth is indirect and unintended, and by no means apparent in the words themselves. This requires a reading between the lines to realize a fleeting visionary instant, as when one suddenly becomes aware that a romance is exposed as hollow at the core or, indeed, never really existed, although this is not seen until a flash of understanding occurs based on a stray comment or unconscious body language. That approach resembles the works of Marcel Proust, for whom the scent of a blossom, or just an appropriately inspired recollection of this sensation, could instantly trigger new levels of memory and self-awareness.

An intriguing affinity with the breakthrough type of turnaround experience depicted in the poetic or narrative remarks of the *Blue Cliff Record* occurs in the final passage of "The Dead," the fifteenth story of *Dubliners* that evokes mystical hearing associated with the lyricism of natural events. Joyce writes with deceptively simple eloquence of the main character's experience of epiphany as a kind of cosmic resonance in dealing profoundly with newfound understanding based on a revelatory view of his wife's past: "His soul swooned slowly as he heard the snow falling faintly through the universe and faintly falling, like the descent of their last end, upon all the living and the dead."[82]

However a basic difference with some of the melancholy implications in Joyce's worldview, which focuses on everyday narratives rather than the adventures of mystical pilgrims, is the conviction as expressed in several Yunmen dialogues of the fundamental level of self-attainment that constitutes the universal potentiality of Buddha-nature. This is conveyed in case 27 on the "Golden breeze" that constitutes the body even when trees wither and leaves fall; case 83 on "Buddhas and pillars communing" symbolizing the unity of ultimate and mundane reality; and case 86 in which Yunmen proclaims, "Everyone has a light," although he acknowledges the conundrum that it appears dark and dim as soon you try to look right at it. This difficulty occurs, he suggests in Joycean fashion, because the function of gazing without genuine insight represents a futile attempt to reduce the pure subjectivity of awareness that encompasses objectivity into a mere entity that stands over and opposed to the perceiver, thereby distorting what should be characterized as a fundamentally holistic act of perception.[83]

# 3

# *Unintended Baggage?*

PART I: YUANWU IN HIS OWN WRITE VIS-À-VIS XUEDOU

## *Yuanwu, A Rhetorical Reviver or Detractor?*

An understanding of the *Blue Cliff Record* is greatly enhanced by capturing the distinctive rhetorical voice of Yuanwu. It stands apart from Xuedou but is intimately related to Xuedou's influence. Yuanwu also greatly impacted Dahui. This crucial autonomous discursive component is, in many appropriations of the text, subsumed or eclipsed by the approaches of predecessor and successor. Yuanwu's views are also sometimes conflated with those of the *Blue Cliff Record* taken as a whole, so that his commentary is overshadowed or conflated with Xuedou's instead of regarded as a discrete component with a purpose and integrity of its own. Moreover, modern views of Yuanwu tend to be greatly affected and sometimes skewed by the prominence of the keyword method in that Dahui's standpoint is applied retrospectively to his mentor's outlook.

This chapter and the next one, covering two parts of the same theme, examine Yuanwu's standpoint in connection and/or disconnection with that of Xuedou and Dahui. The key hermeneutic element in my approach is based on recognizing the importance of the *pingchang*-oriented evaluative method of commentary used throughout the collection, which is not committed—or, to put it more positively, remains astutely uncommitted—to any particular ideology or interpretative style but instead explores diverse possibilities without fixation. On the one hand, Yuanwu appears to be fundamentally consistent with the Chan teaching of Xuedou and Dahui, both of whom also wrote extensive prose and poetic commentaries on gongan, and in their respective ways embraced comparable views of multiperspectivism as a crucial factor for the attainment of Chan awakening. As Jacques Gernet says of one of the main principles of the Song worldview expressed in poetry and painting that can also be applied to Chan, "the Chinese landscape is not viewed from a fixed point. It is a field of vision in which the eye can wander, seeing it from different and changing points of view ... [from] a plurality of perspectives."[1] Yet Yuanwu also clearly demonstrates his own uniquely open-ended stance, which both criticized his predecessor and was apparently attacked by his successor, so that it must be differentiated from these and other major Chan teachers of the period.

Like all great literary accomplishments, religious or secular, the *Blue Cliff Record*, especially the extensive portions of commentary composed by Yuanwu, is in large part the result of many sources of inspiration the author absorbed. These include ideas and styles provided by Xuedou's eloquent verse as filtered through Yuanwu's studies while training with mentor Wuzu, in addition to his reading of collected sayings, such as the *Yunmen Record*, and reference works like the *Lexicon of the Ancestral Garden*. The main question in terms of examining the influence of predecessors is whether Yuanwu eagerly promotes or seeks to distance himself from an emphasis on the kind of elegant poetic language that is highlighted by Xuedou's verse comments and, to a lesser extent, by the compositions of Wuzu and other predecessors that are sometimes cited as part of the collection's prose commentary.

We must consider whether Dahui's drastic change of heart, no doubt emblematic of broader perspectives regarding complicated receptions of gongan commentary, was the justifiable result of "unintended conceptual/discursive baggage." Had it perhaps become all too apparent that the intricate rhetoric of the *Blue Cliff Record* could not be relied upon for conveying, but rather had to be seen as distracting from, spiritual attainment and therefore needed to be discarded? In chapter 6 I discuss evidence indicating that the collection probably did not disappear but was copied, perhaps surreptitiously, and distributed in a secondhand way among interested Chan followers.

Yuanwu was prized for his literary production yet also is seen by some commentators as a precursor to Dahui's emphasis on minimalist discourse. The central query with regard to impact is whether there may have been an underlying sense of consistency and continuity between mentor/creator and student/destroyer in that Yuanwu was possibly all too aware of the limitations of his accomplishment—he was apparently warned of the pitfalls of literary excesses by Dharma brother Fojian. He may well have understood or would even have approved of Dahui's taking the last resort of incineration, had he lived long enough to see this unfold. Might Yuanwu have preferred a less ornate style of expression, as seen in *Wumen's Barrier* produced a century later? Or did the destructive act represent a grave misunderstanding on Dahui's part, or perhaps simply a wide gap that emerged on the matter of the efficacy of discourse between two highly respected yet contested Chan Buddhist viewpoints? Moreover how do circumstances regarding the attitude of his rebellious disciple reflect upon Yuanwu's appropriations of Xuedou and Wuzu?

**Five Theories.** A survey of contemporary literature in the field indicates four current interpretative standpoints regarding Yuanwu's relationships with his main predecessor and successor that seem to be greatly affected, for better or worse, by notions put forth by traditional commentators. The standpoints range the spectrum as follows:

1. The lettered Chan thesis argues that Yuanwu fully embraces and provides a significant degree of rejuvenation for the role of literature, while standing in support of Xuedou and in opposition to Dahui.
2. The prose preference thesis suggests that Yuanwu accepts the importance of Xuedou's verse but deliberately shifts the emphasis away from poetry toward the utility of prose commentary.
3. The stepping-stone thesis maintains Yuanwu's approach, intentionally or not, set the stage for yet did not fully achieve the ideal of Dahui's minimalism.
4. The precursor status thesis indicates that Yuanwu would have appreciated in theory, and perhaps even at least partially anticipated in practice, Dahui's keyword standpoint as a kind of culmination or logical conclusion to his own way of thinking about rhetoric.

The first two of these theses regarding Xuedou are examined in this chapter, and the third and fourth theses dealing with Dahui will be treated in chapter 4. In addition to these differing views of Yuanwu's place as a Chan interpreter, there is a fifth standpoint regarding his legacy that is examined and rebutted in the final chapter:

5. The diminishing impact thesis finds Yuanwu representing an antiquated and highly specialized commentarial method considered a classic example of ornate writing that drifted out of fashion and was rather inconsequential during later stages of the gongan tradition.

According to this standpoint the *Blue Cliff Record* reflects well its era at the formative stage but ultimately exercises a relatively modest effect on the overall development of the gongan tradition.

The key question about Yuanwu's relation with Xuedou concerns what Yuanwu must have had in mind in composing prose comments. Did he feel that the Xuedou verses were so precious to deserve special treatment, as the lettered Chan thesis indicates? Or could he have been thinking that they were abstruse and needed to be brought down to earth to have a greater impact on the training of novice monks struggling with the *One Hundred Odes*, as suggested by the prose preference thesis? The central question in regard to Dahui is whether Yuanwu may have been concerned that his own contribution to literary Chan carried unintended baggage, as the stepping-stone thesis suggests. Would Yuanwu have been repulsed by his former student's actions, or might he have expected that destruction of the text was an inevitable and much-needed remedy for the excesses of literary Chan, as in the precursor status thesis?

These standpoints are all one-sided, according to my understanding, because they tend to place too much attention on the matter of stylistic discrepancies that are mistaken for substantive differences, while overlooking the crucial role of *pingchang*-based commentary conjured in both the poetry and prose sections of the *Blue Cliff Record*. This evaluative interpretative method is conducive to expressing the notion of uncertainty as the basis of an experience of self-realization, which is vigorously advocated throughout the collection's sophisticated rhetorical structures and literary content.

My preliminary conclusion is that while he is ever cautious about relying on the excesses of language (thus reminding us of the keyword method), this does not indicate that Yuanwu would have supported his disciple's far-reaching notion of eliminating all rhetorical baggage, which he feels must be continually explored and corrected rather than rejected outright. Dahui's position toward Yuanwu is much more complicated and nuanced than simple dismissal, especially since he produced his own major gongan commentaries and expositions of Chan dialogues. Yuanwu recognizes that Xuedou's verses are not well understood unless abetted with line-by-line explications, which are deliberately abstruse and provocative, but there is no hint that he considers language necessarily flawed and deficient. It is not the text but, rather, the reader's comprehension that can become either problematic or useful, so the burden of responsibility for assessing the relationship between Yuanwu and others lies in determining how gongan discourse is appropriated on an individuated basis.

    The crucial point is that from the very start of the *Blue Cliff Record* Yuanwu emphasizes the innate limitations of discourse as a possible detriment to awakening while at the same time he shows, perhaps in playful fashion, how verbal prowess used by a powerfully expressive poet-monk can become a constructive enhancement of enlightenment. Somewhat differently from both Xuedou, the versifier of symbolic imagery, and Dahui, the skeptic of rhetoric as an end in itself, Yuanwu takes a guarded approach toward discourse by neither fully ratifying nor denying its applicability. However Yuanwu also generously, albeit critically, explores diverse sorts of expression and their multifarious implications. The primary factor is that Yuanwu at once dismisses both poetic and prose commentary when these are unfortunately not carried out in an efficacious manner—he does not favor one over the other, as a recent scholar suggests[2]—yet praises Xuedou's verse as exceptional, although not without a certain amount of ambiguity underlying this assessment. Through his remarks Yuanwu seeks to carve out a middle position between naïve affirmation and stubborn rejection of literary Chan.

    In order to assess critically the various contemporary theories it is necessary to place in fuller cultural context Yuanwu's body of work in relation to that of Xuedou and Dahui in several ways: first, with regard to appraising some of the major trends and tropes of Chinese literary history that influenced Song Chan discourse; second, by considering how each of the key figures reacted to this intellectual historical environment through the rhetoric contained in their respective writings; and third, through a careful analysis of their thought in key passages culled from the *Blue Cliff Record* and related texts. This multileveled examination helps probe and penetrate the argot game of gongan commentarial typology and terminology, which includes remarks on a host of Chan topics in the work of the three thinkers in relation to how other masters from this and later periods commented on many of the same cases.

## Contradictory Song Literary Perspectives

The first level of analysis considers how debates about the place of rhetoric in gongan commentary have unfolded in the context of the somewhat conflicted and contradictory role attributed to literary discourse in Song China, including but not limited to Chan writings and practices. For most observers the achievements of the *Blue Cliff Record*—whether these are prized or, in some prominent instances, disdained—are attributed to the way its approach to interpreting cases epitomizes lettered Chan in that a preoccupation with achieving rhetorical flair is considered superior to other concerns, including the pursuit of enlightenment that should be the main goal of Chan religiosity. Literary creativity viewed as the basis for both the rises and falls in prestige that the collection has undergone is generally regarded as the product of the affiliation on the part of Yuanwu and Xuedou with a set of discursive methods deeply ingrained in the Northern Song cultural environment.

While this thematic emphasis certainly represents a worthwhile area of inquiry, which is further explored here, the main problem with adapting uncritically an attitude focused almost entirely on the role of literature is that it tends to reinforce the conclusion that the collection's accomplishments are based largely on an art for art's sake outlook instead of the priority of the spiritual quest, a theme that, it is claimed, gets lost or overlooked in the complicated process of its writing styles. It is important to realize, however, that an oft-repeated trope in the history of Chinese literature in which Yuanwu and Xuedou were engaged is the dual themes of celebrating eloquence while being ready and willing to denigrate any sign of its excess. Therefore the *Blue Cliff Record*'s spectacularly mixed reception based on Dahui's actions reflects a creative tension with regard to the fine line between the utility of elegant rhetorical complication and the futility of counterproductive linguistic convolution.

On the positive side, Song literary criticism as expressed in formal comments and as casual musings suggests an appreciation for the sense of harmony and resonance reverberating from good writing that has the seamlessly imaginative impact of the sound of an echo or the ringing of a bell, or of a one-string harp—or, paradoxically, from a Chan standpoint, of a stringless zither or an iron flute played upside down. Productive literature is not just a mimetic depiction of objects, persons, or places but indicates deep reflection based on subjective impressions and self-awareness of circumstances and surroundings. Writing that expresses this quality is cogent and persuasive through adapting either a soothing and graceful or a dazzling and astounding style. It conveys with dexterity in just a single word or succinct phrase a sense of the unity of a whole scene and also indicating the partiality and limitation of human perception and perspectives by offering incongruous or multiple possible resolutions while exalting this condition yet without succumbing to arbitrarily praising relativism or pessimistically wallowing in nihilism.[3]

To achieve this a writer must avoid cliché or the obvious through effectively using ellipsis, allusion, and indirection, and also be able to diagnose
self-critically, akin to medical investigation, his or her own flaws, faults,
and disorders to weed out and repair them through the proper prognosis
and prescription. If an author realizes he is trying, so to speak, to carve an
ax handle with an ax, or to trade jade for garbage—rather than, as in *Blue
Cliff Record* images, to look for iron and find gold, or to hunt a frog and
come up with a whale—then instead of forcing a publication that will not
be conducive he must be willing to take the drastic step of discarding his
efforts. Self-satisfaction is invariably accompanied by a disbelieving sense
so that, as one Song dynasty author bluntly put it, "Whenever I see my old
work, I want to burn the poems I hate."[4]

We also should consider the impact of Neo-Confucianism—even
though its thinkers were at times harshly critical of Chan—for which
study and learning as a means of self-cultivation required respect for
language and meaning. Without the crucial role of discourse, especially
the sayings of classical sages Confucius and Mencius, humanity would
be little if any different than beasts. Words were not, as the Madhyamika
Buddhists claimed, essentially empty. Rather Song Confucians, including Zhu Xi (1130–1200), who first experimented with and then rejected
but ultimately greatly influenced Chan literary styles, affirmed that verbal
expressions were the real conveyors of true meaning and had significant
epistemological power sufficient to affect and facilitate transformations of
reality in decisively cognitive and ethical ways.[5]

Therefore it is crucial to defuse a sense of contrast or conflict between
Chan spirituality and literary rhetoric in that, according to Japanese
Sinologist Iriya Yoshitaka's analysis, the underlying element for both is
contemplative reverie. The most valuable writings of the period for Iriya
were not those that made an "attempt [at] religious statement, but those in
which the poet disports himself in a free, effortless reveling in the Way—
the joyful outpouring of a 'sportful samadhi.'"[6] Nevertheless, a skeptical
view concerning the role of discourse was continuously espoused by expo-
nents of antiliterary Chan, such as Zhenjing Kewen (1025–1102), whose
recorded sayings were read and to some extent appreciated by Wuzu and
Yuanwu, and this standpoint came to the fore during the Southern Song
dynasty with the writings of Dahui.

Dahui's act of incineration, if true, joins a long list of destructive
tendencies in Chan regarding written texts. Tension about writing
can also be found in more subtle fashion in the Chan poetry of Touzi

Yiqing (1032–1083), a Caodong master known for his own gongan collection featuring verse remarks (further commented on in *pingchang* style by Linquan Conglin), who notes wistfully in a poem that was one of a group of three compositions on living at his mountain hermitage, "Though I am in the business of Emptiness,/ I cannot avoid being at the mercy of my inclinations./ For even though I have long been practicing Chan meditation,/ Instead I remain preoccupied with literary content." 雖然所業空,免被才情役.忝曾學參禪.叨以習文義.[7] The dilemma is by no means limited to traditional Chan, because Touzi's wistful reflection has a resonance with *Rhymes of a Rolling Stone* (1912) by modern American poet Robert W. Service, who remarks, "I have no doubt at all the Devil grins,/ At seas of ink I spatter./ Ye gods, forgive my 'literary' sins—/ The other kind don't matter."

In the *Blue Cliff Record*, despite constantly cautioning against misguided understandings of words and letters by insisting that his audience not take literally various conceptual explanations, diagrams, and formulas often used in gongan interpretations, Yuanwu highly values the effect of verbal teaching when used appropriately as a skillful means. In the introduction to case 25 involving the Hermit of Lotus Blossom Peak, he insists, "If your words do not astonish the audience you will fall into the streams of the commonplace" 語不驚群.陷於流俗.[8] Moreover in prose commentary on the case he says of the dilemma of using or not using language, "Although the matter is not found in words and phrases, if not for words and phrases it could not be discerned and one would not perceive the Way. So it is said, 'There is fundamentally no word for the Way, but only through words is the Way revealed.'" 況此事雖不在言句中.非言句即不能辨.不見道.道本無言因言顯道.[9] Moreover in case 81, "People don't realize that in a single activity or a single technique the old masters untied fetters and broke chains in that each and every word and phrase held precious meaning within. . . . If one has the eye and brain of a patch-robed monk he sometimes holds fast and sometimes lets go . . . shifting with the circumstances. . . . [Using] great function and great capacity . . . he is like a clear mirror reflecting the strange or ordinary just as they appear before him." 殊不知.古人一機一境.敲枷打鎖.一句一言.渾金璞玉.若是衲僧眼腦.有時把住. 有時放行. 臨時通變.大用大機.大似明鏡當臺.胡來胡現漢來漢現.[10]

The conundrum about the role of language in relation to imagery regarding the natural landscape is summed up in an anonymous verse cited by Yuanwu in the commentary on case 72: "If words do not break free of the old clichés,/ How will you be able to escape that which conceals and binds?/

White clouds covering the mouth of the valley,/ Deluding so many people about the source." 語不離窠臼.焉能出蓋纏.白雲橫谷口.迷卻幾人源.[11] Yuanwu notes that for the Caodong stream the outlook expressed in this poem is referred to as "transgression" 觸破, a rhetorical technique based on using words as a poison to counteract poison or as a tool of disruption, or a necessarily problematic explanation to help disciples gain liberation from delusion. In case 12 Yuanwu indicates that the role of language, while functioning as a dispensable vessel, is nevertheless irreplaceable and absolutely essential by citing the saying of an "ancient sage" (no doubt Zhuangzi), "The Way basically is wordless but we use words to illustrate the Way. In seeing the Way you can forget about the words [that were essential to get you there]." 道本無言.因言顯道.見道即忘言.[12]

## Lettered Chan Thesis

By considering the *Blue Cliff Record*'s rhetorical structures and content in light of other related texts, the lettered Chan thesis sees Yuanwu epitomizing the *wenzi* approach in a way that was consistent with the poetics of his predecessors and opposed to the antiliterary method. In his study of Juefan's view of literary Chan, for example, George Keyworth argues for a stark contrast with Dahui, "Yuanwu Keqin appears to have been among the most prodigious Chan masters to promulgate these [literary] methods of instruction [by bringing up precedent cases 舉古 (*jugu*)] with his students. Along with Fenyang, Yuanwu Keqin was arguably the premier proponent of using dependence on language to teach his pupils."[13] However, this thesis appears somewhat biased because the primary focus of the *Blue Cliff Record* is on edification in regard to realizing enlightenment rather than erudition based on literary flair.

The career achievements of Xuedou and Yuanwu as Chan monastic abbots and lifelong teachers are vast and complicated and should not be judged by rhetoric alone, no matter how stunning an accomplishment their lyricism may seem. Both writers were remarkable literary talents as evident by their poetic and prose compositions. In addition to his odes, Xuedou contributes capping phrases on fifteen cases in the *Blue Cliff Record*, and Yuanwu occasionally cites selections from some of his other texts. To fully appreciate Xuedou's contributions, we must also take into account varying ways in which later masters commented on Xuedou's remarks or on some of the same cases covered in the *One Hundred Odes*.

Xuedou was thoroughly conversant in the complex rules of Song-regulated verse composition, especially four-line or truncated verse (*jueju*) with its complex guidelines governing every character used in the poem. He utilized this literary form with a genuine skill for conveying the opaque, cryptic style of communication appropriate to the interiority of spiritual awareness at a time when such a facility was highly prized due to extensive interactions between monks and powerful literati intrigued by engagement with Buddhist thought. The *One Hundred Odes* is considered a brilliant example of Song verse that creatively integrates Chan doctrinal explanations and evaluations with lyrical evocations rooted in a strict adherence to the rubrics for rhyme schemes, tonal patterns, and thematic progressions that governed Chinese poetry.

For example, the verse for case 37 featuring lyrical imagery recalls the naturalist Buddhist poetry of Su Shi as Xuedou refers to "The flowing stream making a lute/ Playing tunes and harmonies nobody understands" 流泉作琴. 一曲兩曲無人會.[14] The last line reads, "Evening rain pouring in the pond deepens the autumn waters" 雨過夜塘秋水深.[15] In his prose remarks, Yuanwu mentions that his predecessor and muse, Xuedou, was often regarded as having the talent in aesthetics characteristic of an imperial scholar (literally, "belonging to the Han Lin Academy" of learning that was a highlight of Tang literary culture). Xuedou was also willing to bend or break the rules of the poetic game by using fewer characters in a line or abruptly abandoning the rhyme scheme, not out of ignorance or inability, but from confidence that the spiritual message takes priority over literary style.

An exceptionally gifted writer in his own right, Yuanwu emerged as the ideal commentator who could mine in the sense of de- and reconstructing the vast reservoir of allusions, citations, and references evoked in the source dialogues, as well as by Xuedou's poetry, to carry out a thought-provoking elucidation of obscure and hidden truths embedded in the cases.[16] The works of Xuedou and Yuanwu, both independently and combined, were continually explored and plumbed for deeper meanings by many generations of subsequent interpreters in East Asia.

**Xuedou's Rhetorical Approach.** Compared with the exceptionally eventful lives of Yuanwu and Dahui, which were both characterized by a series of dramatic ups and downs in gaining approval or disapproval during the course of their quest to attain enlightenment, as well as in maintaining status and prestige through difficult social-political upheavals in later stages of their careers, Xuedou's path was rather pedestrian though not without its own set of tribulations and triumphs. His name is a reference to Mount Xuedou, the location of Zisheng temple near Mingzhou (currently Ningbo in Zhejiang province), where Xuedou lived and led an assembly for the last thirty-one years of his life and spawned seventy-eight Dharma successors. In his letters, Xuedou also referred to himself as Chongxian and Yinzhi, and he received the honorary title "Clear Enlightenment" (Mingjue) that appears in the title of his collected writings.

The available Song dynasty biographical records are based primarily on details contained in his funerary inscription.[17] When Xuedou first began learning Buddhist scriptures and treatises, he showed a keen aptitude for understanding the profound meanings in the writings of Zongmi (780–841), but his teacher recommended that he start a southward journey from Sichuan to Hubei where Xuedou met an important Chan master, Shimen Yuncong (965–1032). Xuedou stayed at Shimen's temple for three years, and following this he studied under Zhimen Guangzuo (active 964–1010). Zhimen's sayings are featured in two *Blue Cliff Record* cases, including case 21 in which Yuanwu refers to Xuedou as Zhimen's "true heir," and case 90 where the final line of Xuedou's verse suggests that Zhimen's enigmatic adage remains so perplexing that "Chan houses have been doing Dharma battle over this for many years" 曾與禪家作戰爭.[18]

According to his biographical records, one evening Xuedou asked Zhimen, "The ancient masters did not produce a single thought, so what is the problem?," and he achieved enlightenment after being hit twice by the master's fly-whisk.[19] Following this event he stayed at Zhimen's temple for five years and then traveled throughout Hunan and Anhui provinces while visiting several Chan monks. In 1019 Xuedou was invited to be the abbot of Cuifeng temple located beside Lake Dongting in Suzhou (currently Jiangsu province), where he started his teaching career.[20] Three years later he was invited by an official of Mingzhou to reside at Zisheng on Mount Xuedou.

The complexity of Xuedou's intricate approach to the use of language as a vehicle for expressing enlightenment combines variability in style with an underlying consistency in its use of an evaluative method that is critical and even sarcastic, if disingenuously so, about nearly everyone else's understanding. This approach is accompanied by a profound recognition of the limits of Xuedou's own ability. The theme of rhetorical richness vis-à-vis limitation is highlighted in the *Blue Cliff Record* through an intriguing web of metaphors centering on mythical dragons. The image of the dragon represents the attainment of a supreme accomplishment gained against all odds—in this case, the realization of Chan awakening—and the exercise of deep wisdom in a turbulent world. The Dragon Gate, supposedly located at a waterfall on a mythical mountain associated with legendary Emperor Yu, is portrayed as a barrier that is magically transformed into an entranceway to a transcendent realm. Reaching the gate as symbolic of the goal of attaining enlightenment, rather than the typical meaning the passing imperial exams, is evoked in the main story and verse of cases 49 and 60, in addition to the verse of cases 7, 95, and 99, and the prose commentary of case 100.

In case 95 Xuedou refers to this barrier in ironic fashion in order to chastise Changqing (854–932), the apparent loser in an encounter with Chan adversary Baofu (860?–928), who concludes their dialogue with the simple instruction, "Go have a cup of tea" 喫茶去. Xuedou calls out Changqing's given name, "Chan monk Leng, O Chang monk Leng,/ You've gotten a mark on your forehead while failing to cross the Dragon Gate in the third month." 稜禪客稜禪客.三月禹門遭點額.[21] This comment, which follows the main part of the verse, indicates that gatekeeper Baofu has struck Changqing for being unable to navigate the barrier.[22] Highlighting the exclusivity of entering the gate, which even an apparent adept may miss, is a typical image that is reversed through an emphasis on widespread realization in a verse included in Xuedou's recorded sayings: "The Dragon Gate is ten thousand feet high./ Those visitors who have been able to reach there,/ Must learn to advance and retreat together./ So who among them would fail the exam?" 龍門萬仞.曾留宿客.進退相將.誰遭點額.[23] That sentiment stands in contrast to the view that the Dragon Gate allows no temporary stayers who help one another reach the top, since the barrier demands being crossed only by supreme individual effort.

As a way of characterizing the ongoing challenges of his teaching mission, in cases 3, 14, 18, and 99, Xuedou conjures the related imagery of trying persistently to enter the metaphorical cave located deep within the recesses of the sea where precious jewels of many colors are hidden and guarded by a dark-hued dragon. This imagery is based largely on an early Buddhist sutra about the Naga king and an idiom attributed to Zhuangzi, in which the phrase 探驪得珠 means "to pluck a pearl from the black dragon," that is, to pick out the salient points from a tangled situation or to see through complexity by realizing the nub of the problem. Xuedou says he frequently succeeds in this mission, but the endeavor demands

that a steep price is paid on each occasion for making a grave sacrifice, as
he misleadingly grumbles to his assembly:

> For twenty long, hard years I have suffered,
> By dredging up time and again from the blue dragon's cave for
>    your sake.
> Such is the grief that can hardly be recounted.
> If you want to be a worthy patch-robed monk, you'd better not take
>    this lightly!

二十年來曾苦辛.為君幾下蒼龍窟.屈.堪述.明眼衲僧莫輕忽.[24]

In response Yuanwu asks rhetorically, "How many people are able to go
to the blue dragon's cave to make a living?" 多少人向蒼龍窟裏.作活計.[25]
Also in case 62, Yuanwu notes that looking for enlightenment is like a
black dragon gazing admiringly at a gem.

A very positive message about the potential for accessing the dragon
cave is expressed in a Xuedou verse seeming to belittle the capacity
of language to capture truth that was written in response to the query
of a devoted Chan disciple, with the opening line referring to the odd
number of characters used in typical poetic forms: "One word, seven
words, three or five words./ Myriad phenomena sought after cannot
be grasped./ As the night deepens the moon grows brighter over the
dark ocean./ And the black dragon's jewel can be found in every wave."
一字七字三五字.萬象窮來不爲拠.夜深月白下滄溟.搜得驪珠有多許.[26]
Furthermore in his verse on case 2 in the *Blue Cliff Record* Xuedou
proclaims, "When consciousness in the skull is spent how can joyful-
ness remain?/ In the withered tree the dragon's song is never ending"
髑髏識盡喜何立/枯木龍吟銷未乾.[27] The roar made by the dragon is like
the sound of wind howling in a grove of barren trees that becomes audi-
ble only during a deep level of meditation, which is not to be confused
with a quietist or blissfully passive condition.

To this Yuanwu adds the paradoxical capping phrase, "Hah!
The dead tree blooms again while Bodhidharma travels to the east"
咄.枯木再生花.達磨遊東土.[28] After Xuedou enjoins his audience to, "Judge
for yourself" 君自看, Yuanwu comments, "[All] blind! ... but this is none
of my [literally, "this mountain monk's"] business" 瞎 ... 不干山僧事.[29] As
Yuanwu notes in his prose commentary, Xuedou seems to have crafted his
saying by combining aspects of several different dialogues about how the

dragon's song has endured despite the desolate surroundings that are attributed to Tang masters Xiangyan, Shishuang, and Caoshan. The latter, when
asked what sutra was being recited by the dragon, once replied, "I don't
know the source but I mourn for all those who hear it" 不知是何章句.聞者
皆喪,[30] since the sound can be tremendously agonizing because it causes
one's ignorance to be exposed and rooted out like extracting a painful tooth.
Ironically, as suggested by Dōgen in the "Dragon's Song" (Ryūgin) fascicle
of the *Treasury of the True Dharma-Eye*, the apparent death of the listener
indicates his true rebirth as the basis of spiritual awakening.

In case 20 Yuanwu explains Xuedou's case 18 comment that, "A clear
pool allows no place for the blue dragon's coils." He notes that a fierce
dragon would not remain in still waters since it thrives only amidst tumult
in that, "If it is truly a living dragon it goes where the surge of billowing
waves floods the skies above" 若是活底龍.須向洪波浩渺白浪滔天處去.[31]
In the verse to case 95 Xuedou remarks, "A reclining dragon is not to be
seen in still water" 臥龍不鑒止水.[32] That is why Longya lost his Dharma
battle with Cuiwei and Linji over the query about why Bodhidharma came
from the west. By dwelling in a stagnant pool (literally, "dead water" 死水)
he was susceptible to being struck, literally and figuratively, by adversaries.

Moreover in case 99 Xuedou cautions, "Three thousand sacred seas
remain still and silent by night/ I don't know anyone who enters the blue
dragon's cave" 三千剎海夜沈沈.不知誰入蒼龍窟　三十棒.[33] To the lat-
ter line Yuanwu adds the following capping phrase: "Thirty blows of the
staff and not a single one can be omitted! He's finished bringing up the
topic but, alas, none among you understands! Xuedou has pierced all of
your nostrils, so do not mistake yourself for the pure, unspoiled body of
Buddha." 　三十棒.一棒也少不得.拈了也.還會麼咄.諸人鼻孔被雪竇穿了
也.莫錯認自己清淨法身.[34]

A closely related feature of Xuedou's rhetorical style is the use of a
reversal or inversion of conventional meanings as with the image of
visitors staying for a spell at the Dragon Gate. He did not invent this
technique, which is part and parcel of the deliberately puzzling and paradoxical teaching that, in a phrase cited by Yuanwu, was no doubt inspired
by how Confucius trained a disciple by showing him "one corner of the
room so that thereafter he will find for himself the other three" 舉一隅
不以三隅反.[35] Images associated with the sound of the dragon on a withered tree are but one of countless examples in Chan discourse in which
silence equals speech, death becomes life, or east leads west, last turns
into first, and mountains-rivers are not really mountains-rivers, and so

forth. In the ode to case 82, Xuedou says of the victorious master in the dialogue, "Grasping the white jade whip/ He smashes to smithereens the black dragon's pearl./ If he hadn't destroyed this/ That would have added to its flaws." 手把白玉鞭.驪珠盡擊碎.不擊碎.增瑕纇.[36]

Xuedou, who like Yuanwu is thoroughly committed to the view that upending and upsetting or subverting and tossing aside any and all unconscious presuppositions and conscious expectations is absolutely essential to the teaching mission, takes the process of inversion to another level in several examples of overturning the typical use of seemingly contradictory phrases. The character for upside-down or topsy-turvy 倒, which has a decidedly negative meaning by indicating ignorance or foolishness in the *Lotus Sutra* and other Mahayana texts, is occasionally used in early Chan works, such as Dongshan's record, in more ambiguous ways.[37]

This term often suggests in the *Blue Cliff Record* an experience or phenomenon that is detrimental, such as collapse or comeuppance, like having one's meditation seat thrown asunder 倒禪床 or falling back three thousand feet 倒退三千, but it can also represent a mode that is ironically productive, as in the ability to knock aside the mythical Mount Sumeru 踢倒須彌. In case 48, in which several monks discuss whether the spirit dwelling under the hearth (or the kitchen god) was responsible for one of the group accidentally tipping over 翻 a tea kettle, Xuedou boldly interjects, "At that time I would have kicked over 倒 the tea kettle!" 當時但踏倒茶爐.[38] At the end Xuedou declares while touching base with dragon imagery, "How many times have I crossed the waves of contrary currents?" 逆水之波經幾回, to which Yuanwu caps, "Seventy-two blows of the staff should become one hundred fifty" 七十二棒翻成一百五十.[39]

Another interesting instance of a Xuedou interjection occurs as part of case 19 in the Edo period *Entangling Vines Collection* (*Shūmon Kattōshū*), which includes a dialogue based on the conundrum devised by Xiangyan of hanging by one's teeth from the limb of a tree while trying to answer an urgent inquiry about why Bodhidharma came from the west. Unlike case 5 in *Mumon's Barrier*, which ends with this paradox left unresolved, here "Senior monk Hutou says, 'I am not asking about someone hanging from a tree. Please say something, Master, about before the tree was climbed!' The master gave a hearty laugh. Regarding this Xuedou commented, 'It's easy to speak when up a tree, but hard to speak while beneath one. This old monk is about to climb up a tree. Now bring me your question!'" 有虎頭上座云.上樹即不問.未上樹請和尚道.師呵呵大笑.雪竇云.樹上道即易.樹下道即難.老僧上樹.致將一問來.[40]

A prime instance of a double reversal (or perhaps it functions on more than two levels) is Xuedou's reference in the verse on case 87 to another Zhuangzi-inspired image of "building a carriage behind closed doors" 閉門造車, a deliberately counterintuitive adage implying that even though someone is not looking outside their gate, they can still know perfectly well how to construct a vehicle that will ride effectively on the ruts that were carved into the roads in ancient China without getting stuck or going astray. From a Daoist standpoint, which would have been well known by Song Chan teachers, this image suggests the prevalence of subjective truth over objectivity. The idiom is also used in contemporary Chinese society in an opposite way to indicate the height of folly based on impractical idealism cut off from reality. Apparently in that vein Xuedou pronounces, "By not building a carriage behind closed doors/ The pathway of its own remains wide open and clear" 閉門不造車.通途自寥廓.[41] This implies in a reversal of the original inversion that an effective vehicle would be constructed to ride the thoroughfare so that there is a harmony between subjectivity and objectivity without prioritizing one side over the other. Yet Xuedou's saying still captures the initial meaning that there is no need for an external object, in that a true adept navigates through free and easy wandering along an unobstructed path minus any need for assistance.

Next Xuedou abruptly reverses course once again by admitting, "That's totally wrong!/ Although one's nose may be stuck way up in the heavens it still needs to be pierced [with a ring]" 錯錯.鼻孔遼天亦穿卻, suggesting that he realizes he has erred in his speaking and requires being disciplined. To this Yuanwu caps in a way that is similar to case 11, "Your head has fallen as I strike while exclaiming, 'Your nostrils are pierced through!'" 頭落也.打云.穿卻了也.[42] According to Yamada Kōun's self-reflective comment in regard to the conundrum of expression this means, "No, [his teaching] is not yet the real thing, [Xuedou] tells us. This is [his] way of checking himself in his own self-assured proclamations and saying that there is still a long way for him to go. . . . When I'm in the midst of giving a [sermon] I sometimes tend to get carried away by the force of my own argument. But when I finish I often feel ashamed for talking so much. Nevertheless, it's necessary for me to talk."[43]

Another rhetorical technique employed by Xuedou is to evoke the exclamation 咄, which indicates anguish, outrage, or contempt though often in a mock or deliberately exaggerated way. The exclamation can be translated variously, depending on context, as "Bah," "Tsk," "Humbug," or "Tut," which imply deprecation, or as "Aha," or "Well," which suggest approval even if reluctantly bestowed. This word appears nearly fifty times altogether in the *Blue Cliff Record*, mainly in Yuanwu's capping phrases or prose comments, but Xuedou also uses this expression as a final exclamation that completes the odes to cases 4, 36, and 89. Originally a declarative utterance following the oral delivery of a poem that was recorded by a disciple in attendance, the term appears now in the text's typography as if part of the literary composition. Yuanwu's capping phrases about the use of the term in these three instances indicate, respectively, support or admiration, disapproval or dismissal, and a neutral or impartial stance.

In the verse to case 84, the term is used at the beginning of the poetic comments as part of a partially disingenuous dismissal of Vimalakirti, who has been silenced in the main story by the bodhisattva Manjusri, but is usually considered the everyman hero of the story. Yuanwu remarks that Xuedou cuts through ignorance like a diamond sword, but he also suggests that the expression of exasperation does not go far enough since Vimalakirti deserves "a thrashing with three thousand blows in the morning and eight thousand at night." Another intriguing way of ending an ode is when, in case 81 regarding an imaginary archery match, it is said, "Xuedou raises his voice to exclaim, 'Watch out for my arrow!'" 雪竇高聲云.看箭.一狀領過.[44]

In addition to various verse comments, including those in which he addresses the audience directly to criticize one of the dialogue partners or to scold members of his assembly, Xuedou makes his overall viewpoint known via the use of capping phrases 著語 that are contained in fifteen cases, with other examples no doubt included in the original version but lost over time.[45] In some instances in the *Blue Cliff Record*, the insertion of Xuedou's exclamation may be limited to a single ironic word or phrase, such as the defiant, "I've seen through you" (or "Exposed!") 勘破了 used in cases 4 (two times) and 84, and "Wrong!" 錯 evoked twice in case 31, as well as "Heavens! Alas!" 蒼天蒼天 in case 55. Case 61 includes the ironically menacing, "Xuedou picked up the staff and demanded, 'How many patch-robed monks are there among you who could live and die along with [Fengxue, the main character in the dialogue]?'" 雪竇拈拄杖云.還有同生同死底衲僧麼.[46]

The remark in case 61 is one of eight instances in which Xuedou's capping phrase completes the recorded gongan.[47] In most of these examples his remark serves to wrap up the case as with, "Thanks for your reply" 謝答話, following Changsha's final constructive response to the head monk in case 36; "A pair of mischievous thieves who just cover their ears while trying to steal a bell" 兩箇惡賊.只解掩耳偷鈴,[48] as a putdown to both dialogue partners in case 85; and "Too bad to make such an effort without any result" 可惜勞而無功, a zinger that appears at the end of case 91. The latter example features Xuedou's comments on four masters' reactions to the main dialogue while Yuanwu caps with, "You yourself are included. No doubt it would be even better to dish out thirty blows of the staff!" 兼身在內.也好與三十棒.灼然.[49] Case 18 also contains four Xuedou capping phrases, including as the first instance, "One hand by itself does not make any sound" 獨掌不浪鳴.[50] This saying probably has its origins with Muzhou and became the basis for Hakuin's famous, "Clapping both hands together makes a sound, but what sound does a single hand make?" 両掌相拍って声あり隻手に何の声かある. In modern non-Buddhist Chinese idiom Xuedou's phrase suggests folly rather than acting as trigger to gain enlightenment.

In a couple instances, including case 48 in which Yuanwu calls him the outstanding commentator, Xuedou uses a capping phrase to break down the fourth wall, so to speak, in that he orally addresses the assembly by entering the source dialogue to alter or disrupt its narrative, rather than to complement or complete it, to create a greater sense of urgency in regard to experiencing uncertainty during the quest for self-realization. This goes along with a pattern set by Yunmen, who would sometimes discuss a dialogue by saying, "If I had been there [the outcome would have been different]," a model also followed occasionally by Yuanwu. An example is in case 73 where Yuanwu suggests what he would have done instead on behalf of both the inquiring monk, who he says should have bowed deferentially, and Mazu as respondent, who he says should have struck with the staff unreservedly. For his part Xuedou finishes the ode to case 48 by doubting the abilities of all Chan practitioners while declaring, "Among the gods above and humans below I alone understand the case" 天上人間唯我知, while Yuanwu dares to say, "Then I will snatch away your staff!" 奪卻拄杖子.[51]

Another example is case 42, in which Xuedou comments on a case in which Layman Pang feels that his saying about snow falling has been misunderstood by a monk whom he ends up slapping twice while also hurling insults at him. According to Xuedou's remark directed to the monk, "Why didn't you just go ahead and hit Pang with a snowball when you first asked your question?" 初問處但握雪團便打.[52] However Yuanwu says this is a matter of too little expression provided too late given the circumstances. He cites Librarian Qing's suggestion that contrary to Xuedou's comment the monk should have not even waited to roll up and toss an object; instead he would have been better off strik-ing Pang immediately without hesitation or reservation. Then the verse takes the rather unusual step of starting self-referentially, rather than more typically by citing valuable content from the source dialogue, with Xuedou proclaiming, "The snowball strikes! The snowball strikes!" 雪團打雪團打.[53] In the ode celebrating his own reaction, Xuedou goes on to charge that gods and men, including Pang and even Bodhidharma, are unable to discern the meaning, even as Yuanwu rebuts this by say-ing that his predecessor is no better off since in the end he stays buried in the same pit as all the others.

**Yuanwu's Rhetorical Approach.** Yuanwu was one of or perhaps the most significant leader during the extraordinary flourishing of Song Chan's thriving networks of monastic communities in addition to its expansive engagement with imperial authorities and growing groups of lay disciples, including well-educated and highly cultured scholar-officials.[54] Yuanwu's role was perhaps only surpassed by that of Dahui, who is sometimes con-sidered second in importance in Chan history to the semimythical Sixth Patriarch Huineng (638–713). Taking this sense of intralineal rivalry a step further, according to some assessments, Yuanwu was not just eclipsed, but it can be said for many the master is primarily known through his associa-tion with the most prominent of disciples/critics.[55]

The Chan school suffered through the ups and downs of the era's political turmoil that created fierce competition with various factions of Buddhism and Neo-Confucianism, which offered a harsh critique of what appeared to outsiders to be an endless array of seemingly nonsensi-cal Chan discourse. Both Yuanwu and Dahui are notable in their respec-tive religious quests for surmounting grave challenges and giving voice to confessional expressions of regret and remorse for shortcomings both personal and social during turbulent times. They eventually prevailed and basked in the glow of emotional recovery in addition to institutional rec-ognition, reward, and redemption. By the end of their careers, each was highly regarded by the imperium for displaying a firm commitment to religious discipline in developing innovative literary and/or pedagogical techniques.

Overall, Yuanwu led a very successful monastic career as a tenth-generation Linji school master and abbot, who crossed various cultural and sectarian and social and geographical boundaries in pursuit of Chan spirituality, and he was duly recognized with patronage and titles received from the Northern Song court. Born in Sichuan in 1063 to a family of

Confucians, as a young man he trained to take civil examinations but did not perform so well. He then visited Miaoji temple near his home, and this gave him the feeling that he must have been a Buddhist monk in a previous lifetime. It is said that at an early age Yuanwu's literary acumen developed in connection to musical arts in that he learned to "beat drums, clang cymbals, clap sticks, blow the flute, and sing drama" 敲鼓打鈸擊節吹笛唱戲 with such proficiency that the adults in his village let him become a local member of the prestigious Eight Sounds Association 八音社.[56]

After wide-ranging itinerant travels and struggles to attain awakening, while already in his forties, Yuanwu eventually finished studying and gained a powerful and enduring enlightenment experienced at Dongchan temple in Hubei province under the tutelage of the renowned Wuzu, who had undergone his own prolonged struggles before attaining a realization. This occurred only after Yuanwu was at first dismissed by the master or, in another version, was dissatisfied with Wuzu's teaching and departed from his assembly. He then underwent a sustained period of feverish illness 熱病 (perhaps typhoid fever) because of intense anxiety and disturbance due to an excessive focus on meditation while trying to maintain an itinerant lifestyle. Wuzu, who had advised Yuanwu to return when he was exhausted from struggling with the Chan malady, foresaw this condition. The trauma broke Yuanwu's sense of pride and self-confidence, qualities driving him to succeed but also serving an ego that was an impediment to reaching his spiritual goal. This set the stage for productive uncertainty encompassing profound doubt that led to the ultimate attainment beyond the distinction between selfhood and selflessness.[57]

According to Yuanwu's enlightenment verse recorded in volume 19 of the *Five Lamps Merged Together* (*Wudeng Huiyuan*), which was resoundingly approved by Wuzu as a "great achievement" 大事, "Behind the fragrant curtain colorfully embroidered with golden ducks,/ In the midst of songs [accompanied] with the flute he got drunk and left./ Such a romantic experience of youth,/ Only the lady herself can appreciate." 金鴨香銷錦繡幃.笙歌叢裏醉扶歸.少年一段風流事.祇許佳人獨自知.[58] There is a double-layered story behind this expression. First it is said that a transport clerk, who retired from office and was on his way back to his native Sichuan, came to ask Wuzu to instruct him in the way of Chan and was given a verse containing the two lines, "Repeatedly calling to Xiaoyu actually has nothing to do with her,/ It is only to let 'Lover Tan' (Tanlang) recognize my voice." That poem, in turn, involves a woman who was shy to leave her bedchamber when her lover came and, instead, called out the name of her maid Xiaoyu as a means to let him be aware that she was available. The clerk told Wuzu that he grasped these two lines.

Sometime later Yuanwu, who happened to stand beside them at that time, asked the master for his opinion of the clerk's understanding, and Wuzu said, "He only recognizes the voice." Yuanwu responded, "'It is only to let Lover Tan recognize my voice'—since the clerk has recognized the voice, then what is the problem?" Wuzu asked, "What are the meanings of 'The first patriarch coming from the west' and 'Cypress standing tree in the courtyard'? Hah!" Upon hearing this Yuanwu was suddenly awakened. While walking out he saw a rooster flying to the railing and heard the flapping of wings, as it was about to fly. He said to himself, "Isn't this the voice?" Yuanwu then entered Wuzu's chamber to report to the master through verse his enlightenment experience.[59]

According to case 77 of the *Entangling Vines Collection*:

One evening, as Wuzu Fayan's three disciples Fojian Huiqin, Foyan Qingyuan, and Foguo Keqin were attending to Wuzu at an inn, they and the master talked so late that, when it came time to leave, the lamps were already out. In the darkness Wuzu said, "Each of you please give me a turning-word." Fojian said, "A radiant phoenix dances in the sky." Foyan said, "An iron snake lies across the ancient road." Foguo said, "Watch where you step!" Wuzu commented, "Only Foguo will destroy my teachings!"

五祖演,三佛侍於一亭上夜話.及歸燈已滅.演於暗中曰,各人一轉語.佛鑑曰,彩鳳舞丹霄.佛眼曰,鐵蛇橫古路.佛果曰,看腳下.演曰,滅吾宗者乃克勤爾.[60]

Of his three followers, including Fojian, or Buddha Mirror, who refers to an auspicious omen of renewal, and Foyan, or Buddha Eye, who evokes a seeker's feeling of desperation, it was Foguo, or Buddha Fruit (Yuanwu), who was ranked highest by Wuzu's ironic expression of praise for evoking "a Chan saying frequently written on boards and placed in the entrance halls of Zen temples as a reminder to remain always aware."[61]

After his breakthrough Yuanwu was soon invited to preach at Zhaojue temple in his hometown of Chengdu, the capital of Sichuan, where he began his lectures on the *One Hundred Odes*. This was convenient because Yuanwu also needed to care for his ailing mother as an expression of filial piety, and he would return to this temple for the last five years of his life in 1130. Zhang Shangying, then a chief councilor and Buddhist advocate who repeatedly fell in and out of the imperial court's favor over the course of several decades and had recently been demoted to a regional post in Hunan province,[62] met Yuanwu in Sichuan in the early 1110s. He soon after invited Yuanwu to help lead the temple on Mount Jiashan, although it is not clear that he served as the abbot 方丈 (*fengchang*). This was where Yuanwu's more polished lectures on the *One Hundred Odes* eventually came to form the *Blue Cliff Record*. Yuanwu received the purple robe from Emperor Huizong, a strong patron of cultural arts who traveled to Hunan in part to see the master (although Huizong was already politically weak and ineffective, a condition that a decade later helped precipitate the demise of the Northern Song). In 1114 Yuanwu was symbolically named Foguo Chanshi, or Fruition of Buddha Chan Teacher.

In 1125, the year the *Blue Cliff Record* was compiled and Dahui first came to study with him, imperial authorities appointed Yuanwu abbot of a major monastery, Tianning Wanshou, in the capital of Pianliang (Kaifeng), although with the Jin invasion the next year this assignment did not last long. In 1128 Yuanwu was granted the moniker by which he is best known, Yuanwu Chanshi, or Perfectly Enlightened Chan Teacher, and, joined by Dahui as his main assistant, he served as abbot of Taiping Xingguo temple on Mount Jiang (in present-day Nanjing). Yuanwu also served for a time at Zhenru cloister on Mount Yunju in Jiangxi province after being banished to the south along with Dahui following the fall of the Northern Song before returning to Chengdu in 1130. Yet another imperial title, Zhenjue Chanshi, or Truly Awakened Chan Teacher, was bestowed posthumously.

Another example of his creativity is a verse contained in the *Record* that was composed while Yuanwu resided at Jiangshan temple in Kaifeng. It concerns the core dialogue of case 53 in the *Blue Cliff Record*. Mazu twists his disciple Baizhang's ear while explaining that it is inappropriate to refer to ducks "flying by," since such an expression that is seemingly true to ordinary perception denies the immediacy of momentary experience. According to Yuanwu's poetic expression linking self-realization to natural imagery:

Wild ducks fly by the creek,
Myriad peaks display their wintry hues.

Looking around [Baizhang] does not know where they return,
Yet he cannot help but depend on being struck [by Mazu].
Smashing away the ball of doubt as complicated delusions melt away,
And are carried by the wind directly to the clear sky.
Clouds, mountains, oceans, and moon are unwavering forms,
As a single saying reflecting Chan prevails in all the lands.

野鴨過前溪.千峰凜寒色.相顧不知歸.未免資傍擊.扭破疑團葛怛消
.捎風直下透青霄.雲山海月渾閑事.一語歸宗萬國朝.[63]

In the eighth month of 1135, during the reign of Southern Song Emperor
Gaozong (r. 1127–1162) Yuanwu fell ill and ordered his disciple Daoyuan
(d.u.) to take charge of the monastery. On the fifth day of the month at
the request of his attendants, he composed a verse on his deathbed that is
ironically self-deprecating, which is typical of the genre:[64] My best efforts
[on behalf of teaching the Dharma] are devoid of merit./ There is no need
for me even to leave this verse,/ Other than to show that I accept my fate./
Adieu! Take good care! 已徹無功.不必留頌.聊示應緣.珍重珍重.[65]

In addition to producing seventy-five monastic disciples in the
Linji-Yangqi lineage, it is evident from his voluminous letters 書 used
as a teaching method emulated by Dahui that Yuanwu addressed both
monks and lay followers, who received nearly one quarter of the 145
correspondences contained in the *Essentials of Mind*.[66] Yuanwu was particularly well acquainted with and served as an inspiration for many
of the era's leading scholar-officials, including the grandson of Su Shi
among other prominent figures, several of whom wrote prefaces for
his *Record* that was published before his death in 1134. In one of these
epistles Yuanwu relates a tonsure ceremony then taking place to a classic instance involving Danxia Tianran (739–824). An irreverent seeker
who relinquished a life of success in the secular world before pursuing
the way, Danxia had his head shaved by Shitou after putting down his
hoe one day despite the master's instructions to keep weeding. Later he
gained the precepts from Shitou's rival Mazu and eventually became
known for irreverently using a wooden Buddha statue as firewood on a
cold winter day. Yuanwu's letter ends with this poem: "Danxia spaded
the weeds and burned wooden Buddhas,/ He'd given up a chance to
become an imperial official after meeting [a monk] who split hair by
blowing on it.[67]/ Startling the crowd while overcoming foes he proved
himself a true teacher,/ Who could cast just one fishing rod but capture

a dozen large sea turtles." 丹霞鏟草.燒木佛.宮使捨緣吹布毛.驚群敵勝
真師子.一釣須連十二鼇.[68]

In sum it is interesting to note that, unlike Xuedou, who stayed for his
final thirty-one years in Zhejiang province before it housed the capital, and
Dahui, who ended his career on Mount Jing near Hangzhou, Yuanwu did
not reside in the increasingly prestigious Jiangnan area although during
the course of illness between periods of studying with Wuzu he probably
spent at least a little time wandering there accompanied by Fojian. While
very much affected by the sociopolitical turmoil of the era, Yuanwu completed his career as a Chan master who constructively allied the Emperor
and literati with the local elite in various locations, especially in the capital
of Kaifeng and in Hunan province, along with enabling his fellow citizens
of Sichuan, where he spent the first and the final stages of his life, to gain
a successful intertwining of religious and literary pursuits. Having spread
the Linji-Yangqi stream well beyond its original domain in the southwest
of China to the northern, southeastern, and central regions, another testament to his legacy is that all Rinzai sect lineages in Japan are ultimately
descended from Yuanwu through the travels to and from China during
the late thirteenth-century émigré monk period.[69] This crucial phase of
cultural interaction no doubt contributed to the recovery of the *Blue Cliff
Record* in the early 1300s.

However there is little reason to label Yuanwu a strict representative of
*wenzi Chan* if that term is considered—misleadingly, perhaps—to imply
an attitude of favoring language over and above, rather than in service to,
the spiritual quest. Yuanwu's impartiality toward literature when seen as
an end rather than as a means is indicated in his capping phrases that use
lyrical images for a typical Song Chan trope referring to a Madhyamika
Buddhist fourfold categorization of the relation between words (or expression) and meaning (or intention):

Words get there but meaning does not get there:
In the ancient valley a cold spring gushes while blue pines are laced
   with frosty dew.
Meaning gets there but words do not get there:
Unrooted grass grows on a stone while still clouds hide the
   mountains.
Meaning and words both get there:
White clouds gather in the sky at dawn and water flows under the
   bright moon.

Meaning and words both do not get there:
The blue sky is unspotted by clouds and in green waters the wind
  is spurring waves.

句到意不到.古澗寒泉湧.青松帶露寒./意到句不到.石長
無根草.山藏不動雲./意句俱到.天共白雲曉.水和明月流./
意句俱不到.青天無片雲.綠水風波起.[70]

The first two lines create a sharp contrast between frostiness and growth,
while the third line indicates a realm free of obstruction enhanced by the
final line's image of unrestricted movement.

Yuanwu presents a devastating critique of misinterpretations of Chan
writing and teaching by mentioning, as in a kind of parody of inappropriate gongan discourse, that "when [Tang master] Baoshou held a service
and Sansheng pushed forward some monk the master slapped him and
Sansheng's retort was, 'What does this teach people; isn't it your way of
deceiving the monk?'" 只如寶壽開堂.三聖推出一僧.壽便打.聖云你與麼
為人.非但瞎卻這僧.[71] It is unclear whether in this anecdote, which concludes with Baoshou throwing down his staff and returning to the abbot's
quarters, if Yuanwu is aiming his criticism at a particular commentator.
But it is obvious he attacks anyone's facile understanding that merely
skims the surface and thinks it is profound or, to evoke a variation on a
Chinese saying mentioned in the prose remarks on case 6 in *Wumen's
Barrier*, one who "holds up the head of a sheep to sell the meat of a dog"
縣羊頭賣狗肉.[72]

Yuanwu is consistent with the teaching he gained from Wuzu, which
is found in nearly all examples of Song Chan factions whether embracing or rejecting the role of literary pursuit as an end in itself, since
enlightenment requires the full overcoming of a reliance on discourse
by allowing for no element of conceptual discrimination to enter one's
thinking. Yet he, like nearly all Chan teachers, uses words and letters
as a skillful means. According to the introductory remarks on case 23
of the *Blue Cliff Record*, Yuanwu indicates that his commentaries are
designed to polish the tool of language when it is expressed through
verse comments on cases in order to serve as a device testing the understanding of trainees:

Jade is tested with fire, gold is tested with a stone, a sword is tested
with a hair, and water is tested with a pole. In the school of patch-
robed monks through a single word or a single phrase, a single

encounter or a single state, a single exit or a single entry, a single opening or a single closing, you are able to judge whether someone is deep or shallow, whether he is facing forward or behind. Tell me, what will you use to test him?

玉將火試.金將石試.劍將毛試.水將杖試.至於衲僧門下.一言一句. 一機一境.一出一入.一挨一拶.要見深淺.要見向背.且道將什麼.[73]

## *Prose Preference Thesis*

What is Yuanwu's view of Xuedou's verse comments and their contribution to the Chan discursive process? There is certainly consistency and compatibility in that Yuanwu uses a variety of rhetorical techniques as gestures to end sermons that he learned in large part from Xuedou, such as shouting, picking up the fly-whisk, pounding the meditation seat, or raising the staff while threatening to strike. From a broader view, both figures employ the multiperspectival *pingchang* style of appraisal to redirect the audience toward questioning and probing for themselves from every possible angle each dialogue along with multileveled case comments. Although his role in the *Blue Cliff Record* is not that of a poet, should Yuanwu's remarks on odes by Xuedou, who also composed a considerable amount of prose commentary on gongan, be seen as supporting and enhancing or as denigrating and diminishing the religious significance of poetry?[74] The answer to this is purposefully left unclear and ambiguous in Yuanwu's ironic commentaries because, as part of the evaluative process, he varies from offering high praise to demeaning criticism in remarks on his precursor.

According to the suggestion of Ding-hwa Hsieh, which exemplifies what I refer to as the prose preference thesis, Yuanwu's prose comments on Xuedou's odes are partially a tribute but also in large measure reparative in that the former "tried hard to elevate the value and function of Hsueh Tou's literary composition in the context of Ch'an kung-an instruction and praxis."[75] Hsieh goes further in arguing that Yuanwu could not help but show the flaws of his predecessor. She claims that his aim was to "exculpate Hsueh Tou from the charge of making Ch'an merely a literary activity... which appeared bookish and static," rather than "personal and intuitive," in order to restore the "supremacy of Ch'an Buddhism ... in its unique pedagogical methods."[76]

**Yuanwu Praising and/or Critiquing of Xuedou.** Does Yuanwu add prose commentary to Xuedou out of a belief that there is deficiency embedded in the verses because poetry remains stuck in the realm of lettered

Chan? Yuanwu's approach is captured in Puzhao's preface to the *Blue Cliff Record* that was mentioned in chapter 1:

> Chan Master Xuedou had the true eye that transcends any particular school and goes beyond ordinary standpoints as he upheld the true Dharma by refraining from falling back on conventional views. He took up the hammer and tongs to smelt and forge buddhas and ancestors, and composed verses well above and beyond the nostrils of patch-robed monks. . . . If you do not meet a great master, how can you thoroughly comprehend the profound meaning of the teaching? When the worthy Foguo (Yuanwu) was dwelling at Blue Cliff cloister, students were perplexed and asked him for a penetrating analysis. Taking pity on them this worthy extended his compassion by plunging to the deepest source so as to explicate the essential principles. Directly pointing at the truth he never resorted to one-sided views.

> 其惟雪竇禪師.具超宗越格正眼.提掇正令.不露風規.秉烹佛鍛祖鉗鎚.頌出衲僧向上巴鼻....不逢大匠.焉悉玄微.粵有佛果老人.住碧巖日.學者迷而請益.老人愍以垂慈.剔抉淵源.剖析底理.當陽直指.豈立見知.[7]

This passage suggests that Yuanwu's followers—including at the time Dahui, who it is said had engaged with the *One Hundred Odes* in his early days of silent study some years before training under Yuanwu—greatly appreciated but were invariably confused by Xuedou's verse when it was read without commentary. They were eager for a skillful teacher to break down the structure and content of the poems, and explain each line critically yet open-endedly by allowing for multiple interpretations.

The prose preference thesis is further suggested by Yi-hsun Huang who, in a groundbreaking article highlighting Xuedou's extensive collection of prose commentaries on gongan in addition to verse, argues that there is a basic difference between the use of the two writing styles and that prose is somehow preferable to poetry because it offers clarity and gets to the point rather than being vague and elusive. A short albeit crucial passage, which I argue has been somewhat misleadingly translated and interpreted in some recent renderings including Huang's, appears in the prose commentary to Xuedou's verse on the first case of the *Blue Cliff Record*. Here the first patriarch makes a brazenly iconoclastic quip to the Emperor before departing to cross the Yangzi River and never return to the capital despite the ruler's pleas.

Yuanwu stakes out his view of the role of language in gongan discourse by valorizing the poem, especially its opening segment:

> Xuedou's verse on this gongan is like skillfully performing a sword dance, lithe and limber in midair, naturally never being endangered by the sharp point of the blade. . . . Those who possess the true eye see that by picking up this or considering that, and praising here or bashing there, [Xuedou] needs just four lines of poetry to settle the whole gongan. Generally verse comments (*songgu* 頌古) just take a meandering path to explicate Chan, whereas prose comments (*niangu* 拈古) try to wrap up a gongan by remarking on the case's overall meaning, and that is all. But here Xuedou pinches hard and does not let go.

> 且據雪竇頌此公案.一似善舞太阿劍相似.向虛空中盤礴.自然不犯 鋒鋩.若是具眼者看他一拈一掇一褒一貶只用四句揩定一則公案. 大凡頌古只是繞路說禪,拈古大綱據欵結案而已.雪竇與他一拶.劈 頭.[78]

The key factor in this passage, according to my reading, is that through these and related remarks, Yuanwu seeks to carve out a middle position between naïve affirmation and stubborn rejection of literary Chan. Yuanwu at once dismisses both poetic and prose commentary when, as examples of a strictly lettered approach, these forms of expression are unfortunately not carried out in an effective manner. Settling or wrapping up a case is a desirable goal, but even this effort can easily decline to the level of deficiency. Yet Yuanwu praises Xuedou's verse as exceptional although not without a certain amount of ambiguity underlying this assessment.

In contrast to my reading, some other renderings stress that the passage is intended to reflect a basic difference in quality between verse and prose styles of commentary, or instead see both types of interpretation as either invariably positive or hopelessly unproductive. This is one of several important passages regarding Yuanwu's life and thought—another involving Dahui's enlightenment experience under Yuanwu is discussed in chapter 4—where a seemingly minor discrepancy in translation or slight variation in interpretation of the thorny original expression can convey very different meanings, thus leading to a gap in understandings of the significance of his writings that demand a careful clarification of the syntax.

According to the translation of the last sentence only by Huang, who points out that "Xuedou's style of making remarks is summarized in Yuanwu Keqin's famous work, the *Emerald Cliff Record*": "Generally speaking, verses on old cases just expound Chan in a roundabout way; the general purpose of making remarks on old cases is to bring resolution to those old cases." 大凡頌古只是繞路說禪.拈古大綱據欵結案.[79] In featuring a partial section of the passage while neglecting the last part of the sentence and the beginning of the next one, Huang uses the term "making remarks" in a specific way to refer explicitly to prose in contrast to verse commentary, but this is done without clearly explaining or justifying this distinction in her use of English terminology. She further argues, "In other words, when Chan masters compose verses on old cases, they simply illustrate the meaning of Chan contained in the raised old cases with their own words, in a non-linear fashion with verse. When masters remark [in prose] on old cases, they bring to resolution that which is unsettled in the other monks' questions, responses or even performances in the raised old cases."[80]

A problematic aspect of Huang's version is that she leaves out the final phrase indicating "and that is all" 而已. The expression is crucial because it undermines the notion of the efficacy of both styles of interpretation for those interpreters who lack Xuedou's level of acumen, so that the passage overall does not favor prose over poetry. Huang also does not include the opening phrase of the next sentence, which reinforces that Xuedou's verse is superior to conventional poems that do not convey self-realization in that their meandering or roundabout 繞路 fashion fails to capture the real point of the case. In trying to accentuate the function of prose remarks at the expense of verse comments, she shortens and tends to skew the source passage accordingly.

Another version of Yuanwu's statement that is similarly problematic is in the complete translation of the *Blue Cliff Record* by Thomas Cleary and J. C. Cleary that reads: "Hsueh Tou offers, takes back, praises, and deprecates, using only four lines to settle the entire public case. Generally, eulogies of the Ancients express Ch'an in a roundabout way, picking out the main principles of the old story, settling the case on the basis of the facts, and that is all. Hsueh Tou gives a thrust."[81] While this version does include parts of the passage that are not referenced by Huang, including the end of the main sentence and the beginning of the next one, the problem with the rendering by Cleary and Cleary is that it has the inverse lack of clarity in failing to highlight the distinction between poetic and prose comments by blurring them into the misleading category of "eulogies" (which should only be used to indicate verse). Therefore it is not clear why, despite the praise, Yuanwu feels that there is an advantage in Xuedou's approach to articulating literary Chan.

The real aim of Yuanwu's passage—once again, 若是具眼者看他一拈一掇一褒一貶只用四句揩定一則公案.大凡頌古只是繞路說禪.拈古大綱據欵結案而已.雪竇與他一拶 ...—is not to draw a contrast between poetry and prose, as Huang suggests, or to conflate the two styles, as Cleary and Cleary indicate. Instead, it emphasizes the difference between conventional literature consisting of poetry and/or prose when either style seems forced and thereby false, and Xuedou's insightful verse that captures the meaning in an appropriate way. Yet poetry too could and should be further elucidated by Yuanwu's prose exposition, which supplements and complements rather than conflicts with or contradicts the verse even when it is being critical.

For Yuanwu the genius of the *One Hundred Odes* is that it is neither a roundabout way of talking endlessly without ever getting close to evoking the essence nor a means of reducing gongan to a repeated and memorized formulaic discussion of a doctrinal treatise, as is often found in Fenyang's poetry on cases. Rather it showcases how Xuedou's verse consistently probes the matter and compellingly presses the point to the audience/reader, even though this remains subject to Yuanwu's playful critique. Both Xuedou and Yuanwu composed collections of brief *niangu*-style comments on cases, and these in addition to Yuanwu's lengthier *pingchang*-style remarks are equally evocative yet uncertain in the productive sense of providing manifold standpoints that amplify and enhance his predecessor's poetic comments.

Moreover, in contrast to the prose preference thesis, a careful examination of the *Blue Cliff Record* indicates that for the most part Yuanwu is overwhelmingly positive in regard to the contributions of Xuedou to Chan discourse. In prose comments on well over sixty of the cases, Yuanwu makes a point at least one time in each set of comments to exalt the literary qualities of Xuedou's verses by indicating that Yuanwu is offering aids to understanding through explaining the odes without sacrificing indirection, so that readers of the text are relentlessly challenged and provoked to develop an appropriate insight on their own. However, while Xuedou's verbal sword is said to shine remarkably bright, it is also argued by Yuanwu that for better or worse Xuedou often shows the compassion of a doting granny since a fear of misunderstanding by the audience causes him to descend to their level on occasion to try to clear up deluded apprehensions.

In commentary on the ode to case 4, for example, Yuanwu lavishly acclaims Xuedou as the most authoritative versifier of cases who has the ability to wrap up a gongan with just the first one or two lines of his ode. In this instance Yuanwu notes that Xuedou's verse effectively reflects on three capping phrases—"I've seen through!" or "Exposed!" 勘破了也 used two times, and "Adds frost to snow" 雪上加霜 at the end—that he had interjected into the main dialogue during the course of his sermon:

> When Xuedou composed verses on one hundred gongan, with each case he burned incense and offered it up and that is why his poems have circulated widely throughout the land. He mastered literary composition so that only after he had penetrated a particular gongan and had become fully conversant with its meaning would he set his brush to paper. Why? It is easy to distinguish dragons from snakes but it is hard to fool a patch-robed monk. As Xuedou carefully studied and fully penetrated this case he included three capping comments at unfathomable junctures in the dialogue and then used each of these as the basis of his verse.

雪竇頌一百則公案.一則則焚香拈出.所以大行於世.他更會文章透得公案.盤礡得熟.方可下筆.何故.如此.龍蛇易辨.衲子難瞞.雪竇參透這公案.於節角聱訛處.著三句語.撮來頌出.[82]

In regard to the ode to case 24 that rather uncharacteristically does not evoke directly the words of the main dialogue involving the interaction of the itinerant female Iron Grindstone Liu and her apparent adversary, the established master Guishan, Yuanwu admires the way Xuedou demonstrates evenhandedly the strength of both figures, which is not necessarily the typical approach to this case. Xuedou eulogizes Liu's irreverent actions in the first and third lines and also Guishan's comebacks in the second and fourth lines: "Entering the fortress riding an iron horse,/ The imperial decree declares the six kingdoms are all clear./ Still holding the golden whip she questions a returning traveler;/ In the depths

of the night, which one of them walks the stately highway?" 曾騎鐵馬入
重城.敕下傳聞六國清.猶握金鞭問歸客.夜深誰共御街行.[83] According to
Yuanwu's remark, "Xuedou's verses are universally considered the best of
their kind. Of the one hundred odes, this verse is the most remarkable. It
is the one in the entire collection that to the greatest extent is marvelously
expressed and clearly set forth. . . . Xuedou has the ability to admire the
quick movement [of Liu and Guishan] when they are hurrying along and
also to praise their laid-back tarrying when they are easygoing." 雪竇頌
.諸方以為極則.一百頌中.這一頌最具理路.就中極妙.貼體分明頌出....
雪竇有這般才調.急切處向急切處頌.緩緩處向緩緩處頌.[84]

Yet Yuanwu sometimes critiques Xuedou for saying too much or
not enough, or for being overly indulgent or missing the mark, even
if the scathing reproach is usually delivered in tongue-in-cheek fashion. By emphasizing the inevitability of brambles lying underfoot in
case 1, Yuanwu recognizes, and probably feels Xuedou knows this, that
poetry can at any time become a double-edged sword. Yuanwu suggests
that his predecessor is being overly kind or indulgent of the audience's
weaknesses. When Xuedou adds the exclamation "Speak! Speak!" 道道
at the end of the verse to case 53, Yuanwu caps with, "What is there to
say? Don't expect me to speak in order to teach you" 什麼道.不可也教
山僧道. [85] In his prose comment he remarks, "Xuedou versifies most
impressively, but no matter what he says he still can't leap out either"
雪竇雖然頌得甚妙.爭奈也跳不出.[86]

How we are to understand the overlapping yet distinct interests and
techniques of Xuedou and Yuanwu while recognizing that a key feature
of the *Blue Cliff Record* is the way it reflects the intricate relationship,
sometimes smooth or harmonious and at other times abrasive or chaf-
ing, between the two contributing authors, one of whom is absent and
unable to respond to the different sorts of evaluations his words are receiving? It seems that Xuedou himself varies from using a style of indulging
his readers to one of chastening them, and that Yuanwu adopts the same
twofold attitude toward the *One Hundred Odes* as a way of seeking a balanced approach toward polishing its manner of expression and thereby
establishing a nonauthoritative mode of evaluation enabling his followers
to continue to ponder the meaning of the verses.

In other instances of skepticism pointing to the need for self-realization,
Yuanwu takes Xuedou to task for using his poetry merely "to give footnotes" to the dialogue rather than contributing his own unique standpoint. In case 45 Yuanwu asks whether in regard to the profound sayings

of Zhaozhou, who is the main figure in this dialogue, Xuedou is "a truly creative harmonizer or mere annotator" 下載清風付與誰.[87] On the other hand, in cases 62 and 83 Yuanwu praises Xuedou's compassionate stance in adding notes as part of wielding a sharp-edged sword symbolizing the compelling quality of his rhetoric.

Building on that approach in case 55, Yuanwu suggests that annotation is a positive feature in that, "Xuedou understands how to add footnotes exceptionally well. He is a descendant of Yunmen, with the hammer and tongs to have three sayings present in every single phrase. What is difficult to explain he expresses thoroughly, and what seems impossible to open he is able to break through and open up." 雪竇偏會下注腳.他是雲門下兒孫.凡一句中.具三句底鉗鎚.向難道處道破.向撥不開處撥開.去他緊要處頌出.[88] Here Yuanwu refers to the capacity of Xuedou to capture the main rhetorical technique gained from Yunmen, whom the latter praises as his ideal model according to Yuanwu's remarks on cases 6 and 62. This involves the ability to imply three sayings within just a single phrase. These sayings, as mentioned in case 14 and elsewhere, are similar to Linji's three essentials and serve the function of cutting off the myriad streams of ignorance by undermining conceptual fixations, encompassing heaven and earth with truth through revealing multiple perspectives at once, and following the ephemeral waves by adjusting teachings to the level of the learner; in some explanations the order of the second and third statements is flipped. For Linji, as well as Yunmen, Xuedou, and Yuanwu, once the meaning is contained the words are forgotten.

Yuanwu's overall attitude is perhaps summed up best in case 2, where the ode consists of two back-to-back four-line segments (jueju) followed by a final two-line comment. In commenting on this intricacy Yuanwu provides a mixed assessment of Xuedou:

Although the first four-line verse abruptly cuts off Xuedou has extra ability so he opens up and reveals what is concealed [by adding another verse], but this is like putting a head above a head. . . . At the beginning of the verse Xuedou's approach appears too solitary and steep yet by the end he is overly indulgent. If you can bore right through to see and penetrate the point naturally it will be have the excellent flavor of ghee. But if you do not leave behind one-sided interpretations then you will be lost in confusion and definitely will not be able to understand [Xuedou']s explication of the teaching.

則此四句頌頓絕了也.雪竇有餘才.所以分開結裹算來也.只是頭上
安頭道....雪竇頭上太孤峻生.末後也漏逗不少.若參得透見得徹.
自然如醍醐上味相似.若是情解未忘.便見七花八裂.決定不能會如
此說話.[89]

Case 44 is one of numerous examples of taking the critique even further in that Yuanwu says Xuedou deserves a thrashing for composing one
of his less compelling poetic lines that equivocates the matter at hand by
affirming redundancy in a facile way.[90] At the end of the verse on a dialogue in which Heshan, a disciple of Xuefeng, responds to four questions
posed by a monk with the same answer each time, "Knowing how to beat
the drum" 解打鼓, Xuedou adds this comment, "Let me tell you something: There's no need to be confused, sweet is sweet and bitter is bitter"
報君知.莫莽鹵.甜者甜兮苦者苦. Yuanwu blasts him by remarking, "Even
Xuedou has not seen it in a dream; don't you realize he is just adding frost
to snow? He is being rather crude. We can thank him for his answer but
after all he mistakenly adds a footnote that deserves thirty blows. Has he
ever been flogged? I strike! As with previous instances that is what it takes
to drive away darkness." 雪竇也未夢見.在雪上加霜.爾還知麼.也有些子.
儱儱侗侗.謝答話.錯下注腳.好與三十棒.喫棒得也未.便打.依舊黑漫漫.[91]
The implication is that the reader, just like Xuedou, can avoid punishment
only by being challenged to show spontaneously his or her own genuine
insight.

Some other instances of Yuanwu's harsh critique of Xuedou include
the following examples. In case 21 Xuedou ends the verse by saying
that "one foxy doubt leads to yet another foxy doubt" 一狐疑了一狐疑,
to which Yuanwu caps, "It's you who doubt since you cannot avoid the
impact of a sensation of doubt. I strike while saying, 'Do you understand?'" 自是爾疑.不免疑情未息.打云.會麼.[92] However it remains unclear
whether this admonition is intended for Xuedou or the general audience.
Also when Xuedou ends the verse to case 73 with, "In all the world only I
know" 天上人間唯我知, Yuanwu remarks, "What 'I' do you refer to? I'll
snatch away your staff.... What then will you use to know?" 用我作什
麼.奪卻拄杖子.... 將什麼知.[93] In addition in case 20 Yuanwu suggests
that Xuedou (and the assembly) needs "thirty more years of practice"
更參三十年.[94] When Xuedou ends the ode to the case by "shouting at the
top of his lungs, 'Look right where you are!'" 高聲喝云.看腳下, Yuanwu
adds the dismissive cap, "He draws the bow after the thief has fled. One
time, two times—the repetition of words is not worth paying attention

to." 賊過後張弓.第二頭第三頭.重言不當吃.⁹⁵ In prose remarks Yuanwu says that Xuedou fails to be subtle while an editor's interjection in the text notes, "Yuanwu struck!"

Case 96 offers an interesting, two-sided evaluation of Xuedou by Yuanwu. The case itself is anomalous because it simply mentions "three turning words" 三轉語 used by Zhaozhou although these phrases— "A mud Buddha does not pass through water," "A gold Buddha does not pass through a furnace," and "A wood Buddha does not pass through fire," as well as the prototypical conclusion, "The real Buddha sits within" 真佛屋裏坐—are deliberately left out as unnecessary by Xuedou, who then offers three separate verses. Yuanwu quickly sums up the matter, "If a mud Buddha passes through water it will dissolve; if a gold Buddha passes through a furnace it will melt; if a wood Buddha passes through fire it will burn." 泥佛若渡水.則爛卻了也.金佛若渡鑪. 則鎔卻了也.木佛若渡火.便燒卻了也. He asks rhetorically, "What is so hard to understand about this?" 有什麼難會.⁹⁶ Yuanwu then enunciates, "Xuedou's hundred odes that versify old cases are complicated by making judgments and comparisons; only these three verses directly reflect the vitality of a patch-robed monk. However these poems are nonetheless difficult to understand, so if you can pass through the three odes I will determine that your studies are complete." 雪竇一百則頌古.計較葛藤.唯此三頌直下有衲僧氣息.只是這頌也不妨難會.爾若透得此三頌.便許爾罷參. After lengthy comments that include citing verses by various monks, Yuanwu concludes by noting, "Once cleansed at a primordial level you will naturally see for yourself [Xuedou's] compassion" 淨裸裸地.自然見他親切處也.⁹⁷

**Other Kinds of Remarks.** To understand the rhetorical style of Xuedou and its impact on the overall gongan tradition, it is necessary to consider not only the *One Hundred Odes* in relation to Yuanwu's comments in the *Blue Cliff Record*, or even the intimate connections between Xuedou's gongan interpretations and Yuanwu's view of these as gleaned from other texts such as his *Record of Keeping the Beat (Jijielu)*. We must recognize that this would likely be considered a *vase clos* situation if left separate and isolated from the larger context in which Xuedou's verse and prose remarks have been dealt with extensively by subsequent commentators beginning in twelfth century China and also in Korea and Japan starting from the thirteenth century. These instances sometimes involve several cases found in the *Blue Cliff Record* but also include many other gongan, including several attributed to Xuedou himself in that the tradition of creating encounter dialogues continued to unfold in latter days.

In briefly taking into account a few such examples, it quickly becomes apparent that the same pattern evident in Yuanwu's evaluative approach—that is, citations and evaluations combining high praise with disingenuously severe criticism—can be found in additional sources as well. One instance finds a Xuedou comment cited approvingly in a thirteenth-century Korean text, *Explanations of Prose and Verse Comments of the Chan Gate* (*Seonmun Yeomsong Seolhwa*), a collection of 1,125 gongan first compiled by Hyesim in the 1220s and later enhanced with detailed comments by Gag'un, who added cases for a grand total of 1,463. In the main dialogue, Xuefeng reprimands two monks, but "Xuedou Chongxian says, 'Out of three people, one was saved. If this is not discerned clearly there will be very many people (left) in the dust.'" 雪竇顯拈.三箇中. 有一人受救在.忽若擬不辨明.平地上有甚數.[98]

In another example, Gag'un remarks of a case, "That which completely covers the Dharma realm can only be oneself" 則周羅法界.唯自一人. He follows up this assessment by noting, "An ancient worthy [Xuedou] said, 'The mountain in the spring is, layer upon layer, dazzlingly green;/ The water in the fall is, ripple after ripple, flawlessly blue./ Standing alone in the vast empty space between heaven and earth/ Where is the limit of (my) gaze?' 古德云.春山疊亂青.秋水漾虛碧.寥寥天地間.獨立望何極. Gag'un follows this with his own evaluative comment denying Xuedou's approach, "Ha, ha, ha! What is this? North, south, east, and west, it is all just me." 阿呵呵.是什麼.南北東西唯是我.[99]

An additional instance in the same collection cites Yuanwu's ironic comment on Xuedou's prose remark in regard to a dialogue in which Xuefeng challenges a disciple, who seems to mimic the words of another teacher but also willingly accepts some of the blame for the misunderstanding. In considering Xuedou's "substitute answer, 'I have long known of the reputation of Xuefeng'" 至雪竇代云.久嚮雪峯, Gag'un notes that Yuanwu's more assertively bold substitute answer is, "Then I would overturn his meditation bench!" 後頭被打僧也. However Yuanwu next praises his predecessor, among others, whom he considers to be savvy masters by saying, "Xuedou had a device that could trap tigers" 雪竇有 陷虎之機.[100]

On the other hand, a very different picture emerges with regard to a case known as "Xuedou's 'You People'" 雪竇諸人, in which he argues that just when nothing can be depended on, above or below and to the right or the left, at that moment "a light naturally shines right in front of you, and each of you will be like a wall towering a thousand feet high" 自然常光現前, 个个壁立千仞.[101] In response to this, Xinwen Tanben (1100–1170), a strong advocate of Dahui's pedagogical method, preaches during a sermon in the Dharma hall with a reference to Zhang Dian, a famous ancient calligrapher, as well as a popular folk ditty:

> Xuedou spoke like this to make small children follow the writing model, which is fine. But if unexpectedly he encountered Zhang Dian 張顛 coming forth, who dipped his topknot in the ink and wrote a left-slanting stroke and a right-slanting stroke, he definitely would not see Zhang's spirit even if he searched for it. If it were up to me (Wannian), what would I say? 'Applying thickly the rouge onto her face,/ Satisfied she took the pearl and placed it in her hair./ You do not know the beauty's true face,/ In vain have people been singing [the ditty] Xiaoliangzhou.'"

> 雪竇與麼道.教小兒順朱即得.忽遇張顛出來把頭髻蘸墨打个丿乀定是討精魂不見. 萬年又且如何.濃將紅粉傳了面.滿把眞珠蓋却頭.不識佳人眞面目.空教人唱小梁州.[102]

The scathing attack by Xinwen seems to be matched by a frequently cited case that similarly puts Xuedou in a critical light. According to this story, "Muzhou called out to a monk, 'Great virtuoso!' but when the monk turned his head the master insulted him by saying, 'You board-carrying fellow!'" 睦州喚僧云.大德.僧迴首.師云.擔板漢.[103] This epithet indicates someone who is narrow-minded or simply a blockhead. Xuedou adds a comment, "Muzhou has only one eye. Why? All the monk did was turn his head when he was called. Why does this make him a board-carrying fellow?" 雪竇顯拈.睦州只具一隻眼.何故.這僧喚既回頭.因甚却成擔板.[104] In another version Xuedou adds, "What Muzhou said only made matters more complicated. What fault does that monk have?" 睦州伊麼道.却成多事.這僧有什麼過.

However this rejoinder does not win the day as "Huitang Zuxin [1025–1100] added a comment that Xuedou was the real fool, since 'Xuedou also only has one eye. The monk turned his head as soon as he was called. Why would this not make him a narrow-minded [or board-carrying] fellow?'" 晦堂心拈.雪竇亦秖具一隻眼.這僧一喚便迴, 爲甚麼不成擔板.[105]

Moreover Cuiyan Sizong (1085–1153) assesses the situation with a mixed comment:

> The monk turned his head and did not discern true and false. What can be done about Muzhou, who used his influence to bully an ordinary person? Had Xuedou not testified on his behalf, this monk would have been wronged again. Although this is the case Muzhou has a kind heart. Even if you follow what Xuedou said, it is still okay to call him a board-carrying fellow for turning his head when he was called.
>
> 翠嵓宗拈.這僧迴首.眞虛莫辨.爭奈睦州用勢.欺壓平人. 若無雪竇證明.這僧還同受屈.雖然如是.睦州却是好心.若 據雪竇恁麼道.也好喚迴與箇檐板漢.[106]

It seems for Cuiyan that Muzhou and the monk, in addition to Xuedou, can all be critiqued and also justified in the intricate web of multiperspectival, mutually conflicting yet complementary, gongan interpretations.

# 4

# *Unintended Baggage?*

## *Yuanwu, A Rival or Precursor?*

Continuing from "Unintended Baggage? Part I," this chapter offers an in-depth examination of Yuanwu's distinctive discursive style in relation to Dahui's apparently radical reaction to his teaching methods. This study helps clarify how the rhetoric of uncertainty was developed, especially in light of the oft-debated transition from the Northern Song emphasis on literary Chan to the Southern Song focus on antiliterary approaches. The analysis explores and explains whether Dahui could, or perhaps should, be considered justified—perhaps even according to Yuanwu himself, as some traditional and modern commentators suggest—for incinerating the *Blue Cliff Record*, while recognizing that the complexity of the issue resists letting it be cast in either/or terms.

In a discussion of various traditional standpoints regarding the historical and ideological (dis)connections between Yuanwu and Dahui, I examine, in particular, the interpretative implications of case 12. Dongshan Shouchu 洞山守初 (910–990), a disciple of Yunmen (not the better known Tang master, Dongshan Liangjie 洞山良价, 807–869, founder of the Caodong school) responds to a monk's question, "What is Buddha?" 僧問洞山.如何是佛, by saying inscrutably, "Three pounds of flax" 麻三斤.[1] (See Figure 4.1.) This dialogue along with poetic and prose remarks by Xuedou and Yuanwu seems to come as close as any example in the *Blue Cliff Record* to approximating what Dahui intended with his focus on the keyword technique.

FIGURE 4.1 Calligraphy of "three pounds of flax" by Kazuaki Tanahashi, courtesy of the artist.

The Dongshan dialogue, which is also included as case 18 in *Wumen's Barrier* and in volume 15 of the *Five Lamps Merged Together* (*Wudeng Huiyuan*) of 1252, is a prominent example of what I refer to as a puzzler case in which the teacher responds abruptly and sparingly to a monk's single seemingly innocuous query with an apparent absurdity or non sequitur such that the reply cannot be parsed one way or another. The response renders no follow-up from the inquirer. Almost all versions of the story end with Dongshan's cryptic retort, although one variation (case 172 of Dōgen's *300 Cases Treasury of the True Dharma-Eye*, or *Mana Shōbōgenzō*) is exceptional in concluding, "The monk had an immediate realization (*satoru*) and made a bow" 僧有悟.便礼拜.[2] Most of the puzzlers in the *Blue Cliff Record* involve either Zhaozhou or Yunmen and his followers, although occasionally there are other examples, such as Mazu's responding in case 3 to a monk's question about how he was feeling with, "Sun-face Buddha, Moon-face Buddha" 日面佛.月面佛.

The usual explanation of case 12 is that Dongshan was probably standing in a storage room at the time of the question where he was weighing how much hemp was available since it took three to four pounds to make a Buddhist robe. To highlight that such an interpretation based on logic and practicality is inappropriate some translators simply leave the original expression in transliteration as Másānjīn (J. Masangin). This is similar to the treatment often given to the reply in case 21 of *Wumen's Barrier*, another puzzler gongan in which Yunmen answers a similar question by saying, "A dried turd" 乾屎橛 left as Gānshǐjué (J. Kanshiketsu).

Yuanwu's commentary, building on Xuedou's verse remarks, vehemently denies the role of expediency or seeing the answer in terms corresponding to the situation; neither of these usual explanations for the function of gongan, he argues, serves as a legitimate way of elucidating the meaning of Dongshan's perplexing utterance. The case thus seems to abandon any reliance on language that is compatible with the shortcut path to realization advocated by the keyword method, which similarly bypasses conventional rhetoric. It therefore may lend support to theories suggesting that, rather than occupying a position of contrast or rivalry with his main disciple and also regardless of whether he realized or could have possibly acknowledged this on a conscious or intentional level, Yuanwu embraced a standpoint that paved the way for and eventually culminated in the technique pioneered by Dahui.

My examination finds that assessment to represent a reductionist reading and, instead, stresses that the *pingchang* orientation of Yuanwu's evaluative method—based on awareness of the multiple implications of indeterminacy, a crucial interpretive factor often overlooked or underappreciated—is the key for understanding the contributions of the *Blue Cliff Record* to overall gongan commentary. Yuanwu's discussion of this case, including remarks on Xuedou's verse, resembles Dahui's approach, but in the final analysis his outlook is highly allusive and associative rather than aimed entirely at cutting off all modes of thought. This reading of the complexity of the *Blue Cliff Record*'s rhetoric of uncertainty helps defeat stereotypical impressions of Yuanwu's relation to Dahui, a complex issue frequently reconfigured retrospectively as a matter of concealed compatibility despite obvious dissimilarities between the Chan thinkers.

Classical views of the *Blue Cliff Record* that continue to affect greatly contemporary interpretations tend to see the association between Yuanwu and Dahui in very different ways, encompassing nearly opposite perspectives that stress either difference yet with complementarity or conflict based on innate inconsistency. At one extreme is the view that the two gongan commentators are of separate but equal status since, despite the master-disciple relation lasting about five years, they were simply far removed from one another both conceptually and in terms of the dynamic of the cultural environment that changed dramatically between the 1120s and 1130s: Yuanwu epitomized the literary heights of Northern Song's lettered Chan by building on Xuedou's rhetorical embellishments in appealing to scholar-officials, whereas Dahui represented the skeptical stance of Southern Song Chan in trying to restore a "special transmission outside the scriptures" by applying the keyword technique to the practice of monastic and lay followers alike. A contrary standpoint tends to demean Yuanwu's elaborate discourse by accepting and ratifying Dahui's destructive action as legitimate since his approach to pedagogy surpassed and justifiably replaced what Yuanwu had accomplished, which was more or less relegated to the dustbins of Chan history.

The contrasting perspectives are further variegated in that some evaluations are neutral and balanced in emphasizing the compatibility of the Chan teachers, whether from the angle of highlighting similarity or difference, yet others express a surreptitious or perhaps not-so-hidden value judgment of preference that usually leans toward the priority of Dahui's teaching. There are also a couple of attempted standpoints that, by either applauding or condemning both Yuanwu and Dahui, resist viewing the thinkers as either polar opposites or, contrariwise, as twin sides of a coin. For example, Zhongfeng Mingben argues that no Chan pedagogy, including that of luminaries such as Bodhidharma, Linji, and Deshan, approximates the "gongan (or public case) realized (or manifested)" 現成公案 (C. *xianzheng gongan*, J. *genjōkōan*) during the forty-nine years of the teaching of Sakyamuni. Writing in the early fourteenth century at the time of the reconstitution of the *Blue Cliff Record*, Zhongfeng asks rhetorically:

> Do you mean to say that [Buddhist truth] is something Xuedou could eulogize and Yuanwu adjudicate? Even if the *Biyan lu* had millions of fascicles, how could these add to or subtract from the manifest public case? Of old, Dahui did not fully understand this principle and broke the woodblocks—does this not seem like forbidding a stone woman to give birth to a son? Now could it be that the gentleman who again wants to publish these blocks wants to urge the stone woman to give birth to a child? This is truly laughable![3]

**Sources for Dahui's Action.** Many contemporary approaches to the relation between Yuanwu and Dahui seem to be heavily influenced by Song-Yuan dynasty explications but without necessarily investigating or challenging the basis of their assumptions in historical context. In trying to correct that tendency it should be noted that the main sources for the divergent perspectives are a couple of relatively obscure works, including *Precious Lessons from the Chan Forest* from 1189 and several para-texts (prefaces and afterwords) to the reconstituted edition of the *Blue Cliff Record* from the early 1300s.[4] Since these works reflect traditional biases, they are hardly sufficient to substantiate historical claims.

The locus classicus, or at least the earliest known and apparently only extant Song work that deals directly with the legend of Dahui's devastation of the collection, is a passage contained in *Precious Lessons* that was probably produced in mid-twelfth century, although the full text was not published for a couple of decades. This work, which consists of a series of short excerpts from various Song teachers regarding the causes of disruption and need for reform in then-current Chan training, was initially compiled by Dahui and was amplified and edited by followers after his death.[5] Although it contains expressions by and about numerous masters, including Wuzu and Yuanwu with the latter generally cast in a favorable light, overall this is a work that reflects the agenda of Dahui's lineage.

The crucial passage forms part of the reflections of Xinwen Tanben, a lesser known Linji-Huanglong lineage monk, about the supposedly regrettable condition of the Chan school at the time. Xinwen argues that an overreliance on literary studies made it evident the *Blue Cliff Record* warranted elimination. He begins by pointing out that while eleventh-century commentators such as Fenyang and Xuedou offered stirring verse comments on gongan cases, it was their emphasis on writing skill as an end in itself that eventually led to a severe decline in genuine Chan religiosity:

> During the Tianxi era [1017–1021], by using his talents of eloquence and erudition with splendid intent, Xuedou made innovations while seeking to create new expressions through the use of skillful speech following the example of Fenyang, who [first created the genre of] odes to the ancients (*songgu*). This gained the attention of students at the time so that the style of the Chan lineage from this point on was fundamentally altered to deleterious effect.

天禧間雪竇以辯博之才.美意變弄求新琢巧.繼汾陽為頌古.籠絡當世學者.宗風由此一變矣.

Xinwen further claims that by Yuanwu's time there was no turning back on the part of the leading Chan teachers to restore the path of a special transmission that was persuasively conveyed in the initially unencumbered—that is, without need for elaborate explanations or interpretations—encounter dialogues involving Tang masters:

In the Xuan era [1119–1125] Yuanwu discussed the meaning of [Xuedou's] passages in composing the *Blue Cliff Record*. At that time the greatest masters of the age like Ningdao [n.d.], Sixin [Wuxin, 1043–1114], Lingyuan [Weiqing, d. 1117], and Fojian [Huiqin, 1059– 1117] did not try to challenge this approach. Students of our latter days still treasure [Yuanwu's] words. From dawn until dusk they utter these sayings as if the highest form of learning, but without realizing how wrongful this is or recognizing the unfortunate situation in that it has caused their capacity for thinking to diminish.

逮宣政間.圓悟又出己意離之為碧巖集.彼時邁古淳全之士.如寧道者死心靈源佛鑒諸老.皆莫能迴其說.於是新進後生珍重其語.朝誦暮習謂之至學.莫有悟其非者.痛哉.學者之心術壞矣.

The passage concludes on a triumphal note concerning Dahui's supposedly heroic efforts, undertaken in the Age of the Degenerate Dharma 末法 when true teachings are understood poorly by people incapable of attaining higher spiritual aspirations, although Xinwen does not accompany or link the destruction of the *Blue Cliff Record* to advocacy for the keyword:

At the beginning of the Shaoxing era [1131–1162], Fori (Dahui Zonggao) went to Fujian province and saw that Chan students were being misled. Day and night he pondered the situation of these learners until finally he felt sure about taking the correct course of action. Fori then smashed the woodblocks and tore up the words [of the *Blue Cliff Record*] so as to sweep away delusion, rescue those who were floundering, get rid of excessive rhetoric and exaggeration while destroying false teachings to reveal the true Dharma. Once he did this patch-robed monks gradually began to realize the error of their ways and no longer reverted to conceptual attachments. If not for Fori's farsightedness and compassionate drive to rescue beings in the Age of the Degenerate Dharma, Chan communities today would surely find themselves in great peril.

紹興初.佛日入閩見學者牽之不返.日馳月騖浸漬成弊.即碎其板闢其說.以至祛迷援溺剔繁撥劇摧邪顯正.特然而振之.衲子稍知其非

而不復慕.然非佛日高明遠見乘悲願力救末法之弊.則叢林大有可
畏者矣(與張子韶書).[6]

While the Xinwen passage attributes the loss of the *Blue Cliff Record* directly to Dahui from the standpoint of lavishly praising this deed as salvific of the Chan school, other selections from the *Precious Lessons* further support indirectly the feeling that gongan training had become excessively obtuse. One record indicates that Yuanwu had received a cryptic warning about this from his Dharma brother Lingyuan (d. 1117) that was given an equally terse rebuttal emphasizing that holding to faith and uprightness in the end overcomes inauthenticity:

Lingyuan said to Yuanwu, "Even though a patch-robed monk has qualifications to see the Way, if he does not develop a depth of self-cultivation when he puts his ability to use it is certain to become crude and abrasive. Not only is it of no avail in instructing people to enter the gate of Buddha's teaching I am afraid it will only lead to spiritual decline and humiliation." Chan master Yuanwu replied, "The way of learning is kept in trustworthiness [or faith]. Establishing trustworthiness depends on integrity. . . . The ancients said, 'One may lose clothing and food but integrity and trustworthiness can never be lost.'"

靈源謂圓悟曰.衲子雖有見道之資.若不深蓄厚養.發
用必峻暴.非特無補教門.將恐有招禍辱.圓悟禪師曰.
學道存乎信.立信在乎誠.存誠於中.然後俾眾無惑....
古人云.衣食可去誠信不可失.[7]

Another example is a highly charged passage cited in *Precious Lessons* by Wan'an Daoyan (1094–1164), one of Dahui's main disciples who generally cites Yuanwu in a positive fashion and in this instance does not name him. As part of a wide-ranging repudiation of pervasive false teachings and bad habits, Wan'an remarks that masters from the period were no longer using dialogues for constructive discussion among peers. Instead case interpretations had become a rationale for abbots to take up arbitrarily a contest with any rival or adversary who visited their temple. This was done without due cause since the main purpose was to show off and trumpet one's own technique, the basis of which was left hidden in obfuscation to avoid scrutiny and critique since the rules of this game were invariably weighted in favor of the teacher. Therefore, legitimate doubts were not mitigated by this kind of gongan practice, as challengers to any maestro were intimidated and forced into psychological submission during the exchange rather than gaining insight and illumination.[8]

The other main early source that highlights some of the reasons for the incineration of the *Blue Cliff Record* by giving credit (or blame) to Dahui comes well over a century later. It is impossible to determine whether passages contained in the collection's para-texts merely echoed reports from the *Precious Lessons* or if, by then, there was additional information available to support the assertion that Dahui was responsible for the destruction. The full list of para-texts includes the following items, with brief notations regarding their composition:

- 1128 Preface by Puzhao Bhikkhu, on 3rd month 30th day
- 1300 Preface by Fanghui Wanli of Mount Ziyang, on 4th month 8th day
- 1305 Preface by Zhou Chi, a Liaocheng laymen, overlooking Qiantang Bridge in Zhejiang
- 1304 Preface by Sanjiao Laoren, elder of Three Teachings, on 4th month 15th day
- 1125 Afterword by Guanyu Wudeng
- 14th c. Afterword by anonymous author
- 1302 Afterword by Jing Ri, bhikku of Tiantong, 7th gen. disciple of Yuanwu, in fall
- 1317 Afterword by Xi Ling, bhikku of Jingshan, 8th gen. disciple of Yuanwu
- 1317 Afterword by Fengzi Zhen, an esteemed elder

Some editions of the *Blue Cliff Record* also contain two additional short para-texts: one is an afterword from the eighteenth century testifying to the continuing popularity and reprinting for hundreds of years of the collection in China; and the second is a passage inserted after case 50 by Zhanghui Mingyuan of Yuzhong, who briefly explains the basis for the reconstruction.[9]

The two para-texts from the 1120s are useful for describing the process of the original compilation of the collection some years after the lectures were completed, with Guanyu's postface adding the comment that there was a strong sentiment among Yuanwu's followers that his precious sayings had to be recorded even though he notes they were wary that the truth expressed in his oral sermons could never be captured by words on paper. All seven para-texts from the 1300s, including three of four prefaces and four of five afterwords, clearly state that it was Dahui who incinerated the text. But in their expression of enthusiasm for the rhetoric of the *Blue Cliff Record*, these passages take a decidedly more measured approach than Xinwen's caustic comments by supporting equally the efforts of Yuanwu and Dahui.

The fourth afterword, presented in full below (a section was cited in chapter 1), was composed on the day of a Buddhist assembly to express Xi Ling's reverence for the collection. Although it was apparently written less than two decades after the reconstitution, this piece refers to a long time passing since then, which is either a bit of hyperbole in an era when chronology was not well documented or reflective of a genuine feeling about the richness of the period since Zhang's recovered edition was published. Consisting of three paragraphs that each end with a probing inquiry, Xi Ling's essay contains lavish praise for Yuanwu's work, albeit with a dose of cynicism at the end of the opening section, while he also greatly admires Dahui:

> Chan master Yuanwu commented critically on monk Xuedou's *One Hundred Odes* in order to examine meticulously and reveal the mysterious depths so as to awaken the fundamental mind of advanced disciples to realize the pivotal functions of patriarchs in our lineage. This wondrous knowledge is disclosed and transmitted through a spiritual process that seeks to bring illumination to a dusky cave, like a small toad lifting and shining light on the recesses of a darkened room. How could a seemingly shallow, discriminatory form of expression divulge the ultimate state?
>
> Later Chan master Dahui began to doubt the impact made by the collection when he was giving private instruction to students, who made some skeptical remarks. He then started carefully inspecting the work and felt some of its comments contradicted one another. On further reflection he felt the collection precipitated a decline in spiritual awareness and concluded, "Studying the *Blue Cliff Record* does not lead to enlightenment." Out of concern that his followers would not understand the original underlying meaning but instead focus their attention on its particular use of words, he took it upon himself to burn the text in order to rescue disciples from delusion. Both the composition and the

incineration of the book reflected the same intention. How were there two such [different results]?

[In 1300] Zhang Mingyuan, [a layman] from Yuzhong, by chance got a copy of a handwritten version of the second half of the text and then he also found a version that was recently edited by Xuetang as well as yet another manuscript kept at [Zhaojue temple in] Sichuan. Zhang worked on revising and correcting these fragments so as to compile the three versions into a single new complete edition that, once published, has been passed down and widely distributed for seemingly quite a long time. Based on just a single perusal of this text people with great wisdom will suddenly awaken their original mind and quickly reach the stage of thoroughly removing all doubts. How could this be called a small deed?

圓悟禪師.評唱雪竇和尚頌古一百則.剖決玄微.抉剔幽邃.顯列祖之機用.開後學之心源.況妙智虛凝.神機默運.晶旭輝而玄扃洞照.圓蟾升而幽室朗明.豈淺識而能致極.後大慧禪師.因學人入室.下語頗異.疑之纔勘而邪鋒自挫.再鞫而納款.自降曰.我碧巖集中記來.實非有悟.因慮其後不明根本.專尚語言以圖口捷.由是火之以救斯弊也.然成此書.火此書.其用心則一崵中張明遠偶獲寫本後冊.又獲雪堂刊本及蜀本.校訂訛舛.刊成此書.流通萬古.使上根大智之士.一覽而頓開本心.直造無疑之地.豈小補云乎哉.徑山住持比丘.希陵拜書以為後序.[10]

A similarly evenhanded approach toward the outlooks of Yuanwu and Dahui is found in the preface written in 1304 by Sanjiao Laoren, a monastic elder who was well versed in diverse Mahayana Buddhist teachings and supported a pragmatic approach for evaluating teachings:

> You should realize that the intentions of both masters were correct. Yuanwu was mostly concerned with training future generations of students so he recited Xuedou's verses and commented on them extensively, whereas Dahui was mostly concerned with saving people from burning or drowning so he destroyed the *Blue Cliff Record*. Sakyamuni Buddha spoke the whole great canon of scriptures (or Tripitaka), yet in the end he said he had never uttered a single word. Was he fooling us? Yuanwu's intention was like that of Sakyamuni speaking the scriptures, and Dahui's intention was like that of

Sakyamuni denying that he had ever spoken. . . . Whether a cart is pushed or pulled, the main concern is that it is moved forward.

知此則二老之心皆是矣.圜悟顧子念孫之心多.故重拈雪竇頌.大慧救焚拯溺之心多.故立毀碧巖集.釋氏說一大藏經.末後乃謂.不曾說一字.豈欺我哉圜悟之心.釋氏說經之心也.大慧之心.釋氏諱說之心也....推之輓之.主於車行而已.[11]

According to Sanjiao's essay, which like other passages embraces the implication that the act of destruction should not be disputed or dismissed despite the remarkable rhetorical quality of the collection, Yuanwu and Dahui were equally praiseworthy because they both functioned in accord with Buddhist traditions. Sanjiao concludes, however, by suggesting that whatever is read in a book is not the same as the reality it tries to depict, an analogy that may be construed as a subtle putdown of the discourse used in the *Blue Cliff Record*.

The examples from *Precious Lessons* and the para-texts are clear about their respective attitudes toward incineration, with Xinwen approving of this action by saying the text got what it deserved, and with Xi Ling and Sanjiao giving an impartial account supporting the merits of a crucial work that deserved to be reconstructed while acknowledging that Dahui successfully addressed its demerits. As time went by, the hermeneutic situation became increasingly complicated and variable with commentators like Zhongfeng trying to carve out more nuanced positions. The reason for the disparity of later outlooks involves contradictory factors of lineage and patronage that are somewhat external to the text yet invariably exert an influence on almost all subsequent appropriations of Yuanwu's work as well as controversies surrounding its impact.

One factor concerns the complex legacy of Yuanwu's pedagogical efforts in terms of the sociohistorical background of the ongoing development of Chinese Chan discourse. Despite Dahui's notoriety as the most prominent follower of Yuanwu who undermined his erstwhile mentor, as the lineage of Yuanwu stemming from Baiyun and Wuzu unfolded during the late Southern Song and Yuan dynasties and also greatly influenced the early period of Zen in Kamakura Japan (1185–1333), this school was dominated by adherents of another of Yuanwu's main disciples, Huqiu Shaolong (1077–1136). Huqiu's following, which divided three generations later into the Songyuan (1139–1209) and Boan (1136–1211) streams, eventually included prominent gongan commentators Gaofeng Yuanmiao

(1238–1295), the teacher of Zhongfeng, who had mixed views about the use of the keyword in relation to other styles of training. The ascendancy of this movement left Dahui's fellowship as a collateral line, rather than the main branch of the Linji school, and mitigated some of his influence in China and Japan although the keyword approach was still important.

Members of the lineage via Huqui, some of whom were reclusive and engaged in mountain austerities while others led large monasteries and interacted with the literati elite in an urban setting, generally were non-combative and sought to overcome instead of exacerbate intra- and inter-sectarian divergences in ideology and method. They thus tried to reconcile Buddhist Vinaya or the precepts and regulations for monastic discipline with Chan irreverence and iconoclasm, and the Chan school's poetic discourse with the Pure Land school's *nianfo* recitation.[12] In this context Linji school followers of various stripes were eager to find ways of explaining that the approaches of Yuanwu and Dahui were actually complementary or, contrariwise, that both exhibited a comparable amount of rhetorical or practical deficiency. This attitude often led to linking the two thinkers in creative but sometimes artificial or superficial ways.

Related to that development was the enhanced role the Huqiu-based lineage played during the period of émigré pilgrim-monks, that is, Chinese teachers who traveled to Japan to help transmit and establish the Rinzai sect beginning with Lanqi Daolong (1213–1278, J. Rankei Dōryū) in 1246 and a series of Japanese monastics who traveled to China in the late thirteenth century to study at Five Mountains temples in Zhejiang.[13] All the émigré monks had a keen interest in establishing and maintaining in Japan a strong sense of sectarian identity and the integrity of their school. This no doubt helped lead to the recovery of the lost text of the *Blue Cliff Record* around 1300 because latter followers of the Yuanwu lineage wanted to celebrate their esteemed ancestor. After it was introduced to Japan, the collection was studied throughout the medieval period, especially at temples known as Rinka 林下 (literally, "forest below") that included many non–Five Mountains monasteries belonging to both Rinzai and Sōtō lineages, thus cutting across sectarian divisions.

In a trend that was at once consistent with and contrary to a focus on the compatibility of Yuanwu and Dahui as favored by the Huqiu-based heritage, the rise to dominance of the keyword method among practitioners in China and Japan in addition to Korea contributed to a retrospective reading of the *Blue Cliff Record* by asserting the priority of a minimalist interpretation of gongan. According to that approach, the collection was seen as important mainly in that it formed a part, intentionally or not, of a lengthy but essentially linear teleological progression that led inevitably to the sparse style of discourse epitomized by examples of the keyword that claimed to fulfill Chan's special transmission not bound by words and letters.

Current scholarship greatly influenced by advocacy of the keyword method generally offers two main views of the relationship between Yuanwu and Dahui. One is the stepping-stone thesis, which maintains that Yuanwu's approach was intentionally different but failed and underneath was unintentionally leaning in Dahui's direction, anyway. The other view is the precursor status thesis, which argues that Yuanwu actually did intend, fully consciously or not, to move toward a contraction or reduction of rhetoric but probably realized on some level the extent to which he remained trapped by his era's disposition toward lettered Chan. Therefore Dahui's method brought out the genuine significance of the work of Yuanwu, who would have been willing to acknowledge or even applaud his disciple's new approach.

## Formation of Dahui's Thought

Before critically examining some of the pros and cons of these outlooks and their shared assumption that Dahui surpassed his predecessor, I will take a closer look at Dahui's intellectual development and how this was shaped by interactions with Yuanwu, in addition to related ideological and social factors influencing Song Chan discourse. Although Dahui's initiation of the keyword method in 1134 and destruction of the *Blue Cliff Record* in 1140 seem to represent Southern Song dynasty preferences, his thinking was initially formed and his enlightenment was experienced as part of a prolonged and arduous process of training undergone during the last several decades of the Northern Song. Seeing how this experience attained under Yuanwu had an impact on Dahui's later activities involves exploring controversies about a key passage in records depicting his enlightenment experience.[14]

The overwhelming reputation of Dahui, the thirteenth of Yuanwu's twenty-four monastic disciples,[15] seems to rest more on his approach to meditation than on creating texts despite the ample production of his voluminous gongan records and commentaries. The narrative about him is augmented by how certain elements of his biography encompass the predilections of a towering personality who endured many hardships while also overcoming challenges and accomplishing remarkable feats to become a great religious leader. This is a fascinating and well-documented account that is even more dramatic in its intricate twists and turns than Yuanwu's story in conveying profound disappointments and eventual recoveries during the course of a complicated yet ultimately uplifting and rewarding spiritual journey.

Dahui's narrative covers years of early training with various kinds of Chan masters and friendships with prominent literati like the monk Juefan Huihong and scholar-official Zhang Shangying, who were already closely associated with Yuanwu. Both literati suffered through their own trials and tribulations, including imprisonment and exile due to pressures from the imperial court, which was experienced by many apologists for Buddhism since secular authorities challenged the religion's role during the rule of the last Northern Song emperor, Huizong. The account also includes Dahui's extraordinary realization attained under the mentorship of Yuanwu and subsequent extensive periods of banishment to the malarial south before he returned triumphant at the conclusion of his career to take up the abbacy of Mount Jing, which at the time was the leading Five Mountains temple located west of Hangzhou.

Like Yuanwu, Dahui was born in an era featuring a baffling array of competing teaching lineages and diverse practices circulating among Chan factions. At the beginning of his pursuit of the Buddhist path, he undertook extensive travels to see teachers from both the Linji and Caodong lineages, while coming to distrust the techniques of the latter school as arbitrary and counterproductive.[16] Dahui spent the most time in Jiangxi province training under Zhantang Wenzhun (1061–1115), a master of the Linji-Huanglong branch and a disciple of Zhenjing Kewen (1025–1102), who had also enlightened Juefan. Like Wuzu and others, Zhantang, who had served for ten years as assistant to Caodong school master Furong Daokai (1043–1118), was apparently critical of silent or passive approaches to meditation associated with that lineage, although eventually Dahui would consider this to be an affliction also pervading the Linji-Huanglong stream. As with most other Chan trainees, Dahui is said to have studied the *One Hundred Odes* during his formative stage. Even though he gained Dharma transmission and felt he had developed a strong intellectual understanding of Chan, including going through what he later referred to as "eighteen minor awakenings," the attainment of full and final enlightenment as opposed to fleeting moments of breakthrough proved elusive.

Following the death of Zhantang, Dahui interacted for a time with Juefan, who then was involved in a project with which Dahui assisted to accumulate Zhantang's record. Zhang Shangying suggested that Dahui seek out Yuanwu in the Linji-Yangqi stream for a possible resolution to his never-ending spiritual journey. It took nearly a decade before Dahui was finally able to meet Yuanwu, and their time together lasted just a few years in all, with most of it spent by Dahui as Yuanwu's head monk and assistant at several temples, first in the north and then in the south after the fall of the Northern Song. After realizing his spiritual goal in 1125, ten years following the passing of Zhantang, Dahui's fame spread quickly and widely. A host of scholar-officials vied for the opportunity to study with him. He was awarded a purple robe and the honorific title Fori 佛日, or Buddhist Sun, and he was also often referred to as Miaoxi 妙喜.

The account of Dahui's enlightenment under Yuanwu is inextricably tied historically and conceptually to the teacher's struggles to realize his ultimate religious achievement under the tutelage of Wuzu, so the link between these three thinkers runs deep. Yuanwu presented to Dahui the same case he had received from Wuzu. According to the original dialogue, which appears in the first half of case 32 in the *Entangling Vines Collection*, Tang master Changqing Lan'an (793–883) addresses his assembly with the conundrum, "Being and nonbeing are like wisteria vines clinging to a tree" 有句無句.如籐依樹. Hearing of this, Shushan Guangren (837–909) traveled from Hunan to Zhejiang to present to the teacher a turning word he had devised by asking where being and nonbeing go if the tree falls and the vines wither. But when Shushan misconstrued Changqing's loud laughter in response to the query, he was told to go meet Mingzhao, from whom he received clarification that the teacher had not intended that his sound of amusement be taken as scornful or as a harsh blow like feeling the thrust of a dagger.

According to Tōrei Enji (1721–1792), who wrote of their encounter centuries later, Dahui was skeptical at the beginning, "When [Dahui] first met Yuanwu, he thought to himself, 'I'll complete nine summers, and if he approves me like they have everywhere else, I'll write a treatise on the nonexistence of Zen.'"[17] Dahui's own account highlights a fateful day in 1125, the same year the compilation of *Blue Cliff Record* was completed by Yuanwu's disciples. After a protracted period in which he struggled day and night before finally breaking through another gongan, "East Mountain walks on water" 東山水上行, Dahui was still in the midst of working through the case, "Being and nonbeing are like wisteria vines clinging to a tree." He found that Yuanwu always immediately cut off his responses and those of his colleagues as soon as the words came out of their mouths, for being misguided and dead wrong. No progress whatsoever was being made despite his sustained effort.

One evening Dahui sat in the abbot's quarters with some public officials eating supper, but he was so distracted that he held the chopsticks in his hand and forgot to eat. After Yuanwu made a sarcastic comment that Dahui must be investigating "boxwood Chan" 楊木禪,[18] a metaphor suggesting an earnest but plodding and painstakingly slow-to-awaken style of training, the disciple blurted out, "Teacher, it is the same in principle as a dog staring at a pot of hot oil; he knows he can't lick it but he can't leave it alone, either." 和尚.這箇道理.恰如狗看著熱油鐺相似.要舐又舐.不得.要捨又捨不得. Yuanwu responded approvingly, "You have hit on a wonderful analogy. This is what is known as the Vajra cage [something so hard you cannot get out of it] or the prickly chestnut ball [something that cannot be swallowed]." 老和尚曰.爾喻得極好.只這箇便是金剛圈栗棘蓬.[19]

Yuanwu then brought up how the case of wisteria vines had led to his own enlightenment, and Dahui, who was eager to learn more about this, asked Yuanwu what his teacher Wuzu had said when he inquired about the story 話 (*hua*). Yuanwu was at first unwilling to explain, but Dahui insisted that when Yuanwu discussed it with Wuzu, it was not a private training session because the inquiry took place in front of the assembly. Since it was part of the public record, nothing should prevent Yuanwu from disclosing what transpired. Dahui further reports:

> Yuanwu said, "I asked, 'What about being and nonbeing, which are like wisteria vines clinging to a tree?' and Wuzu said, 'A drawing cannot portray it and a sketch will not be able to depict it.' I asked further, 'What about when the tree falls down and the vines die?' and Wuzu said, 'How intertwined they are!'[20] As soon as I heard him bring this up I understood and exclaimed, "I got it!"
>
> 老和尚乃曰.我問.有句無句如藤倚樹時如何.祖曰.描也描不成.畫也畫不就.又問.忽遇樹倒藤枯時如何.祖曰.相隨來也.老漢纔聞舉便理會得.乃曰.某會也.[21]

However the journey did not end there as Dahui needed to be tested further by the master because the claim that he had a breakthrough to

full understanding could be just the latest example of many such assertions made since the time Zhantang had cautioned that sometimes Dahui
seemed to comprehend when he was awake but lose this capacity when he
was asleep. As with a crucial passage, discussed in the chapter 3, regarding Yuanwu's views of Chan poetic vis-à-vis prose comments from his
remarks on case 1, a single key sentence revealing the dynamic interplay
with Yuanwu at the crucial turning point in Dahui's awakening can be
variously translated and lead to different conclusions concerning the issue
of Dahui's role as either a successor to or a digresser from his mentor.
According to Dahui's account:

> Yuanwu said, "I only fear that you have not achieved a full penetra-
> tion of gongan." I replied, "Please bring up [some cases]." Yuanwu
> then brought up a series of intricate and perplexing gongan, but
> with each one I was able to turn it around and resolve the case again
> and again. This was like setting out on a trip in a time of great peace
> with no worries so that while walking down the road there is noth-
> ing to obstruct the path. Yuanwu said, "You have finally come to
> understand the way. I do not deceive you."[22]

> 老和尚曰.只恐爾透公案未得.老漢曰.請和尚舉.老和尚遂
> 連舉一絡索誵訛公案連舉被我三轉兩轉截斷.如箇太平
> 無事時得路便行更無滯礙.老和尚曰.如今方知道.我不謾爾.[23]

The passage could also be read as indicating that, at the time of the
testing, Dahui was given some "phony (literally, vague and misleading)
gongan cases" 誵訛公案 to ponder as an apparent bluff by Yuanwu to
throw his disciple off the mark. In any event Dahui demonstrated prowess that was bold enough to keep interrupting this sequence with appropriate replies. Two other renderings suggest something a bit different.
One version by Miriam Levering refers to a "series of *gongans* ... [and
Dahui] cut through them in two or three revolutions"; and the other by
J. C. Cleary suggests that Yuanwu presented "several particularly difficult cases in order to question Ta Hui, who replied to them all without
getting stuck."[24]

Although the variation may seem slight, this is significant because the
Levering and Cleary versions indicate an underlying level of sympathy
and continuity between master and disciple that foreshadows—or even
initiates—the development of the keyword method as a series of shortcut

cases posed as barriers that are cut through once and for all, rather than as open-ended cases to be penetrated and resolved in terms of uncertainty. My rendering suggests that at this stage, which occurred a decade before the gongan-introspection approach was developed, Dahui simply gained enough mastery as acknowledged by Yuanwu to be able to recognize and distinguish the authentic from the false. Either way it is clear that Dahui learned from Yuanwu and other teachers a sense that many falsehearted monks merely memorize rhetoric about gongan cases rather than fully absorb and understand their meaning.

Dahui's enlightenment transpired at a very troublesome time for China, and in the very next year of 1126, the capital was moved to Hangzhou, south of the Yangzi River, as a consequence of the attack by the Jurchen (Ruzhen) Jin from the north: the Southern Song dynasty began. Yuanwu and Dahui were exiled to the south at Mount Yunju in Jiangxi province and then to Fujian province, where they may have briefly met Hongzhi, who later became a renowned Caodong master in Zhejiang province. Hongzhi was Dahui's main ideological adversary because of the former's promotion of the method of "silent-illumination" 默照禪 (*mozhao Chan*), although the masters maintained cordial personal relations, and Hongzhi recommended just before his death that Dahui succeed him as abbot of Tiantong temple.

Following this interlude, from 1137 to 1141 Dahui was rehabilitated for a time and served as abbot at Mount Jing where he was prized by imperial authorities for attracting nearly 2,000 followers, but he then suffered a second and more devastating period in exile lasting fifteen years. During that phase, according to a passage in the *Precious Lessons from the Chan Forest*, Dahui was highly successful proselytizing to lay disciples and also was visited by followers, many of whom deserted the Hangzhou area in order to flock to his group. In the late 1140s, Dahui published a collection of correspondences, the *Dahui Shu* 大慧書 and the voluminous gongan collection containing 661 cases known as the *Treasury of the True Dharma-Eye* 正法眼藏 (C. *Zhengfayanzang*, J. *Shōbōgenzō*).[25] In 1157 he returned to the capital where he remained as the head of prestigious Mount Jing for most of the rest of his life.

Another factor promoting Dahui's reputation, which seems to catapult his significance over Yuanwu, is his unsurpassed role as creator of the technique of meditation based on the use of the keyword. This makes him the proverbial godfather of nearly all forms of Chan/Seon/Zen practice in East Asia, along with the spread of the Rinzai school to the West in the twentieth century. Dahui is legendary in that diverse luminaries appropriated his keyword method, such as Jinul in thirteenth-century Korea, Hakuin in eighteenth-century Japan, Xu Yun in twentieth-century China, and modern representatives of the Japanese Sanbyōkyōdan school affiliated with Sōtō Zen, among many others. Although he was criticized by diverse figures such as Dōgen in thirteenth-century and Bankei (1622–1693) in seventeenth-century Japan, among others, countless volumes have been and will continue to be written in praise of or emulating Dahui's teachings.[26] Nevertheless it is still a matter of debate whether the keyword was intended primarily for lay followers or to what extent Dahui may have allowed for monks to undertake other kinds of practices.[27] The degree of prominence accorded Dahui fosters a sense of orthodoxy that tends to cloud our view of Yuanwu's role because the mentor is seen through the lens of how his teaching was taken over by the disciple's multitude of followers, as if Yuanwu somehow anticipated or even perhaps unconsciously sought the destruction of the *Blue Cliff Record* because of its unintended baggage.

According to the biography, the *Annual Chronology of Chan Master Dahui's Life* (*Dahui Pujue Chanshi Nianpu*), beginning in 1134 Dahui reversed his course regarding literary Chan and developed gongan-introspection as a shortcut focusing on a critical word or phrase extracted from a case while discarding the dialogue's full content as an impediment to insight. He continued to preach the keyword approach for thirty years while aggressively bashing other forms of practice. Although there were literally hundreds of gongan to choose from based on his own collections, for the most part, Dahui used only a handful since he believed that clarification of one or two cases was sufficient to attain awakening, especially for lay followers with a limited background in Chan classics or time for meditation.

In addition to cases like Dongshan's "Three pounds of flax," Yunmen's "A dried turd," and Zhaozhou's "Cypress tree standing in the courtyard" 庭前柏樹子 or "Ten thousand things return to the source, but where does the source return?" 萬法歸一一歸何處曇賣, which he often presented together in the same list, the single most important example for Dahui is Zhaozhou's one-word response, "Wu" 無 (J. Mu), or "No," to a monk's query, "Does even a dog have Buddha-nature or not?" 狗子還有佛性也無.[28] This dialogue became the first case in *Wumen's Barrier* and the eighteenth case in the *Record of Serenity*, although it is not cited in the *Blue Cliff Record*, probably because it was not popular until Dahui's attention made it so. Dahui writes extensively of how the inscrutability of the term Wu/Mu heightens one's sensation of doubt 疑情 (*yiqing*) about the pitfalls of conventional language and thought, and the way its unbridled defiance of expectations functions as a knife that ultimately cuts through all conceptual obstructions by leading to a spontaneous breakthrough to awakening.[29]

**Question of Dahui Burning the Collection.** There is no mention in the biography of Dahui or in any text by or about him from the period with the lone exception of the above-cited Xinwen passage that refers to his burning the *Blue Cliff Record* or making disparaging remarks toward Yuanwu for not using the keyword. We can only surmise whether he actually performed this deed, supposedly around 1140, when he was ensconced for a few years at a prestigious temple near the capital between tours of exile in the south, and speculate on some of the possible reasons. It should be acknowledged that this legend would likely not have persisted and spread if there were not a strong sense of reliability to the account given its resonance with Dahui's approach to interpreting gongan.

Lore suggests Dahui caused the incineration of the *Blue Cliff Record* in an era marked by a conscious withdrawal from the Northern Song's longstanding promotion of the elevation of literary pursuit that was, in turn, an antidote to Chinese society's previous emphasis on militarism. The stress on strong martial values rather than on cultural production had been blamed for causing centuries of chaos and conflict, but by the mid-twelfth century, literature was being charged with resulting in collective social stagnation. Idle aesthetic pursuit, it was felt, had led to the capture and death of the last Northern emperor, Huizong; the cession of territory; and the fall of the capital in Kaifeng to the Jurchen Jin, which occurred just at the time of the release of the *Blue Cliff Record* in the mid-1120s.

Claiming to be inspired by Yuanwu's mentor, Wuzu, who may have been enlightened through working on the "Wu" case with Baiyun, more so than by his own mentor, Dahui endorsed the minimalism of meditation based on the keyword technique that extracts a powerful catchphrase from the gongan. The reductionist approach to language emphasizing the transformative function of the sensation of doubt (*yiqing*) as a stepping-stone to the attainment of awakening is usually contrasted with the method of silent-illumination mainly supported Dahui's friend yet rival, Hongzhi, who was an ancestor of Dōgen, and his Dharma brother Qingliao (1088–1151). Dahui was vocal in his attacks, but these were not reciprocated in kind, either out of indifference to the debate or because a straw man of silent-illumination was fabricated. Yet Dahui's textual production was voluminous, which shows that he was also involved to some extent in literary pursuits.

As part of a response to larger social issues during an extended period in which he was exiled to the southeast region, Dahui was concerned that some of his lay and monastic followers were complaining that the *Blue Cliff Record* was too convoluted to be easily comprehended. He felt that their practice of studying the text provided evidence of failing to make much progress toward enlightenment. Dahui saw Yuanwu's work as a "complication" (*geteng*), a term that is often used in the *Blue Cliff Record* either in a positive sense to indicate powerfully expressive discursive devices or in a neutral way as a synonym for the term gongan, which Yuanwu was one of the first to promote. The debate between the standpoints of *huatou* (*watō* in Japanese pronunciation), emphasizing minimal expression, and *geteng* (*kattō*), emphasizing elaborate rhetoric—or of Watō versus Kattō, to highlight the conflicting views—is examined in detail in my recent book, *Like Cats and Dogs: Contesting the Mu Kōan in Zen Buddhism.*

What is the explanation for Dahui's radical action? One theory that diminishes the impact of what he may have done is that the *Blue Cliff Record* in its day, when publishing was still in its infancy in China, was not actually distributed widely beyond a limited readership of his and some other Chan followers.[30] Assuming that the collection did gain a popular following by the 1130s, could it be that Dahui exercised an "unruly temperament," as claimed by Wihelm Gundert, the German translator of the first nearly complete edition of the *Blue Cliff Record* produced in the West?[31] Robert Buswell amplifies this notion by suggesting that Dahui "vehemently lashed out" at the collection, and Juhn Ahn adds that he "launched a virulent attack."[32] Dahui was known as a strict and severe teacher, at times a hothead, since he did not suffer fools gladly when they were "spreading demonic theories."

Or was Dahui simply carrying out a necessary exercise in sectarian reform in the remarkable, but not for Chan so unusual, spirit of Huineng ripping and Deshan burning the sutras? According to Nyogen Senzaki's assessment as part of his remarks on case 89 of *The Iron Flute*, an Edo period gongan commentary with capping phrases and verse comments (C. *songgu*, J. *juko*):

> When Yüan-wu gave a lecture on Hsüeh-tou's selected kōans and poems, he criticized one phrase after another, then published them

all in book form under the title, *Pi-yen-chi*, or *Blue Rock Collection*. After his death, his disciple, Ta-hui, gathered all the publications together in front of the temple and made a bonfire of them. What the teacher builds in shape must be destroyed by the disciples in order to keep the teachings from becoming an empty shell. Western philosophers create their own theory, then followers continue to repair the outer structure until it no longer resembles the original. In Zen we say, "Kill Buddha and the patriarchs; only then can you give them eternal life."[33]

Nyogen embellishes the legend rather significantly with the image of a temple bonfire, which is not mentioned in classical sources.

## Stepping-Stone Thesis

Can we determine Yuanwu's true intention that was perhaps unrecognized at the time by him or others? Was he a supporter of lettered Chan far removed from what Dahui represented? Or could he be considered instead a forerunner consistent and subsumed by the outlook of his disciple, such that the latter's burning of the *Blue Cliff Record* was part of an ongoing process of contraction exercised in Song Chan textuality to which Yuanwu somehow contributed? In a reversal of Keyworth's understanding of the *Blue Cliff Record* as the epitome of a literary approach, Christoph Anderl argues that Yuanwu is "one of the most important precursors of [keyword] Chan" and further suggests that Yuanwu's unconscious leaning was to move away from an emphasis on rhetoric demonstrated by Xuedou. According to this reading, Yuanwu was mainly involved in setting the stage, even if unwittingly, for Dahui's shortcut technique since he had little use for verse as an end in itself because, as Anderl says, "[o]nly the enigmatic and often paradoxical statements seem to qualify as real 'live phrases.'"[34]

Following this line of thought, Ding-hwa Hsieh says that her research seeks to "give much more positive recognition to Yüan-wu K'o-ch'in, the master of Ta-hui Tsung-kao, in the evolution of the mature [keyword] Ch'an." She concludes, "A comparison of Yüan-wu and Ta-hui, moreover, shows that Yüan-wu ... failed to provide an effective solution of how one could succeed" in trying to "eliminate the mental tendency toward conceptualizing *kung-an*," since he "did not specifically mention the investigation of *hua-t'ou* in his teaching." Hsieh nevertheless argues, "Yüan-wu K'o-ch'in's teaching of *kung-an* practice thus marked a turning point in the evolution of Ch'an *kung-an* practice; the task of systematizing the [keyword] technique by giving 'doubt' a specific soteriological role had to wait for his disciple Ta-hui Tsung-kao," who "consistently taught his students to investigate the *hua-t'ou*," and thus "further succeeded in spreading [keyword] Ch'an to the important cultural centers of the Lower Yangtze Valley."[35]

From the perspective of Anderl and Hsieh, it seems that Yuanwu's main contribution lies in representing a necessary stage in the seemingly inexorable process of discursive abbreviation of various styles of voluminous Song Chan records. This extends from (1) brief encounter dialogues based on Tang interactions as included in transmission of the lamp records in the early eleventh century, to (2) gongan cases extracted from lengthier narratives as cited and commented on in the Fenyang and Xuedou collections a few decades later, to (3) pithy capping phrases appended to cases in the *Blue Cliff Record* in the early 1100s, and finally to (4) the keyword as the culmination of the trend toward contraction reached by Dahui by the middle of the twelfth century. Therefore Yuanwu's capping phrases that are cryptic and seemingly indecipherable should be understood not as an expansion of gongan discourse in a novel direction but, rather, as an emerging stage of reductionism through the shedding of rhetorical baggage in the development of the keyword technique; whether or not this would be acknowledged by Yuanwu (if given the hypothetical opportunity to comment) is up for debate since he also contributed introductions and lengthy remarks in prose.

However, even though the seminal Xinwen passage charges that the *Blue Cliff Record* surely got the treatment it deserved, this does not suggest that Yuanwu somehow anticipated or prepared Dahui for the eventuality or even that the keyword method is incipient in Yuanwu's commentary. The para-texts generally do not imply that Yuanwu was unconsciously following a path that would lead to Dahui; rather, their attitude is generally more in line with Keyworth's. But a classical precedent to the stepping-stone thesis appears in a section of Sanjiao Laoren's preface that exerted a strong influence on later interpretations.[36] Sanjiao compares three stages in the development of the tradition of encounter dialogues, leading up to and surpassing Yuanwu's approach as the implied second phase, with the respective tasks of public officials making different kinds of legal judgments. These responsibilities include the roles of:

1. "A local magistrate, who makes a determination about a crime and assigns punishment by not missing a single fact in his investigation to proffer a fair but firm assessment" 如老吏據獄讞罪.底裏悉見情款不遺; this indicates Tang dialogues as sources for gongan cases.

2. "A ranking officer, who carefully reviews a previously determined case and has the capacity to reverse or overturn the judgment, thereby saving a convicted criminal from death [by execution]" 如廷尉執法平反.出人於死; this suggests the poetic and prose comments promulgated in an evaluative approach that is contrary to conventional wisdom.

3. "An imperial official, who promulgates a set of laws so that people reading the regulations can know for themselves how to eradicate evil thoughts as soon as they arise" 如官府頒示條令.令人讀律知法.惡念才生.旋即寢滅; this refers to the keyword method that claims to be proactive rather than reactive.

As Steffen Döll points out, "The respective functions are associated with the examples of head officials, including state employees, criminal officers, and chief administrators. They exhibit an ascending hierarchical order that mirrors China's civil bureaucracy and occurs in respect to the soteriological as well as consecutive/logical order of functions."[37] According to Sanjiao's view of hierarchy the advantage of the third and final function connected with Dahui lies in promoting self-reliance in a way that anticipates and prevents problems based on ignorance and attachment before they occur. However this approach can also be seen as having the disadvantage of being removed and distant both historically and conceptually from the dynamic hands-on situation of the first function, in which the primary role of a master making an assessment while adjusting to circumstances takes place in an unmediated way. It also lacks the urgency of the second function marked by oral sermons delivered with the liberal use of the staff as a symbol of the master's insight and authority in recreating the sense of a live situation.

My appraisal is that Sanjiao's summary, which is rooted in Yuan dynasty Mongol-ruled society two centuries after the *Blue Cliff Record* lectures were compiled, places too much emphasis on bureaucratic occupations. It tends to overemphasize the element of legalist imagery of punishment for crimes, which is used occasionally in the collection as the key for an overall interpretation to the detriment of Yuanwu's primary focus on self-realization based on the ability to transform any and all situations by overturning misguided opinions. Sanjiao's passage stemming from an era during which Dahui's keyword method prevailed may also reflect subtle ideological biases that similarly affected (or, perhaps, infected), directly or indirectly, the views of Xinwen and Wan'an, who must be regarded as Dahui apologists.

**Comparing and Contrasting Rhetorical Approaches.** There are two main interconnected issues for assessing Yuanwu's thought in relation to Dahui's and the possible merits of the notion that the former represented a stepping-stone and/or a precursor to, rather than an opponent of, the keyword method. The first question is whether the treatment of gongan in the *Blue Cliff Record* and related Yuanwu texts shows evidence of foreshadowing the formation of the shortcut technique or, instead, constitutes a distinct approach. The second issue deals with the role of doubt in the spiritual experience of working though cases as seen from Yuanwu's perspective, and the extent to which this may have influenced or strongly resembled Dahui.

My preliminary response to these questions is that there are considerable indications in support of linkages so that the idea that Yuanwu anticipated Dahui, whether or not this was something he intended, is by no means an altogether unlikely inference. Both thinkers produced voluminous works that are of comparable content and quality. Their writings are filled with stories, anecdotes, inscriptions, instructions, poems, and correspondences to monks and layperson. As with Yuanwu and most other leaders from the era, Dahui's thirty-volume recorded sayings as edited by Yunwen (n.d.) in 1171 and presented to Emperor Xiaozong (r. 1163–1189) contains a broad selection of materials required by Chan rules manuals, including formal sermons, informal sermons, general talks for lay believers, and verse commentaries on gongan along with other kinds of poetry. Dahui's collection of letters 普說 (*pushou*) in four volumes of a separate text in addition to similar communications that fill five volumes (13–18) of his record resembles Yuanwu's *Essentials of Mind*. It seems that Dahui gained from his teacher a strong interest in ministering to non-monastics that only increased during his years in exile.

The two Chan teachers closely resemble one another in numerous aspects of their respective discursive styles. These include (1) a common use of shouts along with the waving or throwing down of the staff following a defiant or incongruous statement made to the assembly as a way of demonstratively concluding sermons with a sense of either triumph or disdain, so as to create a live atmosphere that recaptures some of the flavor of source dialogues; (2) a shared rhetorical flair for creatively twisting the ordinary construction of prose and poetic forms of expression in order to make a philosophical point about the experience of awakening; (3) an appreciation for classic masters including Wuzu, who is routinely praised by both teachers for his lucid approach to gongan cases, along with a rousing condemnation of imposters and pretenders because of their false views and misguided standpoints; (4) the shared notion that passing one gongan barrier resolves all others, although Yuanwu suggests this metaphorically while promoting diversity in terms of uncertainty whereas Dahui takes the proposition more literally in encouraging keyword practice based on a single case; and (5) an eagerness to pass judgment in evaluating cases as if filling out a scorecard, so to speak, to appraise the competitive game between Chan contestants.

In the final analysis, however, any suggestion that the mentor led to and was eclipsed by the disciple is overshadowed by contrary evidence demonstrating significant differences between the two thinkers. Yuanwu's *pingchang* approach, for which every possible perspective is potentially viable while none is considered fully reliable, is an example of what is known today as "divergent thinking" 分散思維 based on a freewheeling association of ideas evoking allusive variations of precedent expressions.[38] This outlook is not, in the end, in accord with Dahui's "convergent thinking" 收斂思維, which seeks a resolution for disparities among alternative options by honing in on particular catchphrases to the exclusion of other possibilities.

How different are their respective standpoints? The following passage from the *Essentials of Mind* is an example of Yuanwu's remarks that does seem to recall Dahui in attacking the pervasiveness of ideological and practical defects based on an overreliance on repeated clichés, memorized lists, concocted diagrams, standardized formulas, superficial slogans gained from handbooks, and other examples of rote learning and similarly deficient devices. These inappropriate techniques to which deficient followers resort out of spiritual despair or desperation, or exasperation, all represent the empty talk of blind fools and phonies that is in dire need of being identified and rooted out like a rapacious spreading weed:

> Teachings were often expressed through three mysteries, three essentials, four classifications, four levels of guest and host, the bejeweled sword of the Vajra King, a crouching lion, the shout that does not act as a shout, the probing pole and the reed shade, distinguishing guest and host in a single shout, or illumination and function occurring at the same time. Scholars who just bundle together their notes about all of these kinds of explanations can

hardly fathom that "there is no such sword in the royal storehouse." They look over their notebooks thoroughly, but all they can do with this is just blink their eyes. Surely they consider just the surface evidence to verify they are right, and then they find a skewed angle from which to project their misguided rationale.

是故示三玄三要四料簡四賓主金剛王寶劍踞地師子一喝不作一喝用.探竿影草一喝分賓主照用一時行.許多絡索.多少學家搏量注解.殊不知我王庫中無如是刀.及弄將出來看底只是眨眼.須是他上流契證驗認正按旁提.[39]

In a similar vein, as Juhn Ahn points out, Dahui rails against those who seek to investigate the meaning behind expressions and feel they can attain from a word or half a phrase some "special understanding," "mysterious and sublime understanding," or "secret understanding," which are in the end nothing but false transmissions.[40] Dahui's criticisms were motivated not so much by factional rivalry, Ahn argues, as by what he believed to be the lack of coherence among these miscellaneous inauthentic practices.[41] Many of Dahui's criticisms are included in a one-volume work known as *Chan Master Dahui's Arsenal* 大慧普覺禪師宗門武庫,[42] which was completed posthumously by Daoqian (n.d.) and includes a preface added in 1186 by Li Yong (n.d.). The main term in the title *Arsenal* 武庫 (*Wuku*) of a text containing comments and anecdotes taken from Dahui's talks to his disciples regarding various Chan masters of the past and then-present suggests a combative tone in that the teacher had ample ammunition to defeat his opponents. The weaponry was, of course, verbal or figurative yet highlights the fact that Dahui was associated with political hawks in questions about whether the empire should consider waging with war with the Jurchen Jin to the north.[43]

Despite some similarities, the following sermon from Dahui's recorded sayings is an intricate passage that can be contrasted with Yuanwu's rhetorical style. In particular there are crucial differences in his use of two prominent images for understanding the Chan path for overcoming ignorance to attain enlightenment: tangled vines, which represent a way of thinking about cases; and the double-edged sword, which symbolizes the role of language. Both metaphors are invariably negative for Dahui but are often evoked in positive ways by Yuanwu:

Having or not having [a reliance on] words is like vines clinging to a tree. If the right opportunity has not arrived then language will not be useful. Opportunity fosters language and language is suited to the opportunity. Do not throw sand into anyone's eyes and do not cast water into anyone's ears. There are those who, when hearing it expressed this way, will say, "Once you see the moon don't keep looking at the finger." They do not realize that even if they have at their disposal a ten thousand-mile long hook and a horse a thousand miles long, or if they cover the heavens with their net to catch the giant wave-beating Kun fish of fabled legend, they are like a toad or an earthworm or a blind turtle crawling. Their hook will be used in vain and their net will come up empty. It takes the right kind of person to understand the appropriate situation.

In that vein it has been said, "A killer naturally has a killer's dagger and a life-giving person naturally has a life-giving sword. If there were a killer's dagger and no life-giving sword, then no dead person would be able to live. If there were a life-giving sword and no killer's dagger, then no living person would be able to die. If a dead person can live and a living person can die, then you will be able to shave a turtle's hair or ride on the back of an iron cow and cut off a rabbit's horns beside a stone woman."

Do not get caught up with the strange and peculiar, and do not try to explain the mysterious and mystical. I dare ask all of you, If those who are called the "undead" and "nonliving" can exist, why kill and why bring to life? If these people can neither be killed nor brought to life, then the Dharma is without fulfillment. Even if someone could kill or bring to life, that would still not make him an adept. This kind of activity has nothing to do with the functions of a patch-robed monk. So I ask, What are the attributes of a patch-robed monk? (After a pause), All a monk has is a pair of hardworking hands. Never has a monk prostrated before a disengaged individual." There was much shouting.

示眾.有句無句如藤倚樹.機不到語不副.機副語語投機.眼裏著沙不得.耳裏著水不得.有般漢.聞恁麼道.便道.見月休觀指.不知垂萬里鉤.駐千里烏騅.布漫天網打衝浪鯤鯨.若是蝦蟆蚯蚓跛鱉盲龜.徒勞上鉤徒勞入網.須是恁麼人方知恁麼事.所以道.殺人自有殺人刀.活人自有活人劍.有殺人刀無活人劍.一切死人活不得.有活人劍無殺人刀.一切活人死不得.死得活人活得死人.便能刮龜毛於鐵牛背上.截兔角於石女腰邊.不作奇特商量.不作玄妙解會.敢問諸人.只如不死不活底人出來.且作麼生殺作麼生活.若殺不得活不得.佛法無靈

驗.直饒殺得活得.也未是作家.於衲僧分上了無交涉.且道衲僧有甚
麼長處.良久云. 雖有一雙窮相手.未曾低揖等閑人.喝一喝.[44]

Dahui evokes the image of vines in the negative sense of indicating entanglements that are hopelessly convoluted and counterproductive. He also
suggests that any talk of the relativity or complementarity of the killing
sword and life-giving sword as an example of Chan expression that is used
as a skillful means to reach an end must be condemned and rooted out like
a damaging weed because it leads to a sense of disengagement that fails to
promote awakening.

In contrast to Dahui's rhetorical outlook the *Blue Cliff Record*'s introductory comment to case 12 makes the point that the image of a double-
edged sword, which is conjured by Yuanwu dozens of times throughout
this collection and in many of his other works, does not represent a twisted
paradox propelling a trainee beyond the realm of discourse. Rather it fully
captures the notion that uncertainty is a perpetual condition that one lives
and continually reckons with before, during, and after enlightenment,
which constitutes an ongoing experience that necessitates the loss of conventional self-identity:

> There is a killing sword and a life-giving sword: this is the teaching
> style used by the ancestors that serves as the essential pivot for today
> as well. When you discuss killing it means that not a single hair is
> harmed and when you discuss giving life it means that your own
> selfhood is sacrificed. Therefore it is said, "The thousand sages have
> not transmitted the path above; students are fooled by appearances
> like monkeys grasping at reflections." But tell me, if it is the situ-
> ation that awakening cannot be transmitted why do we make use
> of so many entangled gongan? Those who possess the true eye can
> explain this by contemplating [the case].

> 垂示云.殺人刀活人劍.乃上古之風規.亦今時之樞要.若論殺也.不
> 傷一毫.若論活也.喪身失命.所以道.向上一路.千聖不傳.學者勞形
> .如猿捉影.且道.既是不傳.為什麼。卻有許多葛藤公案.具眼者.試
> 說看.[45]

The term for tangled vines or entanglements 葛藤 in the penulti-
mate sentence can also be translated as "complications," which modi-
fies the quality of the gongan as a literary device that triggers continual

contemplation, sometimes leading to truth and at other times to errancy that in a roundabout way finds its pathway to veracity. This term consists of two characters—one is the destructive vine known in English as "kudzu" as a loan word from the Japanese, which are a detriment to be discarded, and the other is the wisteria, which is redeemed by its beautiful flowers that are cultivated. This sense of the term recalls early Chinese Buddhist thinker Jizang's view that the aim of Buddhism is "deconstructing what is misleading and revealing what is corrective" 破邪顯正.[46] Yuanwu's ironic tone reflects an ambivalent and noncommittal approach toward both language and doubt that lacks—deliberately so, in my reading—the iconic sense of conclusiveness advocated by Dahui's shortcut method, which disdains both thinking and speaking altogether.

By viewing uncertainty as an attitude that is neither strictly positive nor strictly negative the prose commentary of the *Blue Cliff Record* takes a ludic and inconclusive approach to the role of language in relation to the power of doubt as a process of polishing expression without expecting a final resolution. This does not mean there is never a culminating point to Chan training—both Yuanwu and Dahui experienced intense breakthrough instances in the formative stages of their careers—but for Yuanwu, as with Japanese interpreters Dōgen from the Sōtō sect and Daitō (1282–1337) from the Rinzai sect (the latter wrote his own capping phrases on the *Blue Cliff Record* and related collections even though he did not have a chance to travel to China), eloquent rhetoric is likened to the life-giving sword.[47] Ongoing discourse is enhanced and perpetuated through sustained post-realization cultivation as evoked by Dōgen's view in the "*Gabyō*" fascicle that, "Only the picture of a rice-cake 画餅 satisfies hunger,"[48] an inversion of the original Chan saying implying that illusion must be terminated rather than transformed.

## *Precursor Status Thesis*

The hallmark of the precursor status thesis is that the dramatic shift from the *Blue Cliff Record* to the keyword method was intended by master and fulfilled by disciple. As Natasha Heller argues, Yuanwu "laid the groundwork for the *huatou* advocated by his student Dahui. . . . [and] rejects the recitation of a text as well as intellectual probing."[49] According to Robert Buswell, this transition was "the culmination of a long process of evolution in Chan whereby its subitist rhetoric came to be extended to pedagogy and finally to practice."[50] Also:

> Unfortunately the notoriety of Ta-hui's provocative action with regard to his teacher's writings has tended to obscure the revolutionary step made by Yüan-wu in the use of *kung-an*. Yüan-wu was apparently the first to teach that *kung-an* were not simply the dead records of an exchange between ancient Ch'an masters, and thus suitably the focus of literary endeavors. Rather, they should be used as if they were directly pointing to the mind of each and every individual—that is, as a statement of immediate, contemporary relevance guiding one toward enlightenment.[51]

While there is much merit in this view—I fully agree that both Yuanwu and Dahui in their respective ways sought to restore the atmosphere of a live situation to gongan commentary and training—a careful analysis of the rhetorical structures of their respective works for the most part shows a significant disparity between approaches. This gap should, in my assessment, be acknowledged and examined, and not be either exacerbated by highlighting Dahui's apparent destruction of the collection as confirmation that it lacked value or concealed through an effort to find undercurrent compatibility between masters based on the priority of the keyword method.

**Does Yuanwu Support the Keyword?** Some passages from the comments on case 12 do seem at first to support the notion that Yuanwu was an incipient keyword proponent, or a "key-phrase-ologist," but in the final analysis this claim is not substantiated. In apparent compatibility with Dahui's emphasis on minimalism, Yuanwu notes that "so many monks have misunderstood this case" 這箇公案.多少人錯會.[52] Following Xuedou's remarks that "To understand Dongshan in terms of presenting the matter corresponding to conditions at the time/ Is like a lame tortoise or a blind turtle entering an empty valley" 展事投機見洞山. 跛鱉盲龜入空谷,[53] Yuanwu maintains that gongan cases must not be misunderstood as intellectual endeavors or construed for what is contained in words alone.

Xuedou's verse further suggests that the "good response" 善應 from Dongshan came out like a golden crow 金烏急 (symbolizing the sun) swooping by or a jade hare 玉兔速 (the moon) bounding along, that is, spontaneously and swiftly without preparation, reflection, or hesitation. To this Yuanwu caps, "Like a bell rung when struck or a valley resounding with an echo" 如鐘在扣.如谷受響.[54] But he also maintains that the case is misinterpreted:

> It really is hard to chew on, since there is no place for you to sink your teeth into because it is bland and flavorless. The ancients had many answers to the question, "What is Buddha?," such as "The one in the shrine," "The thirty-two auspicious marks," and, "A bamboo rod on a mountain forest of staffs." In contrast to these Dongshan said, "Three pounds of flax." He could not be stopped from cutting off the tongues of the ancients.
>
> 直是難咬嚼.無爾下口處.何故淡而無味.古人有多少答佛話.或云.殿裏底.或云.三十二相.或云.杖林山下竹筋鞭.及至洞山.卻道麻三斤.不妨截斷古人舌頭.[55]

Yuanwu proclaims the superiority of Dongshan's expression because it does not attempt to answer the question either with a direct reference to the qualities of Buddha, as in the first two responses, or with indirect imagery, as in the third example.

The rest of the commentary revolves around identifying various misapprehensions of the case, as Yuanwu delineates four kinds of wrong views that if followed to the end would cause the Chan school to disappear:[56]

> Literalism: "Many people base their understanding on the words uttered and say that Dongshan was in the storehouse at the time weighing out flax when the monk questioned him, and that is why he answered in this way." 人多作話會道.洞山是時在庫下.秤麻.有僧問.所以如此答.
>
> Contrariness: "Some say that when Dongshan is asked about the east, he answers about the west." 有底道.洞山問東答西.
>
> Misdirection: "Some say that since you are Buddha and yet you still go ahead and ask about Buddha, Dongshan answers this in a meandering way." 有底道.爾是佛.更去問佛.所以洞山遶路答之.
>
> Realism: "There are those dead people who have a way of saying that the three pounds of flax is itself Buddha." 死漢更有一般道.只這麻三斤便是佛.

According to Yuanwu, "These interpretations are all irrelevant. If you seek this way from Dongshan's words you can search until the Future Buddha Maitreya is born on earth and still never see it even in a dream." 且得沒交涉.爾若恁麼去洞山句下尋討.參到彌勒佛下生.也未夢見在.[57] After rejecting the series of common misconceptions, Yuanwu continues by evoking a Zhuangzi-like view of the discardable quality of the tool of language since:

> Words and speech are just vessels to convey the way. Far from realizing the intent of old masters people today just search amid words, but what can be gained from this? An adept said, "Originally the path is wordless; with words we illustrate the path. Once you see the path, the words are immediately forgotten." To get to this point you must go back to your own original state. Just this "three pounds of flax" is like the single track of the great road leading to [the ancient capital of] Chang'an. As you raise your feet and put them down there is nothing that is not this path. This case is generally like the story of Yunmen's "Cake" 餬餅 [case 77], which is also unavoidably difficult to understand.

> 何故言語只是載道之器.殊不知古人意.只管去句中求.有什麼巴鼻 .不見古人道.道本無言.因言顯道.見道即忘言.若到這裏.還我第一 機來始得.只這麻三斤.一似長安大路一條相似.舉足下足.無有不是 .這箇話.與雲門餬餅話.是一般.不妨難會.[58]

If we stopped reading there, then the approach taken by Yuanwu might appear quite similar to the keyword method in favoring concentration on a critical slogan dislodged altogether from any conceptual background, although here and elsewhere he prefers the term "turning word of old masters" 古人答一轉語 to *huatou*.[59] The dismissal of misunderstandings generated by excess verbiage is reminiscent of Dahui, but Yuanwu also has a very positive estimation of verses by both Wuzu and Xuedou, whom he says exhibit "thoroughly penetrating insight" 雪竇見得透.[60] An important example appears in Yuanwu's capping phrases for the main dialogue. Of Dongshan he writes, "Clearly his straw sandals are worn thin as he points to a pagoda tree while accusing a willow tree of being the basis for measurement." 灼然.破草鞋.指槐樹罵柳樹.為秤鎚.[61] The key factor in this passage is the way Yuanwu defends divergence by evoking the image of measurement, so that an understanding of the case necessarily involves association and allusion.

In the prose section Yuanwu says, "Dongshan does not reply lightly to this monk. . . . Great or small, he responds accordingly, never daring to make a careless impression." 洞山不輕酬這僧. . . . 大小隨應.不敢輕觸.[62] The emphasis on the efficacy of literary expositions apropos to the moment constitutes a significant departure from Dahui. Yuanwu then cites "a verse from my late teacher Wuzu," which reads, "The cheap-selling board-carrying fellow,/[63] Weighs out three pounds of flax./ With a hundred thousand years' worth of unsold goods,/ He has no place to put it all." 五祖先師頌云賤賣擔板漢.貼秤麻三斤.千百年滯貨.無處著渾身.[64] This verse, he says, can "do away with your defiled feelings and thoughts, or judgments based on gain and loss, and when these are completely purified once and for all you will spontaneously understand." 爾但打疊得情塵意想.計較得失是非.一時淨盡自然會去.[65]

Moreover Yuanwu particularly exalts Xuedou's verse comments evoking his teacher Zhimen's cryptic naturalist remarks on Dongshan's saying, including "Flowery groves, clusters of brocade" 花簇簇錦簇簇 and "Bamboo trees in the south, hardwood trees in the north" 南地竹兮北地木. To these Yuanwu caps, "That's putting a head above a head" 頭上安頭.[66] More positively Yuanwu maintains, "All at once Xuedou spilled his guts by presenting them to you." 雪竇一時.突出心肝五臟.呈似爾諸人了也.[67] If it were not for Xuedou's literary endeavor, "the whole school of Bodhidharma would be wiped off the face of the earth" 達磨一宗掃地而盡.[68] Yuanwu then cites an anonymous Chan verse and a second verse by Xuedou while maintaining that "Xuedou is someone who has transcended worldly attachments . . . Xuedou easily goes to where the barriers are broken and the hinges are smashed in order to reveal a small teaching that enables you to see." 雪竇是出陰界底人 . . . 雪竇輕輕去敲關擊節處.略露些子教爾見.[69] Furthermore Xuedou is able "to smash the feelings and opinions" 破人情見[70] of those who persist in lingering over "delusion" 迷 by insisting on finding hidden symbolism in three pounds of flax, which is a way of thinking that only Xuedou's verse seeks to overcome.

Finally, in assessing Xuedou's eight-line verse that ends after referring to an obscure historical anecdote about whether it is more productive to laugh or cry with the provocative exclamation, "Ha!" 咦, Yuanwu remarks that "just the first three lines are sufficient for understanding the whole poem" 若論他頌.只頭上三句.一時頌了: "I ask you, since the whole realm is nothing other than three pounds of flax, why does Xuedou still express so many entanglements? It is just because his compassion is excessive that he is like this." 我且問爾.都盧只是箇麻三斤.雪竇卻有許多葛藤.只是慈悲忒殺.所以如此.[71] For Yuanwu, it is Xuedou's fear of possible misunderstandings on the part of the reader that causes him to get down in the weeds of discrimination to compose verse comments that are uplifting and effective in overcoming misconceptions.

Yuanwu's affirmative view of Xuedou's poetry is further supported by Tenkei Denson's interlinear comments composed six centuries later in Edo period Japan that praises the verse to case 12, "This brings out the great meaning of the koan. Everyone, open your eyes and look!" In regard to the "Ha!" appearing at the end of this ode, Tenkei writes avidly of the reversals and inversions that are commonly found in Xuedou's poems as a means of dismissing any tendency to take matters too seriously in a way that would cause an attachment to the form rather than intent of discourse: "Setcho [Xuedou] implies that his lengthy discussion is also laughable; he has turned the whole verse around and thrown it over onto the Other Side. Other Side? What 'Other Side'? Other Side of what? Try to find your nose! This is a living wave of Setcho's river of Zen."[72] In light of Tenkei's comments along with other examples in the *Blue Cliff Record*, it is probably not surprising that Yuanwu caps Xuedou's final expression of his poem with the deliberately disingenuous critique, "Bah! What is this? I strike!" 咄是什麼.便打.[73]

In contrast to Yuanwu's approach, a short verse in Dahui's record highlights the keyword aspect of the utterance by saying, "Dongshan's 'Three pounds of flax.' How can fool's gold be compared with the real thing?/ ... The ancestral teacher's saying is like a well-placed lancet/ Causing a dragon to flail violently in a basin of water./ Or like threading fine hair through the eye of a needle./ Everyone who strives has some gain and some loss/ But by counting up words while neglecting intimacy/ They fail to see a goose amid the clouds." 洞山麻三斤.真金不博金.頌祖師投針話龍猛盂中水.提婆毳上針.人人爭得失.箇箇話疏親.不睹雲中鴈.[74] The images of the acupuncture lancet and the sewing needle, along with the overall criticism of words, drive home the point that "Three pounds of flax" is beyond conceptualization or discursive reasoning.

A remark on Dongshan's saying that is included as case 52 of the prose commentary section of Yuanwu's recorded sayings also does not indicate a keyword orientation. This passage opens with images of reflection-response in the first two sentences that recall Yuanwu's comments on case 12 about immediacy, while the third sentence may remind us of Dahui. But the remarks in the last two sentences emphasize that any and all expressions supporting divergent rhetorical directions can ultimately lead to realization if they do not miss the mark:

The bell rings in the valley and the moon is reflected in water like a mirror holding an image. You should not approach a situation in terms of anticipating an opportunity; why would you scratch before feeling an itch? Iron turns to gold in an instant when one favors the straight and forgoes the bent. A single shot of an arrow kills two birds and a single slap to the ear draws a pool of blood in the hand. You people do not realize that when the vast heavenly net is cast wide and far it does not miss any catch.

僧問洞山.如何是佛.山云.麻三斤.鐘在扣谷受響.池印月鏡含像.曾非展事投機.豈是預搔待痒.點鐵成金舉直措枉.一箭-鵰一雙.一摑血一掌.君不見疏而不漏兮恢恢天網.⁷⁵

As a bit of additional evidence that during the Song dynasty the keyword method was not monolithically accepted as the only way of viewing Dongshan's utterance, I cite here several short verse comments contained in the *Jeweled Compendium of Chan Verse Comments* (*Chan Songgu Lianzhu Tongji*) that was reprinted in 1392. While not necessarily stellar examples of poetry, these are primarily notable for leaning more to the side of Yuanwu's allusive style of thinking, although they are characteristically ambiguous enough to defy easy interpretation:

To a question about Buddha he says, "Three pounds of flax."/ Austere monks are wary of tea left out over night./ After the Cold Food festival in springtime,/ Raucous winter crows are calling out among the ancient trees. (By Haiyin Xin). 問佛三斤麻.齋僧怕夜茶.春來寒食後. 古木噪寒鴉. (海印信).⁷⁶

It is obvious that weights and measures do not mislead people,/ So do not let the pupils of your eyes glare with anger./ Thirty-six thousand days occur over a hundred years./ When times are joyful then rejoice! (By Baiyun [Shou]duan) 斤兩分明不負君.眼中瞳子莫生瞋.百年三萬六千日.得忻忻處且忻忻. (白雲端).⁷⁷

Venerable Dongshan does not neglect knowledge./ By answering a question about the Buddha Dharma with "Three pounds of flax."/ As nothing is gained from the surface of your answer, people get upset./ But for those who gain insight the saying has verily contributed to killing people['s ignorance]. (By Miaofeng Shan). 洞山老勿疏親.答佛法麻三斤.無面目得人憎.見得徹賺殺人. (妙峰善).⁷⁸

**What About Doubt?** In what may seem similar to Dahui's emphasis on the role of doubt, Yuanwu sometimes cites his teacher Wuzu's saying, "Not doubting words and phrases is your great ailment" 不疑語句.是為大病, and in the commentary on case 12's verse he notes that "Xuedou's grand-motherly kindness necessitates that he smash your sensation of doubt" 雪竇老婆心切.要破爾疑情.[79] The notion of doubt has a rich history in Chan as used in the record of Linji; other Tang sources; and by post-Dahui thinkers in China, such as Dufeng (c. 1400–1480),[80] Boshan (1575–1630), and Weilin (1615–1702);[81] among many others in Korea and Japan as well. Furthermore Neo-Confucian thinkers in the twelfth century, such as Zhu Xi, emphasized the importance of doubt in cultivating spiritual awakening. But there are naturally different shades of meaning for the notion, so it is important to look beyond superficial similarities to avoid conflating the various standpoints.

One contention I dispute is that the approach of Yuanwu, who is said by a supporter of the thesis that he anticipated Dahui by casting doubt "as the primary obstacle that Ch'an practitioners should make an effort to overcome,"[82] approximates yet falls short of his disciple's focus such that "the task of ... giving 'doubt' a specific soteriological role had to wait for his disciple Ta-hui Tsung-kao."[83] This evaluation appears to judge Yuanwu by the standard of the presupposed superiority of Dahui's approach. It is misleading to believe that Yuanwu intends but does not quite achieve an emphasis on experiencing doubt as representative of an unproductive dead-end that, when taken to its logical conclusion, triggers awakening. That contention seems to miss the valuable quality of the rhetoric of uncertainty, which explores multiple perspectives while clinging to none. The contrast is that Dahui views doubt as a kind of iconic experience that leads to a single breakthrough, whereas Yuanwu sees it as an ironic pivot or turning point in an ongoing constructive engagement with the tangled vines (C. *geteng*, J. *kattō*) of language that provisionally yet renewably lead to transcendence.

For Dahui the experience of doubt forces an awareness that a gongan is basically unintelligible and cannot be thought about or understood rationally, no matter how hard one tries. This fosters bewilderment, anxiety, consternation, and the desperation of feeling that there is no exit or possibility for return to conventional thinking. Doubt usefully creates the impression that "someone's head is on fire" or "a rat is trapped in a corner" to force an advance to a new level of understanding. In a couple of prominent cases (5 and 46) in *Wumen's Barrier*, Shishuang's "Leaping from a

100-foot pole" 百尺竿頭進步 demands that one demonstrate his true self and Xiangyan's "Man up a tree" 人上樹 highlights that one who hangs over a precipice will lose his life if he answers an impossible question or his integrity if he does not. Dahui also uses the analogy of wrongly naming or not naming a bamboo comb as an example of intensifying the sensation of doubt to its breaking point:

> Calling this a bamboo comb creates friction and not calling this a bamboo comb is defiance. Not expressing through words and not expressing without words; not expressing through thinking and not expressing through speculating; not expressing by getting up and walking away: Everything is left unexpressed. If you want to snatch the bamboo comb I will let you go ahead and snatch it. . . . An elder from Zhoufeng remarked, "Somebody read the monk's bamboo comb story and said it was like they had confiscated all his property and yet asked for more possessions." What a wonderful metaphor this is! When you have nothing left and nowhere to go, you will simply have to die. In throwing yourself into a river or jumping into fire, once you have given up life you will be ready to die. Only after you have died will you gradually begin to come back to life again.

> 喚作竹篦則觸.不喚作竹篦則背.不得下語.不得無語.不得思量.不得卜度.不得拂袖便行.一切總不得.爾便奪卻竹篦.我一且許爾奪卻....有箇舟峰長老云.某看和尚竹篦子話.如籍沒卻人家財產了.更要人納物事.妙喜曰.爾譬喻得極妙.我真箇要爾納物事.爾無從所出.便須討死路去也.或投河赴火.云得命方始死.得死了卻緩緩地再活起來.[84]

As indicated by the death-and-resurrection imagery of this passage, which recalls Yuanwu's severe illness before his awakening and a Chan saying about "bringing horses back from the dead" and Dahui's frequent references to the "great death" 大死 (*dasi*), doubt represents a supreme opportunity to encounter frustration productively. An instant of symbolic demise is, to cite another of Dahui's favored analogies, like a snowflake that melts immediately coming into contact with a red-hot stove. Through this experience Dahui advocates what is commonly referred to in Chan/Zen circles today by the Japanese term *kenshō* 見性 (*jianxing*) or *satori*, or spontaneously "seeing into one's true nature" in a way that kills off all afflictions and attachments. This instantaneous breakthrough is also evoked in *Wumen's Barrier* by a brief prose comment on case 8, in which Yangqi stream predecessor Yue'an hypothetically deconstructs the structure of a cart. Wumen remarks, "If anyone can directly clarify this topic, his eye will be like a shooting star and his activity like a flash of lightning." 若也直下明得眼.似流星機如掣電.[85]

The result of a productive use of doubt is reinforced in the following letter that Dahui composed in responding to lay disciple Lu, who apparently inquired about the significance of distrusting language:

A thousand doubts or ten thousand doubts after all are just one doubt. If doubt is shattered on the basis of the keyword then a thousand doubts or ten thousand doubts are shattered all at once, but the keyword is not shattered . . . If you abandon the keyword, doubt will arise whenever you pick up any other discourse [words and letters]. Doubt will arise on the basis of the scriptures, doubt will arise on the basis of the gongan of masters, and doubt will arise amid all worldly worries and cares (Skt. *klesa*).

千疑萬疑.只是一疑.話頭上疑破.則千疑萬疑一時破.話頭不破...
若棄了話頭.卻去別文字上起疑.經教上起疑.古人公案上起疑.日用
塵勞中起[86]

Doubt for Dahui is positive yet dangerous, with great potential for stirring awakening but when misunderstood it may lead to destructive results as with the Chan malady.

Yuanwu also emphasizes the productive effect of being dazed and confused by the rhetorical context one is surrounded by and reflecting on. Yet he sees doubt functioning in an even more exacerbated sense than Dahui as an ongoing process of reckoning with uncertainty. For Yuanwu doubt is a means of realizing the frustration and futility of discourse. But instead of leading to an ultimate sense of despair and desperation, doubt leads one to circle back and reexplore the multifarious possibilities for expressing the Dharma. Therefore, to recast gongan metaphors, all situations of leaping and dangling are fulfilled by constructive engagement with uncertainty.

For example in a capping phrase on the first line of Xuedou's verse comment on case 21, "Zhimen's lotus flower, lotus leaves" 智門蓮花荷葉, Yuanwu writes in sardonic fashion that Xuedou wanted simply but generously to expose the truth of the paradoxical case, "The granny is eager to see the gongan resolved because the splendor of the text is obvious" 老婆心切.見成公案.文彩已彰.[87] Following this remark Xuedou says in the last two lines of the verse, "Is it north of the river or south of the river, you can ask the old king/ Someone with suspicion [the doubt of a fox] is suspicious of another who holds suspicion." 江北江南問王老/ 一狐疑了一狐疑. [88] Yuanwu comments with a capping phrase, "Even if you try to bury [doubt] in a foxhole, of course you are still going to have doubt. You can't avoid having the sensation of doubt as soon as you draw a breath. Having struck [someone in the assembly] I ask, 'Do you understand?'" 一坑埋卻.自是爾疑.不免疑情未息.打云.會麼.[89]

Yuanwu concludes the prose commentary on case 21 by demanding that those who know only doubt in infinite regress will never be able to extricate themselves from doubting in a way that could be seen as the antithesis of Dahui's emphasis on heightening doubt. According to Yuanwu, "You are like wild foxes who are full of doubt while walking over thin ice on a river. Listening for the sound of water you think if there is no sound it must be safe to cross the river. But how will those with the doubt of a fox ever be able to leave it behind to attain peace?" 如野狐多疑.冰凌上行.以聽水聲.若不鳴方可過河.參學人若一狐疑了一狐疑.幾時得平穩去.[90]

## *Further Reflections on Yuanwu in his Own Write*

Ideological discrepancies and linkages between Yuanwu, his predecessor, Xuedou, and his successor, Dahui, have been examined in terms of the intellectual historical context of the transition from the height of literati influences on the Chan school in the Northern Song to the period of competition for lay followers with Buddhist and non-Buddhist religious movements that accompanied an antiliterary outlook of the Southern Song. The *Blue Cliff Record* comes right in between these two historical arcs as it was published at the time of the culmination of the first trend and the onset of the following one. It may seem that Yuanwu has one foot in each camp, and that is why there is a rather bewildering set of views seeing him variably as supporting or refuting each of the preceding and succeeding standpoints: Yuanwu considers Xuedou as either a doting granny or precious provocateur, and probably would estimate Dahui's ultimate act of destruction in a range stretching from utter disbelief to at least partial relief.

Where does Yuanwu stand in relation to Dahui and between his connections with Xuedou at the beginning of the gongan tradition and Wumen at the end of the initial arc of composing poetic-prose commentaries on cases? My conclusion regarding Yuanwu's position is threefold in encompassing shifting and contended literary, textual, and ideological perspectives. First, Yuanwu's complex and nuanced approach vis-à-vis both Xuedou and Dahui, each of whom is a complicated figure difficult to categorize neatly, should not be seen in black-and-white terms as being for or against any particular viewpoint in that there are multiple gradations in these ideological relationships that need to be analyzed as fully as possible. Here is a list of possible interpretations suggesting how Yuanwu can be regarded in relation to predecessor and successor, which I mention inconclusively:

- Fully supports Xuedou's verse and adds interlinear comments as another "granny."
- Begins to move away from Xuedou through his prose commentary.
- Cautions against "indulging . . . in writing elusive poetry or elegant prose."
- Takes a critical stance that helps set in motion Dahui's approach.
- Is ultimately a precursor much more consistent with Dahui than not.
- Remains eclipsed by Dahui's shortcut standpoint.
- Gives way to the approach in *Wumen's Barrier*, which expresses "true" Chan poetry.[91]

Second, Yuanwu seems to strive for and, in my estimation, is able to strike a distinctive middle ground regarding the benefits and pitfalls of Chan rhetoric. His standpoint resists being pigeonholed based on sectarian biases or presumptive opinions often derived from subsequent appropriators of the Song giants that tend to infuse contemporary scholar-practitioner interpretative stances with a leaning toward either supporting or refuting a sense of polarity while overlooking other areas of linkage and disjuncture. From my perspective Yuanwu precedes and surely helps shape but does not necessarily represent a precursor to Dahui's views in the sense that he would have been a supporter of the keyword method. Whereas Dahui proffers a prescriptive approach mainly for lay followers to participate in the gongan-introspection style of meditation, the emphasis of commentary in the *Blue Cliff Record* is on instructing monastic disciples regarding the multiple levels of meaning embedded in cases selected by Xuedou,[92]

Therefore the approach of the *Blue Cliff Record* needs to be understood in the context of other kinds of compendia and commentaries on gongan, each of which expresses a different outlook:

- Authoritative, in *qingqui* 清規 (monastic rules) texts that provide regulations without cases.
- Informative, in *chuandeng lu* 傳燈錄 (transmission of the lamp) and *yulu* 語錄 (recorded sayings) compilations that include encounter dialogues.
- Instructive, in various formal 上堂 and informal 示眾 or 小參 sermons that use cases.
- Ruminative, in *songgu* 頌古 (verse) and *niangu* 拈古 (prose) comments based on the notion of entanglements 葛藤.
- Prescriptive, in *huatou* 話頭 as expressed in general talks 普說 or letters 書 answering queries of lay disciples.

In this list I place Yuanwu's primary approach in the ruminative category in that the tangled vines of conceptualization are cast aside but only after being worked through based ratiocination. The term *geteng/kattō* 葛藤 has a long and rich history in Chinese letters, as the image of the kudzu 葛 was also long evoked in poetry and cultural lore to suggest fertility because of its seeds and the "ties that bind," in that the fiber was used to make sandals for wedding ceremonies and came to imply postnuptial conjugal relations in addition to the new entwinements of the bride with her in-laws.[93]

Despite these positive associations, in Song literary criticism, *geteng* did function as a negative designation suggesting a mistrust of language as unclear or muddy, or a clouded and troubled mind lost in delusion and despair because of hankering after shadows and apparitions and a failure to see reality as it is. Dahui uses the term in the critical sense of suggesting the futility of trying to weed out destructive tendrils, and the term also appears that way in some secular treatises on poetry criticism 詩話 (*shihua*) by referring to verse encumbered with words and letters that become obstacles blocking, rather than vehicles breaking through, the crutch of expression to attain freedom from conceptualization. While promoting tangled vines, Yuanwu over and over again issues a caveat emptor to the effect that rhetoric may at any time degenerate into formulaic cliché or lead to bickering about deluded views.

The third element of my conclusion is that there remains, after all is said and done, much common ground linking Yuanwu with Dahui in that they tend to see language as a poison to counteract poison or delusion to bury delusion. For both, it is crucial to keep challenging assumptions and upending a reliance on conventions so that rhetoric functions as an antidote to the arrogance, impatience, naivety, and superficiality of the quotidian life of established cultural norms. Both masters do not want a trainee to resort to the object-less realm of no-mind 無心 (wuxin), which is a false state of quietude that actually creates the nervous tension and anxiety of profound underlying disquiet concealed by a lack of attentiveness.

Furthermore, the thinkers agree in emphasizing that a single moment of awakening, which provides clear evidence 證 (zheng) of insight into that which is not readily revealed, is coterminous with a multiplicity of awakenings, as expressed by Yuanwu's comments on case 21:

> When someone asked about the time or season the old masters at once gave a question or a reply that was so timely and attuned that it put to rest all concerns. Pursuing words and following after phrases is not relevant. If in the midst of words you can penetrate through words and in the midst of meaning you can penetrate through meaning, or if in the midst of an encounter you can penetrate through the encounter and can let go and let yourself live freely—only then will you be able to understand Zhimen's answer in this dialogue.

何處有伊問時節也.古人一問一答.應時應節無許多事.爾若尋言逐句.了無交涉.爾若能言中透得言.意中透得意.機中透得機.放令閑閑地.方見智門答話處.[94]

As George Keyworth notes, irrespective of discrepancies between them, "Without the erudition of Chan masters like Fenyang, Xuedou, Yuanwu Keqin, Dahui Zonggao, later generations of Chinese, Korean, and Japanese Chan, Seon, and Zen masters would not have known their forefathers' sometimes impious, yet always pithy, sayings and actions from which to extract Chan meditation practices."[95] Their approaches, whether seemingly scholastic or minimalistic, recall the immortal inunction of Zhuangzi regarding language and awakening: "Nets are employed to catch fish; but when the fish are caught the nets are forgotten. Traps are set to catch hares, but when the hares are caught the traps are forgotten. Words are employed to convey ideas; but when the ideas are expressed the words are forgotten. I wish to meet someone who has forgotten words, so that I might have a word with this person!" 荃者所以在魚.得魚而忘荃.蹄者所以在兔.得兔而忘蹄.言者所以在意.得意而忘言.吾安得忘言之人而與之言哉.

As a final comment on the comparison, it seems the role of irony is not distinctive to the *Blue Cliff Record*, in which the rhetorical outlook remains ever playful and resists getting pinned down to one particular viewpoint while demanding that the reader meet the challenge, as it is also found to a great extent throughout *Wumen's Barrier*. How about Dahui? John Wu argues that Dahui "gave an excellent exposition of Chuang Tsu's idea that Tao is not only beyond speech but beyond silence as well [in that] there is silence in speech, speech in silence; there is action in inaction, inaction in action." But he also says in a Chan-style putdown, "He is like a singer whose voice is high-pitched and loud; but one feels that it comes from the throat rather than the diaphragm."[96] Despite his apparent lack of irony in many passages, we must not sell short Dahui's own considerable rhetorical skills, as in the use of parallelism, metaphor, and imperative in the bamboo comb passage cited above.

Yuanwu's outlook is unique and distinctive from that of both predecessors and successors, and he should not be either conflated with or eclipsed by other thinkers. At the same time, I believe that regardless of Song Chan masters' differences there is an underlying consistency based on a basic notion that is succinctly conveyed by case 178 of the *Entangling Vines Collection*. In this terse exposition an ancient worthy says, "Buddha's teaching is expressed through the power of reason, but Bodhidharma's intention is expressed through devices 機 (*ji*) that break through barriers 關 (*guan*)" 古德曰.佛教説理致.祖意説機關.[97] In other words pre-Chan Buddhist ideas consisted primarily of doctrines articulated in terms of logical principles that could be argued and debated. However Chan gongan, no matter how they may be interpreted or applied, disclose meaning in a way that stands beyond yet remains embedded in words through the use of expedient measures such as "Three pounds of flax," which remove barriers at strategic checkpoints leading to an unimpeded experience of enlightenment.

As Musō Sōseki points out in *Dialogues in a Dream (Muchū Mondō)*, "The policy [of using devices] was to 'watch the wind and set the sails accordingly.'"[98] He also notes that "students who prefer teaching through principle tend to demean teaching through devices, and those who prefer teaching through devices tend to demean teaching through principle." In contrast to that false division Musō suggests, "A kōan is simply a skillful means (*upaya*); if one imposes interpretations upon the different expressions of this skillful means, one obscures what the masters are truly attempting to convey. ... When a clear-eyed master expresses a teaching, it is impossible to define it either as 'teaching through principle' or 'teaching through devices.'"[99]

The comprehensive outlook Musō endorses can be further applied to bridging supposed gaps between the rhetorical style of Yuanwu, who is critical of all tactics yet committed to none, and the method of Dahui, who came to expound among manifold possible interpretations just one technique, or so some of his followers claim. Disputes between these and other thinkers need to be seen in light of connections fundamental to all teachers of Chan devices, even as an awareness of such linkages should not be allowed to overshadow clear areas of difference or discrepancy between approaches. Let this be food for further thought!

# 5

# *Sharpening a Sword*

CASE STUDIES OF REPRESENTATIVE GONGAN

## *Diversity and Divergency*

To set the stage for case studies of representative gongan it is important to take into account the textual and theoretical context of Chan lineages and their assorted approaches at the time of the composition of the *Blue Cliff Record*. Chan rhetoric of uncertainty is greatly enhanced in that the gongan featured with explanations in the *Blue Cliff Record* are wide-ranging in thematic content and rhetorical structure because so many different topics and mindsets are included. The cases are also rich in literary quality based on the use of assorted interpretative genres and styles at once building on and playing off one on another to disrupt and dislocate the audience's fixed views through the use of irony, paradox, and misdirection.

Yuanwu completed his initial studies of the *One Hundred Odes* while training under mentor Wuzu at the turn of the twelfth century with just a couple of decades left in the rule of the controversial last Northern Song emperor, Huizong. Yuanwu quickly came into his own as an interpreter who had the confidence and wherewithal to offer original remarks in an ongoing series of oral sermons covering the entirety of Xuedou's text. This process was soon fulfilled during the period from 1111 to 1112 while Yuanwu resided at Mount Jiashan, although he continued to revise his talks over an extended period prior to final compilation and publication.

By the time he delivered the first lectures that were collected by enthusiastic disciples, Yuanwu was no doubt well aware of the seemingly unlimited array of encounter dialogues featuring diverse kinds of pedagogical devices attributed to so many different schools and their masters.[1] In almost each and every instance any given gongan was presented with a slight or perhaps more than minor twist or discrepancy reflecting how a certain technique might be construed or applied by appropriators. Variability in interpretation was an essential component of the originality of Chan thought but could become confusing. How Yuanwu dealt with the complexity of materials and outlooks is key to understanding the development of the *Blue Cliff Record*'s *pingchang*-based approach to making comments on cases. Evaluative remarks show that Yuanwu responded to diversity by flexibly surveying and celebrating while also critically analyzing and assessing an exploding variance of ideological views and pedagogical procedures developed by numerous Northern Song Chan lineages. His primary aim was to avoid having highly personalized remarks fall prey to endless factional disputation and discord.

Yuanwu's multilevel method combines formative elements in highlighting sectarian variations with a reformative approach that ingeniously revises or invents new uses for traditional terminology and symbols in order to promote a transformative mission of awakening learners from dogmatic slumber to explore intricate gongan as the pathway to attaining an experience of enlightenment. His prose and capping-phrase remarks seek to justify diverse teachings and techniques while at the same time dismissing intellectual views, including those of luminaries such as Yunmen and Xuedou when they rely on clichés and stereotypes. Yuanwu says repeatedly—and his peers agree—that all Chan exercises are essentially devoid of meaning in themselves but function instead as a skillful tool grounded in genuine self-realization to gain credibility or otherwise be discarded as unnecessary baggage. By avoiding succumbing to a conforming slant that might reduce all gongan to a single line of interpretation, Yuanwu embarks on the deconstructive or reformative task of undermining and overturning any and all misguided standpoints.

The main advantage of divergent thinking evident in Yuanwu's approach to the gongan commentarial tradition is the seemingly illimitable variation of aims and perspectives that are examined from nearly every possible angle through enigmatic and often idiosyncratic assessments of the significance of Chan exchanges and verses about them. Without clinging to any tenet or method, Yuanwu took up one ancient encounter dialogue after another and turned them into a "samadhi of self-fulfilling enjoyment" 自受用三昧 (*zishouyong sanmei*).[2] However, Yuanwu's outlook implicitly acknowledges a disadvantage embedded in discursive divergence in that, as valuable as an attitude based on noncommittal adaptability is for inspiring trainees to extricate from one-sided positions to break out and breathe the fresh alpine air of spiritual freedom, to evoke a Nietzschean saying, the ambiguity and indecision inherent in this open-ended experience also leads to significant challenges threatening to derail its efficacy.

The sheer multiplicity of cases and comments reflecting long-lost denominational schisms, which were increasingly fostered during the eleventh and twelfth centuries by the initial widespread distribution of texts due to advances then being made in publishing in China, caused the interpretation of a vast array of gongan perspectives to be baffling and bewildering. The proliferation of manuscripts produced by various compilers and editors, appearing in different versions that sometimes included printing discrepancies or errors, articulated distinctive teaching styles as part of widespread competition among miscellaneous schools. While this led to a creative expansion and ongoing reinvigoration of Chan discourse, the degree of instability engendered could also be obstructive because of the lack of standardization or regularity.[3]

Diversity among the Five Houses of Chan was probably first recognized and examined with some degree of concern in regard to shortcomings based on the deficiencies of many then-current teachers by Fayan Wenyi in his tenth century text *Ten Normative Treatises on the Chan School* 宗門十規論 (*Zongmen Shiguilun*). Both Fenyang and Xuedou in the eleventh century reacted by creating an even greater extent of variety through composing replacement answers 代語 (*daiyu*) or alternate answers 別語 (*bieyu*) for gongan, in addition to odes 頌古 (*songgu*) and prose remarks 拈古 (*niangu*). In the early twelfth century, Yuanwu tried to provide some consistency without effacing diversity through expansive evaluative comments filled with contradiction and irony. Coming a generation (and, in an important sense, an era) later, Dahui placed much more emphasis on uniformity through initiating the keyword method. Nearly a century after Dahui, Wumen compiled a gongan collection that gave voice to concise keyword-oriented verse and prose comments.

A hundred years after that, Zhongfeng was disturbed by flaws in the system since he found that many Chan masters of his day frequently taught gongan "contained in the various Ch'an texts as if these were primers used in elementary schools. This was, of course, counterproductive, for the very purpose of these *kung-an* was to force one not to use one's intellect to understand them," so in response he "did not regard even the most famous *hua-t'ou* as sacrosanct."[4] For example when Zhaozhou answered, "Cypress tree standing in the courtyard,"

Zhongfeng said that there was no deeper significance behind the cypress tree; Zhaozhou could just as easily answered "water flows leisurely in the creek" or "peach blossoms are red on the hill."[5] This indicates that the interpretation of gongan has not been, and probably never should become, a settled matter, even though efforts to squelch relativism sometimes result in a kind of dogmatism that intrudes into the interpretative process.

To cite one among seemingly countless examples of how hermeneutic vagueness rooted in the principle of uncertainty regarding gongan evaluation can appear to reflect a perplexing inconclusiveness, let us consider back-to-back cases contained in Yuanwu's *Record of Keeping the Beat* commentary on Xuedou's prose remarks that highlight responses to a monk's query, "What can be expressed completely in just one word?" 一言道盡時如何.[6] Noting that the sequence in this collection seems out of chronological order in that Muzhou was Yunmen's teacher and thus likely spoke first, case 53 indicates that Yunmen says, "Ripped apart!" 裂破, to which Yuanwu caps, "What's that?" 道什麼. Then Xuedou comments not through speaking but by "[s]napping his fingers three times" 雪竇彈指三下, and Yuanwu caps, "This came only after words of explanation" 也是隨語生解. In case 54 of the same text, Muzhou replies, "I am found in the pouch of a begging bowl" 老僧在你鉢囊裏, and Yuanwu caps, "It's a double case" 兩重公案. Xuedou comments again with a gesture by interjecting, "Laughing out loud, Ha! Ha!" 雪竇呵呵大笑, and Yuanwu caps with, "Compare that!" 猶較些子.[7]

What is the relation between the distinct replies proffered by Yunmen and Muzhou along with Xuedou's nonverbal reactions? To make matters even more complicated, Yuanwu's prose remarks defy the reader to neither conflate nor separate the answers of the core dialogue while trying to comprehend intuitively Xuedou's state of mind:

> Muzhou always used an ability to answer like a lightning bolt.... Tell me, Was this the same as or different from Yunmen's answer? If you say different, then the Buddha Dharma will be of two kinds; but if you say the same, then why are there two answers since there is only one question? You must penetrate to where there is no doubt and then you will be able to see thoroughly.... When Xuedou "laughed out loud, 'Ha, Ha!,'" what was the reason behind this? Try to discern it.

睦州尋常機如掣電...且道與雲門答處.是同是.若道是別.
佛法有兩般.若道是同.為什麼問處則一.答處兩般.須是透
到無疑處方見徹...雪竇呵呵大笑.是什麼道理.試辨看.[8]

For a small glimpse of the extent to which the gongan tradition
has encouraged divergent thinking to proliferate with additional
layers of complexity, we can consider briefly Dōgen's interpretation of these cases that are included in vol. 2.133 of his *Extensive
Record* of sermons delivered in Chinese (*kanbun*) in the Dharma
hall at Eiheiji temple (then known as Daibutsuji). Here the order
of responses begins with Muzhou's words while Yunmen's reply
is changed to, "Ripped apart from long ago until now!" 裂破古今.
According to the record, rather than trying to explain what any of
this means since that might result in a sense that logic prevails,
"Dōgen throws his fly-whisk down on the ground while saying,
'Great assembly, do you understand this fully? If you do not understand then it is regrettable that I even bothered with this fly-whisk.'"
擲下拂子階前便云.大眾還会麼.若也未会.可惜許.一柄拂子.[9]

A similar example of inconclusiveness is found in the verse to case
31 in the *Blue Cliff Record*, in which Xuedou deliberately contradicts
himself in back-to-back lines, "Each and every gate has a path that is
empty and desolate/ No, it is not desolate" 門門有路空蕭索.非蕭索.
Yuanwu's capping phrase states, "Fortunately [Xuedou] has a place to
turn around" 賴有轉身處, but nevertheless, "I strike" 便打.[10] The final
line of the poem suggests, "An adept seeks a remedy even if he has
no illness" 作者好求無病藥. However this part of the verse can also
be read as, "The adept seeks but there is no medicine for his disease,"
or more emphatically, "The enlightened man must take medicine for
the illness of 'having no illness.'"[11] Since everyone including the awakened suffers from some sort of ailment, if the adept considers himself immune then such a belief in itself constitutes a form of disease.
Gongan interpretation seeks to avoid the futility of "hanging a medicine bag on the back of a hearse" 喪車背後懸藥袋,[12] which is a state
similar to "pulling the bow after the thief has fled" or "falling into
secondary status" 落在第二.

Another example of seemingly unresolvable ambiguity is in the *Record
of Linji*, in which the master reacts to the unconventional behavior of a trick-
ster figure known as Puhua 普化 (literally, "Universal Transfiguration"),

showing that a single ambiguous word or phrase can lead to nearly opposite conclusions about the whole passage. The text covers the exploits of
the prototypical ninth-century leader but can perhaps be considered a
Song Chan composition because it was first included as a section of the
*Tiansheng Transmission of the Lamp Record* (*Tiansheng Guangdenglu*) of 1036
and was not published as an independent work until 1120, just a few years
prior to the publication of the *Blue Cliff Record*.[13] Linji had a mixed assessment ranging from acceptance and admiration to exhaustion and exasperation with Puhua, who joined his assembly for a while yet frequently tried
to one-up the master before passing away in mysterious fashion:

> One time Puhua was going around the streets of the town ring-
> ing a little bell while calling out, "When there is brightness I strike
> the brightness; when there is darkness I strike the darkness; when
> there are four quarters and eight directions I strike like a whirl-
> wind; and when there is vast sky I strike like a wheelhouse." Linji
> told his attendant to go and, as soon as he heard Puhua say those
> words grab him and ask, "When nothing at all happens then what?"
> Puhua pushed the attendant aside while saying, "Tomorrow there
> will be a great feast at Dabei cloister [a small temple in the city]. The
> attendant returned and told this to the master who said, "I've always
> had to wonder about that fellow."

> 因普化.常於街市搖鈴云.明頭來.明頭打.暗頭來.暗頭打.四方八面
> 來.旋風打.虛空來.連架打.師令侍者去.纔見如是道.便把住云.總不
> 與麼來時如何.普化托開云.來日大悲院裏有齋.侍者回.舉似師.師
> 云.我從來疑著這漢.[14]

The phrase 疑著 in the final sentence is taken to mean that Linji "had
my doubts or suspicions," thus indicating a modest extent of disapproval
or at least wariness. But it could also suggest the opposite according to
some translations in which Linji "held wonder for" or "was in awe of" the
controversial Puhua.

As Juhn Ahn astutely observes, Song Chan was characterized by a "cri-
sis of authority in reading and learning"[15] because, despite the fact that
voluminous textual sources and interpretative resources were available as
never before due to mass printing, diversity and divergence did not lead
to either a unifying ideological vision or an overarching pedagogical standard. A sense of coherence that could bridge apparently incommensurable

or conflicting viewpoints, some of which may have gained an endorsement from reigning emperors or influential men at court, was simply not generated by the fragmented and dispersed Chan institution, thus "opening a door for sheer arbitrariness or irresponsibility."[16]

Gongan functioned at the forefront of contestation in that they "were, indeed, used as emblems of factional identity and style"[17] so that, as Juefan once regretted, "a hair's breadth of differentiation" could lead one view to be labeled authentic while a plausible alternative was dismissed as a "crazy" 狂 or "wild fox" 野狐 interpretation. As *Wumen's Barrier* remarks in the verse on case 21, "In a blink of the eye the opportune moment is lost forever" 貶得眼巳蹉過.[18] The stakes were incredibly high, yet no altogether convincing explanation could or would be given for judgments made.

Meanwhile the bane of single-flavored, tunnel-vision-based thinking on the part of stubborn fools and incorrigible phonies, who failed to realize their limitations, went hopelessly uncorrected. There was no other recourse than delivering "thirty blows of the stick" 三十棒 for faux disciples who out of ignorance fell back on stale formulas, indecipherable diagrams, memorized lists, recited ditties, or other examples of rote learning carefully catalogued into neat typologies while they frantically tried to fake their way through contested spiritual barriers. The blows were unfortunately also richly deserved by deceptive teachers who, based on arrogance, feigned that they were unconcerned and above the fray in evoking ordinary, everyday reality just-as-it-is 平事禪 (*pingshi Chan*) as a rationale for taking a laissez-faire stance. Therefore flogging, whether literal or more likely figurative, was fitting punishment for hopeless pretenders who gave away their deficient status by "having jowls big enough that they could be seen from behind" 腦後見腮.[19] This is like the comment in the verse to case 6 of *Wumen's Barrier*, "He makes the bad look good, as if holding up the head of a sheep but selling the meat of a dog" 壓良爲賤.懸羊頭賣狗肉.[20]

The sayings of Linji, who is usually depicted in paintings with an intimidating scowl and is known for instructing disciples to "kill the Buddha," contains some of the harshest condemnation of misfits, including "students, who come from every quarter to try in a host-and-guest context to test the teacher's understanding with a single phrase, or presumptuous disciples, who pick out some clever words to challenge [the master's] authority" 如諸方有學人來.主客相見了.便有一句子語.辨前頭善知識.被學人拈出箇機權語路.[21] Teachers are also scathingly criticized when they trot out a trivial and worthless "bag of tricks" 境塊子, including "a series of actions, such as raising a whisk, holding up a stick or shouting, or gestures such as snapping the fingers or winking the eye, to test the student's ability to distinguish the sham from the real,"[22] which is exactly what they themselves are incapable of fathoming. In many instances the disciples know better yet keep up the pretense in order to sustain the illusion of temple hierarchy, while in other examples the learners are an embarrassment but the teacher holds onto them just to preserve his paltry group of followers.

On the other hand, in case 34 Yuanwu remarks ironically that to have true awareness beyond conceptualization, it takes acting "like a simpleton to understand the gongan lest you chase aimlessly after words with no end in sight" 如癡似兀.方見此公案.若不到這田地.只在語言中走.有甚了日.[23] However, the commentary on this case, in which Yunmen pronounces that the dialogue held by Yangshan Huiji (813–890) and a monk shows "they had a conversation in the weeds" 有落草之談,[24] also mentions several examples of meaningful nonawareness. Xuedou eulogizes the poet Hanshan (9th c.), who "forgot his way home" 忘卻來時道 after ten years of travel, and Yuanwu cites a stone grotto worker 石室行者, who was so pure that he declined an invitation from Emperor Suzong (r. 756–762) and so aloof that "he forgot the movement of his feet when he was treading the pestle" 每踏碓忘移步.[25]

**Swords and Songs.** The largely unforgiving approach reflected in the *Record of Linji* could be summed up by the phrases, "When I dislike I strike," and "When in doubt I shout" (the latter could also be "I shout to incite doubt"),[26] and Yuanwu frequently mentions these methods as well. But he combines an emphasis on advancing and holding firm through scolding and controlling disciples with the opposite view of letting go or releasing them to demonstrate compassion. According to the pointer to case 85 both extremes can be appropriate attitudes based on the particular circumstances involved in teaching: "To touch iron and turn it into gold or to touch gold and turn it into iron, to suddenly capture and to suddenly discharge—that is the staff of a patch-robed monk." 點鐵成金.點金成鐵.忽擒忽縱.是衲僧拄杖子.[27] Ultimately the trainee must seize the day by taking responsibility for his own quest. The issue becomes, what does it take to get disciples to be able to reach the stage of self-determination?

Xuedou and Yuanwu put forth a studied uncertainty about their respective (and collective) evaluative enterprises. Xuedou's odes vary from using a style of indulging his readers to one of chastening them, and Yuanwu adopts the same twofold attitude in interpreting the odes as a way of seeking a balanced approach that establishes an antiauthoritative form of instruction so followers can decide for themselves. To cite the image of the double-edged blade, or "sword that kills and gives life" 殺人刀活人,[28] which appears in seven cases including 12, 15, 16, 31, 34, 54, and 60 (with images of wielding a sword used dozens of times in all),[29] whatever is true from one perspective may, or perhaps must, be reversed or inverted based on different levels of perception.

In other words vinegar and honey are used equally and evenhandedly but selectively as incentives for training in order to create a sense of moderation, a situational outlook with which Linji and other masters concur. The *Blue Cliff Record* preface by Fanghui Wanli from 1300 refers to the "grandmotherly kindness" 老婆心切 of both Xuedou and Yuanwu along with that of Zhanghui Mingyuan who, he says, "revived dead ashes by reprinting the text" 燃死灰復板行.[30] Yuanwu appreciates kindheartedness when it is needed as reflected in a teacher's willingness in case 34 "to get down in the weeds" 入草求人 by addressing a disciple at a level only he can understand, so long as this does not lead to an indulgent spoonfeeding approach. On the harsher side, Yuanwu admires an adept's "ability to capture tigers and rhinos while distinguishing dragons from snakes, or between the underbelly and limbs" 有擒虎兕定龍蛇底手腳,[31] but this approach must not degenerate into an excessively demanding authoritarian position.

Generally a sword is evoked as the main image of the harsher or more challenging and imposing side of a teacher-student relationship, which is often compared to that of lord and vassal; it requires a sharp blade of incitement to provide proper instruction. The image of singing reflects the flexible or more responsive and nimble side evident among adepts, who maintain collegial associations as peers seeking to harmonize their respective thoughts.

In case 7 Yuanwu remarks that to be qualified as a master, "You must be the kind of person who does not turn his head even when flogged repeatedly with a stick, and has teeth like sharp swords that are as big as a tree with a mouth full of blood" 除非是一棒打不回頭底漢.牙如劍樹.口似血盆.[32] In reversing a traditional Buddhist idiom about nonviolence, Yuanwu says, "Only with the ability to kill a man without blinking an eye can one become Buddha right where he stands" 有殺人不眨眼底手腳.方可立地成佛.[33] Similarly in his *Arsenal* Dahui writes, "Wuzu treated people like he had a blade wrapped in cloth. If you stumbled across him he stabbed you in the throat and killed you. What about [Wuzu's teacher] Zhenjing Kewen (1025–1102)? If [the blade] touched the leg then he killed you on the leg, if it touched the hand then he killed you on the hand, and if it touched the throat then he killed you on the throat." 五祖為人.如綿裹一柄刀相似.纔 挨著便將咽喉.一刺刺殺爾去也.若是真淨.腳上著也即腳上殺爾.手上著 也即手上殺爾.咽喉上著也即咽喉上殺爾.[34]

In commenting on the verse to case 38, in which Linji schoolmaster Fengxue (896–973), while giving a talk at a prefectural government head-quarters where he received the governor's approval, responds with strikes and a shout to questions raised by an elder named Lupi, Yuanwu remarks, "In Fengxue's one phrase [about the "iron ox" 鐵牛, which today means "tractor"] he is immediately equipped with the spear and armor of the three mysteries [propagated by Linji]; with seven accouterments at his side it is not easy to oppose him." 風穴一句中.便具三玄戈甲.七事隨身.不輕酬他.[35] Furthermore, Yuanwu says that "Xuedou's verse on this case seeks to bring out the active edge 機鋒 of the Linji line" 後面雪竇要出臨濟下機鋒,[36] by evoking the fanciful image of great waves billowing in waters near a mythical castle to highlight that "just a single shout was all that [Fengxue] needed to cause the breakers to reverse 倒 their course" 只消一喝.也須教 倒流.[37]

Yet Yuanwu makes clear that a sword is used both for killing and giv-ing life, so that even in causing death an element of compassion is dis-closed. According to Urs App's analysis of Yunmen, who served as the main role model for Xuedou and Yuanwu, "Though Yunmen's provoca-tions are often as sharp, precisely aimed, and deadly threatening as a razor blade set against one's throat, permitting no movement whatsoever, they are by no means meant to discourage the student. On the contrary, by unsettling and shocking the student, by calling his very self into ques-tion"[38] this approach exposes the trainee's spiritual dilemma that is based on self-imposed inability and destabilizes this condition so he can let go of conceptual fixations.

Yuanwu appreciates that "Xuedou's odes are like the jewel sword of the Diamond King striking all at once" 雪竇頌古.偏能如此.當頭以金剛王寶劍. 揮一下了 by saying something provocative or outrageous. He also argues, "Xuedou follows up with a more moderated tone. But, despite any appar-ent discrepancy, ultimately there are not two different understandings." 雖 然如此.畢竟無有二解.[39] The constrained tone used by Xuedou is mainly symbolized by images associated with music, such as singing or playing an instrument, which highlights the rhythmic harmony and melodic tune-fulness linking adepts. Chan masters use this technique inventively to merge with the tempo set by a predecessor, but the skill also allows them to freely adapt or change the rhythm either as reproach or simply to create a new effect for a different audience. This is part of the time-honored East Asian tradition that considers emulating, while at the same time surpassing, to be the highest compliment paid a forerunner.

Yuanwu's two major works interpreting Xuedou's gongan comments highlight the musical metaphor. The term *pingchang* 評唱 used in the *Blue Cliff Record*, which refers to the rearranging of Chan teachings in a literary critical style, indicates comments that are made by singing alternately with a colleague whether he or she is present at the time. This was a popular way of disseminating scholarly and religious viewpoints during the Northern Song when performance halls proliferated which featured edifying entertainers who utilized the *pingchang* method as key to their discourse.[40] Also the term *jijie* 擊節 in the title of *Record of Keeping the Beat* is related to the phrase *jijie tanshang* 擊節嘆賞, which suggests showing appreciation while listening to the recitation of a poem or a piece of music by marking time to the cadence with one's hand as on a seat or counter.

Commenting on the verse to case 39, Yuanwu says, "Xuedou sizes up the audience to create his rhythm by making the lute strings vibrate while plucking out the tune. With each and every phrase he enunciates a judgment. What an ode expresses is no different from what is conveyed through various sorts of prose (*niangu*) commentary." 雪竇相席打令.動絃別曲.一句一句判將去.此一頌.不異拈古之格.[41] In remarks on case 92 about a mythical sermon involving the World Honored One and Manjusri, Yuanwu's introduction says of an adept's ability, "One who can discern the tune as soon as the lute strings move is hard to find even in a thousand years" 動絃別曲.千載難逢,[42] and he adds, "Beating the drum, playing the harp, two masters meet each other in familial harmony" 打鼓弄琵琶.相逢兩會家.[43] The ode for case 37 includes lines that praise the musical quality of nature, "The flowing stream makes a lute,/ One tune after another but nobody understands" 流泉作琴.一曲兩曲無人會, to which Yuanwu caps, "Hear it? ... All the tones and meters are completely clear" 聞麼 ... 五音六律盡分明.[44]

In case 22 Yuanwu analogously cites a verse by Zhenjing, who was known for his criticism along with Wuzu's of passive or annihilationist views of meditative training known as "unconcerned Chan" 無事禪

(*wushi Chan*).[45] This gongan involves a dialogue between Xuefeng and Changqing about the fearful turtle-nosed snake that seems to be misunderstood by Xuansha but is later settled by Yunmen when he throws down his staff and makes a gesture of fright as if it were a serpent. Zhenjing's ode, which ends by favoring Xuansha, opens with the lines, "Beating the drum, strumming the lute,/ Two men of understanding meet,/ And Yunmen is able to harmonize,/ But Changqing is misguided/ So the ancient tune does not rhyme." 打鼓弄琵琶.相逢兩會家.雲門能唱和.長慶解隨邪.古曲無音韻.[46] In an ironic example of musical imagery Yuanwu's prose remarks on case 27 asks whether Yunmen "responded [as a superior] to a monk's question, or was instead harmonizing [as a peer] with him" 且道雲門為復是答他話.為復是與他酬唱,[47] and then says that either view of the master's cryptic saying causes one to "plunge into a ghost cave" 依舊打入鬼窟裏去.[48]

To cite a couple of other examples of the use of musical metaphors, during the Northern Song the Caodong school, as derived from a passage in the record of founder Dongshan, was associated with a phrase evoking improvisation as a symbol for Chan insight, "Drumming and singing arise together" 敲唱双拳 (J. 敲唱双び拳ぐ).[49] This saying refers to a mysteriously subtle communion between teacher and disciple based on the unmediated activity of inquiry and response, or calling out and receiving a spontaneous reply. In addition two Sōtō monks compiled one of the major kōan collections of Edo era Japan known as *The Iron Flute Played Upside Down* 鐵笛倒吹 (*Tetteki Tōsui*).[50] The incongruous title, which is based on a saying derived from various Song sources, consists of two paradoxical compounds linked together: *tetteki*, which indicates an "iron flute" that like the stringless lute, another Chan symbol borrowed from poet Tao Yuanming (365–427), cannot actually be played because there is neither mouthpiece nor finger holes; and *tōsui*, which further highlights contradiction by indicating that the flute is "blown on upside down."[51]

In the preface to the translation of this text from 1939, making it probably the first example of a traditional kōan collection rendered almost completely into English with comments added, Senzaki Nyogen 千崎如幻 (1876–1958) cites a verse by Xuedou called "For a Monk Playing Harp" 贈琴僧, which I have modified to read: "A great aged, clear sound is coming from your fingertips,/ As the moon hovers above the pines and the night grows cold on the veranda./ The melancholy melody makes many a listener weep./ Don't play anymore unless a soundless sound is conjured." 太古清音發指端.月當松頂夜堂寒.悲風流水多嗚咽.不聽希聲不用彈.[52]

As Senzaki points out, this verse most likely evokes a passage from chapter 41 of Laozi's *The Way and Its Power* (*Daodejing*), "The greatest square has no corners,/ The greatest talents ripen late,/ The greatest music has no sound,/ The greatest images have no form./ The Dao is hidden and without name,/ Yet it is only the Dao that nourishes and completes all things." 大方無隅.大器晚成.大音希聲.大象無形.道隱無名.夫唯道,善貸且成. Therefore Senzaki's citation of Xuedou suggests that the iron flute, like one hand clapping, refers to a muted expression that is unbound by established notions of melody and tone, yet in reflecting the standpoint of self-realized awareness it can and must be conveyed eloquently by using rhetorical conventions borrowed in part from musicality.

## Chan Themes and Schemes

Yuanwu says he yearned mightily for the idealized era of the early Tang masters whose teaching style he says was pure and unsullied as it existed prior to discrepancies caused by Chan factions branching off in so many different directions. According to the commentary to case 25:

> After attaining the path the old masters dwelled in thatched huts or stone grottos where they ate the roots of wild greens boiled in broken legged pots while passing the days. Never seeking fame and fortune they were without pretense but in accord with circumstances. They would impart a turning word out of gratitude for the benevolence of Buddhas and ancestors in order to transmit the Buddhist mind seal.
>
> 古人既得道之後.茅茨石室中.折腳鐺兒內.煮野菜根喫過日.且不求名利.放曠隨緣.垂一轉語.且要報佛祖恩.傳佛心印.[53]

In those times it was said that adepts generally resisted or refused to have their words recorded, so that disciples would have to eavesdrop from under a chair or while hidden somewhere in the room to write the expressions down surreptitiously.

Eventually recorded sayings and related compositions were compiled, edited, and often given prefaces by famed literati in addition to monks who were usually skillful poets. During the Song dynasty some of these newly published texts featured a proliferation of cryptic formulas without providing much explanation. The *Record of Linji* includes "three statements" 三句, "three mysteries" 三玄門, "three essentials" 三要, "four shouts" 四喝, "four propositions" 四料, "fourfold relations of guest and host" 四賓主, and more. Dongshan's record was known for "three roads," "three kinds of fall," and "five positions of lord and vassal." No doubt it was not the intention of the masters to have their teachings reduced to named designations.

As the first to compose odes along with prose remarks on cases, Fenyang included in his poetry intricate references to some of the other teaching formulas, especially the five positions. Xuedou eschewed this approach and was better versed in the use of literary images and rhymes than Fenyang. Xuedou did not evoke specific Chan principles but preferred to use cultural allusions and metaphors. Probably the main reason that Yuanwu's Dharma brother Foyan was said to teach by telling stories rather than examining cases was that he tried to avoid delving into the obscurities of variant methods. Yuanwu sought to capture a sense of the original consensus that connected Chan lineages in the golden age of the Tang—or was retrospectively imagined to—while acknowledging diversification but for the most part without rancor or discord.

Yuanwu says, "Chan gongan from past to present are extremely diverse like a forest full of thickets" 自古及今.公案萬別千差.如荊棘林相似.[54] Trying to insist on consistency between factional teaching methods is a less important criterion to use in making gongan evaluations than highlighting and appreciating the particular strengths and areas of integrity of each approach. In a friendly rivalry in case 51 between Xuefeng (822–908) and his Dharma brother Yantou (828–887), who were then both under the tutelage of the dynamic leader Deshan (782–865), Yantou appears to prevail in the contest and Yuanwu writes, "If you can penetrate this case then no one on earth can harm you and all the Buddhas of past, present, and future will salute you. But if you cannot penetrate it you must learn to heed Yantou's saying, 'Xuefeng was born in the same lineage as me but he did not die in the same lineage,' since in a single sentence an abrupt turnaround is spontaneously expressed." 爾若透得去.天下人不奈何.三世諸佛.立在下風.爾若透不得.巖頭道.雪峰雖與我同條生.不與我同條死.只這一句自然有出身處.[55] The key to the power of Yantou's expression is the way he at once links to and distances himself from his colleague.

The problem with claims of uniformity is further indicated in case 16, which deals with Jingqing's use of the symbol for the process of awakening through the image of a mother hen pecking to break into a shell as the baby chick taps to break out. This represents a process of mutuality and simultaneity known in Japanese pronunciation as *sottaku dōji* 啐啄同時, which is sometimes compared to adepts clashing swords so as not to harm but to enhance and reinforce one another's positions in the match. Yuanwu says in a cap to the verse in case 31, "East, West, South, and North all have the same family style" 東西南北一等家風,[56] but Xuedou opens the ode to 16 with, "Ancient Buddhas each had their own family ways" 古佛有家風, to which Yuanwu caps, "Don't slander dear old Sakyamuni" 莫謗釋迦老子好.[57] In the next line Xuedou suggests that for Jingqing, who is asked by a monk to break in the shell but ends by calling the trainee a "man in the brambles" 也是草裹漢, "the initial reaction to receiving praise comes to denunciation" 對揚遭貶剝.[58] Yuanwu remarks, "Xuedou's first line contains the whole verse" 雪竇一句頌了也, but adds that with the second line, "Xuedou shows deep knowledge of the case so he is able to complete the verse in just the first two lines. After that he too gets down in the weeds to explain things more clearly for [those who still do not understand]." 雪竇深知此事.所以只向兩句下.頌了.末後只是落草為.爾注破.[59]

In case 11 involving a dialogue between Mazu and Baizhang, Yuanwu emphasizes the particularity of insight as developed and transmitted in a lineal context by remarking, "You must see for yourself how father and son act in that house before you begin to understand." 須是親見他家父子行履處始得.[60] Similarly in case 64, the second half of the cat gongan in which Zhaozhou places his sandals on his head when told by Nanquan of his killing of the feline to stop monks from quarreling, which is the topic of case 63, "The masters are singing and clapping together but just a few know this tune so they add error upon error." 唱拍相隨.知音者少.將錯就錯.[61] Furthermore Yuanwu remarks that as an example of "the turnaround of old masters" 古人轉處,[62] "Father and son meet each other and harmonize the edges of their blades, so that when Nanquan raises the head Zhaozhou immediately understands the tail." 他父子相投.機鋒相合.那箇舉頭.他便會尾[63] Appreciating the relationship between Nanquan and Zhaozhou does not require that one should abandon his or her own lineal position; on the contrary, "You must bring forth your own family treasure and only through that perspective will you see the great function of [Zhaozhou's] total capacity." 須是運出自己家珍.方見他全機大用.[64]

Since for Yuanwu the goal of gongan studies is to gain liberation from any and all fixed standpoints, but without necessarily rejecting the efficacy that specific techniques demonstrate, a major part of his mission is to put in context and evaluate the complexity of the remarkable degree of diversity he encountered. Disparity is viewed from the multiperspectival outlook of cultivating divergent thinking that reflects the notion of uncertainty, whereby all standpoints are explored without bias or attachment but none is accepted as fully satisfactory.

Very much related to this aim is a more basic effort made by Yuanwu to keep his audience abreast of various theories, events, personages, and activities that are helpful in making sense of each case by fostering an openness to manifold hermeneutic angles. As highly as the *Blue Cliff Record* is regarded as an interpretative masterpiece, it is also an important and resourceful reference work that, like the *Lexicon of the Ancestral Garden* compiled by Muan just a few years before, contributes to the process of collecting a wide variety of materials related to the sources, symbols, and themes of cases and the interlocutors of the source dialogues in light of their background in training and predilections for practice. Yet, unlike Muan, Yuanwu is much more than a categorizer of inventory regarding principles and symbols since his inventive spirit relentlessly assesses and creates novel forms of commentarial expression that keep a steady focus on addressing each gongan, not for the sake of intellectual clarification or historical explanation but as a vehicle to attain enlightenment.

In examining how Xuedou and Yuanwu reacted to diversity and disparity within Chan, the remaining sections of this chapter look briefly at examples of three commentarial components used to construct the rhetoric of uncertainty in the *Blue Cliff Record*:

1. A foundational level, in which interpretative remarks play an informative role by presenting key aspects of each of the Chan lineages while critically examining without preference or detraction the formative elements of their pedagogical methods.

2. A transitional level, which is reformative in exploring the multivalent quality of words to disrupt and overturn stale or stereotypical interpretations through a reinvention or inversion of conventional meanings, and also has a performative dimension that brings out the expressivity of nonverbal gestures.

3. A transcendent level, which is transformative by highlighting opportune moments of strategic pivoting as demonstrated by adepts in dialogues; and deconstructive or deformative, by promoting a self-realized approach to the attainment of awakening while avoiding the pitfalls of relativism.

## *Foundation: Formative and Informative Elements*

Many Song masters were sometimes disturbed by and critical of their counterparts yet, for the sake of perpetuating the potentially fragmented Chan school, they generally cultivated an ecumenical and favorable outlook embracing ideological diversity. With no apparent ax to grind they sought means of coexistence, cooperation, and harmony rather than competition with rival standpoints. In addition to Fayan's *Ten Normative Treatises on the Chan School*, a few other important works showcasing the variety of lineages included *Genealogies of the Five Houses* 五家宗派 (*Wujia Zongpai*) by Tanying 曇穎 (989–1060) and *Record of the Forest Groves* 範林間錄 (*Linjianlu*) by Juefan from 1107, both of which were highly influential on Yuanwu. Also *Eyes of Humans and Gods* 人天眼目 (*Rentian Yanmu*) by Huiyan Zhizhao 晦巖智昭 (n.d.) from 1188 includes Yuanwu's writings among many other Chan representatives. As these and related texts show, by the eleventh century the Guiyang school died out while the Fayan and Yunmen schools were on the rise but then rather quickly faded, even as their founders remained inspiring prototypes because of the ongoing publication and circulation of their records. The Linji school gained strength in the twelfth century and then split into the Yangqi and Huanglong factions, which tended to compete with the revived Caodong school in a contestation that somewhat affected Yuanwu and was exacerbated by Dahui.

**Informative Elements.** According to a summary of the various lineages by Fayan, who does not depict his own school's approach, Caodong takes "drumming and singing as function," Linji features "reciprocation as its technique," Yunmen involves "covering and cutting off the streams," and Guiyang uses "squares and circles as silent expressions."[65] Fayan maintains that the founders of the schools were genuinely free from rancor, but their descendants turned teaching devices and contrivances into a means of bolstering their own traditions, thereby creating conflicts with adversaries and causes for mutual attack. He reminds his readers, "The great Dao is without directions and the currents of the Dharma have the same flavor." Concerned that Chan awakening would get lost amid that array of different styles, he suggests that nothing prevents lineages from blending harmoniously.

Nearly four centuries after Fayan, Zhongfeng agrees that "differences among the five schools were mainly due to the different personalities of their founders"[66] rather than their teachings. He characterizes the lineages somewhat differently in that the style of Guiyang is "cautious and strict," Caodong is "delicate and refined," Linji is "penetrating and sharp,"

Yunmen is "lofty and classic," and Fayan is "simple and clear." Certain that none of the founders had any conscious intention of establishing a separate lineage, Zhongfeng argues that "a school naturally came into being when like-minded individuals were attracted by the style of one meditation center, stayed together and formed a distinctive tradition."[67] Therefore sectarian bickering is utterly ridiculous: "If the patriarchs of the five schools should know of this in their great silent samadhi, they would surely cover their noses in laughter."

The outlook of Wuzu is preserved in case 84 of the *Entangling Vines Collection*, in which a monk asks about each of the Five Houses and the master responds with succinct, seemingly unflattering comments: in the Linji school, "Mortal offenders of the five sins hear the peal of thunder" 五逆聞雷; in Yunmen, "Scarlet banners flutter" 紅旗閃爍; in Caodong, "Messages are sent but never reach the house" 馳書不到家; in Guiyang, "A broken monument lies across an old road" 斷碑橫古路; and in Fayan, "A night watchman breaks the curfew" 巡人犯夜.[68] Although Wuzu appears to leave no lineage, including his own Linji stream, off the hook of criticism, his disingenuously dismissive remarks are meant to be interpreted positively to highlight Linji's tendency toward irreverence, Yunmen's skill in testing disciples, Caodong's silent contemplation, Guiyang's deliberately puzzling expressions, and Fayan's use of words to transcend language.

Yuanwu's short essay *Essentials of the Five Houses of Chan* 五家宗要 (*Wujia Zongyao*), cited in full from volume 6 of the *Eyes of Humans and Gods*, evokes the ecumenical spirit of Fayan and Zhongfeng without the irony of Wuzu's passage. Yuaanwu opens with a statement that captures briefly the main teaching method of each school:[69]

LINJI: Complete activity has a great function. Students are tested with sticks and shouts circling round or with the tip of knives and swords. Transmitting the path occurs in the flash of lightning. 全機大用. 棒喝交馳.劍刀上求人.電光中垂手 (臨濟).

YUNMEN: The North Star conceals itself and the golden wind reveals itself. The three statements are discerned from an arrowhead flying in mid-air. 北斗藏身.金風體露.三句可辨.一鏃遼空 (雲門).

CAODONG: The paths of monarchs and officials converge while the crooked and straight merge with each other. The bird's flight is untraceable and golden needles sew jade threads. 君臣合道.偏正相資. 鳥道玄途.金針玉線 (曹洞).

GUIYANG: Teachers sing in harmony as father and son are of a single lineage. Brightness and darkness circle round each other but this is disclosed by neitherwordsnorsilence.師資唱和.父子一家.明暗交馳.語默不露(溈仰).

FAYAN: Hearing sounds enlightens on the path and seeing forms illumines the mind. The Chan blade is hidden in a phrase as the voice [of Buddha] is conveyed through words. 聞聲悟道.見色明心.句裏藏鋒.言中有響 (法眼).

In the second part of the essay, Yuanwu celebrates diversity by emphasizing the underlying principle of appropriate responsiveness to circumstances to which all adepts adhere. He is also highly critical of any possible one-sided or self-serving misuse of a teaching style or device that should ideally reflect impartiality and be conveyed through impersonal communication because otherwise it allows weeds, symbolizing struggles with ignorance, to grow untended:

Each of the Five Houses expresses Chan through it own voice and tone in establishing a marvelous gate that can be seen despite changing techniques and shifting styles from thousands of directions and hundreds of perspectives. All techniques exemplify calling out from amid nothingness. The melody initiated by dynamic activity (*ji*) is like a roaring stream that does not leave behind any trace. Turning a cloth inside out reveals its true material that disentangles complications (*geteng*). A thousand soldiers are easy to find, but a single general is hard to come by. Entering into the weeds to assist people by responding to opportunities is what connects the schools on a single thread. But pursuing this based on ambition deviates from the path of selfless expression and gets stuck in a rut. If obstructed or deluded by fixation the spiritual tip of the jeweled sword encountered through face-to-face meetings fails to tend to the flock.

五家改聲換調.展托妙門.易俗移風.千方百面.盡向無中唱出.曲為初機.若是俊流.不留朕跡.掀翻露布.截斷葛藤.然則千兵易得.一將難求. 入草尋人.聊通一線.機前有準.擬向則乖.句下無私.動成窠臼.靈鋒寶劍覿面堂堂.滯殼迷封.不堪種草.

**Formative Elements.** Although Yuanwu appreciates all the various houses as coexisting with more or less equal status, it is also clear from the *Blue Cliff Record*'s comments that some lineages are, in effect, more equal than others. Yunmen's style is particularly favored although not without occasional criticism. In case 6, which is the first example of a Yunmen dialogue featured in the collection, the master uses the phrase, "Every day is a good day" 日日是好日, in response to his own challenge to "say something about the days after the fifteenth day of the month" 十五日已後道將一句來. Yuanwu appreciates that Yunmen frequently used the device of "three-word Chan" 三字禪, which includes the utterances "Observe!" 顧, "Reflect!" 鑒, and "Ha!" 咦 evoked in response to certain circumstances. He also says that Yunmen sometimes uses "one-word Chan" 一字禪 with exclamations like "Exposed!" 露 or "Universal!" 普.[70]

Yuanwu furthermore mentions several times in regard to Yunmen and his followers, including Xuedou, that "in every single phrase he utters three implications are embedded . . . that constitute the 'touchstone of this house'" 一句中三句俱備 . . . 家宗旨.[71] The three implications of each Yunmen saying are based on "the saying that covers heaven and earth, the saying that follows the waves, and the saying that cuts off myriad streams" 函蓋乾坤句.隨波逐浪句.截斷眾流句.[72] The first implication suggests the universality of the Dharma, the second skillfully adjusts to and guides an inquirer based on his particular situation, and the third blocks all discriminative activities of the learner's mind. While the first implication encompasses all possibilities, the second and third implications, which are sometimes listed in reverse order, seem to correspond to what Yuanwu refers to as an adept's ability to release or control his trainee. Yuanwu argues that Yunmen's open-endedness "does not give rise to multiple propositions or exclamations, but those who have not yet penetrated the case expect me to carry on that way" 此事無許多論說.而未透者.卻要如此.[73]

Yuanwu also thinks highly of the Guiyang school's style, which is cited mainly in three gongan. Case 24 involves an encounter between Guishan Lingyou (771–854), founder of the school along with his disciple Yangshan, and a mysterious female practitioner known as Iron Grindstone Liu (n.d.) to symbolize her distinctive way of crushing opponents. One day Liu, who was living in a hut down the road, visits Guishan, who reacts by making a pun on her name as a gentle putdown.[74] Liu asks if Guishan will be going to a communal vegetarian feast being held the next day at Mount Wutai, a famous pilgrimage site for seekers of inspiring esoteric visions of bodhisattva Manjusri that forms the topic of case 35. Both parties must have known this was an unrealistic request, since the sacred Buddhist site was located hundreds of miles away and also was generally forbidden to

Chan travelers because it might distract from their focus on meditation (although that injunction was often disregarded).[75] Guishan responds by lying down on the ground and stretching out as if, according to Yuanwu's capping phrase, an arrow had shot him, and Liu quickly goes as if on her way to visit the mountain.

Even though it appears that Guishan's nonverbal response makes him the victor of the Dharma battle, Xuedou's poetic evaluation is characteristically ambiguous. In the verse cited in chapter 3 (140–141), it is difficult to determine with certainty from its grammar to which interlocutor his ode refers. Yuanwu argues that each line of the verse highlights the four main developments in the case, so that the actions in lines one and three indicate Liu's approach and probing questions, whereas Guishan's response is suggested by the second line and the ode concludes with their perplexing farewell gestures.

Yuanwu's capping phrase on line three, "Both are supported by a single walking staff as they call to each other while going and coming together" 一條拄杖兩人扶.相招同往又同, shows that the apparent adversaries involved in a contest are in fact dialogue partners engaged in a process of compatibility and mutuality that brings out the best in each other. His prose remarks reinforce this view: "This old lady understands Guishan's teaching method, which involves pulling thread and stretching string or letting go and gathering in. The two answer back like mirrors reflecting each other, but without any image to be seen. With each and every action they fully complement one another, and with each and every phrase they are completely in accord." 這老婆會他溈山說話.絲來線去.一放一收.互相酬唱.如兩鏡相照. 無影像可觀.機機相副.句句相投.[76]

Yuanwu mentions a couple of other standpoints indicative of the Guiyang tradition that are evident in the case: one is called "the merging of perspectives" 境致; and the other is "a blocking (or obstructive) phrase" 隔身句 in that "the meaning is understood despite the fact that the words seem to get in the way" 意通而語隔.[77] He also emphasizes that the apparent obscurity of Liu's initial question should not be misconstrued as a "matter of unconcern" 無事 and points out that "only one who is well versed in this lineage will be able to understand it thoroughly" 唯是知音方會他底只 by breaking through the apparent hindrance of her words.[78]

Two other cases that derive at least in part from the Guiyang school involve Zifu Rubao (n.d.), a lesser known disciple of Yangshan, who draws a circle in both instances. It is generally said that circles and other kinds of figures or diagrams were routinely used in this lineage, which at one time held a master list of ninety-seven circular symbols in all, each with its own set of commentaries.[79] The use of circles as an instructional device was also associated with Caodong school techniques for explicating the five positions of lord and vassal. Another use of the symbol is found in case 69, in which Nanquan draws a circle while he and two companions are on their way to visit National Teacher Huizhong, to whom the origins of teaching through circles is attributed, but neither Nanquan nor Huizhong were affiliated with the Guiyang school.

As part of his response to the main dialogue involving a rhinoceros fan in case 91, Zifu draws a circle with the character for ox symbolizing enlightenment placed inside. In case 33 Zifu is approached by ministry official Chen Cao, who was fond of testing monks and once conversed with Yunmen about his interest in the *Lotus Sutra*, and the master responds by drawing a circle. When the minister protests, Zifu closes the door. Despite Xuedou's capping phrase inserted in the case, "Chen Cao has only one eye" 陳操只具一隻眼,[80] Yuanwu refers to the minister as an "adept" 作家, and he does not let Zifu off the hook and challenges him to "draw another circle" 也好與一圓相.[81] Yuanwu then questions Xuedou's perhaps overly positive assessment even as he also praises the poet-monk for having "an eye on top of his head" 頂門具眼. This case is characterized as "discerning the target amid words while concealing ability through phrases" 言中辨的句裏藏機, which recalls the assessment of Guiyang school teaching styles in case 24.[82]

Although Dongshan is only mentioned in one case (43) in the *Blue Cliff Record*, he and the Caodong lineage with various references to the technique of the five positions is cited or alluded to directly or indirectly numerous times, including cases 5, 7, 16, 20, 22, 31, 48, 49, 61, 66, 72, 73, 81, 83, 89, 97, and 99. Unlike Dahui's scathing critique of the Caodong approach, Yuanwu acknowledges differences of opinion and in practice but for the most part does so in a respectful and noncombative way. Case 43, in which Dongshan easily handles a monk's questions about avoiding cold and heat with a paradoxical response that receives commendation from Yuanwu, provides an opportunity for the commentator to explore Dongshan's view of the fivefold relation of absolute and relative while emphasizing that "naturally lineal members have an understanding based on the explanations of their house, so Xuedou makes use of that approach in crafting his verse." 自然會他家裏人說話.雪竇用他家裏事頌出.[83] The ode culminates in an image, symbolizing the inquirer's foolishness, of a swift black dog known for outracing any wily hare that bounds up the stairs in hopeless pursuit of the brilliant moonlight, which represents Dongshan's perplexing response.

Case 20 is probably the main example in which the Caodong school is directly criticized, although not without a degree of ambivalence. Here Dongshan follower Longya's (835–923) question, "What is the meaning of Bodhidharma coming from the west?," results in his being hit with a meditation brace (or chinrest) by Cuiwei (n.d.) and also with a cushion by Linji (note that the order is reversed in the telling of the story in the *Record of Linji*).[84] In both instances, as well as in a follow-up dialogue noted in the prose commentary, Longya responds, "It's okay for you to hit me but after all there isn't any meaning to Bodhidharma coming from the west" 打即任打.要且無祖師西來意.[85] Yuanwu does not favorably evaluate Longya's encounter, calling his question "an old tale known everywhere" 諸方舊話, and his concluding comment a matter of "drawing his bow after the thief has fled" 賊過後張弓. The drastic actions of Cuiwui and Linji are deserved as "fitting punishment for [Longya's] crimes" 一狀領過, yet Yuanu also admits, "It is a pity to strike this kind of dead fellow" 可惜打這般死漢.[86]

It is clear that Longya is being criticized for not showing his own initiative. He seems overly ritualistic by not seizing the opportunity to demonstrate his Chan pivot and so should be struck to alert him to his deficiencies. In support of the critique, Yuanwu's prose remarks present six previous evaluations of the dialogue, including one by Xuedou who says, "I would have picked up the brace and cushion and thrown them right in front of [Cuiwei and Linji]" 我當時如作龍牙.待伊索蒲團禪板.拈起劈面便擲.[87] Cleary and Cleary note that this may be a one-sided assessment, since "Tenkei Denson sometimes remarked that Yuan Wu was not thoroughly familiar with the devices of the Tung lineage, and did not realize that there is a turning point, a pivot, in each rank."[88]

However Yuanwu's approach is complicated. On the one hand, he charges that Longya "only acted as a disciple in the Dongshan lineage" by remaining passive during the exchanges, "and if he wanted to be a disciple of Deshan or Linji [with whom he had also studied] then he would have realized there is an active side as well" 只做得洞下尊宿.若是德山臨濟門下.須知別有生涯.[89] Yet Yuanwu also comments that while he did not agree with Longya, he should accept for different reasons the view that there is no meaning to Bodhidharma coming from the west. Yuanwu concludes that Longya "does the best he can" 不妨盡善, but "falls into secondary status" because he does not follow the old masters who, with "each word and every phrase" 一言一句, were able "to make the most of horizontal and vertical, and thereby attain illumination and function" 有權有實.有照有用.[90]

Another Caodong school–based view of a gongan is found in the comments on case 81, which involves Yaoshan Weiyan (745–828), an ancestor of Dongshan. Yuanwu mentions that the opening query from a monk who asks about shooting the so-called elk of elks, the king among deer with horns sharpened on the rocks of cliffs so that they are like swords, thus making it nearly impossible for man or beast to confront this creature, would be "interpreted in the Caodong tradition as 'a question that uses things' or as 'a question testing the host' evoked in order to illustrate the inquirer's present capacity" 洞下謂之借事問.亦謂之辨主問.用明當機.[91] But, as with some other examples of designations of specific teaching styles, no additional details of the techniques are provided. This is either because audiences at the time would have been readily able to understand these categories and did not need further explanation or because some materials were lost or left out of the text, either purposely or unavoidably.

There are a number of additional examples of teaching methods cited briefly and without much explanation throughout the *Blue Cliff Record* commentaries, some in conjunction with a particular lineage while others cross sectarian lines. One is the notion discussed in case 17 of using "flavorless words, flavorless phrases, and flavorless conversations, which choke people and leave them no room to breathe" 可謂言無味句無味.無味之談.塞斷人口.無爾出氣處. This approach, which tends to be associated with the Yunmen school, is also mentioned in cases 12, 22, 30, 44, and 58.[92] In addition Yuanwu cites the model of fishing, or of one who holds a fishing pole yet is often frustrated by seeking a big and impressive catch while ending with a toad in the mud, as in cases 22, 33, 38, 62, 74, 82, and 91.

Another device cited in case 25 is the use of "three seals." According to Yuanwu "when [a stubborn learner] meets an adept face-to-face the master tests him by using three essential words for sealing space, sealing mud, and sealing water. That way the master can determine whether teaching is like trying to fit a square peg into a round hole without there being enough space for it." 若到作家面前.將三要語印空.印泥印水驗他.便見方木逗圓孔.無下落處.[93] The seals are used to identify superior trainees who have an attainment leaving no trace, to correct incorrigible novices whose self-deception invariably does leave traces, and to test midlevel practitioners who have gained partial understanding that is not fully traceless. These functions recall Yunmen's three phrases and also resemble a similar tract in the *Record of Linji*.

In case 7, in which Fayan enlightens a monk by simply repeating the inquirer's name, Yuanwu refers to the method as "arrowheads meeting" 箭鋒相拄, which is preferred by this school "since it does not use the five positions of lord and vassal or the four propositions" 更不用五位君臣.四料簡.[94] A technique similarly highlighting the Chinese character for the sharp edge or point of an instrument 鋒, whether meant literally to refer to an arrow or sword or figuratively to symbolize one's mental capacity, is found in case 75. Here a monk representing the early Northern school of Chan engages with master Wujia from the rival Southern school and end up hitting and insulting each other, perhaps unsurprisingly to their mutual satisfaction. In this instance no lineal preference is indicated by the dialogue, the verse, or the prose commentary. Following a line in Xuedou's ode, Yuanwu characterizes the technique as "dialogue partners exchanging action points with perfect continuity so that they fuse through reciprocal enhancement into unity" 兩箇機鋒互換.絲來線去.打成一片.[95]

**Gongan and the Public Domain.** The writings of Xuedou and Yuanwu may appear to proffer a philosophy of timeless mystical significance based on the turnabout capacity of a handful of skilled Chan adepts and poet-monks that is immune to the variability of change taking place amid the vagaries of historical events. However, an important aspect of the discourse of the *Blue Cliff Record* is the framing of some of the teaching methods not only in terms of lineal rivalries and/or compatibilities among the Five Houses but also in light of the fuller social behavioral context of public life in Song China. At that time all traditional institutions and communal associations were governed by forces reflecting the shifting sands of political rule and were regulated based on their ability to promote civil affiliations. Factors controlling or constraining the growth of the Chan school included complex relations between state and church, which was subject to governmental priorities. In a highly competitive religious environment, the imperium alternately supported Buddhist rituals, including Chan meditation and monastic discipline, as a means of relief and release from conflict or rejected them by snubbing or purging these practices for representing a foreign, escapist ideology that fostered an irreverent antinomian and antifamilial worldview.

Over a dozen cases, including 1, 3, 6, 11, 13, 25, 34, 38, 40, 44, 61, 66, 67, and 69, can be interpreted as expressing either explicitly or between the lines a message about the standing of Chan pedagogy in regard to some of the prevailing administrative implications from the pre-Tang era through the Song dynasty. Several gongan reflect the idea of there being positive and cordial relations with rulers and officials, who appreciate and learn from Chan adepts despite the baffling and blasphemous quality of their teaching. In the *Blue Cliff Record*'s first case, Bodhidharma abruptly upends all the assumptions about good deeds and personal identity held by Emperor Wu, founder of the Liang dynasty of southern China, for which he eventually receives the ruler's reluctant praise and an invitation to return after departing the area, to which the first patriarch is not known to have responded.

In case 67 Xuedou and Yuanwu compare Bodhidharma, at least indirectly, to Fu Daishi, a sixth-century Buddhist teacher during a period that was prior to the rapid growth of Chan during the Tang dynasty. Fu was invited by the same ruler to give a sermon on the *Diamond Sutra*. Instead of speaking he shook the lectern and descended from the platform 揮案一下.便下座, thereby mystifying the emperor, who appears somewhat mollified by the assurances of an elder priest also in attendance. Yuanwu says of Fu's action that, "By not bothering to express the meaning, he was like a shooting star that lights up the sky and then disappears by seeming to be, yet is not entirely, on the mark." 直得火星迸散.似則似是則未是.不煩打葛藤. Yuanwu concludes ironically, "Fu's crime should be listed on the same indictment [as Bodhidharma], so I strike" 正好一狀領過.便打.[96]

The prose commentary on case 34 mentions a stone grotto worker, who turns down the invitation of Emperor Suzong in the mid-ninth century, for which he is praised; and in case 40 Nanquan teaches a government official named Lu Xuan, who attains a high level of understanding from studying Chan with him. Case 69 features Nanquan joined by Dharma brothers Guizong and Magu traveling from Jiangxi province south of the Yangzi River, where they studied under Mazu, to visit National Teacher Huizhong, who was located in the capital city of Chang'an to the far north. Once Nanquan stops in the road and pays homage by drawing a circle that is in accord with the esteemed leader's teaching style, the travelers agree it is not necessary to complete the journey; Xuedou at first approves, yet in the end questions the group's decision.

In a later period, during the Five Dynasties (907–960), according to Yuanwu's remarks on case 6, Yunmen received the support of King Liu of south China, who was awakened by Yunmen's presentation of the gift of an empty box and then appointed the master leader of Lingshu monastery. There Yunmen succeeded his own teacher, who had been a close advisor to the monarch but died apparently of his own volition rather than succumb to pressure applied by the ruler asking for advice about waging an imminent battle. Also case 38 contains a sermon that was delivered by Fengxue during the same era at a local government headquarters in Hubei province where the Linji school was starting to become ascendant. The narrative introducing the dialogue refers to the master's teaching that day as a "Dharma hall sermon" 上堂云, which is a term usually reserved for a monastic setting but here serves as a fine example of the "public preaching of Chan" 公說禪.

Chan's institutional relations with the government were not always a rosy affair, and along with other schools of Buddhism, it often suffered slings and arrows during unstable political times. This was especially true when the notorious Huichang era persecution of all foreign religions transpired in 845 at the hands of fanatical Emperor Wuzong; thousands of temples including their libraries were shuttered or destroyed and hundreds of thousands of monks and nuns were forced to return to lay life. Case 11 includes a discussion of Xuanzong, the younger brother of Wuzong, who, before succeeding to the throne in 846, was regularly ridiculed by his sibling for traveling with master Xiangyan to Mount Lu and other Chan sites. In additional examples, case 25 refers to Shandao as a monk who was laicized in 845 but continued to preach; in case 44 it is asked ironically why the protector spirits of temples were not available to help during the period of suppression; and case 13 reflects on the victims of accusations of heresy during purges that took place in ancient India as a way of commenting on troubling public events in contemporary China.

Several decades after the Huichang persecution there were stages of political turmoil and social upheaval that greatly affected Chan leaders, so that a peaceful and thriving institutional period would not come to pass until the eleventh century. In case 66 Yantou asks a monk, who says he has come from the capital, whether he gained the sword of Huangchao, a notorious rebel whose weapon was considered a gift from heaven that inspired him, after failing to pass the exams, to overthrow the government and kill the imperial family while briefly declaring himself emperor in 874 before being driven out of Chang'an seven years later. Yantou had lived through the 845 persecutions as a young man and worked as a ferryman before practicing Chan. When the monk says that he does hold this sword, Yantou sticks his neck out while making a loud shout, and afterward the monk declares that the master's head has indeed fallen while Yantou laughs heartily. The act of lying down while feigning that his head was chopped off by the monk's faux blow recalls Yantou's final gesture before his death in 887. Even though he lived in Hubei province far from the capital, there were disturbances in the area so his assembly fled, but Yantou remained practicing meditation in solitude. It was said that when captured and killed by rioting bandits he gave a great shout.

Meanwhile in case 66, after the initial encounter with Yantou, the monk consults Xuefeng, who in hearing the story quickly strikes with the staff. Xuedou writes, "Thirty blows of the cane lets him off too easy" 三十山藤且輕恕,[97] and reinforcing this assessment Yuanwu says that Xuefeng should have beaten the monk until his staff was broken. Yet Yuanwu also praises the pesky inquirer with, "Yantou and Xuefeng, supposedly so great, were on the contrary exposed by this rice-eating Chan follower" 大小大巖頭雪峰倒被箇喫飯禪和勘破.[98] Xuedou ends his ode, "To take advantage is to lose the advantage" 得便宜是落便宜, to which Yuanwu caps, "This wraps up the case" 據款結案.[99]

Perhaps the single most significant yet perplexing example of the *Blue Cliff Record* commenting on Chan's unfortunate affairs with the state is found in the ode to case 3. In the source dialogue when asked by the temple superintendent how he is feeling during a bout of illness Mazu replies, "Sun-face Buddha, Moon-face Buddha" 日面佛.月面佛. This cryptic saying is usually taken to suggest a unity of the eternal (solar) and ephemeral (lunar) aspects of ultimate reality. The second line of Xuedou's verse asks rather mysteriously, "The Five Sovereigns and Three Emperors, what kind of people were they?" 五帝三皇是何物,[100] and Yuanwu notes this passage was censured by Emperor Shenzong (r. 1068–1085) for appearing to give preference to religious leaders in a way that subverted imperial authority.

The censure referred to in case 3 must have occurred sometime after the death of Xuedou and during a phase in which the government was for the most part enthusiastically supportive though cautiously supervisory of the Chan school. Yuanwu also remarks that Xuedou's controversial query derives from a line by Tang poet Chanyue excoriating the behavior of a particular prince. The royal's luxurious dress and accessories used for hunting as sport, all while he scorned the plight of the peasants laboring in the fields, stood in sharp contrast to the supposedly caring attitude of mythical rulers of old China. This citation indicates there was a long-lasting set of tensions between Chan independence, frequently expressed in terms of disingenuous blasphemy toward its own and secular leaders, and ongoing oversight and regulation of all religions enforced by the state, which might easily misinterpret or take offense at an otherwise innocent (or perhaps not so much) comment made by a Chan teacher.

## Transition: Performative and Reformative Elements

In *The Language of the Chan School* (*Chanzong Yuyan*), modern scholar Zhou Yukai explains with many intriguing examples over a dozen types of verbal and nonverbal expressions that are frequently used in Chan writings.[101] These include various elicitations through the use of body language, shouting, and hitting, in addition to communications via nonsensical words or eloquent but enigmatic phrasing, and more. The perplexing forms of expressions emerge from some degree of closure to trigger creativity while avoiding deceptive or distracting practices pigeonholed as foxy or crazy. In that vein Yuanwu boldly claims of his method for examining and evaluating encounter dialogues, "I always show people how to observe clearly the dynamic moment of pivotal activity whereby a turnaround is able to smash through any barrier." 山僧尋常教人覷這機關轉處.[102]

Transitional rhetorical elements embedded in the *Blue Cliff Record* are aimed at unsettling conventional understandings of words and phrases through the inventive or reformative use of neologisms and wordplay while also resorting, when language fails to overcome conceptual entanglements, to various unvoiced or ritual performative acts and gestures that upset the stereotypical comportment of arrogant fools and stubborn phonies who were infecting Chan training routines. Through resourceful verbal maneuvers and imaginative nonverbal movements any outlook that resembles an ordinary worldview is turned radically upside down and inside out, not to establish yet another fixed opinion reflecting ignorance but to free an interlocutor from attachment to particular perspectives.[103]

As Yuanwu says in case 20, because the intellectual and/or emotional views of regular practitioners are so deeply rooted, a master's exploits exert a distinctively disturbing effect in appearing "to reverse the great ocean, kick over Mount Sumeru, scatter the white clouds with shouts, and break up empty space; straightaway, with a single device and a single object the tongues of everyone on earth are cut off." 掀翻大海.踢倒須彌.喝散白雲.打破虛空.直下向一機一境.坐斷天下人舌頭.[104] He also suggests in case 8 that for those trainees who are better prepared, "If someone suddenly comes forward right now to overturn meditation seats while scattering the

great assembly with shouts, this should not be considered mystifying."
如今忽有箇出來.掀倒禪床.喝散大眾.怪他不得.[105]

The phrase in the passage above that literally means "a single device
and a single object" 一機一境 (*yiji yijing*, or sometimes 機境, *jijing*) and is
used frequently and functions in Yuanwu's rhetoric as a special compound
to indicate the exceptional kind of activity of an adept that expresses much
more than what is actually being said or done. Examples include such gestures that a Chan master uses as teaching devices in replying to questions
as "twinkling the eyes," "raising the eyebrows," and "raising the staff,
the whisk, or the gavel."[106] Moreover Yuanwu uses a variety of verbs that
convey the capacity to disrupt inflexible standpoints, such as "to reverse"
掀翻, "to kick over" 踢倒, "to scold and scatter" 喝散, and "to break up
(or through)" 打破. Yuanwu also makes it clear that anyone, including
himself, could be subjected to this comeuppance. In commenting on case
79, he criticizes Touzi (819–914), who strikes an impertinent monk for
asking whether breaking wind reflects the voice of Buddha, because he
stops the assault before "his staff is broken" 拄杖未到折.[107] Then, in capping Xuedou's lines about ignorant people who die while playing in the
tide, "Suddenly come back to life/ As a hundred rivers surge backwards
with a roar" 忽然活.百川倒流鬧活活, Yuanwu says, "My meditation seat
shakes as, startled and stunned, I too fall back three thousand miles"
禪床震動.驚殺山僧.也倒退三千里.[108]

**Performative Elements.** We have seen many examples within the
source dialogues that evolved into cases whereby a dramatic form of enact-
ment, such as striking and scolding, or threatening to inflict harm with a
stick, sword, arrow, or a dangerous animal like a snake or tiger, or reacting
with feigned fear or as if a victim of these dangers, is crucial to the impact
of the encounter. In that sense the action of the exchange reflecting an
adept's ability to pivot on the spot or a novice's lack of capacity for this—
or the interplay in which one party heightens their facility or is exposed
for faking it through the challenge presented by the other—speaks more
loudly than words in terms of sending the reader/audience a powerful
message regarding what is needed to attain self-realization. Therefore the
term gongan seems to function in such a context less as a noun referring
to a prearranged discursive entity than as a verb capturing spontaneous
behavior during lively dialogues and debates. Even if we believe that many
of the accounts were literary devices invented long after the supposed
event took place, these techniques must have originally exuded a sense of
vitality and immediacy that can only be surmised.[109] We can imagine, for

example, the effect felt at the time when Heshan (891–960) said simply but forcefully, "Knowing how to beat the drum" 解打鼓, four consecutive times in reply to a monk's persistent queries about the nature of truth and transcendence.

By the time monastic ritualism was encoded in Northern Song works, especially the *Rules for Chan Gardens* (*Chanyuan Qinggui*) from 1103 as the most authoritative example, collecting the vast storehouse of dialogues was for the most part completed. There was also a clear sense of how pedagogical practices should be conducted. Whether delivering formal sermons before the full assembly in the Dharma hall 上堂 or teaching individuals or smaller groups in the more informal settings of the abbot's quarters 入室 or monks' hall 小參, in addition to other types of delivery, each style had its own set of rules regulating content and demeanor. It is clear from textual and contextual evidence that, although nearly a century apart, both Xuedou through poetry and Yuanwu through prose and capping-phrase comments presented their remarks on one hundred gongan while giving formal sermons, but they also sought ways to break the mold when it came to behavioral codes and instructions by acting spontaneously in a live situation at critical moments. When the text of the *Blue Cliff Record* is read today as words on paper (or in digital form), this extemporaneous activity probably cannot help but come across as having at least a partially scripted or premeditated quality. But if properly appreciated, it provides a distinctive flavor that approximates the immediacy of the moment. This is still emulated in the delivery of Chan/Zen/Seon sermons today, although the deliveries are often rehearsed, thus giving the impression that what started as the antithesis of ritual—unfortunately, for some observers or participants—has come to epitomize it.

A key example showing Xuedou's performative stance is case 91 about a rhinoceros fan, in which the remarks of four interpreters of the main dialogue are cited and Xuedou caps each one. This section of the case recalls case 18, and Xuedou's impromptu expression following the delivery of his ode resembles the approach taken in case 60. After the usual four-line *jueju*-style verse, and with Yuanwu's capping comments later appended to make it appear from a typographical standpoint that this is an extension rather than a supplement to the poem, Xuedou challenges "every member of the Chan group to give a turning word" 請禪客各下一轉語. Disappointed when a monk interrupts to "instruct the assembly to go practice in the hall" 大眾參堂去—it is not clear whether this refers to the meditation hall, which would be conducted in silence, or to another room for private interviews, which would break the momentum of the group session, but in either case against the grain of hierarchy it alters Xuedou's expectation—the master "steps down" 便下座.[110] Yuanwu adds that he should have instead dished out thirty blows with the staff.

One textual indicator of examples of Yuanwu's unplanned delivery is the occasional use of the phrase, "after a pause" 良久, probably during which there were questions or comments raised by the audience that were undocumented. Or perhaps Yuanwu allowed the assembly to wait a brief interval to heighten the sense of drama before he spoke again. In case 11 such a suspension of words is noted in the prose remarks on the dialogue just before the verse is presented; Yuanwu comments on the image of piercing nostrils as a sign of discipline: "As soon as I speak this way I have already lost my head. People, where are your nostrils? (A pause) They've been pierced!" 山僧恁麼道.已是和頭沒卻了也.諸人鼻孔在什麼處.良久云.穿卻了也.[111] At the end of case 22 the text says that "the master struck" after asking the assembly some perplexing rhetorical questions, and case 47 concludes in similar fashion but adds the exclamation, "Blind!," while cases 47 and 77 also feature a pause before the final biting comments proffered by Yuanwu.

Another case shows both Xuedou and Yuanwu demonstrating a performative element as the latter's approach intertwines with his predecessor's. At the end of the ode to case 81, which involves the story of "a monk who collapses" 僧放身便倒 when he pretends to be hit once by master Yangshan (751–834), Xuedou says, "Look—an arrow!" 看箭. Yuanwu notes that "after telling the story [in verse] in the Dharma hall Xuedou wrapped it up in a single bundle by calling out loudly ... and at that moment everyone sitting or standing in the assembly was unable to stir." 雪竇是時因上堂.舉此語束為一團話.高聲道一句云 ... 坐者立者.一時起不得.[112]

**Reformative Elements.** One of the most important features of the rhetoric of uncertainty occurs on a microlevel discourse in which Yuanwu flexes a flair for being a wordsmith, who skillfully twists or reverses the conventional meaning of a character, compound, or phrase, as well as a broader symbol, theme, or set of allusions, in order to uncover the appropriate while also exposing the inauthentic implications for experiencing self-realization. In his hands all manners of expression are tossed topsy-turvy to be reoriented or suited to a particular context. The effect of this inventive phrasing suggests that any and every moment can become an opening for achieving a fundamental breakthrough if handled fittingly by at least one of the parties in a dialogue, which involves hierarchical, liminal, momentary, and subjective factors regarding truth manifested in the setting of a contest rather than standing independent as a set goal that floats above the fray. In the fleeting disorderly moment of interpersonal interplay, spiritual destiny is realized. Yuanwu's evaluations are based on discerning whether an opportunity has been seized or lost, and how in the ephemeral situation of competition true reality is to be recognized. One who gets the point immediately and without hesitation will be able to "get up and go" 剔起便行,[113] but missed chances are severely critiqued.

A key example of verbal dexterity is the inventive use of the term gongan, which only appears one time in Xuedou's text in the ode to case 64. Prior to Yuanwu, the preferred word for what we now consider to be a case was 則 (*ze*), which functioned more as a counter for items (dialogues or stories) than as an evocative indicator of a complex nexus of exchanges enhanced by various layers of commentary with variable implications and applications. Intriguing divergences from the core meaning of gongan are suggested by the utterance, "It's a double case" 兩重公案, which first appeared as a Tang Chan expression and was further conjured by Yuanwu to indicate twice the complication and thus two times the possibility for either sinking into delusion or attaining awakening. In a capping phrase to case 16 Yuanwu exclaims, "It is a double case, a triple case, a quadruple case!" 兩重公案.三重四重了也.[114] He also uses both 現成公案 (*xiancheng gongan*, J. *genjōkōan*) and 見成公案 (*jianchen gongan*)—the first character varies from "realize" to "see"—to suggest an open-and-shut case or a condition whereby the meaning of the dialogue becomes apparent as an epiphany right before one's eyes.[115]

Perhaps the main example of Yuanwu's stylish way with words is seen in his extensive use of the term 機 (*ji*),[116] which is included in "encounter dialogue" 機緣問答 (*jiyuan wenda*) and appears several hundred times throughout the *Blue Cliff Record* in various contexts, often by itself but also as part of a compound. In addition to its literal meaning of "trigger," referring to the workings of a mechanical device—probably originally this was a loom used for weaving, which was developed in early Chinese society and keeps the mechanism functioning on its own without human effort—the word also indicates "potential," "innate aptitude," "activity," "moving power," "opportunity," "occasion," or more broadly, "having a knack for an encounter," that is, the innate capacity to carry out an engagement in which a spiritual breakthrough transpires.[117]

In the *Blue Cliff Record* the term *ji* suggests the fleeting moment in which an adept turns circumstances freely and resolutely as an opportunity to enact radical change by undertaking a dramatic, transformational turn or pivot from accepting the falsity of illusion to expressing true reality. An example is the following verse attributed to ninth-century master Muzhou: "Chan practitioners experience an opportunity that is profound,/ That profound opportunity appears and then fades./ If you wish to grasp teaching prior to the opportunity,/ See identity expressing itself through differentiation." 禪者有玄機.機玄是復非.欲了機前旨.咸於句下違.[118] According to case 16 in the *Record of Serenity* (which corresponds to case 31 in *the Blue Cliff Record*), "[Magu] sees the opportunity and acts" 見機而作 without hesitation or deliberation interfering with his response. Although the term is used in a positive sense by Yuanwu, it also has a negative meaning in the *Record of Linji* that says, "What is my purpose in speaking this way? I do so only because followers of the Way cannot stop their mind from running around everywhere seeking and go scrambling after the worthless contrivances 機境 (*jijing*) of the ancients." 山僧與麼.意在什麼處.祇爲道流一切馳求心不能歇.上他 古人閑機境.[119]

Yuanwu innovatively expands the meaning of the term to suggest whatever is apropos to the occasion of the encounter dialogue by coining or evoking several compounds. These include *jifeng* 機鋒, in which *feng* indicates a "razor-like blade" so the word symbolizes a knack for repartee that is sharp and biting, yet the profound upheaval it conveys is subtle and not too weighty; and *jijing* (the same term that is used negatively by Linji), in that every inner potential 機 and every external object 境 become matched and merged. According to a saying from the period, each of the various Chan schools has an answer for every occasion 禪家一機一境.[120] Both terms in this compound can refer to subjective and objective phenomena producing, individually and together, an effect that cannot be rendered conveniently in a single English expression.[121] Another example also used in Yuanwu's other writings is "total working" or "whole effect" 全機 (*quanji*), which was borrowed by Dōgen to serve as the title of a prominent short fascicle of his *Treasury of the True Dharma Eye* known in Japanese as "Zenki."

Yuanwu also sometimes inverts various images involving sight, such as "blink an eye" 眼定動 for ignorance, "one-eye" 一隻眼 for lack of insight, and "blindness" 瞎, so that they indicate true seeing that transcends ordinary vision; moreover the word for "error" 錯 suggests a creative misunderstanding that leads to a fuller level of awareness. Another term conjured in contradictory ways is a word whose very meaning is suggestive of such irony, that is, "upside down" or "reversed" 倒. In Mahayana scriptures, including the *Lotus Sutra*, this character signifies deluded or false understanding, as in compounds for "distortion" 顛倒夢想, "confusion" 顛倒, and "mistaken attachment" 倒執. This negative implication is also clear in a prominent Dongshan dialogue that is cited in the commentary to case 99. For the most part, in Yuanwu's hands, the term indicates exactly the ability to subvert and invert conventional views that any adept is expected to demonstrate in order to confront and convert his trainee. Therefore the word functions multifariously as the descriptor of a condition, an injunction to overthrow misguided standpoints, and an indicator of the upset felt by those who have had their status quo capsized by Yuanwu's clever rhetoric of uncertainty.

A mainstay of *Blue Cliff Record* rhetoric is the notion that any and every thing can teach a lesson in Dharma if it becomes an integral component of a Chan adept's capacity to exert *ji* at the right time and place. Yuanwu explores several different discursive sectors to convey consistently the transition from the problem of attachment to the solution of realization. These include the medical paradigm of diagnosing illness that is cured by medicine and results in wellness; the legal template of the occurrence of crime leading to an investigation, indictment, judgment, and finally either punishment or release; and military strategy involving ways of escaping from traps and attacks by exercising craftiness that exposes an opponent's weaknesses and overcomes their strengths.

In many dialogues with commentaries key aspects of monastic life and its ritual activities are transformed into pedagogical devices. These include references to (1) ceremonial objects, like staffs, bells, drums, robes, bundles, seats, benches, cushions, and bowls; (2) clerical routines, such as daily and seasonal rites; practice during retreats; or traveling over pathways for periods of itinerancy at mountain hermitages or to visit pilgrimage sites, between temples to learn from or challenge a new master, or flee areas mired in political turmoil;[122] (3) animals either living on temple grounds including cats and dogs that are scavengers and companions, lurking nearby the compound as pesky intruders such as foxes, inhabiting the generally rural local territory such as cows and oxen, occupying more remote or mysterious places like rhinoceroses, playing a potentially harmful role like snakes and tigers, or dwelling as mythical creatures such as dragons in secluded caves or the high seas; and (4) scriptures, especially the *Lotus Sutra*, which are in principle not part of Chan's "special transmission" 別傳 that distances from conventional Mahayana doctrinal teachings even though, directly or otherwise, scriptures continue to infuse the worldview that informs gongan discourse

To briefly consider a few key examples, there are several different kinds of staffs that play a prominent role in core dialogues or remarks by symbolizing either a master's pure experience attained in the wilderness or an image of his authority in an institutional setting. These include the monk's metallic ringed or sounding staff 錫杖 (Skt. *khakkhara*) in case 31; the walking staff 拄杖子 gained from travels in the forest in cases 25 and 60, in which it transforms into a dragon that swallows the universe; the stick 棒 for delivering thirty or more blows in several dozen cases recalling a typical punishment in the Chinese legal system; and the ceremonial fly-whisk 拂子 in cases 4, 11, 21, and 38. In case 18 Xuedou says, "A rough-hewn (or mountain) staff" 山形拄杖子 in response to a comment by Danyuan (n.d.), and Yuanwu notes, "An ancient [Fengxue] said, 'If you know the staff the work of your whole life's study is complete'" 古人道.識得拄杖子.一生參學事畢.[123] Yuanwu also strikes with the fly-whisk in a capping phrase to the verse in case 32, and he raises it ominously in cases 63 and 88.[124] Case 68 indicates that "Baizhang bequeathed his staff and whisk to Guishan, whereas Huangbo received the master's meditation seat and cushion" 百丈當時. 以禪板蒲團付黃檗. 拄杖拂子付溈.[125]

Some of the sutras cited or alluded to in the *Blue Cliff Record* include the *Diamond Sutra* in cases 4 and 97, the *Huayan Sutra* in cases 37 and 80, the *Surangama Sutra* in cases 32 and 46, the *Vimalakirti Sutra* in cases 7, 40, 62, and 65 (with Vimalakirti also mentioned in 84, 86, and 92), and the *Yuanjue Sutra* in case 31. There is a small group of gongan in which the *Lotus Sutra* makes its influence felt. The last two lines of Xuedou's ode to case 19 compare the "appropriate teaching" 對揚 of "raising just one finger" 豎一指 to "Casting a piece of driftwood into the dark sea/ Finding a blind tortoise amid the night waves" 曾向滄溟下浮木.夜濤相共接盲龜.[126] Yuanwu remarks in a way that is similar to case 12, "The *Lotus Sutra* says, '[Teaching] is like a one-eyed tortoise sticking its nose through a hole in driftwood so that it won't sink or drown.'"[127] This image suggests that a visually impaired amphibian surfaces the water at the precise moment a floating board with a tiny opening passes by, symbolizing the exceedingly rare opportunity to hear Buddhist teaching, to which only a few humans have the capacity to respond.

The first line of the verse comment on case 97, which deals mainly with the significance of a *Diamond Sutra* passage, refers to the *Lotus Sutra*'s parable of a jewel sewn into a pocket that is also referenced in a dialogue in Yunmen's record in which someone asks the master, "How about the pearl in the cloth container?" and he responds, "You tell me!" 問如何是布袋裏真珠.師云.説得麼.[128] In case 50 a monk asks Yunmen, "What is every atom samadhi?," and the master replies, "Food in the bowl, water in the bucket." The final lines of Xuedou's ode read, "If you doubt/ If you hesitate/ You are like a rich man's son with no trousers" 擬不擬.止不止.箇箇無褌長者子,[129] which alludes to the parable of the impoverished son who does not have britches from the fourth chapter of the *Lotus Sutra* and also recalls a famous poem by Hanshan. In prose remarks on case 33,[130] one of a couple of instances (another is 95) of direct references, Yunmen asks if the rumors were true that Chen Cao had studied the *Lotus Sutra*, and he instructs the minister to abandon this as Chen Cao bows while admitting the error of his ways.

**Interpreting Cases 14–15.** These back-to-back gongan, involving seemingly complementary Yunmen dialogues, feature innovative wording that highlights the teachings that are either appropriate to the occasion or upside down 倒. The cases evoke some of the same principles underlying the *Lotus Sutra* and can, in turn, be interpreted in light of the scripture's view of the One Voice of Buddha expressed in chapter 16 on "The Lifespan of Tathagata":[131]

Case 14. A monk asks, "What are the teachings of a lifetime?" (Even now the matter is not finished. This temple lecturer does not get the point and is entangled in a nest of complications). Yunmen says, "A timely (or appropriate) statement." (An iron hammerhead with no hole for the handle. Seven flowers bloom but eight wither.[132] An old rat gnaws on raw ginger). 舉僧問雲門.如何是一代時教 (直至如今不了.座主不會.葛藤窠裏).雲門云.對一説 (無孔鐵鎚.七花八裂.老鼠咬生薑).

Case 15. A monk asks, "What about when there is no current activity and there are no current phenomena?" (Taking a leap he falls back three thousand miles). Yunmen says, "An untimely (or inappropriate, literally "upside down") statement." (It is an even score. That's what comes out of the convict's mouth

so he cannot be let go as he is covered in overgrown weeds).
舉僧問雲門.不是目前機.亦非目前事時如何 (跳作什麼. 倒退三千
里).門云.倒一説 (平出.款出囚人口.也不得放過.荒草裏橫身).[133]

These puzzlers originally appeared in different sections of Yunmen's recorded sayings, rather than consecutively, and the nuance of the second exchange in that text is a bit different from the *Blue Cliff Record*'s version: "A monk asks, 'What about when there is no deep mystery and nothing to be seen?' 問不是玄機.亦非目擊時如何.[134] Whereas case 15 seems to emphasize the phenomenal world in both phrases of the query while also making a distinction between movement and stillness, the exchange in Yuanwu's record highlights two altogether different realms, one metaphysical or transcendent and the other physical or immanent. In both versions the point is that opposites are negated, thus indicating the emptiness of all categories.

Conventional interpretations see the cases as representing two sides of the same coin, with each capturing its own portion of the whole truth. This is reflected in Xuedou's verse comments that refer in case 14 to getting "one side of a tally" and in case 15 to "divvying up a single token." The question in the first dialogue refers to the teachings of the Buddha's lifetime. Remarks in the *Lexicon from the Ancestral Hall* point out that Yunmen was probably thinking of a classification of various teachings then current in the Tiantai school in order to bring consistency and continuity to disparate doctrines and methods by attributing them to specific phases and occasions of the Buddha's life. As Cleary and Cleary explain, according to the analysis of Zhiyi, Buddha's teaching was divided into five periods: the first stage was the mythical phase of the *Huayan Sutra* when he directly expressed his own realization under the tree of enlightenment; in the second stage, since no one at the time could fully understand the initial teaching, the Buddha expounded the *Agamas* for twelve years to suit elementary capacities; in the third stage he preached a transition from the lesser to the greater vehicle known as universally valid scriptures; in the fourth stage he taught the transcendence of wisdom; and in the fifth stage he preached the *Lotus Sutra* and *Great Nirvana Sutra*.[135]

Yunmen's answer to the monk's query suggests that the Buddha's teaching is responsive and appropriate: there is one and only one message, but it is conveyed variably based on the interlocutor's level of understanding in his or her own era. However the capping phrase expresses typical

Chan irony that indicates Yunmen's answer is ineffective by offering three images of futility, including an incongruous tool, withering blossoms, and a rodent self-destructively eating food he would ordinarily reject. Nothing should be taken at face value, and the dialogue exemplifies the uselessness of words rather than an exalted vision of truth.

The monk in case 15 is said to be the same as in the previous case, which stresses that the teachings of the Buddha's age are established according to the total capacity of hearers in terms of their situational context. The absence of present activity and phenomena could be taken to mean that perceiver and the perceived are unified by virtue of realizing the universal mind of Samadhi, whereby all things are void of own-being. Even though the questions and answers are parallel in the two gongan, the response in case 15, as shown in Figure 5.1, constitutes a riddle that contrasts with yet complements the previous case. "Turn that statement around!" or "A topsy-turvy statement!" are just two possible alternative translations of Yunmen's answer.[136]

In prose commentary Yuanwu remarks that the point of the fifteenth case's question was abstruse and misleading so that the response needed to be that way as well, as a paradoxical instance of corresponding or appropriate teaching. Yuanwu goes on to say that the reply of Yunmen, who is a "fellow with eyes," is an example of "riding the thief's horse in pursuit of the thief." When Xuedou's verse refers to, "Thirty-three ancestors [28 from India and 6 from China, with Bodhidharma playing a double role]

FIGURE 5.1 "An untimely statement" by Kazuaki Tanahashi, courtesy of the artist.

entering the tiger's den," Yuanwu's capping phrase says with irony, "I alone can know. A single leader is hard to find; all others are nothing but a band of wild fox spirits." 唯我能知.一將難求.野狐精一隊.[137] Therefore, both cases in seemingly opposite ways reflect utter frustration with any and all forms of discourse.

Yuanwu preempts an attempt to offer a revised interpretation with a stern warning about conceptualizing case 14 that is almost as severe as some of the *Lotus Sutra*'s notoriously harsh admonitions regarding misrepresentation: "People who often misunderstand and say, 'Buddha's preaching was appropriate to the conditions of one time.' . . . enter hell as fast as an arrow flies."[138] On the other hand, Yuanwu offers a rationale for seeking alternative explanations when he wonders in the introduction to the case, "Tell me, since [Dharma] is not transmitted [through words], why then are there so many entangled dialogues (*geteng* gongan)? Let those with eyes try to explain." 且道.既是不傳.為什麼.卻有許多葛藤公案.具眼者.試說看.[139]

With that qualifier I propose three main elements of a One Voice approach to interpreting cases 14 and 15 based on the *Lotus Sutra*: (1) Since Buddha is eternal there is no point in referring to his lifetime as a single previous event in that the full lifespan of Tathagata covers an incalculable amount of time encompassing all possible periods, phases, and stages of past, present, and future—he is living and breathing at any given time, including this moment. (2) His teachings are unified and unwavering yet invariably undergo continuing modification and modulation of content and style without sacrificing consistency or integrity, but not necessarily in a logical or historically bound sequence as implied in theories by Zhiyi and other Chinese Buddhist thinkers. (3) Nothing expressed in a Chan dialogue stands apart from or fails to participate in conveying fundamental Buddhist teachings that target a particular audience but remain beyond any distinction of what is timely and untimely.

A One Voice approach is supported by references in the *Lotus Sutra* to "hearing the gentle voice of Buddha" 聞佛柔軟音. Although this can indicate that full understanding is limited to what can be communicated only between enlightened parties, the implication as drawn out by Dōgen's diverse commentaries on the scripture is that universal potentiality qualifies everyone who engages with Dharma on any level as a full-fledged Buddha.[140] Even if they have misunderstandings—and everyone, including Buddha at times, does—the carrying of a board over one's shoulder symbolizing a blind spot is turned around as an epiphany so that errors or untruth represent productive standpoints of investigation and explication leading to truth.

The meaning of case 14, according to the One Voice approach, is related to the opening section of Yunmen's record titled "Responding to Occasions" 對機 (*xuanji*) and is similar to the notion of 機宜 (*jiyi*) that is mentioned in *Blue Cliff Record* cases 6, 8, 9, 12 and 61, which implies knowing what to do under any given circumstance or, to cite another Zen saying, "speaking in tune with the particular occasion." This reading of the case suggests that responsive expression is directed either toward enhancing or maintaining an opposition to whatever view has been offered in moments of encounter, points of decision-making, or modes of debate. An appropriate teaching eminently suited to meet the circumstances and capacities of listeners hits the mark through Yunmen's one-word barriers. Yuanwu points out Yunmen's distinctive capacity in case 47, "He does not turn his back on questions in that, by responding to the time or adapting to the season with a word or a phrase, a dot or a line, he invariably finds a place to show himself" 更不辜負爾問頭.應時應節.一言一句.一點一畫.不妨有出身處. [141]

What about case 15? From the standpoint of a One Voice approach, its emphasis is on interpreting multiple aspects of perception understood from shifting perspectives; since the timely teaching of case 14 must encompass untimeliness, the untimely teaching of 15 is also beyond dichotomization. Topsy-turvy pedagogy is expressed in several other gongan attributed to Yunmen, such as case 27 on a "Golden breeze" in commenting on withering trees and falling leaves; case 39 on the "Flowering hedge" in response to a query about the pure body of Buddha; case 47 on "Six is not enough" in response to a query about Dharmakaya; and case 77 on "Cake" in response to a query about what transcends Buddhas and patriarchs. Additional examples are case 21, in which lotus flowers and leaves are deliberately conflated; case 46, which uses the term topsy-turvy to refer to human delusions about sensations of the phenomenal world; case 68, in which masters' names are purposefully though playfully reversed; and case 87, in which medicine and illness are seen as interdependent.

While case 14 speaks of hitting its target in suitable fashion, case 15 suggests upending the mark by turning it upside down and inside out in contrary or contradictory fashion. Therefore, the reply in case 14, which not only talks about but constitutes an appropriate teaching, is enhanced by the seemingly inappropriate reply of case 15, which in being unsuited or unfit to its occasion is exactly what makes it apropos. Nikkyō Niwano suggests a musical simile based on section 33 of the *Sutra in Forty-Two Sections* 四十二章經: "A harp emits no sound/ If the strings are stretched too much./ It also sounds nothing/ If they are stretched too little./ Only when the strings are stretched just right,/ All music is in tune."[142] From the standpoint of the One Voice interpretation, inversions and reversals invariably apply and can lead via a creative process of disentangling entanglements 葛藤 (*geteng*) to an experience of realization since no matter what Buddha says or does not say it is expressive of truth. It seems that if one is not yet a Buddha then nothing is communicative; but since everyone is fundamentally Buddha at all times, then whatever is expressed or is not expressed discloses truth in a timely and/or untimely way.

Let us next consider some additional examples by Yuanwu and other Song interpreters that represent a tiny selection from the vast number in the Chan corpus of comments sometimes filled with irony and contradiction on the two cases. In response to the first question Yuanwu says in his remarks, "Preserved in the dragon's palace within the sea are gold writings and jade treatises. Teaching with the right technique at the opportune moment overcomes barriers and keeps the rhythm. Over forty-nine years [the Buddha] used the same voice at more than three hundred assemblies of our school with appropriate phrases adapted to circumstances cutting through iron." 海藏龍宮金文玉牒.逗器觀機破關擊節.三百餘會振綱宗.四十九年同箇舌.阿剌剌對一說.諦當之言如截鐵.[143] His teacher Wuzu writes, "An appropriate statement captures the teaching of the entire Buddhist cannon in five thousand and forty-eight volumes, and enables the wind, flowers, snow and moon to circulate freely. But iron grows quickly on the back of a diamond skull." 對一說.卷盡五千四十八.風花雪月任流傳.金剛腦後添生鋐.[144] A monk named Longmen 龍門 remarks, "How transcendent is an appropriate statement, which fills up emptiness with a ball of iron. Hunger comes unnoticed and food appears like thunder but everyone gathers to fight over it, gnawing and biting." 對一說何卓絕.塞虛空一團鋐.飢來不顧飯如雷.箇箇聚頭爭嚙齧.[145]

On the question in case 15 Yuanwu writes, "It takes a thief to catch thief, or a wedge to remove a wedge, like the bird's traceless path amid clouds, the reflection in a mirror, or the clear image of the moon in water. A teacher shows his student how to break free of delusion, just as a cat finds its path to safety by climbing a tree, with live words as upside-down statements that upend foxes from their den." 是賊識賊以楔出楔.鳥跡空雲鏡象水月.教兒師子迷蹤訣.上樹老貓安身法.活鱍鱍倒一說.

等閑翻卻狐狸穴.[146] According to a monk named Zhengjue 正覺, "An upside-down statement reveals a person's pure essence. Nary a cloud is in the sky yet a snowball is hurled down. How exceptional! This old Chan master bites his tongue." 倒一說.清人骨.萬里無片雲.拋下一團雪.別別.老大禪翁甘滅舌.[147] Yexuan 野軒 writes, "An inappropriate statement provides ample talk that does not allow anyone in the capital to miss the opportunity. But in the four seas and nine continents people are stumbling along. After flying out from the dragon's lair, they bore into an ant hill." 倒一說這饒舌.無端都把天機泄.四海九州徒蹴蹴.飛出龍宮鑽螳穴.[148]

## *Transcendence: Transformative and Deformative Elements*

The first four lines of Xuedou's verse comment on case 82, in which, in response to a monk's query about whether the indestructible Dharmakaya endures after a human body decomposes, master Dalong (n.d.) makes a brief poetic remark that highlights evanescence, "Mountain flowers blooming like brocade, valley streams rolling along tinged with indigo" 山花開似錦.澗水湛如藍 are interesting.[149] This is one of numerous passages in the *Blue Cliff Record* suggesting that lyricism at once embodies and trumps all other forms of expressiveness: "He asked without knowing./ And the answer was still not understood./ The moon stays clear as the wind blows high above/ Wintry pines sitting atop the ancient peak." 問曾不知.答還不會.月冷風高.古巖寒檜.[150] Yuanwu remarks that the verse was in a sense completed with these four lines, but Xuedou composed additional comments since he did not trust his assembly's ability to comprehend. The natural imagery in lines three and four that build on Dalong's reply recalls the truisms of straightforward Chan statements such as, "My eyes are horizontal and nose is vertical" or Yunmen's saying in case 83, "Clouds gather over southern mountains, and rains fall on northern mountains" 南山起雲, as a self-response to his query, "The old Buddha communes with the pillar—what kind of spiritual activity is that?" 古佛與露柱相交.是第幾機.[151]

**Transformative Elements.** These examples of deceptively simple Chan sayings reinforce an emphasis on transformative experience as a realm manifested in the everyday physical world but with a mysterious element beyond ordinary understanding that can best be disclosed through lyrical expressions. However, Yuanwu's commentary shows that an adept's level of awareness is only valid so long as it is accompanied by deformation of whatever viewpoint has been temporarily constructed, including any sort of veneration of naturalism. According to the One Voice approach natural images, which in the end are no more or less effective than untimely expressions with contradictions and reversals, must be subject to a continuing process of unpacking and deconstructing their discursive stance.

Case 46 is a prime example of a dazzler case in that, with each counterpoint, various commentators try to determine who is ahead in the competition based on the ability to maneuver freely and effectively when encountering irony and paradox. A monk responds, "The sound of raindrops" 雨滴聲 to the question posed by Jingqing, "What is that sound outside the door?" 門外是什麼聲.[152] When Jingqing challenges this reply by saying, "Everyone is topsy-turvy because they delude themselves by chasing after things" 眾生顛倒迷己逐物, the monk inquires whether this condition also applies to the master, who says, "It used to, but I no longer delude myself" 洎不迷己. Jingqing concludes, "Liberating oneself may seem easy but the path of casting it all aside is surely difficult." 出身猶可易.脫體道應難.[153] This thought-provoking declaration suggests that since a momentary breakthrough offers an insufficient glimpse of truth it must be enhanced through a fully unimpeded level of awareness.

Yuanwu's remarks cite a couple of other instances in which Jingqing was given similar answers, such as "The sound of a quail" 鵓鳩聲 and "The sound of a snake eating a frog" 蛇咬蝦蟆聲, and then he points out that it is a mistake to "view this case as a matter of tempering words" 公案. 諸方謂之鍛煉語.[154] Although that method of training is mentioned only this one time in the entire collection, without a clear definition provided, we can imagine that it involves a complex pedagogical process comparable to that of creating the edge of a sword that is sharp and unyielding yet flexible and adjustable to the circumstances of the battle. Yuanwu also argues against seeing the case in terms of "(a) clarifying the eye of Dao, (b) clarifying sound and form, (c) clarifying the mind-source, (d) clarifying the forgetting of feelings, or (e) clarifying exposition because, while those approaches may offer detailed explanations, in the end they fester as extraneous ways of talking about the experience." 一明道眼.二明聲色.三明心宗.四明忘情.五明展演.然不妨子細.爭奈有窠臼在.[155] Only after giving these and additional examples of deficiencies does Yuanwu praise the lyrical final lines of Xuedou's ode: "Whether or not there is understanding/ Mountains to the south and to the north drive the torrential rain." 曾不會.

南山北山轉雨霈.[156] This captures eloquently the meaning of Jingqing's concluding statement.

Returning to remarks on case 83 involving a Yunmen saying, Yuanwu says he admires the master for offering instruction that feels "like sparks flying and lightning striking" 如擊石火.似閃電光, and also points out that Librarian Qing asked of this case, "Where in the entire canon can you find such a teaching?" 慶藏主云.一大藏教還有這般說話麼.[157] Yet here, as in other instances, Yuanwu takes great pain to dislocate and dispel several kinds of misrepresentations although these devices are not given much of an explanation about how they function. One view he refutes is that of "calling out from amid nothingness" 無中唱出, which is also dismissed in case 37, despite the fact that it is promoted in the last paragraph of Yuanwu's *Essentials of the Five Houses of Chan*.

Yuanwu notes that Yunmen should not be considered beyond reproach or the need for revision since his teaching can lead to a false view of "unconcern" 無事 that claims all things are essentially the same. Yuanwu cites Wuzu who said, "Supposedly so great a figure Yunmen really didn't have much guts. If it were me I would have just said that [the communion of Buddhas and pillars] is the eighth level of mental activity [as in Yogacara Buddhism]." 大小雲門元來膽小.若是山僧.只向他道第八機. 他道.古佛與露柱相交.是第幾機.一時間且向目前包裹.[158] In a capping phrase to the verse in which Xuedou calls Yunmen "a golden-haired lion everyone should behold" 金毛獅子大家看, Yuanwu refers to him as "one of the dogs" 是箇狗子.[159] Rather than asserting the equality of ultimate and everyday reality, Yuanwu suggests that ongoing assessments about ranking the participants in dialogues and poets who comment are needed. Similarly, according to the concluding contradictory lines of Xuedou's ode, "Suffering is joy, joy is suffering./ Who says fine gold is no better than worthless dung?" 苦中樂.樂中苦.誰道黃金如糞土.[160]

**Deformative Elements.** Case 7 is a puzzler consisting of a brief exchange between Fayan and an inquiring monk and is particularly instructive of Yuanwu's evaluative approach integrating hermeneutic elements that are formative, in explaining lineage by highlighting various interpretations of the master's teaching style; reformative, by using creative rhetorical devices to comment on the core dialogue and poems by Xuedou and others; and transformative, in exploring the role of uncertainty. The case with capping phrases reads:

A monk asks Fayan (What's he saying? The handcuffs give evidence of his crime.),[161] "Huichao is my name. What is Buddha?" (What's he saying? His eyeballs are popping out.) Fayan responds, "You are Huichao." (He comes out with this according to his way of teaching. It's like chewing on an iron bar. He goes right up to [the monk] and takes him down.) 僧問法眼(道什麼.櫓枷過狀)慧超咨和尚.如何是佛(道什麼.眼睛突出)法眼云.汝是慧超(依模脫出.鐵餕.就身打劫).[162]

This exchange conveys the thrust-and-parry-based combative atmosphere of a typical encounter dialogue, which resembles the clash or competition of a sword fight, a chess match, or an intense one-on-one bout testing the wit and wherewithal of adversaries to attain transcendence disclosed at pivot moments. Yuanwu's capping phrases reinforce the impression that Fayan has bested Huichao, an otherwise unknown novice, by answering in a way that is least expected.[163]

Yuanwu's analysis of the case and Xuedou's view of it begins by evoking in the introduction the mystical notion of "a single word before sound" 聲前一句 that has not been transmitted by a thousand sages but if understood, manifests true Dharma activity every instant. This notion resembles other Chan ideas, such as the "last word" 末後句 evoked in case 51 by Yantou in a dialogue with his colleague Xuefeng and "Yunmen's one word" 雲門一言 cited in cases 3, 6, 8, and 47. The implication is that no matter what is said or left unsaid in any encounter falls short of expressing the truth so that any praise for Fayan's reply must be seen in light of this qualification, yet truth can be conveyed effusively by a seemingly innocuous word or phrase if it suits the context or matches the occasion.

In his prose commentary on the main case, Yuanwu lavishes additional praise on Fayan, known for his large assembly and tremendous influence on Chan monastic institutional identity based on a jocular style of teaching, but not to the detriment of the now enlightened inquirer. Yuanwu also dismisses interpretations that reduce Fayan's cryptic words to a logical formula, such as the view that "Huichao is Buddha," by arguing that one who truly understands the "whole activity" 全機 of the master must not "make intellectual interpretations" 作情解 and should be like "someone who does not turn his head when struck" 除非是一棒打不回頭底漢.[164] While this section seems to confirm and support the master, who "has the ability to break in and smash out at the same time" 有啐啄同時底機, the interpretation quickly gets a little more complicated by casting doubt, however subtly, on Fayan's judgment.

Yuanwu mentions a couple of instances in which Fayan uses the same technique of repeating the obvious, one of which was the occasion of the enlightenment of Tiantai Deshao, who until then had been a wandering monk and who composed the following verse that is acknowledged as an expression of succession by the master: "Atop the summit of Tongxuanfeng Peak/ Is beyond the [ordinary] human world;/ Outside of mind there are no dharmas/ Green mountains fill the eyes." 通玄峰頂.不是人間.心外無法.滿目青山.[165] This lyricism resembles Fayan's poem cited in case 2 of the *Record of Serenity*, "Wherever I go the frosty night's moon/ Falls as it may onto the valleys ahead./ The Big Dipper hangs down its handle at night over fresh waters." 到頭霜夜月.任運落前溪.河淡斗垂夜柄. This verse recalls another saying, "The clear autumn moon turns its frosty disc." 秋清月轉霜輪.[166]

Even though, according to Yuanwu's account, Fayan immediately approves of Deshao's verse, which refers to a peak in the Tiantai mountain range in Zhejiang province, the four lines can also be read as an apparently inauthentic form of boasting: "Now that I stand at the peak [from having grasped the teaching to the fullest extent],/ I no longer belong to the everyday realm./ There are no dharmas outside my mind,/ All I see on every side are the green mountains." Rather than a direct apprehension of the natural world encompassing all possible directions, this rendering evokes the image of a trainee who claims to have transcended the world but probably cannot return to ordinary life, a crucial goal as suggested by the image of entering the marketplace as the last of the *Ten Oxherding Pictures* in the version by Guoan, who was in Yuanwu's lineage. Deshao's words were carved into the side of a cliff by Zhu Xi (1130–1200), the famous Neo-Confucian scholar who visited the region in the early 1150s while he was still an admirer of Chan teaching (*Chanxue*) before he became a fierce critic.

While variant readings of the verse reflect a reformative hermeneutic element, it is significant from a formative interpretative standpoint that Yuanwu has worked Deshao into the commentary since Deshan proved to be the most influential of Fayan's disciples who contributed to keeping the school alive as the most prominent Chan lineage for well over a century, especially in the Wuyue (currently Zhejiang province) region. Fayan's support indicated that his follower would eventually hold sway with rulers. Deshao, who produced forty-nine disciples including the eminent exegete Yongming Yanshou, became the main advisor to the young regent Zhongyi (929–988, aka Qian Hongchu), about whose leadership there was a tradition of Buddhist prophecies; as Preceptor of the Wuyue state, he was the "undisputed spiritual guide" of this region.[167] Despite any skepticism regarding the spiritual merit of Deshao's verse, which is also discussed extensively in the commentary on case 32 of the *Record of Serenity* and whose final image is evoked in numerous Chan passages (including a capping phrase to case 91 in the *Record of Serenity*), from the standpoint of the *Blue Cliff Record* commentary taking an inclusive, ecumenical approach toward various lineages, Deshao's vital role in the process of lineal transmission is surely confirmed.

Xuedou's verse highlights transformation: "In the river country the spring wind does not stir/; Partridges are chirping from deep within the flowers/ At the three-tiered dragon gate where fish transform into dragons/ Fools keep on scooping out pond water at dusk." 江國春風吹不起.鷓鴣啼在深花裏.三級浪高魚化龍.癡人猶戽夜塘水.[168] Note that "river country" refers to Fayan's location in Nanjing just south of the Yangzi River, an area that was part of Jiangnan 江南 where both the Tiantai and the Song Chan schools were based. The final two lines evoke the image of the Dragon Gate (also mentioned in cases 49, 60, and 95), which seems to have been sadly misunderstood by Huichao, who looks in vain for fish that have been released, although perhaps Xuedou refers not to the monk but to those who lack his newfound awareness.

The natural images of the first two lines of the verse, with their intertextual allusions to other Chan texts alluding in turn to traditional Chinese poetry, are very much ambiguous and particularly draw Yuanwu's attention through his equally inconclusive capping phrases and prose comments. In *pingchang* remarks Yuanwu dismisses typical misrepresentations of the poem, such as seeing the first line as representing Samadhi and the second as idle talk, or conversely, the first line as a failure to inhale the fragrance of the flowers and the second line as a correction but still not the truly authentic sensation that remains available yet hidden from view. Is there allegorical significance in these lines? The aim of Yuanwu's comments is to keep readers expecting the unexpected while rejecting the supposed tried and true by suggesting that the "two lines are a single expression" 此兩句只是一句.[169]

The overall impact of Yuanwu's evaluation is complex and somewhat contradictory, no doubt deliberately so in order to cultivate the creative tension of uncertainty, by encompassing a transformative function that calls into question and deconstructs stereotypical views of the outcome of the encounter and a more pragmatic formative function in certifying the lineage based on Fayan's style of teaching. Yuanwu highlights the school's approach based on "arrow points meeting" 箭鋒相拄, so that "the case can be understood as soon as it is brought up by those who have practiced this technique for a long time" 這般公案.久參者.一舉便知落處.[170] But, we might wonder, not by others?

However the case's formative function is superseded, according to my reading, in that the main aim of the transformative function is to show that the final arbiter of truth is not based on interpreting verbiage contained in the case or the commentary or by either adhering to or transgressing the lines of transmission. Instead, it resides in the capacity of one's own inner self 自己 (*ziji*), yet only after shedding all biased or one-sided attitudes. "Look at the old masters who have gained awakening," Yuanwu says of Deshao's verse, "and consider what is the basis [of the experience]? It is not enough for me to try to explain the teaching; you yourself must attune your spirit all day long. If you can attain spiritual fulfillment the way [the old masters] did then someday your understanding will be sufficient to extend your hand to aid others, and this will not be considered a difficult matter." 看他古人.恁麼悟去.是什麼道理.不可只教山僧.須是自己二六時中.打辦精神.似恁麼與他承當.他日向十字街頭.垂手為人.也不為難事.[171] This outlook based on self-discovery is reinforced by Tenkei's comment on the case's verse stating that the "mystic principle of Buddhism is 'you are you.'"[172] Those who do not get the message and try to fake their way will be exposed as phonies, as in the retort, "You empty-headed fool!" 這掠虛頭漢[173] at the end of case 10, or "Wild fox spirits!" 野狐精 in case 93 and elsewhere.

It is interesting to note that case 68 deals with a similar dialogue about the use of personal names, in this instance involving masters Yangshan and Sansheng. The latter seems to outsmart his senior colleague, but by laughing heartily at an apparent putdown Yangshan comes off as the same level as the partner, which is acknowledged in the commentary. Yuanwu emphasizes that Xuedou places the responsibility for understanding on the reader: "All at once he has finished adding explanations for you, but nevertheless no one in the world can grasp it. They do not know what [Yangshan] is thinking, and I myself do not know his state. Do any of you know? 一時與爾注解了也.爭奈天下人啗啄不入.不知落處.縱是山僧也不知落處.諸人還知麼.[174]

Therefore the strength of Yuanwu's rhetoric of uncertainty lies in a willingness not to reduce any expression to a single vision of truth but to let every angle make its argument so that the complexity and relativism of uncertainty carries the day, including the sometimes complementary and at other times conflictive interaction between formative and transformative elements of gongan commentary. In remarking on Xuedou's verse after citing a query about the imagery that was raised by Librarian Qing, Yuanwu demands, "For me it is not necessary to stay [with any view] but I am asking you: Having transformed into a dragons, where do the fish now abide?" 我也不必在.我且問爾.化作龍去.即今在什麼處.[175]

We are left to ponder whether Yuanwu's query references Huichao, who is awakened, or Fayan, who demonstrates his knack for the pivot, or Xuedou, whose poem captures the essence of their encounter. Or perhaps Yuanwu himself, despite his denial earlier in the sentence, is the target of the remark. Does it refer to the select few who are awakened or to the multitudinous disillusioned or discouraged readers and learners of gongan discourse, who need to be shaken loose of their fetters with enough blows to break apart the stick?

# Questions are in the Answers

## ENDURING LEGACY IN RELATION TO TEXTUAL CONTROVERSIES

### *Impressions and Influences*

The primary aim of this chapter is to dispel one more stubborn stereotype that tends to create a misimpression about the ongoing impact exerted by the *Blue Cliff Record* on the unfolding of the gongan tradition. This assumption suggests that the appeal of the collection's elaborate rhetoric was probably limited to its original cultural context so that the text quickly faded in significance, almost never to be duplicated or followed again. It is as if no self-respecting Chan/Zen master would dare take up this task because such discursive intricacy in the end defaults to a kind of doctrinal simplicity that distracts and detracts from a single-minded focus on attaining awakening. A proper appraisal of this view necessarily involves examining the issue of how and when the *Blue Cliff Record* first entered Zen practice in Japan, where for centuries it served a variety of interpretative functions that probably helped stimulate the recovery of the lost Chinese text in the early 1300s. Therefore the last section of the chapter provides a critical summary of some of the main facts and legends, especially the account of the *One Night Blue Cliff* attributed to Dōgen, as much as these elements can be ascertained and distinguished, regarding the matter of transnational transition and transformation so that various issues concerning the history and ideology of the text can be appropriately linked.

An example of the stereotypical view of the *Blue Cliff Record*'s legacy (or supposed lack thereof) is evident in Mario Poceski's otherwise excellent recent account of the writings of Mazu, which notes rather dismissively

that "the question about the meaning or purpose of Bodhidharma's coming from India to China is repeated ad nauseam throughout Chan literature. . . . That includes the various *gong'an* collections, such as *Bi yan lu*,
where it is featured prominently in several cases. The question is about a
formulaic and clichéd as is possible to imagine. That much for the Chan
School's vaunted creativeness and originality."[1] In addition to questioning
the value of the collection's supposedly innovative oratory, Poceski suggests that the *Blue Cliff Record* and other prominent texts from the Song
dynasty do not

> serve as user-friendly collections of plain and direct words of ancient
> wisdom. In fact, their highly complex structure, along with their
> convoluted contents and the ostentatious language they deploy, are
> among the distinguishing features of *gong'an* collections such as *Bi
> yan lu*. . . . Consequently, among other things, these texts seem to
> have been meant to showcase the literary talents and intellectual
> creativity of their authors, as well as to focus attention to the pecu-
> liar brand of Chan they were promulgating.[2]

Chan sayings, this argues, should be "plain and direct" in order to convey
the meaning of enlightenment, whereas the *Blue Cliff Record*'s rhetorical
flair is merely "ostentatious."

Poceski's comments tend to demean an emphasis on literary prowess
as an end in itself, which was supposedly a distinctive feature of Song
dynasty discourse that particularly infiltrated the genre of gongan collections. But he fails to acknowledge that the role of *pingchang* or evaluative
commentary, which is revelatory in deliberately indirect fashion of an experience of self-realization, is the real basis of the *Blue Cliff Record*'s approach
to interpretation. The aim of this rhetoric was never user-friendliness, a
recently coined term that is framed by the contemporary era's specific
needs and demands for instructing clients/customers on how to use hi-
tech products. The rhetoric is, instead, meant to be deliberately disturbing
and disruptive to overcome fixations and attachments by assessing from
various angles diverse layers of remarks that had built up around gongan
cases. This helps inspire each and every member of the audience to take
full responsibility in grappling with spiritual conundrums to reach his or
her own conclusion, which in the final analysis is no firm standpoint at
all. The *pingchang* approach continued to influence case commentaries in
Song-Yuan China as well as throughout the medieval, early modern, and

modern eras in Japan (and, to a large extent, Korea). The use of evaluative reactions, whether expressed eloquently or in a more minimalist fashion in prose, poetic, capping phrase, or some other type of commentary such as calligraphy, not only did not die out but was also sustained during all developmental stages of the gongan tradition.

Before looking more closely at how the pervasive influence of the *pingchang* method affects a proper understanding of the impact of the *Blue Cliff Record*, it is important to summarize the debunking that has been carried out in previous chapters for two other misleading views regarding the collection. The first assumption, that Yuanwu somehow favored the utilization of prose commentary to defuse and reorient the merit of Xuedou's highly allusive and elusive verse remarks, is undermined by comparable qualities embedded in Yuanwu's extensive capping phrases, as well as the fact that he composed nearly as much poetic commentary as Xuedou, who in turn wrote the same amount of prose commentary as Yuanwu.

Yuanwu's comments include published letters in the *Essentials of Mind* (*Xinyao*), a twenty-volume recorded sayings text that contains dozens of prose and verse remarks on gongan, and additional interpretations of Xuedou's prose remarks on gongan cases that are contained in *Record of Keeping the Beat* (*Jijielu*). Musical imagery embedded in the terms *pingchang* and *jijie* referring to two kinds of prose commentary illustrates an underlying connection with the rhymes and rhythms of verse as well as nonverse remarks that may have been chanted. Nearly all great Chan masters were skilled in both styles of *songgu* and *niangu* comments. Therefore the *Blue Cliff Record* does not mark a transition from one type to the other, but both praises and appraises Xuedou's poetry with Yuanwu's prose, in turn, becoming subject to subsequent commentator's evaluative responses that were carried out in various literary genres.

The second assumption that the *Blue Cliff Record* deserved its fate of apparently being destroyed is enunciated by Thomas Cleary, who sees this event as part of the typical dialectical Chan process of "cooperation by opposition" or "point-counterpoint" in that "[s]o dramatic was the influence of Yuanwu's *Blue Cliff Record* that it came to be widely recognized as authoritative, with the consequence that it was often memorized and quoted without being studied and employed; therefore Dahui, recognized heir of Yuanwu himself, had the book burned . . . in order to break up the current fixation on Yuanwu's formulations."[3] As previously discussed a typical corollary to this standpoint is the precursor thesis which indicates that Yuanwu was already leaning toward and may have secretly instructed

Dahui in the value of the keyword approach, so that Yuanwu would have been indifferent or even in favor of the destruction.

Part of the argument against this assumption is that any evidence that the collection based on live sermons tried to pose as an exclusive authoritative scripture to be relied upon by disciples at the expense of receiving direct oral teaching gained in face-to-face encounters with an acclaimed mentor is scanty and speculative at best. One of countless examples of passages that I believe helps defuse the precursor thesis, by reflecting the noncommittal, never-boxed-in, flexibility of the rhetoric of uncertainty, is the following commentary from a Dharma hall sermon included in Yuanwu's record on source dialogues involving masters Nanyuan and Jingqing in regard to the notion of the simultaneous pecking into and breaking out of a shell that is also evoked in the commentary on case 16 in the *Blue Cliff Record*.[4] When asked by a monk about "the eye [or subjectivity] that pecks in and breaks out at the same time" 啐啄同時眼, Yuanwu responds, "Smashing through the thousand-year-old wild fox den" 打破千年野狐窟; and when probed about "the function [or objectivity] of pecking in and breaking out at the same time" 啐啄同時用 he replies, "Overturning the black dragon and taking something away with you" 掀翻驪龍領下物. When then asked, "What would happen if your Chan meditation cushion is suddenly overturned by your student?" 忽被學人掀翻禪床時如何 Yuanwu's retort is, "You have fallen back three thousand miles" 倒退三千.

The passage concludes with a poetic evocation of ambiguity, which alludes to the Jingqing dialogue about raindrop sounds featured in case 46, in addition to an ironic injunction against any misappropriation or false transmission of the core experience of awakening. "Sometimes layers of clouds gather and sometimes there is pouring or persistent drizzling rain without letting up" 有時生層雲.有時需微雨, Yuanwu says. "Consider the mind and the phenomenal realm—are they contained within the mind, or are they evident outside the mind? There is a row of brightly colored mandarin ducks yet you fail to see them, so do not try to pass your golden needle on to others." 是心耶是境耶.為復在心內.為復在心外.鴛鴦繡出徒君看.不把金針度與人. In this non–*Blue Cliff Record* passage by Yuanwu, as in the gongan collection, there is no attempt to be direct and user-friendly since such a goal defeats the purpose of Chan discourse that is based on gaining awakening by engaging with indeterminacy.

# The Legacy's Historical and Theoretical Components

In contrast to any view asserting that the *Blue Cliff Record* was only popular in its short-lived heyday, it can well be shown that the collection was certainly one of several factors and, quite possibly, the single main factor affecting the millennium-long development of the gongan tradition in helping form and fashion the ample reservoir of texts and interpretative techniques. This tradition is, after all, a continuing conversation about the purposefully uncertain meaning of cases for which the sayings of Xuedou and Yuanwu function as perhaps the most frequently evoked, though by no means only, background story or reference point for further interpretations. Overall the *Blue Cliff Record* has outlasted and/or taken priority over all other gongan collections, including *Wumen's Barrier*, and no doubt remains the "premier Chan writing" that was revived in China and reinvigorated in Japan by diverse scholars, monks, and lay adherents.[5]

**Table 6.1 Timeline for the *Blue Cliff Record*'s Ongoing Legacy**

12th c. Text created, edited, published, disseminated, and destroyed all within a thirty-year span

13th c. Emulations of *pingchang*-style commentary produced in China, Korea, and Japan

14th c. Prominence gained among Japanese Rinzai monks, especially Daitō and Musō

15th c. Zeami and Ikkyū in Japan, in addition to "Hekizen-Hekigan-Hekigo" sequence of cases

16th c. Tianqi's commentaries in China, and Missan (esoteric) applications in Japan

17th c. Initial Edo period commentaries and collections as well as other cultural influences

18th c. Leading scholastics from Rinzai and Sōtō sects write extensive commentaries

19th c. Early beginnings of academic textual-historical studies of Chan/Zen literature

20th c. Numerous modern translations and analyses by scholars and monks in Japan and China

21st c. New approaches to applying *pingchang*-style remarks to traditional Chan/Zen texts

Table 6.1 provides a concise century-by-century overview of some of the major highlights that reflect the remarkable degree of impact wielded by the collection.

This table shows some of the various and vigorous ways in which the evaluative rhetorical style developed by Xuedou and Yuanwu, which was often overshadowed by the keyword method initiated by Dahui, remained alive and well through the works of a multitude of later commentators representing both the Linji/Rinzai and Caodong/Sōtō schools in addition to various sub-factions. Those who have followed in the footsteps pioneered by the *Blue Cliff Record*, either directly or indirectly, include in the thirteenth- and fourteenth-centuries Wansong Xingxiu and his disciple Linquan Conglun in China in addition to Korean monk Gag'un plus Dōgen and Daitō in Japan. After this came a variety of medieval Japanese preachers and poets, Edo period commentators such as Hakuin and Tenkei, along with modern interpreters like Xu Yun in China and Yamada Mumon in Japan, among numerous other worldwide examples.

My discussion is based on dividing the chronology into four main thematic periods, beginning with the phase of (1) textual emulations created in China, Korea, and Japan in the centuries shortly after the *Blue Cliff Record*'s composition. The stages continue with (2) medieval Japanese applications of teaching methods based on, yet containing elements that go beyond, the use of the actual text; and (3) early modern appropriations of interpretative styles by diverse inventive thinkers and cultural figures. The final phase involves (4) more recent adaptations of the text's methodology and ideology in ways reflecting modern academic or religious practical concerns. For each period I will provide brief citations of representative examples of Chan/Zen expressions that disclose some of the key aspects of influence.

**Early Emulations.** The period of textual replications of the evaluative style covers a couple of centuries of publications advanced in three countries. These works demonstrate that the rhetoric of uncertainty pioneered and polished in the *Blue Cliff Record* in the early 1100s did not vanish. This is particularly evident in the dynamic decade of the 1220s, one hundred years after the original release, when dramatic developments took place in China, Korea, and Japan where texts were prepared or planned that closely adhered to the multilayered evaluative style of gongan commentary and sometimes included the term *pingchang* 評唱 in the title.

The most significant example of such a gongan collection designed specifically to be considered the "Caodong schools's version" of the *Blue Cliff Record* was the *Record of Serenity* (*Congronglu*)—full title: 萬松老人評唱天童覺和尚頌古從容庵錄—by the prominent master Wansong Xingxiu (1166–1246). The text as derived from the verse remarks (*songgu*) on one hundred cases originally created by another eminent leader of the Caodong school, Hongzhi Zhenjue (1091–1157), follows almost exactly the *Blue Cliff Record*'s formula of containing seven sections for each case: an (1) introduction, the (2) gongan selected by Hongzhi with (3) Wansong's capping phrases followed by his (4) prose comments, and (5) Hongzhi's verse with (6) Wansong's capping phrases followed by (7) prose remarks.[6]

The story of the formation of this text is fascinating in that Wansong was located for decades in territory controlled to the north of China by the Jurchen Jin dynasty, which lasted from 1115–1234 and was responsible for the loss of Northern Song areas. Wansong had been invited to come to the Jin capital of Tatu (aka Yanjing, current Beijing) in 1193 by a ruler who was intrigued by the idea of promoting Buddhism as a means of cultivating civilization for his people in their encounters with the Han Chinese. Wansong remained there for the rest of his life, while gaining a number of important monastic and lay disciples, through the time the Jin was defeated by the invading Mongols, who under Genghis Khan (?–1227) had pretty much gained control over the city nearly twenty years before.

Wansong's distinctive approach to Chan theory and practice was initially bred in the Five Mountains temples of Zhejiang province, and his monastic disciples in the north carried forth the Caodong school standpoint that otherwise was dying out in the south where Yuanwu's Linji-Yangqi lineage had come to prevail. One of Wansong's main lay followers was the well-educated and philosophically astute Khitan diplomat Yelü Chucai (1190–1243), an important advisor to Genghis and his son Ögödei. Yelü helped convince Wansong that there needed to be an outstanding published record of his teachings in order for Caodong Chan to compete with various rivals, especially Tibetan Buddhism in addition to other movements including Daoism and the increasingly influential Christianity. Yelü, who endorsed the unity of the Three Teachings (Buddhism, Confucianism, and Daoism) as a response to complex and shifting political circumstances, strongly encouraged Wansong to include many references to Chinese classics. Despite his underlying loyalty to the superiority of his own lineal affiliation, Wansong found commonality with Yelü's vision through his portrayal of Caodong Chan as the root ideology for which other religions, both Buddhist and non-Buddhist, were considered branches.

In a compelling analysis, Yelü maintained, as did Zhongfeng Mngben and others, that there was mainly complementarity rather than conflict among various Chan teaching techniques. He commented on the strengths and weakness of the Yunmen school, which was surprisingly still popular at the time even in the north and emphasized incisive instructions but also showed a tendency toward biased assessments. The Linji school, according to Yelü, was based on seizing opportune moments for instruction through risk-taking that could decline into sheer recklessness, and the Caodong school highlighted the role of clear apprehension that could be diverted to over-attention to fine details. Yelü maintained that all three lineages were of equal value, and he also assessed their compatibility with other Buddhist schools that disciplined the mind, whereas Daoism focused on nature and Confucianism emphasized social concerns. Wansong disagreed with Yelü's full-fledged ecumenism, but he did try to incorporate an even-handed approach, as did Yuanwu in his own way, while subtly asserting the priority of Caodong.

Although Wansong was at first reluctant to create the work prescribed by Yelü, over a number of years he produced a polished collection of gongan comments on Hongzhi's Xuedou-like cases with verses that emulated the style of the *Blue Cliff Record*. Wansong's sermons were delivered and edited at Congrong-an hermitage in Bao'en temple. According to some accounts an early manuscript was lost, but in 1224 Wansong's masterpiece was published and soon after was widely distributed in the northern territory while also gaining the attention of Mongol rulers. Kublai Khan (1215–1294), who practiced a brand of ecumenism that fostered dynamic debates among various religious factions, eventually supported the *Record of Serenity*'s standpoint.

However Wansong's text was not well known among Chan practitioners in Zhejiang province at the time Dōgen was visiting China from 1223 to 1227; nor was this work transmitted to Japan until the sixteenth century, unlike earlier transmissions of the *Blue Cliff Record* and *Wumen's Barrier*, which arrived in Japan via Shinchi Kakushin 心地覺心 (1207–1298) following his travels to China in the mid-thirteenth century. Dōgen had no awareness of the work when he studied gongan literature on the mainland (and may have been exposed to a handwritten copy of the then-defunct *Blue Cliff Record*). The connection between Wansong and the Sōtō sect in Japan was not made until the Edo period when sociopolitical pressures under the Tokugawa shogunate about the status of each Buddhist tradition caused new scholastic reformers to appreciate that Wansong had asserted a strong sense of sectarian identity.[7]

Because of these now long-standing linkages, much has been written in modern Sōtō scholarship about the distinguishing features of the *Record of Serenity*'s view of language in expressing enlightenment vis-à-vis the *Blue Cliff Record*, and many of the arguments presented ring true.[8] The main issue usually considered in such studies is whether and to what extent Wansong, following the ideals of Hongzhi, preferred the path of silent-illumination (*mozhao*) and recommended a passive approach to meditation and quelling a reliance on verbal communication, despite his extensive use of rhetorical flourishes.[9]

Here I mention briefly a few key points in regard to a comparison of the rhetorical techniques evident in the two texts. As shown in Appendix 3, they share at least thirty cases, although in some instances the versions are different. For example, case 91 of the *Blue Cliff Record* on "Yanquan's Rhinoceros Fan" includes four comments on the main dialogue by later masters in addition to capping remarks on each remark by Xuedou, whereas these eight comments in all are cited in case 25 of the *Record of Serenity* in the section of prose commentary rather than as part of the main gongan. As per Table 6.2, Wansong was well aware and took into account the commentaries of Xuedou and Yuanwu, which are frequently

Table 6.2  *Record of Serenity*
Case Commentaries Citing
the *Blue Cliff Record*

| CONGRONGLU | BIYANLU |
| --- | --- |
| 30 | 29 |
| 36 | 3 |
| 50 | 51 |
| 53 | 11 |
| 60 | 24 |
| 71 | 8 |
| 78 | 77 |
| 80 | 20 |
| 85 | 18 |
| 88 | 94 |
| 92 | 62 |
| 99 | 50 |

mentioned and sometimes critiqued. Based on extensive research, it seems the *Record of Serenity* is a rare text from the period (1140–1300) during which the *Blue Cliff Record* was supposedly out of circulation that cites directly Yuanwu comments culled from at least a dozen cases. Wansong also sometimes cites Yuanwu's *Record*, and Xuedou's words in part from his recorded sayings are mentioned in thirty-three cases.[10]

One difference between the two collections is that the kind of homiletic exuberance so much in evidence in the *Blue Cliff Record* functions on a more modest level in the work by Wansong. While he cites numerous examples of Yunmen, Xuedou, and others raising their staff in a threatening or ironic way, or using it to draw a line or circle in the dirt, or to fling it down, Wansong wields the stick or fly-whisk to admonish rival thinkers or to caution his current audience far less frequently than in the *Blue Cliff Record*. However there are several instances in which this pedagogical device is evoked. For example, at the end of the comments on Hongzhi's verse in case 29, Wansong declares, "Be careful not to use affirmation or denial, or gain or loss, to determine triumph and defeat. Doing so would resemble watching a pearl rolling in a bowl while blinking your eyes so that you miss the instant of movement." An editor interjects, "Wansong struck the meditation seat with his fly-whisk and said, 'That's it!'" 慎勿以定奪得失決斷勝負.如珠走盤.眨眼蹉過也.師以拂子擊禪床云.了.[11]

Another disparity is that in many examples of commentary in the *Record of Serenity* it appears that Wansong, who was writing a century after Yuanwu and was prodded by Yelü to be as ecumenical in spirit as possible, cites many more examples of predecessor comments on the cases being covered than are generally found in the *Blue Cliff Record*'s sections of prose remarks. Therefore Wansong's text functions as an even richer storehouse of various teachings and techniques that were current during the Southern Song representing the methods of each of the Five Houses and other kinds of instruction.

Nevertheless, it can well be argued that the evaluative method and intent to express self-realization underlying the two gongan collections is essentially the same. Wansong's capping phrases include novel zingers that match Yuanwu's scathing irony, such as case 74 that says, "Shut that dog's mouth!" 合取狗口, and "Don't daydream!" (literally, "don't have an eye for [imaginary] flowers") 莫眼華. In addition he likes to use onomatopoeia in making some comments, as with the introduction to case 65 that exclaims, "Tut, tut! Pshaw, pshaw! Puff, puff! Whoosh, whoosh! So vague and confusing, it is impossible to chew on and difficult even to approach."

吒吒沙沙.剝剝落落.刀刀蹶蹶.漫漫汗汗.沒可咬嚼.難為近傍.且道.是甚麼話.[12]

As Thomas Cleary points out, "The more fundamental purpose of Wansong's commentaries, naturally, is the elucidation of meanings in the text.... The context in which the meaning intended in Chan usage is defined is the context of the Chan outlook; this becomes perceptible by observing the structure of the sayings or anecdotes presented."[13] While largely agreeing with this observation, it is my contention that the key point for Yuanwu and Wansong is not merely a matter of aggregating and juxtaposing diverse sayings and anecdotes that feature a common conceptual structure, however much that may contribute to the audience/reader's contemplation of cases. Instead their basic aim goes beyond citing anecdotes based on the all-important role of the commentator's evaluative reactions. Like Yuanwu, whom he sometimes critiques with deference to his lineal ancestor Hongzhi, Wansong uses the approach of appropriating someone else's wording or narrative in order to apply it from his own critical standpoint. However, Wansong does not playfully debunk Hongzhi the way Yuanwu frequently zaps Xuedou, who was not from his lineage.

An example of Wansong's evaluative approach occurs in case 34 on a Fengxue saying that includes the following capping phrase as part of the main gongan (this resembles case 61 of the *Blue Cliff Record* but the passage is considerably modified based on the citation from Hongzhi's text), "Xuedou held up his staff [and said to the assembly], 'Who lives in this dusty place?'" 雪竇舉拄杖.意在立塵處. Wansong's prose remarks then cite Xuedou's complete verse commentary that is also included in the *Blue Cliff Record*, which concludes, "The feel of a pure wind blowing for thousands of miles can only be known by oneself" 萬里清風只自知. At the end of the section, Wansong suggests that while "Xuedou does not lose anything at the gateway of serving Buddha" 雪竇於佛事門中不捨一法, he only gets half the point of the case as this is complemented by Hongzhi's verse that "brings out both sides together all at once" 一併拈出.[14]

To cite a few other instances of Wansong's evaluative responses to Xuedou and Yuanwu, in case 50 (corresponding to *Blue Cliff Record* case 51) he praises both figures,[15] but case 53 (11) says, "Xuedou's ode and Foguo [Yuanwu]'s appraisal are quite thorough but they still miss the true meaning of the case in the original record. Tiantong [Hongzhi]'s interpretation in his ode is the most complete version." 雪竇頌.佛果評唱.最詳.尚闕本錄上堂正意.天童頌出.極盡善盡美.[16] Similarly case 78 (77) cites Yuanwu favorably, or so it seems at first but concludes, "I say that if you want the hammer that smashes off fetters and chains then refer to Tiantong's verse." 萬松道.若要敲柳打鎖鈷鏈.問取天童頌古.[17] Additionally in case 99 (50) Wansong maintains, "In his verse Tiantong breaks open the skin on one's face." 天童擘破面皮.頌云.[18]

Wansong's production of gongan commentaries was prolific as he authored several texts, including another with the term *pingchang* in the title known as *Record of Getting to the Point* 萬松老人評唱天童覺和尚拈古請益錄 (shortened: *Qingyilu*).[19] This collection is parallel to Yuanwu's *Keeping the Beat* by including Wansong's commentaries on Hongzhi's prose remarks on one hundred cases with a total of seven levels of interpretation. Wansong also published two additional texts, *Tongxuan's One Hundred Questions* 通玄百問 (*Tongxuan Baiwen*) and *Qingzhou's One Hundred Questions* 青州百問 (*Qingzhou Baiwen*), in which a monk asks a series of questions to which Wansong gives concise and cryptic gongan-like responses. Both collections were first published in the 1240s, but sometime later Wansong's equally prolific disciple Linquan added verse comments for each question and answer.[20] Linquan's odes usually open by restating the response and sometimes are irregular in terms of the number of characters per line. To cite one example of this approach to an evaluative style of commentary:

> Question: If walking the path of profundity is like hiking rugged mountain roads then where do we find flat terrain? [Wansong's] Answer: Four corners of the compass.
>
> [Linquan's] Verse: Four corners of the compass/ Invade heaven with thorns and thistles./ Footless men made of stone do not need to exert themselves,/ But [for the rest] it is difficult to penetrate this barrier./ Only when freely walking back and forth in all directions can one explicate its meaning.

問.行玄猶是涉崎嶇.如何是平坦處.答.東西南北. 頌.東西南北.侵天荊棘.沒足石人.不消勞力.更須透過那重關.自在縱橫方脫纏.[21]

Wansong's answer literally means, "East, west, north, south," thus recalling Zhaozhou's "Four Gates" that appears as case 9 of the *Blue Cliff Record*.

Linquan became a prominent figure during the early decades of the Yuan dynasty (1279–1368), who by citing various gongan won a series of debates that were sponsored by Kublai Khan and held with Tibetan Buddhist and Daoist adversaries. He produced two seven-section *pingchang* collections based on case-with-verse texts initially composed by noteworthy Northern Song Caodong school predecessors. One is the *Empty Valley Collection* 林泉老人評唱投子青和尚頌古空谷集 (shortened: *Kongguji*) derived from odes by Touzi Yiqing (1032–1083), and the other is the *Vacant Hall Collection* 林泉老人評唱丹霞淳禪師頌古虛堂集 (shortened: *Xutangji*) derived from odes by Danxia Zichun (1064–1117), who was the teacher of Hongzhi.[22] These two collections along with Wansong's *Record of Serenity* and *Record of Getting to the Point* are included in a compendium known as *Evaluative Reactions of Four Houses* 四家評唱 (*Sijia Pingchanglu*). All four collections are very much indebted to the rhetorical structure of the *Blue Cliff Record*, although they use additional expressions from non-Buddhist sources while ultimately endorsing the Caodong standpoint.

Jumping ahead in time for an important though little-noted development in China during the late Ming dynasty, Tianqi Benrui 天奇本瑞 (?–1508) produced two *pingchang* commentaries consisting mainly of capping phrases that cover both Linji and Caodong lineages: *Notes on Xuedou's Odes* 螢絕老人天奇直註雪竇顯和尚頌古; and *Notes on Tiantong [Hongzhi]'s Odes* 螢絕老人直註天童覺和尚頌古. There may have been other examples of this genre that were lost over time or not included in the Buddhist canon. To show differences between the approaches in some of these texts let us consider the dialogue between master Fayan and his disciple Huichao that comprises case 7 in the *Blue Cliff Record*.

According to Yuanwu's *Record*, which provides a slightly different version of the brief exchange than appears in the *Blue Cliff Record*, "A monk says, 'I, Huichao, ask the Reverend, What is the Buddha Dharma?' and Fayan replies, 'You are Huichao.'" 僧問法眼慧超咨和尚.如何是佛法.眼云.汝是慧超. Yuanwu remarks by mentioning various examples that suggest resolution by means of appropriate reciprocity: "Something received is returned, sickness is treated by taking effective medicine, hunger is conquered by eating a royal meal, sauce is flavored with salt, and a snowy day is heated by burning coal." 還委悉麼.病遇良醫.饑逢王膳.醬裏得鹽.雪中送炭.[23]

The dialogue appears as case 92 in Linquan's *Empty Valley Collection*; cited here is the introduction, case with capping phrases, and Touzi's verse comment with capping phrases:

Introduction: Searching afar rather than near is like spending in vain to buy straw sandals or preferring the false to the true. To compensate for karmic debt incurred by opening your mouth you must convey directly the right place, but who can express it?

Case: A monk asks Fayan, "What is Buddha?" (Stop talking about what is outside your domain.) Fayan replies, "You are Huichao." (Don't be mistaken about what you know.)

Verse: It is difficult to ask for directions on a perilous route. (Those who are not weary from labor and hardship do not realize this.)/ Someone encountered on the way to the northern village points to the south. (It's done out of compassion with talk that gets down in the weeds.)/ An unlimited number of people come and go to Chang'an. (Even if you bend your fingers and count the numbers you can't get them all.)/ But who can pass through the barrier without first ringing the bell. (Lacking proper credentials in the end they fail to make the grade.)

示眾云.搜遠不搜近.空費草鞋錢.宜假不宜真.枉償口業債.抄直打快處.誰能道得.舉僧問法眼.如何是佛 (休分外).眼云汝是慧超 (莫錯認).頌曰.巇嶮行時問路難 (不是苦辛人不知).有人相指北村南 (慈悲之故.落草之談).長安無限人來往 (屈指從頭數莫真).幾箇無鈴過得關(不有憑由.終成敗闕).24

This version expresses a comparable degree of uncertainty to the *Blue Cliff Record*, but without including the personalized "here's what I think" interpretative element featured by Yuanwu.

Tianqi comments on this in *Notes on Xuedou's Odes*. A key feature of this text, which gives capping phrases on Xuedou's verses also used in the *Blue Cliff Record*, is the function of an ironic remark that "wraps up" 總結 each of the cases like a legal brief for a public record:

Case: A monk asks Fayan, "What is Buddha?" (Asking for instruction.) Fayan replies, "You are Huichao." (Bringing up the head of the matter.) (The main meaning is brought up at a hurried point. Illumination grabs the rabbit in its hole.)

Brief: Arrows and blades fly toward each other.

Verse: In the river country the spring wind does not stir, (All the people of the country are calling out. They don't get the meaning.)/ Partridges are chirping from deep within the flowers (Asking for instruction today by bringing it up in an everyday way)./ At the three-tiered Dragon Gate where fish are transformed into dragons, (This is the spot where Huichao is enlightened as he hears the thunder and becomes [a dragon].)/ Fools keep on scooping out pond water at dusk. (The unwise get emotional over words, just like scooping out pond water late at night in the name of fishing.)

僧 問 法 眼 . 如 何 是 佛 ( 請 益 ). 眼 云 汝 是 慧 超 ( 當 頭 一 提 )
( 主 意 急 處 一 提 . 旨 明 就 窩 打 兔 ). 總 結 ( 箭 鋒 相 拄 ).
江國春風吹不起(盡國人呼.未曾著意). 鷓鴣啼在深花裏(今日請益.
平常一提).三級浪高魚化龍(慧超悟處.聞雷而化).癡人猶庤夜塘水(
無智之人逐語生情.如乎深夜庤水取魚).²⁵

Another monumentally important thirteenth-century *pingchang*-oriented text is Korean monk Gag'un's (n.d.) *Explanations of Chan Verse Comments* (*Seonmun Yeomsong Seolhwa*, C. *Seonmun Yeomsong Shuohua*), an expanded supplement on 1,463 cases for the *Collection of Chan Verse Comments* (*Seonmun Yeomsongjip*, C. *Chanmen Niansongji*) by Hyesim (1178–1234). Hyesim was the successor to Jinul (1158–1210), who had established the keyword technique as the mainstream of the Seon school especially for the Jogye Order. Gagun's extensive prose commentaries on Chinese gongan not only resemble Yuanwu remarks but in many ways also surpass them in terms of the intricacy applied to dissecting each and every phrase of the main cases along with various interpretations, including those of Xuedou and Yuanwu.

During the thirteenth and fourteenth centuries in Japan, Dōgen (1200–1253) and Daitō (1282–1337), representing the emerging Sōtō and Rinzai sects respectively, helped introduce to Japan the role of *pingchang* interpretations of kōan cases by producing highly inventive prose and capping-phrase commentaries greatly influenced by the *Blue Cliff Record*. These two and many other prominent Zen masters of the era also composed Sino-Japanese (*kanbun*) poetry in the style initiated by Fenyang and Xuedou for interpreting encounter dialogues and related spiritual matters.

Daitō is best known for establishing the importance of the *Blue Cliff Record* as a standard Rinzai scripture by, like Tianqi, polishing the style of capping phrases on the writings of Xuedou, Yuanwu, and other Song Chan works that are featured in several of the Rinzai master's main texts. These collections include *Essentials Words for Careful Study* 參詳要語 (*Sanshō Goyō*), in which Daitō caps a sermon filled with irony for the opening of a temple that was originally delivered by Xuedou during his abbacy in Zhejiang province; *Capping Phrases on the Blue Cliff* 碧巖下語 (*Hekigan Agyō*), which comments on every line of the main cases but not the verse or prose comments; and *One Hundred Twenty Cases* 百二十則

(*Hyakunijūsoku*), which includes thirty-five *Blue Cliff Record* cases that are capped with different phrasing than is included in the aforementioned collection. As Kenneth Kraft notes of his contribution to the tradition of kōan commentary, Daitō "expresses the irreverent reverence of Zen, capping the discourse record of the distinguished master Hsüeh-tou with such phrases as 'Hsüeh-tou has opened only one eye,' 'Hsüeh-tou has not yet gotten that far,' or 'Do not make a mistake because of Hsüeh-tou.'" And he applies this principle to himself as well: each time he reconsiders a kōan, he caps it freshly, without reference to his earlier responses.[26] It is also said that in 1325, Daitō won a debate with Tendai school monks that was crucial in establishing Zen as the main sect in Japan by uttering a capping phrase from *Blue Cliff Record* case 47, "An octagonal millstone flies through the air" 八角磨盤空裏走.[27]

Moreover Daitō's approach, Kraft points out, highlights the crucial role of taking responsibility for self-realization based on uncertainty, "Each time that he caps a line of a Ch'an discourse record, he is putting himself on the line as well. Daitō's written capping phrases are the textual equivalent of the live demonstrations that take place in the master-disciple encounter."[28] Lest it seem that Daitō follows the Linji school model of criticism more vigorously than Caodong school interpreters like Wansong or Linquan, such an assessment would not apply to Dōgen, whose work's relation to the *Blue Cliff Record* is discussed near the end of the chapter.

**Medieval Applications.** The medieval era in Japan saw two levels of new applications of the teachings of the *Blue Cliff Record*: one through the high culture of fine arts, including garden design, theatrical theory, and poetry; and the other with everyday monastic training methods based on listening to sermons while working with kōan cases, sometimes in esoteric or cultic fashion. As to the second level, once the era of masters who were capable of closely emulating the *Blue Cliff Record*'s interpretative style began to subside, many Japanese preachers known as Shōmonosha (literally, "Commentators") frequently commented in various ways on Yuanwu's text along with the *Record of Linji*, *Wumen's Barrier*, and *Eyes of Humans and Gods*. These sermonizers often represented the Rinka temples, which covered Sōtō and Rinzai institutions including Dōgen's Eiheiji and Daitō's Daitokuji that stood outside the elite Rinzai-only Five Mountains (Gozan) systems in Kyoto and Kamakura that were supported by the government. Two somewhat overlapping training models were created during this period. One was the style of "Hekizen-gan-go" 碧前巖後 sequential study, which included a series of usually one hundred kōan to be contemplated by monks prior (*zen* 前) to studying cases from the collection (*gan* 巌), which was followed (*go* 後) by another set of one hundred cases. The second model included Missan (esoteric) comments passed down in oral fashion or through informal writing on "strips of paper" (*kirigami* 切り紙) that were often deliberately indecipherable to one not schooled in a particular lineage's teaching method.[29]

One of the main contributors to medieval high culture was Musō Soseki (1275–1351), Daitō's contemporary, who by the onset of the Muromachi (1333–1573) era played an equally important role in establishing the prominence of Zen temples in Kyoto by creating his own monasteries highly ranked in the Five Mountains network. Like Daitō, Musō was well versed in Chinese texts without the benefit of traveling to the mainland. This followed the émigré period in the late thirteenth century during which their teachers either came from China (Yishan Yining/Ishan Ichinei for Musō) or studied for a number of years on the mainland (Daiō, who trained under Xutang, for Daitō). In *Dialogues in a Dream* 夢中問答集 (*Muchū Mondōshū*), a set of conversations about Zen theory and practice, Musō refers to the *Blue Cliff Record* and other works by Yuanwu, including his *Record* and the *Essentials of Mind*.[30]

Perhaps the most interesting feature of Musō's appropriation of the *Blue Cliff Record* is the way he integrated the symbolism of several cases into the creative design of his two most famous temple gardens.[31] For example the "walking garden" at Saihōji, also known as the Moss Garden (*Koke Teien*) because of its multiple shadings of fine greenery, was "formerly two paradise-gardens [on an estate], which Musō changed into what is today a symbolic representation of Zen's ideal land as described in the *Hekiganroku*."[32] Musō did this by creating a space that corresponded to case 18 on the building of a "seamless monument," with landscapes constructed on two levels separated by a gate.

By creating a very different type of garden to be observed from the veranda outside the abbot's quarters at Tenryūji, ranked at the top of the Five Mountains, Musō's design incorporates a vertical waterfall (no longer active) with a carp stone placed to show ascension to reflect the Dragon Gate from case 49 (also cited in 7 and 60). The garden includes a horizontal series of stones in the water below, thus indicating Zhaozhou's bridge as featured in case 52. The message of both temple garden designs is that Zen discourse is a matter of ascending 向上 to transcend the world and attain enlightenment, while at the same time descending 向下 to fulfill the bodhisattva's compassionate vow of bringing the release of wisdom to ordinary humans and other sentient beings. The twin themes are thoroughly grounded in Yuanwu's views.

Noh theater playwright/theorist Zeami (1363–1443) frequently evoked aphorisms culled from the *Blue Cliff Record*, including "Piling snow in a silver bowl" from the gongan in case 13 and "Describing fully the scene of clouds on the mountains and the moon over the sea" from the verse to case 53. Another medieval Zen master, the eccentric Ikkyū (1394–1481), cites the *Blue Cliff Record* in several of his *kanbun*-style poems. For example verse 69 in the *Crazy Cloud Collection* 狂雲集 (*Kyōunshū*), which alludes to the ode to case 3 on Mazu's "Sun-face Buddha, Moon-face Buddha," is part of a small group of poems on the worthlessness of scriptures:

> From the beginning the sutras have no function other than wiping
>     excrement.
> The treasury in the dragon palace of the sea makes light of words
>     and phrases.
> Take a good look at the one hundred cases in the *Blue Cliff Record*,
> Still struggling to find their proper place in this turbulent world.

経巻元除不浄籌.竜宮海蔵弄言詮.看々百則碧巌集.狼籍乳峰風月前.[33]

This *songgu/juko*-style poem cites a verse from the twelfth century discussed in chapter 1, which was originally inscribed on a stele at Xuedou's grave and seems to be a rare example of referring to the *Blue Cliff Record* during the phase when it was not being circulated.

Ikkyū made comments on the loss of the *Blue Cliff Record* in two other poems included in the *Crazy Cloud Collection*. Verse 72 is titled, "Chan Teacher Dahui Burns the *Blue Cliff Record*" 大恵禅師焚碧巌集: "Old man Miaoxi [Dahui] will be famous for a thousand years to come/ For polishing Zen to the greatest extent possible./ A beast was once stabbed by the King of Wu,/ But, sadly, the sword that did the piercing did not have eyes." 妙喜老人千歳名.宗門潤色太高生.子胥曽受呉王戮.可惜鐲鏤無眼睛. The last two lines allude to the ancient legend of a weapon that was used for revenge by a monarch, but this led to the perpetrator's violent death, so that the sword is an instrument that kills indiscriminately. Verse 138 is titled, "Reading the *Blue Cliff Record* Preface" 読碧巌集序: "Come to the mountain and express teachings worth a thousand pieces of gold,/ The light of a single torch is salvific from the ancient past to the present./ Stop talking about principles of a doctrine based on cold ashes,/ Zen training is fully manifest though [the text's] grandmotherly kindness." 來山言教価千金.一炬看来救古今.休向寒灰成議論.宗乗滅却老婆心.

**Edo Appropriations.** During the Edo period marked by a resurgence of Zen scholasticism based on learning Chinese texts while rejecting the previous era's trend toward esotericism, monks from both sects produced monumental commentaries on the *Blue Cliff Record* by using the *pingchang* method toward the original collection. The *Tenkei Teishō*, also known as *Tenkei's Sermons on "Yuanwu's Evaluative Remarks"* ("*[Engo] Kokugon Hyōshō*"),[34] or simply the *Blue Cliff Record Lectures* 碧巖錄講義 (*Hekiganroku Kōgi*), was composed by Sōtō master Tenkei Denson 天桂傳尊 (1647–1735). Tenkei was controversial in his sect because of his criticism of some fascicles in Dōgen's *Treasury of the True Dharma-Eye* that recalls a scathing analysis by Rinzai scholiast Mujaku Dōchū 無著道忠 (1653–1755), who similarly claimed that Dōgen did not understand Chinese, Tenkei's work was matched by Hakuin's *Secret Notes on the Blue Cliff Record* 碧巖録秘抄 (*Hekiganroku Hisshō*),[35] among numerous examples from the period including the concise commentary, *Discussing the One Hundred Blue Cliff Cases* 碧巖百則辧 (*Hekigan Hyakusokuben*) by Hakuin's main disciple, Tōrei Enji 東嶺圓慈 (1721–1792).

Edo period Japan also saw the publication of several important gongan works influenced by the *Blue Cliff Record*. The Rinzai sect's *Collection of Zen Entanglements* 宗門葛藤集 (*Shūmon Kattōshū*) from 1689 contains forty-five cases, or about one-sixth of the total, from the Chinese compilation. The Rinzai *Zen Phrase Books* 禪林句集 (*Zenrin Kushū*), published in 1688, was based upon an earlier anthology of 5,000 Zen phrases known as the *Ku Zōshi* 句雙紙 compiled by Tōyō Eichō 東陽英朝 (1438–1504), who drew materials from sutras, recorded sayings of Chinese masters, Daoist and Confucian texts, and Chinese poetry. The phrases were arranged according to length, beginning with single-character expressions and continuing with phrases of two characters through eight characters, with interspersing parallel verses of five through eight characters. Tōyō's work circulated in manuscript form for several generations until the seventeenth century when it was first published in 1688 under the new title. In addition the Sōtō sects's *The Iron Flute Played Upside Down* 鐵笛倒吹 from 1783, takes in its one hundred kōan only a few cases from the *Blue Cliff Record*, but its use of verses with ironic capping phrases clearly derives from the Chinese collection's interpretative approach.

An intriguing example of the continuing impact of Xuedou and Yuanwu in the Edo period can be seen in a passage from what is considered Tōrei's master work for the way it describes the entire Rinzai curriculum of practice, *Treatise on the Inexhaustible Lamp of Zen* 宗門無盡燈論 (*Shūmon Mujintōron*), which was written in classical Chinese but is read according to Japanese *kanbun* syntax. Tōrei's remarks, which cite cases 71 and 77 from the *Blue Cliff Record*,[36] recount a conversation held between Yuanwu and his prominent lay disciple Zhang Shangying, who comments that he disapproved of Xuedou's interpretation in his recorded sayings of an oft-cited case about the function of the fly-whisk (also mentioned in remarks on case 11 in the *Blue Cliff Record*). In this gongan Baizhang is shouted at by Mazu and goes deaf for three days. According to Xuedou's prose comments:

> The virtues of Chan are strange and mysterious so these days many divide the teachings into various factions but few can trace their origins. It is said that Baizhang was enlightened with a shout. Is this the end of the matter or not? Even though the characters for "crafty" (刁) and "knife" (刀) are similar, and the characters for "fish" (魚) and "foolish" (魯) are almost the same, if one is smart there is no way to dupe him. It is like when Mazu said, "Later on, when you open your trap, how will you be able to help people?" Baizhang raising the fly-whisk resembles bugs boring wood [to form a pattern] or pecking in and out at the same time. Does everyone want to experience being deaf for three days? Highly refined pure gold does not change its color.

> 奇怪諸禪德.如今列其派者甚多.究其源者極少.總道百丈於喝下大悟.還端的也無.然刁刀相似.魚魯參差.若是明眼漢.瞞他一點不得.只如馬祖道爾他後開兩片皮將何為.百丈豎起拂子.為復如蟲禦木.為復啐啄同時.諸人要會三日耳聾麼.大冶精金應無變色.[37]

Zhang tells Yuanwu he disagrees with the implication of permanence in the final assertion regarding the status of gold. Yuanwu, who in a capping phrase on this passage in *Record of Keeping the Beat* says that Xuedou is "mistaken,"[38] recites his own poem. The end reads, "If a lion cub's spiritual power unleashes a counterattack/ Even highly refined pure gold loses its color" 師子神威恣返擲.百煉真金須失色. Yuanwu then says to himself, "Is that so? Is that so? Bah!" 有麼有麼.咄.[39] Zhang is pleased and remarks that Yuanwu has fully captured the teachings of yore. However these matters are never so simple since Dōgen takes Yuanwu to task in the fascicle, "Deep Faith in Causality" ("Jinshin Inga"), for another of his verses that claims the stability of gold's color; meanwhile Dōgen's mentor Rujing affirms change in a way that recalls Yuanwu's introduction to case 31.[40]

A very different example of the *Blue Cliff Record*'s influence on Edo discourse is found in a haiku from 1773 by Buson 蕪村 (1716–1784), one of several dozen verses in his collection highlighting "seasonal words," in this case for autumn: "Morning glory!/ In each petal deepens/ An abyss of indigo" 朝がほや一輪深き淵の色 (*Asagao ya/ Ichirin fukaki/ Fuchi no iro*). The haiku has a preparatory note indicating the author was inspired on the occasion of viewing blossoms by a saying from case 82 in the gongan collection, "Valley streams are filled with indigo" 澗水湛如藍.[41] The image of ephemerality represents an answer to a monk's query about the indestructible body of the Dharmakaya, and this sense is enhanced by the way Buson evokes the forlorn quality of bluebell flowers that bloom brightly yet fade quickly.

**Modern Adaptations.** It is not feasible to capture the multitudinous ways the *Blue Cliff Record*'s influence has been felt in the modern era. As has been said of the author of *Alice and Wonderland*, "To be honest, a book that hunted for [Lewis] Carroll in every crevice, in every art form, would never end. Oh, the places he goes!"[42] One place to find the Chinese gongan collection is a reference in Natsume Soseki's *The Gate* (*Mon* 門). Near the end of the novel the disillusioned Sōsuke visits a Zen temple and is intrigued upon seeing Gidō, a youthful and thoughtful monk studying the kōan text (which Soseki refers to as *Hekiganshū*) by the fireside light. "Sōsuke wonders to himself if, instead of getting trapped in his own random thoughts, as he had the previous night, and overtaxing his mind, it would not be a lot simpler to borrow some standard texts used in this denomination and get the gist of it by reading." Soseki continues:

> But when he suggested this course to Gidō, the monk rejected it out of hand. "Reading over texts is no good at all," he said. "In fact, to be honest, there is no greater obstacle to the true spiritual practice than reading. Even people like me who have gotten to a certain stage—we may read *Hekiganshū*, but as soon as the text goes beyond our level, we don't have a clue. . . . Reading things is a snare and a delusion—you really should just forget about it."[43]

Gidō finishes by recommending that if Sōsuke feels he must study something it should an easier text, like *Prodding Progress Through the Zen Barrier*

禪関策進 (C. *Changuan cejin*, J. *Zenkan sakushin*), which was compiled as a primer for neophytes in 1600 by the Chinese monk Yunqi Zhuhong 云栖袾宏 (1535–1615) and was popular in Japan due to the efforts of Hakuin.

Despite this kind of cautionary note echoing age-old warnings regarding its inaccessibility, the *Blue Cliff Record* is being studied today more extensively than ever in China and Japan in terms of both scholarship and monastic training techniques, especially in streams of the Linji/Rinzai school. For example, commentaries based on *pingchang*-style rhetoric enunciated by modern Chinese monk Xu Yun 虚云 (1840–1959), whose remarkable life spanned several eras as he survived persecution to continue to preach the Dharma in communist China, represent just one of innumerable prominent examples of the enduring legacy of the *Blue Cliff Record*'s rhetorical devices.[44] In addition to the ample production of modern translations into Chinese or Japanese and various kinds of reference works related to deciphering the collection, other instances of its ongoing influence include countless sermons currently being given at head and branch temples in streams of the Rinzai sect in Kyoto and throughout Japan. Those oral discourses are sometimes rehearsed with a prepared script to ensure the preservation of authenticity as inspired by Yuanwu's seemingly impromptu style of commentary, although this pretense of spontaneity may appear contradictory and self-defeating to some observers.

Also Yamada Mumon 山田無文 (1900–1988), former abbot of the Myōshinji temple representing the Daiō/Daitō lineage in Kyoto, is one of several prominent modern Rinzai leaders among other interpreters of various stripes who have made detailed commentaries on the *Blue Cliff Record*.[45] There have been numerous contemporary annotations and translations of this and related kōan texts. Members of Sōtō Zen generally no longer study the collection in detail, although scholars affiliated with the sect have produced leading research on its historical significance including its impact on the formation of Dōgen's approach to kōan interpretation.[46] The Sanbyōkyōdan movement has posted to its website translations with comments on all cases in several gongan collections, including the *Blue Cliff Record*.

On the other hand, an impressive recent development by former American Sōtō leader John Daido Loori of Zen Mountain Monastery, in collaboration with Japanese translator Kazuaki Tanahashi, was Loori's new commentary on Dōgen's collection of the *300 Case Treasury of the True Dharma-Eye* 真字正法眼蔵 (*Mana Shōbōgenzō*). The original Dōgen text is a list of kōan cases compiled without comments in 1235 near the beginning of his career; Dōgen apparently created this text in preparation for his voluminous later interpretations. Loori recreated Yuanwu's rhetorical style by providing his own inventive prose, verse, and capping-phrase remarks in that sequence. According to Loori's work, which was first delivered as oral sermons before his assembly, capping phrases ("Notes") to the Huichao-Fayan dialogue in case 252 read: "1. Although this is an old question, it's worth bringing it up again. 2. This kind of answer is sure to be misunderstood and provide a nest for future generations." The paradoxical "Capping Verse" says, "In breaking in and breaking out, chick and hen do not know each other. / Not knowing each other, they naturally know how to work together.[47]

## One Night Blue Cliff *and Dōgen's Role in the Transition to Japan*

Understanding the early textual history of the *Blue Cliff Record* is difficult to determine because of the abrupt reversals of fortune the collection underwent, which left in their wake a series of unanswered questions about its construction and destruction in addition to how and when it was transmitted to Japan. To what extent was Yuanwu himself involved in editing and publishing the collection, since this was apparently centered at Mount Jiashan over fifteen years after his tenure there? Did Dahui commit the act of defiling his teacher's magnum opus, and if so, was it a radical deed or simply part of a pattern in which Chan masters were said to burn the sutras, destroy their notes, and refuse to allow disciples to record their sayings?

Also to what do we attribute the recovery of the text around 1300 and how was that effort related to influences from Chinese Chan teachers traveling to Japan, often at the behest of political leaders including the Hōjō shogunate, in addition to Japanese priests making the reverse journey during the period of émigré monks in the second half of the thirteenth century? Many of these topics tend to get shaded or distorted by sectarian enunciations based on rival standpoints concerning the value (or lack of value) of the *Blue Cliff Record*'s style of discourse, and whether Yuanwu's rhetoric is seen either as a stepping-stone leading to or as an obstruction delaying the supposedly inevitable development of Dahui's minimalist approach.

The question of how and when the *Blue Cliff Record* made its transition to Japan revolves around the issue of whether this took place in the

1220s with Dōgen's mysterious *One Night Blue Cliff*, as is argued by proponents of the validity of this version, or rather as late as the 1320s when the recovered Chinese text found its way to Japan and was soon appropriated through Daitō's capping phrases and Musō's garden designs, as German translator Wilhelm Gundert maintains.[48] Perhaps both theories have some validity in representing different routes to the same end. As shown in Table 6.3 Xuedou's *One Hundred Odes* was circulating independently and was published in Japan as early as 1289. Could there also have been knowledge by Japanese pilgrims such as Dōgen or Daiō, who spent six years studying with Xutang, a leading figure in the Yuanwu lineage, of the larger gongan collection prior to the time of its reconstitution?

Dōgen's role in the process of transmission is crucial because he was the first Japanese Zen monk to collect and comment extensively on kōan literature based on a wide variety of sources he mastered during his travels to China from 1223 to 1227. While it is certainly possible or even likely that he adopted the *pingchang* evaluative interpretative style of the *Blue Cliff Record* without actually having seen or copied this text, Dōgen's direct link to the collection is supported by the modern discovery of an alternative version generally referred to as the *One Night Blue Cliff* that he supposedly brought with him upon his return to Japan. Dōgen's putative rendition was supposedly kept at Eiheiji temple until a late thirteenth-century fire caused it to be moved to another location. According to the Sōtō sect's account, after a few decades, during which the manuscript may have fallen into the hands of a Rinzai abbot, it ended up at Daijōj temple, a Sōto monastery associated with fourth patriarch Keizan Jōkin (1268–1325) and his disciples located in Ishikawa Prefecture north of Eiheji. Although for centuries this version was kept as a sectarian secret stored in the temple repository and not disclosed despite persistent rumors and queries, the text was finally examined in 1937 and published in 1942 by D. T. Suzuki under the title *Yuanwu's Keeping the Beat to Smash the Barriers at the Blue Cliff* 仏果碧巌破関撃節 (*Bukka [C. Foguo] Hekigan Hakan Gekisetsu*). It is now a national treasure held at an Ishikawa prefectural museum in Kanazawa city with a photofacsimile also available at Komazawa University in Tokyo.[49]

In 1963 Itō Yuten produced an edition of the *One Night* version featuring a passage-by-passage comparison with the Taishō version.[50] According to Itō's analysis of the origins of the text, as indicated in Table 6.4, there were originally three versions of the *Blue Cliff Record*, which is also suggested by the 1125 postface, including renditions from Yuanwu's stays at Zhaojue, Daolin, and Jiashan temples. Itō argues that the *One Night* version was a variation based on the Daolin temple version that was essentially the same

**Table 6.3 Early Textual Formation and Question of Transmission to Japan**

Biyanlu(ji)/Hekganroku(shū) Timeline

1026/38—Completion of Xuedou's *One Hundred Odes* (*Baize Songgu*)

1102—Yuanwu's Reflections and Sermons at Zhaojue Temple in Chengdu

1108—Comments on Xuedou by Muan in *Lexicon of Ancestral Garden* (*Zuting Shiyuan*)

1111–12—Yuanwu's Sermons Delivered at Mount Jiashan

1112–15—Additional Sermons Delivered at Daolin Temple

1122—Notion of "Literary Chan" (*Wenzi Chan*) Promoted by Juefan Huihong

1125—First Postface Composed at Jiashan

1127—Yuanwu Exiled to South Along with Dahui

1128—Initial Publication of Text at Jiashan, with Preface

1130—Yuanwu Retires to Chengdu, and Perhaps Additional Sermons Given

1135—Yuanwu Dies

1140—Text Destroyed (apparently by Dahui)

1189—*Precious Lessons of Chan Forest* (*Baoxuan Chanlin*) attributes Destruction to Dahui

1224—Wansong Cites the *Blue Cliff Record* in *Record of Serenity* (*Congronlu*)

1227—Dōgen's *One Night Blue Cliff* (*Ichiya Hekigan*) Copied on His Departure from China

1267—Daiō's Return to Japan from Studies under Xutang

1289—Japanese Five Mountains Edition (Gozan-ban) of *One Hundred Odes*

1300–17—Reconstitution of Text with Additional Prefaces and Postfaces

1326—Introduction of Text to Japan (according to Gundert vol. 1:25)

1331—Daitō's Capping-Phrase Commentaries

1340s—Musō's Temple Gardens at Saihōji and Tenryūji

1345—*One Night* Version Apparently Moved from Eiheiji Temple to Daijōji Temple

1472—First Mention of *One Night* Version in *Kenzeiki*

1752—Copying of *One Night* Attributed to Hakusan Gongen in Menzan Zuihō's *Teiho Kenzeiki*

1803—Illustrated Edition of *Teiho Kenzeiki Zue* Enhances Menzan's *One Night* Legend

1937—D. T. Suzuki Views and Soon Publishes the *One Night* Version

1963—Itō Yuten Provides Comparison of *One Night* and Taishō Editions

as the mainstream version but with some minor yet crucial structural and wording differences.

Table 6.5 highlights differences in the sequence of the two versions, with the *One Night* edition linking case to verse rather than separating

### Table 6.4 *Blue Cliff Record* Versions

| Versions | Places and Dates of Sermons | Ordering of Contents* |
|---|---|---|
| 1. In Chengdu 成都** Biyanji 碧巖集 changed to Biyanlu 碧巖錄= Taishō 48.2003, 10 vols. | At Zhaojue temple 昭覺寺Handwritten manuscript held in Chengdu, Sichuan, from 1130–1135 | A. Prefaces to collection<br>1. Introduction 垂示<br>2–3. Main case w. capping phrase 本則 + 着語<br>4. Case prose commentary 本則評唱<br>5–6. Verse w. capping phrase 頌 + 着語<br>7. Verse prose commentary 頌評唱 |
| 2. Fuben 福本*** One Night 一夜碧岩 aka<br>3. Bukko Hekigan Hakan Gekisetsu 仏果碧巖破関擊節 2 vols.**** | At Lingquan temple 靈泉院<br>Original version at Mt. Jiashan 夾山 in Hunan 1111–1112, and Daolin temple 道森寺 in Sichuan 1114–1118 | Presumably basically the same as the common (Taishō) version<br>A. Case name 題名<br>1. Introduction 示衆<br>2–3. Main case w. capping phrase 本則 + 着語<br>5–6. Verse w. capping phrase 頌 +着語<br>4. Case prose commentary 本則評唱<br>7. Verse prose commentary 頌評唱 |

*Each kōan is first raised (舉 as main case), then praised (頌 verse), and then appraised (評唱 prose evaluative comments), but the sequence of this varies between the two main versions.

**Also known as the Gozan-ban edition that was the basis for Japanese Five Mountains temple masters' remarks.

***From fifteenth-century commentary, supposedly of the original set of sermons and apparently used in Edo period *shōmono*-style commentaries in Japan that is not divergent from the Taishō edition.

****Correspondence between Daolin version and *One Night* version is asserted by Itō Yūten (1963), 26–27, based on manuscript long held at Sōtō Zen's Daijōji temple repository in Ishikawa Prefecture; generally, this is close to the Taishō edition but there is no preface, the cases each have a title, there is some minor variation in wording throughout, and the order of 28 cases varies (see also https://www.pref.ishikawa.lg.jp/kyoiku/bunkazai/syoseki/2.html).

**Table 6.5 Comparison of Mainstream and *One Night* Versions**

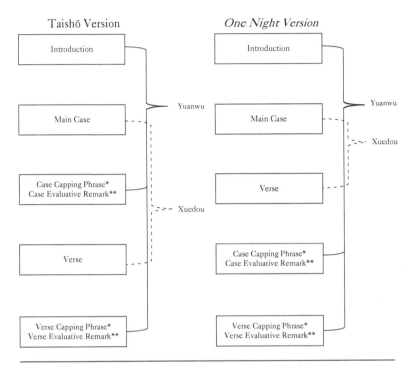

*Notes embedded in text.*
**Reference materials and interpretation.*

them through the appearance of capping phrases and prose commentary placed in between. In addition Table 6.6 shows that the *One Night* version's sequence of cases differs in thirty-eight instances as it follows the pattern of the original version of the *One Hundred Odes*, which varies from that of the *Blue Cliff Record*, thus giving a sense of authenticity to the alternative edition.

However this documentation does not establish firmly a direct connection of the *One Night* version to Dōgen, who cites the *Blue Cliff Record* only a handful of times and never mentions the title, even though his writings feature numerous citations with sometimes-critical comments of other works by Xuedou and Yuanwu.[51] On the other hand, a small piece of evidence that does appear to connect Dōgen is that in a few instances he uses wording that is almost identical to the *One Night* version. One key example occurs in the "Sustained Practice" ("Gyōji") fascicle of the *Treasury of the True Dharma-Eye*. Here a lengthy passage of prose commentary discusses

Table 6.6  Taishō and *One Night Blue Cliff Record* Case Differences

| Case Name* | Taishō Version | One Night Version |
|---|---|---|
| Getting Huangchao's Sword | 66 | 68 |
| Great Adept Fu Expounds a Scripture | 67 | 69 |
| What's Your Name? | 68 | 70 |
| Nanquan's Circle | 69 | 71 |
| Guishan Attends Baizhang | 70 | 72 |
| You Shut Up Too | 71 | 73 |
| Baizhang Questions Yunyan | 72 | 74 |
| Permutations of Assertion and Denial | 73 | 75 |
| Jinniu's Ricc Pail | 74 | 76 |
| Wujiu's Unjust Beating | 75 | 80 |
| Have You Eaten? | 76 | 81 |
| Yunmen's Cake | 77 | 82 |
| Sixteen Badhisattvas Bathe | 78 | 83 |
| All Sounds | 79 | 84 |
| A Newborn Baby | 80 | 85 |
| Shooting the Elk of Elks | 81 | 86 |
| The Stable Body of Reality | 82 | 66 |
| The Ancient Buddhas and the Pillars | 83 | 67 |
| Vimalakirti's Door of Nonduality | 84 | 87 |
| A Tiger's Roar | 85 | 88 |
| The Kitchen Pantry and the Main Gate | 86 | 89 |
| Medicine and Disease Subdue Each Other | 87 | 90 |
| Three Invalids | 88 | 91 |
| The Hands and Eyes of Great Compassion | 89 | 92 |
| The Body of Wisdom | 90 | 93 |
| Yanguan's Rhinoceros | 91 | 78 |
| The Buddha Ascends the Seat | 92 | 79 |
| Daguang Does a Dance | 93 | 77 |

* Based on Cleary and Cleary, *The Blue Cliff Record*.

how Xuanzong, who succeeded his ruthless brother Wuzong as emperor, was persecuted for his spiritual prowess and interest in Buddhism when the jealous sibling was still in power. According to case 11 in the Taishō version, "Xuanzong was beaten almost to death, thrown out into the back gardens and drenched with filthy water to revive him." In a more fanciful *One Night* version that is consistent with "Sustained Practice," "Wuzong summoned Xuanzong and ordered that he immediately be put to death for having climbed up onto the throne of Wuzong's father in the past. His corpse was placed in a flower garden behind the palace and waste matter was poured over it, whereupon he came back to life."[52]

There are two main reasons to argue against linking Dōgen to the *One Night* version. The first reason is based on textual evidence or, rather, the lack of it. Dōgen produced two kōan collections during the mid-1230s, a period when he was still seeking to find his own distinctive rhetorical voice before the main comments on cases were composed for the *Treasury of the True Dharma-Eye* and the first seven volumes of the *Extensive Record*: the first text was the *300 Cases* collection, a preparatory listing of kōan without any remarks; and the other was Dōgen's *Verse Comments* (*Eihei Dōgen Juko*, vol. 9 of the *Eihei Kōroku*), which includes one or two four-line poems for each of 90 kōan (for a total of 102), a style Dōgen abandoned after this project. Both texts seem to show a deep familiarity with many of the cases cited in the *Blue Cliff Record*, as do Dōgen's later writings, but he does not cite the Chinese collection.

According to Table 6.7, which is based on the research of Ishii Shūdō, Dōgen did not use the *Blue Cliff Record* as the source for a single one of the kōan cited in the *300 Cases* and also probably did not reference the Chinese collection in the *Verse Comments* collection, even though he cites other works by Yuanwu and Xuedou over forty times in the *300 Cases*. There are thirty cases that are the same in the two collections.[53] In addition Dōgen refers to the writings of Yuanwu a couple of dozen times in *Treasury of the True Dharma-Eye* and *Extensive Record*, but in these instances he invariably mentions passages from the *Record* or *Essentials of Mind* rather than the *Blue Cliff Record*. The main source for Dōgen is the *Zongmen Tongyaoji* collection from 1093. Could it be that any textual connections represent a coincidence since Dōgen drew from the same voluminous body of materials contained in dozens of transmission of the lamp, recorded sayings, and other miscellaneous Chan texts from the Song dynasty that also are reflected in the *Blue Cliff Record*?

The second argument against linkage is historical and involves a deconstruction of the fundamentally nonfactual basis for traditional sectarian claims that center on what is generally referred to as a "legend" 伝説 (*densetsu*) concocted from hagiographical materials crafted centuries after Dōgen's death.[54] It is said in sectarian biographies, mainly the *Kenzeiki*

Table 6.7  Textual Influences on the *Mana Shōbōgenzō*

| Mana Shōbōgenzō Vol. | 1 | 2 | 3 | Total |
|---|---|---|---|---|
| BIYANLU | o | o | o | o |
| Jingde Chuandenglu | 13 | 19 | 10 | 42 |
| Dahui Yulu | 9 | o | 2 | 11 |
| Hongzhi Yulu | 7 | 19 | 17 | 43 |
| Huangbo Yulu | 2 | o | o | 2 |
| Liandeng Huiyao | 4 | 3 | o | 7 |
| Tiansheng Guandenglu | 1 | 1 | 1 | 3 |
| Tongyaoji | 45 | 43 | 41 | 129 |
| Xuedou (Songgu/Yulu) | 1 | 1 | 1 | 3 |
| Yuanwu Yulu | 10 | 7 | 21 | 38 |
| Zhengfayanzang | 1 | 5 | 1 | 7 |
| Uncertain | 7 | 7 | 6 | 20 |
| TOTAL | 100 | 105 | 100 | 305 |

Adapted from Ishii Shūdō, *Chūgoku Zenshū Wa* (572). Additional texts considered include the *Linjilu* and *Zhaozhoulu*. Notes: (1) Although the text is often called the *Sanbyakusoku* or *300 Cases*, the actual total varies slightly; and (2) the *Tongyaoji* has been variously dated 1093 or 1133 but was available to Dōgen as an independent text even though its contents were folded into the *Liandeng Huiyao* of 1183 and eventually lost as a discrete textual entity.

from 1472 (with variations and revisions until 1803), that Dōgen copied the collection in a single night. As shown in Table 6.8 the original version of the *Kenzeiki* does not mention divine assistance but in later editions several mythical elements of the account began to be included. Dōgen received the help of a deity in copying, which took place just after he received medicine from the Japanese folk deity Inari, who came to China to provide tonic for an ailment, and just before he embarked by boat on an arduous journey, during which he was assisted through a storm by the grace of Guanyin/Kannon, bodhisattva of the island of Putuo Shan near the coast.

The earliest mention of a deity assisting Dōgen in making a copy refers to Daigenshūri Bosatsu 大權修理菩薩 (C. Daquanxiuli Pusa), who was associated with waterways and travelers, especially at Ayuwang temple near the port of Ningbo, where seafaring monks and other travelers transported between China and Japan. By the time of this reference the deity that originated in China had become established as a protector god at many Japanese Sōtō and Rinzai temples. One version of *Kenzeiki* refers simply to a local god or *dojishin* 土地神 (C. *tutishen*), which is a generic term for

Table 6.8  *Kenzeiki* and *One Night Blue Cliff* Deity

| *Kenzeiki* Version | Deity |
| --- | --- |
| 1472 *Kenzeiki* | No deity mentioned |
| 1530 manuscript | Daigenshūri Bosatsu |
| 1589 manuscript | Dojishin |
| 1680 manuscript | Hakusan Myōri Gongen |
| 1694 manuscript | Daigenshūri Bosatsu |
| 1738 manuscript | Daigenshūri Bosatsu/Dojishin |
| 1752 *Teiho Kenzeiki* by Menzan | Hakusan Gongen |
| 1803 *Teiho Kenzeiki Zue* | Hakusan Gongen |

*Notes:* (1) The 1680 manuscript gives a longer version of how the Hakusan deity was dispatched from Daijōji temple in Japan to aid Dōgen in China. (2) In all the early *Kenzeiki* manuscripts the anecdote about the *One Night Blue Cliff* appears a few sequences prior to Dōgen's departure from China (see Kawamura's 1975 edition, 26–27). But in the *Teiho Kenzeiki* (Kawamura, 31–32) as well as the illustrated *Teiho Kenzeiki Zue*, this is depicted as the last event in China that takes place just after the Inari deity visits Dōgen in China to provide some medicine and before the trip back to Japan during which One Leaf Kannon miraculously helps Dōgen through a storm at sea; neither episode is mentioned in previous versions of the text. (3) The 1589 manuscript known as the Zuichō-bon and considered by Kawamura to be the most reliable source is the only one that does not identify the god with a famous deity.

an autochthonous deity who inhabits and guards most Buddhist temples in East Asia, while another version links this divinity with Daigenshūri.

In the 1680 manuscript a lengthier narrative changes the reference to the avatar Hakusan Myōri Gongen 白山妙理権現, the tutelary god of the sacred mountain in Echizen province near where Eiheiji was built that has long been used for retreats by monks from the temple. The 1752 version of *Teiho Kenzeiki* by Menzan Zuihō, the leading Edo period Sōtō scholiast who added many hagiographical ingredients in his extensively annotated version of the text, refers to the divinity as Hakusan Gongen and specifies that he helped complete the last twenty cases. The *Teiho Kenzeiki Zue* (1803), an illustrated version that gained wide popularity, reinforced Menzan's account. Some hagiographical materials go further by introducing into the legend the idea that Rujing secretly disclosed the *Blue Cliff Record* after Dōgen's awakening experience in 1225 at an early stage of their interaction while studying gongan literature together.

In considering arguments for and against the notion that the *One Night Blue Cliff* is a legitimate version, we must recognize that even if the text is a valid, albeit unorthodox, edition of the original Yuanwu publication, which no doubt has been altered over the centuries, that circumstance would not prove that it is attributable to Dōgen. A different theory supported in part by Itō's examination of textual history is that this version may have entered Japan in the early 1300s around the same time as the edition that is now included in the Taishō canon, and it became associated with the Sōtō sect situated mainly to the north of Kyoto while Rinzai temples in the capital held the mainstream version; meanwhile most Rinka temples used the mainstream version.

**Outlines of a Theory.** Based on fieldwork and textual research that cannot help but rely to some extent on various legendary accounts, I believe that Yuanwu was probably not directly involved in the publication process as the production and distribution was handled locally by monks at Jiashan temple over a decade after he taught there, as shown in Figure 6.1.[55] Moreover Yuanwu, who was never invited to become a leader of one of the prestigious Zhejiang area temples, may have been considered controversial by imperial authorities, and the *Blue Cliff Record* was thought of as subversive for opening with a case in which the emperor is snubbed by Bodhidharma and for also including as case 3 Xuedou's comments that were banned by an eleventh-century ruler for seeming to give priority to Buddhas over and above regal leadership. Regardless of what Dahui may or may not have done, the *Blue Cliff Record* circulation likely was quite limited from the beginning and then got cut off by the mid-twelfth century due largely to suspicions about the political implications of its religious message.

FIGURE 6.1 Jiashan's temple production of *Blue Cliff Record*. Jiashan temple, courtesy of the author.

Whatever happened, the text did not disappear altogether. Might Dōgen have been exposed to a surreptitiously kept copy of the collection that he brought home as a kind of contraband? We have to take into account that all the Five Mountains temples he visited in Zhejiang province were by then under the sway of Yuanwu's lineage (rather than Dahui's) that had been spread by his other main disciple Huqiu. It is plausible to think that abbots located at these sites would have clandestinely kept copies of the *Blue Cliff Record* and also had a strong urge to pass on this and related materials to Japanese pilgrims so that Yuanwu's teachings could gain traction in a new land. This trend seems supported by the existence of the "Floating Yuanwu," the first half of an enlightenment certificate given by Yuanwu to Huqiu in recognition of the latter's spiritual achievement, which is the oldest extant document handwritten by a Chan master. The text depicts the spiritual lineage of Chan by explaining its beginnings in India, transmission to China, and division into different schools during the Song dynasty. Tradition says this document was placed inside a paulownia wood canister and drifted ashore on the coast of Satsuma (current Kagoshima Prefecture), and it is now held at Daitokuji temple in Kyoto.

That scroll's arrival in Japan represents yet another myth that sometimes gets conflated with the legend of the *One Night* coming across the waters, as it similarly highlights the larger issue of transnational transition. It is also interesting to note the Chinese émigré monks coming to Kamakura, especially Lanxi Daolong (1213–1278), founder of Kenchōji, and Wuxue Zuyuan (1226–1286), founder of Engakuji, fled China, unlike Wansong and Linquan ensconced in Beijing, because of their trepidation in the face of Mongols. The *Blue Cliff Record* was recovered during the Yuan dynasty when controversies surrounding Xuedou and Yuanwu would have subsided and been eclipsed by the impetus of followers of the latter's lineage to transmit their leader's work to Japan.

Some modern scholars suggest that the way out of the impasse about determining the validity versus the spurious quality of an edition that is extant and may or may not correspond to what is called the *One Night* version copied by Dōgen is to undertake a thoroughgoing demythologization that avoids dispute about origins by emphasizing instead the symbolism driving various accounts of the text. This hermeneutic move maintains that the legend of the *One Night* version, stripped of references to divinities and other miracles, underlines the crucial role Dōgen played in introducing the burgeoning field of gongan/kōan commentary to his native country whether he actually saw, let alone copied and brought over, the

*Blue Cliff Record*. William Bodiford points out in *Sōtō Zen in Medieval Japan* that Dōgen used more than 580 kōan in his teachings.[56] In the *Treasury of the True Dharma-Eye* alone, Dōgen elaborates on at least fifty-five cases quoted in their entirety as he cites more than 280 dialogues. In the sermons included in the *Extensive Record*, ninety-nine kōans are quoted and over one hundred more are mentioned at least briefly in addition to the ninety in Dōgen's *Verse Comments* collection.

Dōgen was immersed in Song dynasty Chan works, and his own writing cannot be understood without referencing this,[57] yet he also realized that he needed to adapt these materials rapidly and effectively to capture and convey the rhetoric of uncertainty for an assembly of Japanese monks largely untrained in reading Chinese classics. That explains why he generally does not use the verse or capping-phrase styles from the *Blue Cliff Record*, although there are some prominent exceptions as in his *Verse Comments*. From my perspective the underlying point of demythologization is that Dōgen's expansive prose remarks on Chinese Chan sayings and scriptures feature the ironic, evaluative spirit of capping phrases even if these were not produced in the strict sense of the *Blue Cliff Record*. Dōgen is a master of the *pingchang* method in transmitting the legacy, if not necessarily the text itself, of Yuanwu's seminal gongan collection.

To conclude with a few examples of how Dōgen adopted the evaluative approach of the *Blue Cliff Record* let us consider some aspects of his interpretative treatment that at times praises and on other occasions criticizes Xuedou and Yuanwu. Xuedou is appreciated in several fascicles of the *Treasury of the True Dharma-Eye*, especially "King of Saindhava" ("Ōsaku Sendaba"), "Tangled Vines" ("Kattō"), and "Why Bodhidharma Came from the West" ("Soshi Seiraii"). However in a passage from the *Extensive Record* vol. 3.196, Dōgen takes Xuedou's view to task along with four other masters. He opens the sermon by relating the last part of the story, told more extensively in the "Reading Others' Minds" ("Tajintsū") fascicle, in which the National Teacher Nanyang Huizhong is not visible on a third challenge presented to the Tripitaka Master Da'er, who claims to have witnessed Huizhong's activities the first two times he was asked.

Dōgen cites various interpretations of why Da'er failed the third time and finishes the series with Xuedou's ambiguous saying, "Nowhere to be found! Nowhere to be found!" 敗也敗也; this could refer either to Huizhong's ability to escape detection or to Da'er's inability to see what was right before his eyes. In characteristic *pingchang*, or "But I think . . ." fashion, Dōgen concludes, "These five respected elders have not yet understood the story. If you ask me about it, that would not be the case. Suppose the National Teacher were present now and wished to examine the Tripitaka Master by asking, 'Tell me, where is this old monk?' On behalf of the Tripitaka Master I would say, 'This autumn morning the frost is cold. I humbly wish that the venerable teacher's health and activities will be filled with blessings.'" 遮五位老人,未会遮一段因縁在.若是永平即不然.而今国師現在欲試驗三蔵,国師向三蔵道汝道老僧即今在什麼処,代三蔵道.即辰季秋霜冷.伏惟和尚法候動止万福.[58]

Similarly in *Extensive Record* vol. 2.179, which resembles the discussion in the "Turning the Dharma Wheel" ("Tembōrin") fascicle, Dōgen cites an anecdote in which the World-Honored One (Sakyamuni Buddha) says, "When one person opens up reality and returns to the source, all of space in the ten directions vanishes." 一人発真帰源,十方虚空悉皆消殞. He then cites several masters who interpreted this saying, including his teacher Rujing and Yuanwu who recast it as, "When one person opens up reality and returns to the source, in all of space in the ten directions flowers are added on brocade." 夾山圓悟禪師道,一人発真帰源,十方虚空錦上添華. Dōgen concludes with a Fayan-school type of emphasis on the rhetorical power of redundancy, "Five previous venerable teachers made their remarks but I have a comment that is not like theirs: 'When one person opens up reality and returns to the source, all of space in the ten directions opens up reality and returns to the source.'" 前来五位尊宿道是恁麼,永平有道与前不同.一人発真帰源,十方虚空発真帰源.[59]

On the other hand, Dōgen greatly admires several sayings from Yuanwu's *Record*, including "Life is the manifestation of total activity, and death is the manifestation of total activity" 生也全機現,死也全機現, which is cited in the "Total Activity" ("Zenki") and "Learning the Way through Body-Mind" ("Shinjingakudō") fascicles.[60] In "Summer Retreat" ("Ango") he praises a Yuanwu saying, and in "Arhat" ("Arakan") he eulogizes the authenticity of his monastic lifestyle. Also in "Spring and Autumn" ("Shunjū") Dōgen appreciates a Yuanwu verse: "The bowl sets the pearl to rolling and the pearl rolls in the bowl./ The absolute within the relative, and the relative within the absolute./ The antelope holds onto a tree branch by its horns, thereby leaving no trace,/ While the hunting dogs circle the forest aimlessly and in vain." 盤走珠珠走盤.偏中正正中偏.羚羊掛角無蹤跡.獵犬遶林空踉蹌.[61] Dōgen remarks, "The expression, 'The bowl sets the pearl to rolling,' is unprecedented and incomparable! It has rarely been heard in past or present. Hitherto people have spoken as if the pearl rolling around in the bowl were something unceasing." いま盤走珠

の道.これ光前絶後.古今罕聞なり.古來はただいはく.盤にはしる珠の住著なきがごとし.[62] However, Dōgen gets the last word by reversing the meaning of the final two lines, while following the logic of the opening lines, expressing Yuanwu's conventional evocation of a story about how an antelope can escape becoming prey. According to Dōgen, "The antelope is now using his horns to hang onto emptiness, and the forest is now circling the hunting dogs." 羚羊いまは空に掛角せり.林いま獵狗をめぐる.[63]

Finally, we can briefly compare Dōgen's evaluative interpretations made in live situations with a prime example of the way Yuanwu introduces his own outlook into commentary on case 88 about the understanding of a blind, a deaf, and a mute person, for which Xuedou's verse ends with, "Do you understand or not?/ An iron hole-less hammerhead" 還會也無.無孔鐵鎚. It is said that in rapid succession, "Master Yuanwu holds up his whisk and asks, 'Do you see?' He raps once on the meditation seat and asks, 'Do you hear?' Then he steps down from his seat and asks, 'Can you speak?'" 師舉拂子云.還見麼.遂敲禪床一下云.還聞麼.下禪床云.還說得麼.[64]

In a similar passage in *Extensive Record* vol. 3.231, "Dōgen holds his staff upright and says, 'This is the ultimate expression of all dharmas.' Holding the staff horizontally he says, 'This is the deepest source of Buddha Dharma.' 舉杖云.諸法之至極.橫杖云.仏法之源底. After citing the Four Noble Truths, Dōgen declares he will show how to go beyond these, and for each of the truths "Dōgen pounds his staff one time" 卓杖一下. At the end he proclaims, 'Although this is going beyond Buddhas and ancestors I ask, What does it mean?' Dōgen then pounds his staff two times." 這箇雖是仏祖向上事,且道,永平意作麼生.卓杖両下.[65]

An intriguing example of Dōgen's use of rhetorical reversal, which was probably learned from *Blue Cliff Record* models, is in *Extensive Record* vol. 7.503 where he cites Rujing's verse on Yunmen's "Dried turd" dialogue that says, "Yunmen shit it out of his mouth [literally, "from the opposite end]" 雲門倒屙一橛屎. Indeed! Then, while using the same rhyme scheme, Dōgen rewrites part of his mentor's poem by including a subtle inversion of some aspects of its meaning,[66] so that Rujing and Yunmen have been one-upped and overturned in his evaluative reaction to this particular example of rethinking gongan entanglements. Let us perpetuate the *pingchang* evaluative process!

# Blue Cliff Record *Lineage Chart*

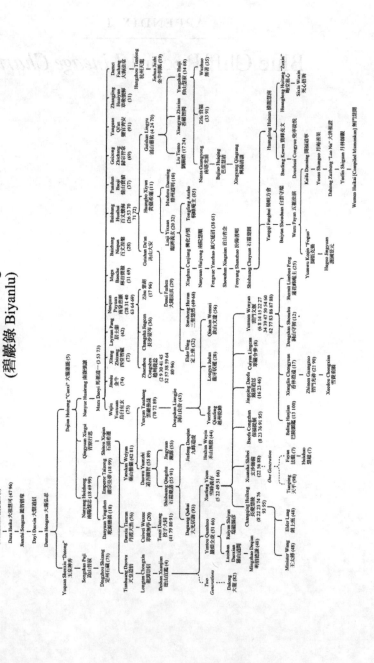

Blue Cliff Record Lineage Chart
(碧巖錄 Biyanlu)

# Blue Cliff Record *Cases with Notes*

| Title (Based on Cleary, 1998) | Dialogue Participants | With Intro, or Comments? |
|---|---|---|
| 1. Emperor Wu Questions Bodhidharma | Emperor Wu, Bodhidharma, Master Zhi | |
| 2. Ultimate Way Is Without Difficulty | Zhaozhou, Monk | |
| 3. Master Ma Is Unwell | Master Ma, Temple Superintendent | |
| 4. Deshan Carrying His Bundle | Deshan, Guishan, Head Monk | Xuedou |
| 5. Xuefeng's Grain of Rice | Xuefeng | |
| 6. Every Day Is a Good Day | Yunmen | NO Introduction or Comments |
| 7. Huichao Asks about the Buddha | Huichao, Fayan | |
| 8. Cuiyan's Eyebrows | Cuiyan, Baofu, Changqing, Yunmen | Yunmen |
| 9. Zhaozhou's Four Gates | Monk, Zhaozhou | |
| 10. The Phony | Muzhou, Monk | |
| 11. Gobblers of Dregs | Huangbo, Monk | |
| 12. Three Pounds of Flax | Monk, Dongshan | |
| 13. The School of Kanadeva | Monk, Baling | |

| Title (Based on Cleary, 1998) | Dialogue Participants | With Intro, or Comments? |
|---|---|---|
| 14. An Appropriate Statement | Monk, Yunmen | NO |
| 15. An Upside-Down Statement | Monk, Yunmen | |
| 16. The Man in the Weeds | Monk, Jingqing | |
| 17. The Living Meaning of Chan | Monk, Xianglin | |
| 18. The Seamless Monument Emperor | Taizong, Huizhong, Danyuan | NO, Xuedou |
| 19. One Finger Chan | Juzhi | |
| 20. The Living Meaning of Chan | Longya, Cuiwei, Linji | |
| 21. Lotus Flower, Lotus Leaves | Monk, Zhimen | |
| 22. The Turtle-Nosed Snake | Xuefeng, Changqing, Monk, Xuansha, Yunmen | Yunmen |
| 23. The Summit of the Peak of Wonder | Baofu, Changqing, Jingqing | Xuedou |
| 24. Guishan and Iron Grindstone Liu | Iron Grindstone Liu, Guishan | |
| 25. The Hermit's Staff | The Hermit of Lotus Blossom Peak | |
| 26. Sitting Alone on the Mountain | Monk, Baizhang | NO |
| 27. Body Exposed in the Autumn Wind | Monk, Yunmen | |
| 28. Truth That's Never Been Spoken | Nanquan, Master Nirvana | NO |
| 29. It Goes Along With It | Monk, Dasui | |
| 30. Big Radishes | Monk, Zhaozhou | NO |
| 31. Magu Carrying His Ringed Staff | Magu, Zhangjing, Changqing, Nanquan | Xuedou |
| 32. Elder Ding Stands Motionless | Elder Ding, Linji, Monk | |
| 33. Zifu's Circle | Chen Cao, Zifu | Xuedou |
| 34. Where Do You Come From? | Yangshan, Monk, Yunmen | NO, Yunmen |
| 35. Dialogue of Manjusri and Wuzhuo | Manjusri, Wuzhuo | |

| Title (Based on Cleary, 1998) | Dialogue Participants | With Intro, or Comments? |
|---|---|---|
| 36. Roaming in the Mountains | Changsha, Head Monk | NO, Xuedou |
| 37. There's Nothing in the World | Panshan | |
| 38. The Workings of the Iron Ox | Fengxue, Elder Lupi, Governor | |
| 39. The Flowering Hedge | Monk, Yunmen | |
| 40. Like a Dream | Officer Lu Xuan, Nanquan | |
| 41. One Who Has Died the Great Death | Zhaozhou, Touzi | |
| 42. Good Snowflakes | Layman Pang, Chan Student Quan | Xuedou |
| 43. No Cold or Heat | Monk, Dongshan | |
| 44. Knowing How to Beat the Drum | Heshan, Monk | NO |
| 45. Zhaozhou's Shirt | Monk, Zhaozhou | |
| 46. The Sound of Raindrops | Jingqing, Monk | |
| 47. Six Do Not Take It In | Monk, Yunmen | |
| 48. Overturning the Tea Kettle | Minister Wang, Elder Lang, Mingzhao | NO, Xuedou |
| 49. Golden Fish Passed through the Net | Sansheng, Xuefeng | |
| 50. Every Atom Samadhi | Monk, Yunmen | |
| 51. What Is It? | Xuefeng, Monk, Yantou | |
| 52. The Stone Bridge | Monk, Zhaozhou | NO |
| 53. Wild Ducks | Mazu, Baizhang | |
| 54. Yunmen Extends Both Hands | Yunmen, Monk | |
| 55. Daowu's Condolence Call | Daowu, Jianyuan, Shishuang, Taiyuan Fu | Xuedou |
| 56. One Arrow Smashes Three Barriers | Chan student Liang, Qinshan | |
| 57. The Stupid Oaf | Monk, Zhaozhou | |
| 58. Zhaozhou Can't Explain | Monk, Zhaozhou | NO |
| 59. Why Not Quote It Fully? | Monk, Zhaozhou | |
| 60. The Staff Changes into a Dragon | Yunmen | |

| Title (Based on Cleary, 1998) | Dialogue Participants | With Intro, or Comments? |
|---|---|---|
| 61. One Atom | Fengxue | Xuedou |
| 62. Within There Is a Jewel | Yunmen | |
| 63. Nanquan Kills a Cat | Nanquan | |
| 64. Nanquan Questions Zhaozhou | Nanquan, Zhaozhou | NO |
| 65. An Outsider Questions the Buddha | Outsider, The Buddha, Ananda | |
| 66. Getting Huangchao's Sword | Yantou, Monk, Xuefeng | |
| 67. Great Adept Fu Expounds a Scripture | Emperor Wu, Great Adept Fu, Master Zhi | NO |
| 68. What's Your Name? | Yangshan, Sansheng | |
| 69. Nanquan's Circle | Nanquan, Guizong, Magu | |
| 70. Guishan Attends Baizhang | Baizhang, Guishan | |
| 71. You Shut Up Too | Baizhang, Wufeng | NO |
| 72. Baizhang Questions Yunyan | Baizhang, Yunyan | NO |
| 73. Permutations of Assertion and Denial | Monk, Mazu, Zhizang, Baizhang | |
| 74. Jinniu's Rice Pail | Jinniu, Monk, Changqing | Xuedou |
| 75. Wujiu's Unjust Beating | Monk, Wujiu | |
| 76. Have You Eaten? | Danxia, Monk, Changqing, Baofu | |
| 77. Yunmen's Cake | Monk, Yunmen | |
| 78. Sixteen Bodhisattvas Bathe | Sixteen Bodhisattvas | NO |
| 79. All Sounds | Monk, Touzi | |
| 80. A Newborn Baby | Monk, Zhaozhou, Touzi | NO |
| 81. Shooting the Elk of Elks | Monk, Yaoshan | Xuedou |
| 82. The Stable Body of Reality | Monk, Dalong | |
| 83. The Ancient Buddhas and the Pillars | Yunmen | NO |

| Title (Based on Cleary, 1998) | Dialogue Participants | With Intro, or Comments? |
|---|---|---|
| 84. Vimalakirti's Door of Nonduality | Vimalakirti, Manjusri | Xuedou |
| 85. A Tiger's Roar | Monk, The Hermit of Tongfeng | Xuedou |
| 86. Kitchen Pantry and the Main Gate | Yunmen | |
| 87. Medicine-Disease Subdue Each Other | Yunmen | |
| 88. Three Invalids | Xuansha, Monk, Yunmen | Yunmen |
| 89. Hands and Eyes of Great Compassion | Yunyan, Daowu | |
| 90. The Body of Wisdom | Monk, Zhimen | |
| 91. Yanguan's Rhinoceros | Yanguan, Attendant, Touzi, Zhimen, Baofu | Xuedou |
| 92. The Buddha Ascends the Seat | The Buddha, Manjusri | |
| 93. Daguang Does a Dance | Monk, Daguang | NO |
| 94. Not Seeing | The Surangama Sutra | |
| 95. Three Poisons | Changqing, Baofu | |
| 96. Three Turning Words | Zhaozhou | NO |
| 97. Diamond Sutra's Scornful Revilement | The Diamond Sutra | |
| 98. Tianping's Travels | Tianping, Xiyuan | |
| 99. The Ten Body Controller | Emperor Suzong, Huizhong | |
| 100. Baling's Sword | Monk, Baling | |

# APPENDIX 3

# Blue Cliff Record *Cases* *in Other Chan/Zen Texts*

| Blue Cliff Record | | Record of Serenity* | 300 Cases** | Verse Comments** |
|---|---|---|---|---|
| 1. | The Emperor Wu Questions Bodhidharma | 2 | | |
| 2. | Ultimate Way Is without Difficulty | | | |
| 3. | Master Ma Is Unwell | 36 | | |
| 4. | Deshan Carrying His Bundle | | | |
| 5. | Xuefeng's Grain of Rice | | | |
| 6. | Every Day Is a Good Day | | | |
| 7. | Huichao Asks about the Buddha | | 252 | 7 |
| 8. | Cuiyan's Eyebrows | 71 | | |
| 9. | Zhaozhou's Four Gates | | 46 | 21 |
| 10. | The Phony | | | |
| 11. | Gobblers of Dregs | 53 | 202 | |
| 12. | Three Pounds of Flax | | 172 | 68 |
| 13. | The School of Kanadeva | | | |
| 14. | An Appropriate Statement | | 95 | |
| 15. | An Upside-Down Statement | | 95 | |
| 16. | The Man in the Weeds | | | |
| 17. | The Living Meaning of Chan | | | |
| 18. | The Seamless Monument | 85 | | |
| 19. | One Finger Chan | 84 | 245 | |
| 20. | The Living Meaning of Chan | 80 | 205 | |
| 21. | Lotus Flower, Lotus Leaves | | | |
| 22. | The Turtle-Nosed Snake | 24 | | |

| Blue Cliff Record | Record of Serenity* | 300 Cases** | Verse Comments** |
|---|---|---|---|
| 23. The Summit of the Peak of Wonder | | | |
| 24. Guishan and Iron Grindstone Liu | 60 | | |
| 25. The Hermit's Staff | | | |
| 26. Sitting Alone on the Mountain | | | |
| 27. The Body Exposed in the Autumn Wind | | | |
| 28. The Truth That's Never Been Spoken | | 249 | |
| 29. It Goes Along With It | 30 | 24 | 83 |
| 30. Big Radishes | | | |
| 31. Magu Carrying His Ringed Staff | 16 | | |
| 32. Elder Ding Stands Motionless | | | |
| 33. Zifu's Circle | | | |
| 34. Where Do You Come From? | | | |
| 35. The Dialogue of Manjusri and Wuzhuo | | 127 | |
| 36. Roaming in the Mountains | | | |
| 37. There's Nothing in the World | | | |
| 38. The Workings of the Iron Ox | 29 | | |
| 39. The Flowering Hedge | | | |
| 40. Like a Dream | 91 | | |
| 41. One Who Has Died the Great Death | 63 | 136 | |
| 42. Good Snowflakes | | | |
| 43. No Cold or Heat | | 225 | 74 |
| 44. Knowing How to Beat the Drum | | 186 | |
| 45. Zhaozhou's Shirt | | | |
| 46. The Sound of Raindrops | | 286 | |
| 47. Six Do Not Take It In | | | |
| 48. Overturning the Tea Kettle | | | |
| 49. Golden Fish Passed through the Net | 33 | 52 | |
| 50. Every Atom Samadhi | 99 | 158 | |
| 51. What Is It? | 50 | | |
| 52. The Stone Bridge | | | |
| 53. Wild Ducks | | 182 | |
| 54. Yunmen Extends Both Hands | | | |
| 55. Daowu's Condolence Call | | 289 | |
| 56. One Arrow Smashes Three Barriers | | | |
| 57. The Stupid Oaf | | | |
| 58. Zhaozhou Can't Explain | | | |
| 59. Why Not Quote It Fully? | | | |

| Blue Cliff Record | Record of Serenity* | 300 Cases** | Verse Comments** |
|---|---|---|---|
| 60. The Staff Changes into a Dragon | | | |
| 61. One Atom | 34 | 214 | |
| 62. Within There Is a Jewel | 92 | 295 | |
| 63. Nanquan Kills a Cat | 9 | 181 | 76 |
| 64. Nanquan Questions Zhaozhou | 9 | | 76 |
| 65. An Outsider Questions the Buddha | | 170 | |
| 66. Getting Huangchao's Sword | | | |
| 67. Great Adept Fu Expounds a Scripture | | | |
| 68. What's Your Name? | | | |
| 69. Nanquan's Circle | | | |
| 70. Guishan Attends Baizhang | | | |
| 71. You Shut Up Too | | | |
| 72. Baizhang Questions Yunyan | | | |
| 73. The Permutations of Assertion and Denial | 6 | 108 | 78 |
| 74. Jinniu's Rice Pail | | | |
| 75. Wujiu's Unjust Beating | | | |
| 76. Have You Eaten? | | | |
| 77. Yunmen's Cake | 78 | | |
| 78. Sixteen Bodhisattvas Bathe | | | |
| 79. All Sounds | | | |
| 80. A Newborn Baby | | | |
| 81. Shooting the Elk of Elks | | | |
| 82. The Stable Body of Reality | | | |
| 83. The Ancient Buddhas and the Pillars | 31 | | |
| 84. Vimalakirti's Door of Nonduality | 48 | | |
| 85. A Tiger's Roar | | | |
| 86. The Kitchen Pantry and the Main Gate | | 80 | |
| 87. Medicine and Disease Subdue Each Other | | | |
| 88. Three Invalids | | 203 | 34 |
| 89. The Hands and Eyes of Great Compassion | 54 | 105 | |
| 90. The Body of Wisdom | | | |
| 91. Yanguan's Rhinoceros | 25 | | |
| 92. The Buddha Ascends the Seat | 1 | 141 | |
| 93. Daguang Does a Dance | | | |
| 94. Not Seeing | 88 | | |

| Blue Cliff Record | Record of Serenity* | 300 Cases** | Verse Comments** |
|---|---|---|---|
| 95. Three Poisons | | 298 | 64 |
| 96. Three Turning Words | | | |
| 97. The Diamond Sutra's Scornful Revilement | 58 | | |
| 98. Tianping's Travels | | 284 | |
| 99. The Ten Body Controller | | 26, 159 | |
| 100. Baling's Sword | | | |

*Record of Serenity* by Wansong, 1224.

**300 Cases—(Mana Shōbōgenzō) by Dōgen, 1235.

***Verse Comments—(in Dōgen's *Extensive Record* vol. 9), 1236.

# APPENDIX 4

# *Timelines: Yuanwu*

1063  Born in Pengzhou, Sichuan with early family background in Confucian thought

1075  Demonstrates ability to memorize a thousand words per day of classics

1080  Interested in Buddhism, leaves home and becomes a monk at nearby Miaoji temple

1081  Studies Chan at Zhaojue Monastery in Chengdu

1085  Begins lengthy period of study of Buddhism in Sichuan, first on doctrinal teachings and then with various Chan masters from Yunmen and Caodong schools plus streams of Linji; leads to training with Zhenjue Weizheng, who literally draws drops of blood in attempt to awaken Yuanwu

[1089]  Dahui Zonggao (1089–1163) born in Anhui

1091  Leaves Sichuan and studies with Huanglong Huinan, among others,; initial unsuccessful meeting in Anhui with Wuzu Fayan of Yangqi stream, who critiques Yuanwu's wit and predicts his future illness, a Chan malady that leads Yuanwu with Dharma brother Fojian Huiqin back to Wuzu

1092  Travels to Jiashan in Jiangsu where he contracts typhoid fever and suffers mightily, and returns to study under Wuzu then located at Mount Huangmei in Hubei; at some point in the process of working with Wuzu studies intensively Xuedou's *Baize Songgu* with Librarian Qing and others

1095  Attains enlightenment under Wuzu, who appoints him first seat and regards him as true heir to his lineage, as reflected in two accounts: one involves the "sound of lover" and a rooster's crowing, and the other involves cutting a tree and being scolded by the teacher; other disciples/heirs of Wuzu include Foyan Qingyuan and Fojian Huijin

1101  Completes study with Wuzu, who dies in 1104

1102  Returns to Sichuan to care for aged mother, and rejoins Zhaojue Monastery to preach; begins first phase of making formal comments in sermonson *Baize Songgu*

1105  Following Wuzu's death in 1104, becomes the eleventh patriarch of the Linji lineage

1111  In Hunan instructs noted literati Zhang Shangying (a.k.a. Zhang Wujin), recently demoted from official post, and this helps bring fame for his teaching methods; invited at Zhang's behest to reside in Lingquan Monastery on Mount Jiashan in Hunan, where during two summer retreats he gives lectures on *Baize Songgu* that become the basis of *Biyanlu*

1112  Continues lectures on Xuedou; discussions with Zhang include Huayan mutual interpenetration

1114  Moves to Daolin Monastery in Tanzhou, Sichuan and continues lectures on Xuedou

1117  Twelve years of comments based on twenty years of studies on *Baize Songgu* concluded, and later published by disciples

1121  Purple robe and title Fruition of Buddha (Foguo) bestowed by N. Song Emperor Huizong; also Dahui Zonggao visits Zhang Shangying, who recommends that he study with Yuanwu

1123  Assigned to Taiping Xingguo Monastery on Mount Jiang in Jiangsu by imperial order

1124  Moves to Wanshou Monastery in Kaifeng in Hebei by imperial order and receives gifts

1125  *Biyanlu* completed by disciples with afterword by Guanyu Wedeng, who comments on twenty years of studies as well as tension between spiritual realization and language; Dahui, studying with Yuanwu, quickly attains enlightenment from intense interactions with gongan cases

1126  Moves to Tongyou Monastery on Mount Jin in Jiangsu to escape the fall of the N. Song

1127  Moves to Jiangxi with Dahui accompanying him as first seat; deemed "Perfectly Enlightened Chan Master" (Yuanwu Chanshi) by S. Song Emperor Gaozong

1128  *Biyanlu* published with preface added by Puzhao Zhongyan; appointed by imperial order to temple on Mount Yunju in Jiangxi and is accompanied by Dahui as "first seat"

1129  At Mount Yunju in Jiangxi had conflict with rival Guoan Shanwu, as reported by Dahui

1130  Returns to Sichuan and is invited to become head of Zhaojue Monastery

1133  Geng Yanxi collects and composes preface to Yuanwu's collection of sayings

1134  *Recorded Sayings* (*Yuanwu Foguo Chanshi Yulu*) published with preface by Zhang Jun

1135  Falls ill, gives control of Zhaojue to his disciple Daoyuan; dies on 8/5, leaving 73 lay followers and 55 monastic disciples

# *Timelines: Xuedou*

980  Born in Yizhou (currently Sichuan) on the 4/8

998  Following the death of his parents, leaves home to become a Buddhist monk under Puanyuan Renxi

1000  Listens to Yuanying at Daci temple lecture on the *Sutra of Complete Enlightenment*; asks questions but is not satisfied by the answers

1004  Xuedou leaves Sichuan and travels to Xiangzhou

1011  Serves as head monk in Mount Lu as well as Jingde temple

1014  Becomes abbot at Cuifeng temple near Suzhou in Jiangsu

1020  Receives letter of introduction to Zeng Hui, an official of Mingzhou (currently Ningbo), from Chan master Yunyin Shan

1021  Zenghui invites Xuedou to move to Mount Xuedou's Zisheng temple, as recorded in the *Puquan ji*; Menren Wenzhen begins the compilation of *Xuedou Kaitanglu*; the production of the *Songguji* 頌古集 also begins

1031  On 5/5 Xuedou writes a preface to his *Recorded Sayings*; the quote, "A single flame perpetuates a thousand lamps and advances the five branches [of Chan]," appears therein.

1036  The *Tiansheng Extensive Transmission of the Lamp* in 30 volumes is published, with the emperor bestowing a poem as its preface; Su Dongpo [Su Shi] (d. 1101) is born in Sichuan

1052  On 6/10 Xuedou dies; on 7/6 he is buried

1053  The Mingjue Stupa 明覚塔 is constructed, and the *Xuedou Houlu* is compiled with a preface written by Ruyu

1065  Lu Xiaqing writes Xuedou's funerary inscription; compiled by Huishi

1108  Muan Shanqing publishes the *Zuting Shiyuan* in 8 volumes; Xuedou's seven-volume collection was already in print

1111  Yuanwu starts his lectures on *Baize Songu* (*One Hundred Odes*) at Jiashan temple

1205  Deyun 德雲 of Mount Xuedou adds introduction to *Recorded Sayings* and publishes it at temple

# *Notes*

CHAPTER 1

1. I am grateful to William M. Bodiford for pointing this out in several personal communications and showing me a series of cover designs for various editions of the text over the centuries that reflects this change. I was surprised at first and found that some of the Japanese specialists I conversed with were also unaware, but once this was noted I invariably saw that early Chinese and Japanese versions did indeed use "*Biyanji/Hekiganshū.*" It is only a matter of speculation in regard to the reasons for the alteration, but one can imagine that in Edo society the term "record" (*lu/roku*) may have carried a certain level of prestige. In considering this matter I am reminded of the cryptic Bob Dylan line about a mysterious character in a complex narrative from the song "Brownsville Girl": "The only thing we knew for sure about Henry Porter is that his name wasn't Henry Porter"; see bobdylan. com (accessed July 5, 2015).

2. T48:148c20. All translations of *Blue Cliff Record* passages cited here have been checked against Thomas Cleary and John C. Cleary, trans., *The Blue Cliff Record*, 3 vols. (Boulder, CO: Shambhala, 1977), as paginated consecutively and reprinted in a single volume in 2005, in addition to numerous other references; see notes 68 and 72 for various sources, both primary and secondary.

3. T48:160a116–17. I agree with Thomas Cleary's comments in the introductory essay to his translation of the *Book of Serenity* (Hudson, NY: Lindisfarne, 1990), 39: "In the Chan understanding, no expression or view can ever be complete, and Chan literature explicitly warns that dialogue and difference among Chan adepts are not to be understood in terms of either/or, win/lose choices. . . . sayings are not necessarily direct comments on or illustrations of the statements they are added to; sometimes they are designed to shift the reader into a different view-point or shed light on the same point from a different angle."

4. T48:142c21.

5. T48:170a1.

6. T48:205b14.

7. T48:205c7.

8. T48:209c1–3; see the discussion in Sonja Arntzen, "The Poetry of the *Kyōunshū* 'Crazy Cloud' Anthology of Ikkyū Sōjun" (PhD diss., University of British Columbia, 1979), 8–10.

9. Arntzen, "The Poetry of the *Kyōunshū*," 10.

10. Sueki Fumihiko, "Sōdai Zenseki no Bunkenteki Kenkyū: *Hekiganroku* wo toshite," *Kaken Kenkyū Deetabeesu* (1989–1991); https://kaken.nii.ac.jp/d/p/ 01450002.ja.html (accessed May 29, 2015). Sueki was first part of a team led by famed Chan scholar Iriya Yoshitaka of a still-standard modern Japanese translation (*gendaiyaku*) and annotation of the collection. Ogawa Takeshi, who specializes in premodern Chinese linguistics, criticized this version in the 1990s, and Sueki was motivated to do his own partial translation along with a monograph on the text.

11. Cited by Arntzen, "The Poetry of the *Kyōunshū*," 136 (altered); she points out this inspired a verse about the collection by Ikkyū (1394–1481); the last line literally refers to "Breast Peak" 乳峰, but I have rendered it based on the meaning of the metaphor. I appreciate Professor Ishii Shūdō, an expert on Song Chan literature who is emeritus at Komazawa University, for discussing and confirming some of this in a conversation on May 27, 2015, and also Didier Davin for helping me locate the original Ikkyū poem. The verse on Xuedou is included in the *Collection of Wind and Moon by the River and Lake* 江湖風月集 (C. *Jianghu Fengyueji*, J. *Gōko Fūgetsushū*) of 1288, part 2, verse 7; this is a compilation of Chan verses published in the fourteenth century that gained importance in Japan.

12. Over the past decade and a half, significant research has been produced in China that in many ways surpasses Japanese scholarship because of a greater familiarity and facility with the traditional sources, but in other regards is heavily dependent on what has been accomplished in Japan and in some cases repeats its strengths and some of the weaknesses that are often based on ideological arguments inherited from centuries of sectarian scholasticism.

13. This claim may be valid historically, but it is sometimes misleadingly associated with Yuanwu, who probably was not involved in promoting tea. A famous calligraphy attributed to Yuanwu reading, "Tea and Chan have the same flavor" 茶禪一味 is a revered idea in Chan, although the attribution is no doubt spurious and may have been invented at Jingshan temple in Zhejiang province, which was long dominated by Yuanwu's lineage yet was not a place he ever visited. Both Jiashan and Jingshan have separate claims to cultivating tea, which is being revitalized in China these days, but chances are none of this involves Yuanwu.

14. Sichuan province, which produced Su Shi and many other eminent Northern Song writers along with Yuanwu's mentor Wuzu, and also served as the location

for the publication of a major edition of the Tripitaka in the late tenth century, had become a hub of literary activity. This was probably due in large part to an influx of elite monks from the Tang capital of Chang'an following the Wuzong persecution in 845 of Buddhism and all other foreign religions, which drove members of the clergy and other intellectuals to escape to the next large city to the south that incorporated various kinds of regional influences.

15. This term stemming from the *Zhuangzi* and other early texts can suggest a disparagement of deceased speakers who are no longer relevant, but it is used in the *Blue Cliff Record* to indicate the unsurpassable behavioral models of Tang masters whose stories are recounted yet never fully explained.

16. See Yi-hsun Huang, "Chan Master Xuedou and His Remarks on Old Cases in the *Record of Master Xuedou at Dongting*: A Preliminary Study," *Chung-Hwa Buddhist Journal* 22 (2009), 69–96.

17. Xuedou was enlightened by another Sichuan native, Zhimen (940–1031). Fourteen cases feature Yunmen and four other instances, for a total of eighteen cases, include his sayings as a comment to a previous dialogue; see Nagai Masashi, "Xuedou no Goroku no Seiritsu ni Kansuru Ikkosatsu (part 2)," *Bukkyōgaku Kenkyū Nenpō* 7 (1973), 11–20.

18. T48:194a28–b2; see various publications by Urs App, especially "The Making of a Chan Record: Reflections on the History of the Records of Yunmen," *Zen Bunka Kenkyūjo Kiyō* 17 (1991), 1–90.

19. T47:545a17; the section title 對機三百二十則 refers to 320 such cases.

20. Cited by Juhn Y. Ahn, trans. and John Jorgenson, ed., *Collected Works of Korean Buddhism* vol. 7–2 (Seoul: Jogye Order of Korean Buddhism, 2012), 249 (altered). This work renders the *Seonmun Yeomsong Seolhwa* and notes that the extant text is the *seolhwa* (explanation of the stories) attached by Gag'un (n.d.) not only to the 1,125 cases in thirty fascicles that he received from Hyesim (1178–1234) but to additional ones for a total of 1,463 cases.

21. T48:140a13–14; the image of corners alludes to a famous Confucius saying to his disciples.

22. T47:674b1.

23. See *Setchō Hyakusoku Juko*, Zen no Goroku vol. 15, eds. Iriya Yoshitaka, Kajitani Sōnin, and Yanagida Seizan (Tokyo: Chikuma shobō, 1981).

24. Based on my visit and discussion with one of the head monks in May 2014.

25. T47:712c28–713a2.

26. See the passage, 多知多解.轉生煩惱.古人或拈古頌古一則因緣; X67:227a24.

27. Victor Sogen Hori, *Zen Sand: The Book of Capping Phrases for Kōan Practice* (Honolulu: University of Hawaii Press, 2003); and Kenneth Kraft, *Eloquent Zen: Daitō and Early Japanese Zen* (Honolulu: University of Hawaii Press, 1992).

28. Christoph Anderl, "Chan Rhetoric: An Introduction," in *Zen Buddhist Rhetoric in China, Korea, and Japan*, ed. Christoph Anderl (Leiden: Brill, 2012), 46.

29. T47:607c13; the title of the text, 汾陽無德禪師頌古代別, refers to the three styles of commentary: verse comments (頌古); substitute (代) words; and alternate (別) words.

30. See An-yi Pan, *Painting Faith: Li Conglin and Northern Song Buddhist Culture* (Leiden: Brill, 2007).

31. Morten Schlütter, *How Zen Became Zen: The Dispute Over Enlightenment and the Formation of Chan Buddhism in Song-Dynasty China* (Honolulu: University of Hawaii Press, 2009).

32. T48:203a8–9.

33. For a full discussion of some of the main elements of the extensive traditional symbolism associated with the Dragon Gate see Norris Brock Johnson, *Tenryū-ji: Life and Spirit of a Kyoto Garden* (Albany, CA: Stone Bridge Press, 2012), especially the tenth chapter. Johnson provides a helpful description of how Musō Soseki designed the temple garden to evoke the proverbial gate, but he does not delve into the linkage with cases in the *Blue Cliff Record* that will be mentioned in chapter 6. Another of Johnson's publications on a different Musō garden makes the connection: "Mountain, Temple, and the Design of Movement: Thirteenth-Century Japanese Zen Buddhist Landscapes," in *Landscape Design and the Experience of Motion*, ed. Michael Conan (Washington, DC: Dumbarton Oaks Research Library, 2003), 157–185.

34. T48:182b24.

35. John R. McRae, *Seeing Through Zen: Encounter, Transformation, and Genealogy in Chinese Chan Buddhism* (Berkeley: University of California Press, 2003), 130–131.

36. T48:224b3–6; the verse follows the regulated four-line poetic pattern of opening-development-turnabout-conclusion 起承轉合(結).

37. T47:670a20. Soon before he died, when his grief-stricken attendant monk requested a parting gatha, Xuedou replied, "My only regret in this life is that I talked too much"; cited in Charles Egan, trans., *Clouds Thick, Whereabouts Unknown: Poems by Zen Monks of China* (New York: Columbia University Press, 2010).

38. T47:712c15–16.

39. T48:185b15.

40. T48:179a23. The following dialogue also mentioned in this case is interesting: "Haven't you heard that a monk once asked Changqing, 'What is the eye of a man of knowledge?,' and he said, 'He has a vow not to scatter sand.' Baofu said, 'You must not scatter any more of it.' All over the world venerable old teachers sit on carved wood seats, teaching with blows and shouts, raising their whisks, knocking on the seat, exhibiting spiritual powers and acting as masters. All of this is scattering sand. But say ye, how can any of it be avoided?" 不見僧問長慶. 如何是善知識眼.慶.云有願不撒沙.保福云.不可更撒也.天下老和尚據曲彔木床 上.行棒行喝豎拂敲床.現神通作主宰.盡是撒沙.且道如何免; T48:179b6–10.

41. Xuedou composed seven texts in all with prose comments on about 300 cases, and in most instances is parsimonious in that the remarks are often limited to just one or two sentences. One of these texts composed later in his life became the basis of Yuanwu's additional prose commentary in *Record of Keeping the Beat* (*Jijielu*).

42. T48:141a2–3.

43. T48:141a11–12.

44. T48:141a4–5.

45. T48:141b1–3.

46. T48:141a22–24.

47. T48:161a29–b1.

48. T48:161b4–6.

49. As cited by Musō Soseki in Thomas Yuhō Kirchner, trans., *Dialogues in a Dream* (Kyoto: Tenryū-ji Institution for Philosophy and Religion, 2010), 181; Yuanwu is referred to here as an "ancient master," and the original passage is from T47:757a.

50. The seven layers to be discussed in chapter 2 are (1) introduction, (2) case with (3) capping phrases and (4) prose remarks, (5) verse with (6) capping phrases and (7) prose remarks. In the so-called *One Night Blue Cliff* (*Ichiya Hekigan*) edition supposedly copied in a single night with the aid of a local deity and brought back from China by Dōgen and secretly preserved at the Sōtō sect's Daijōji monastery in northwestern Japan, the sequence is somewhat different as it follows the original *One Hundred Odes* in that the verse immediately follows the case, which can convey a different impression to the reader; see discussion in chapter 6.

51. Chi-chiang Huang, "Elite and Clergy in Northern Sung Hangchou: A Convergence of Interest," in *Buddhism in the Sung*, eds. Peter N. Gregory and Daniel A. Getz, Jr. (Honolulu: University of Hawaii Press, 1999), 297.

52. McRae, *Seeing Through Zen*, 122–123.

53. Wuzu's three main disciples, Fojian, Foyan, and Foguo, all gained this moniker.

54. The friendship between Su Shi and the eminent Chan monk Foyin Liaoyuan, who lived for a long spell on an island mountain, Jinshan, in the Yangzi river in Zhejiang province and was highly regarded for his literary talents as well as for drinking wine while composing verse, is arguably the most celebrated example of the spiritual and artistic exchanges between scholar and monk of the era; their relationship, as chronicled by Juefan and celebrated in many other records, probably began in 1079; see Pan, *Painting Faith*, 114–115.

55. Juefan's (aka Shimen) text from the 1120s, *Shimen's Literary Chan* 石門文字禪 (*Shimen Wenzi Chan*), probably coined the term literary Chan.

56. This style is truncated in the sense that in according with traditional Buddhist gatha it constitutes half of the more typical eight-line verse, and thus does not include couplet parallelism that characterizes the longer style; see William M. Bodiford, "The Rhetoric of Chinese Language in Japanese Zen," in *Zen*

*Buddhist Rhetoric in China, Korea, and Japan*, ed. Christoph Anderl (Leiden: Brill, 2012), 300–301.

57. T48:188c09–12.

58. The commentary by Yamada Kōun of the modern Sambōkyōdan school points out an interesting discrepancy between the mainstream version of the text and the version in the *One Night Blue Cliff* edition; see http://www.sanbo-zen.org/Heko54.pdf (accessed January 26, 2015).

59. It is also included as one of the "Three Greatest Chan Masterpieces" 禪門三大奇景, in addition to the *Platform Sutra* attributed to Sixth Patriarch Huineng from the late eighth century.

60. T48:139a17.

61. T48:0139a5–18.

62. T48:139a12.

63. Kenneth Kraft, *Eloquent Zen*, 131.

64. Heinrich Dumoulin, *A History of Zen Buddhism, India and China* (New York: Macmillan, 1988), 249.

65. A. V. Grimstone, "Introduction," in Katsuki Sekida, trans., *Two Zen Classics: Hekiganroku, Mumonkan* (New York: Weatherhill, 1977), 18–19.

66. Cleary and Cleary, *The Blue Cliff Record*, xxiii; see also *Zengaku Daijiten*, 1109–1111.

67. Ishii Shūdō, *Chūgoku Zenshūshi Wa: Mana Shōbōgenzō ni Manabu* (Kyoto: Zen bunka kenkyūjo 1987), 572.

68. Western translations include: R. D. M. Shaw, trans. and ed., *The Blue Cliff Records: The Hekigan Roku, Containing One Hundred Stories of Zen Masters of Ancient China* (London: Michael Joseph, 1961) (partial translation leaving out the prose comment, but with Shaw's annotations, of all one hundred cases); Wilhelm Gundert trans., *Bi-Yän-Lu: Meister Yüan-wu's Niederschrift von der Smaragdenen Felswand, verfasst auf dem Djia-schan bei Li in Hunan zwischen 1111 und 1115 im Druck erschienen in Sïtschuan um 1300*, 3 vols. (Munich: Karl Hauser, 1954, 1965, 1973) (includes sixty-eight cases all with annotations); Katsuki Sekida, *Two Zen Classics* (includes introduction, case, and verse for all cases along with extensive annotations often derived from the prose commentary that is not translated); Cleary and Cleary, *The Blue Cliff Record* (the first complete translation is still reliable and very useful for researchers yet has some minor questionable passages, though rarely actual errors, throughout); Thomas Cleary, *The Blue Cliff Record* (Berkeley, CA: Numata 1998) (also a complete translation that in most instances duplicates the Cleary and Cleary version, but in other instances changes it, sometimes for the better but in other cases to the detriment, plus this version includes four prefaces but not the five postfaces, and it also lacks the use of notes and the inclusion of monk biographies among other explanatory materials); and Daisetz T Suzuki, trans., "The *Hekigan-roku (Pi-yen Lu)*," *The Annual Report of Researches of The Matsugaoka Bunko* 26 (2012) (includes twenty-two cases). In

addition there are two translations of portions of the original text supplemented with Edo era comments by Hakuin Ekaku and/or Tenkei Denson: Thomas Cleary, trans. *Secrets of the Blue Cliff Record: Zen Comments by Hakuin and Tenkei* (Boston: Shambhala, 2000); and Zenrin R. Lewis, trans., *The Blue Cliff Record Coming through Hakuin: The First Twenty Cases* (Jackonsville, FL: Zen Sangha Press, 2013). There are also efforts to use the text as the source or inspiration for further reflections in poetry or prose, such as David Rothenberg, *The Blue Cliff Record: Zen Echoes* (Albany: State University of New York Press, rpt. 2001). A valuable scholarly source on the text is Ding-hwa Evelyn Hsieh, "A Study of the Evolution of *k'an-hua* Ch'an in Sung China: Yüan-wu K'o-ch'in (1063–1135) and the Function of *kung-an* in Ch'an Pedagogy and Praxis" (PhD diss., University of California, Los Angeles, 1993).

69. See especially Ding-hwa Evelyn Hsieh, "Yuan-wu K'o-ch'in's (1063–1135) Teaching of Ch'an *Kung-an* Practice: A Transition from the Literary Study of Ch'an *Kung-an* to the Practice *K'an-hua* Ch'an," *Journal of the International Association of Buddhist Studies* 17/1 (1994): 66–95; Huang, "Chan Master Xuedou and His Remarks on Old Cases"; and Caifang Zhu, "The Hermeneutics of Chan Buddhism: Reading Koans from *The Blue Cliff Record*," *Asian Philosophy* 21/4 (2011), 373–393.

70. Note a passage that appears near the beginning of the *Linjilu* and is repeated in numerous texts, "[A monk] asked, 'Master, of what house is the tune you sing?'" 問.師唱誰家曲; see Thomas Yūhō Kirchner, ed., *The Record of Linji*, trans. Ruther Fuller Sasaki (Honolulu: University of Hawaii Press, 2009), 120. For a discussion of how sounds of percussion devices (drums, bells, boards) in addition to other noises, such as those of animals, stimulate Chan awakening, see Guo-Jing, "Realization through Hearing in Chan Literature," trans. Jeffrey Kotyk, *Journal of Chinese Buddhist Studies* 27 (2014), 129–179. For another perspective on musicality in Buddhism, see Wei-Yu Lu, "The Performance Practice of Buddhist Baiqi in Contemporary Taiwan" (PhD diss., University of Maryland, 2012).

71. T48:140a11.

72. In addition to a variety of modern Japanese translations (*gendaiyaku*) with annotations, such as Iriya Yoshitaka et. al., eds. *Hekiganroku*, 3 vols. (Tokyo: Iwanami bunko, 1994–96), some important examples of Japanese scholarship include: Katō Totsudō, *Hekiganroku Daikōwa*, 15 vols. (Tokyo: Heibonsha, 1939–40), the first 12 volumes are on *The Blue Cliff Record* and the final 3 are on the *Gateless Gate*; Sueki Fumihiko, *Hekiganroku o Yomu* (Tokyo: Iwanami seminaabukks 73, 1998); Ogawa Takashi, *Zoku: Goroku no Kotoba, Hekiganroku to Sōdai no Zen* (Kyoto: Zen bunka kenkyūjo, 2010); and Ogawa Takashi, *Goroku no Shisōshi: Chūgoku Zen no kenkyū* (Tokyo: Iwanami shoten, 2011). See also Iriya Yoshitaka et. al., eds., *Setchō Hyakusoku Juko*. Sueki has also published *Gendaiyaku Heikiganroku*, 2 vols. (Tokyo: Iwanami shoten, 2001–03). Contemporary Chinese scholarship produced or reprinted in Taiwan includes Huang Yun-chung, *Chanzong*

*Gongan Tixiangyong Sixiang Zhi Yanjiu* (Taipei: Taiwan zuesheng shuju yinxing, 2002); Yinshun, *Zhongguo Chanzong Shi* (Taipei: Zhengwen chubanshe, 1971); and Zhou Yukai, *Chanzong Yuyan* (Taipei: Zongbo chubanshe, 2002). A recent annotated edition is *Biyanlu*, eds. Yang Cengwen and Huang Xianian (Zhengzhou: Zhongzhou guji chubanshe, 2011).

73. Itō Yuten, *Hekiganshū Teihon* (Tokyo: Risōsha, 1963), an edition based on Suzuki Daisetz T., *Bukka Hekigan Hakan Gekisetsu* (Tokyo: Iwanami shoten, 1942).

74. The course titled 《碧巖錄》哲學專題討論, or Seminar on the Philosophy of the *Blue Cliff Record* was taught by Professor Chenping Kun; for course description see https://nol.ntu.edu.tw/nol/coursesearch/print_table.php?course_id=12420M6520&class=&dpt_code=1240&ser_no=89932&semester=102-2 (accessed October 23, 2014).

75. George Albert Keyworth, III, "Transmitting the Lamp of Learning in Classical Chan Buddhism: Juefan Huihong (1071–1128) and Literary Chan" (PhD diss., University of California at Los Angeles, 2001) notes a text that refers to taking "writing and make it as beautiful and brilliantly shining," 150; Foyin was at times critical of a foolish dependence on words and letters.

76. Keyworth, "Transmitting the Lamp of Learning in Classical Chan Buddhism," 165.

77. Cited by Jan Yün-hua, "Chinese Buddhism in Ta-tu," in *Yüan Thought: Chinese Thought and Religion Under the Mongols*, eds. Hok-lam Chan and Wm. Theodore de Bary (New York: Columbia, 1982), 405, from the *Kongguji* collection. Yün-hua notes the ecumenical style of Linquan's two main collections in citing masters from a wide variety of Chan lineages, but this is true for most other major gongan collections as well.

78. T48:139a24–27.

79. Yuanwu tested Dahui on the case, "Being and nonbeing are like wisteria vines clinging to a tree" 有句無句如藤依樹; T47:83b08–13.

80. McRae, *Seeing Through Zen*.

81. Anderl, "Chan Rhetoric," 42.

82. T48:150a03.

83. T48:148a22–24.

84. T47:525c27.

85. T48:141a2.

86. T48:141a7.

87. T48:141a08–10.

88. T48:141a09–10.

89. T48:186a17–18.

90. T48:186a16–17.

91. T48:160a16.

92. T48:165c14.

93. T48:166b16.

94. T48:166b19.

95. T48:166b19–20.
96. T48:166c24–25.
97. For example between the lines of case 97 Xuedou says, "I've seen through him!" 勘破了也; T48:220c21–22.
98. The two sorts of prose comments reflect a somewhat different structure and aim, with remarks on cases being more investigative and explanatory in regard to how the case originally developed and has been recorded in Zen texts and those on verses more concerned with a kind of literary critical approach to Xuedou's literary skill and rhetorical acumen.
99. T48:140b5.
100. T48:141b3.
101. T48:155c2.
102. T48:211c17.
103. T48:155a18.
104. Ernst Cassirer, *Language and Myth* (New York: Dover, 1953), 31.
105. T48:139b3–7.
106. As quoted in Howard Edson, *What Color Is Your Paradigm: Thinking for Shaping Life and Results* (n. p.: Management Advantage, 2003), 184.
107. T48:139a24.
108. Ishii Shūdō's final (farewell) lecture delivered at Komazawa University, Tokyo (January 24, 2014), "Saishū Kōgi: Chūgoku Zen to Dōgen Zen— Sono Renzoku to Hirenzoku to nitsuite" 最終講義—中国禅と道元禅— その連続面と非連続面とについて ("Chinese Chan and Dōgen Zen: Regarding Their Continuities and Discontinuities"); cited by permission of author.
109. Kirchner, *Dialogues in a Dream*, 102.
110. Another usage is the compound 論機論境.

### CHAPTER 2

1. Yanagida Seizan, "The Development of the 'Recorded Sayings' Texts of the Chinese Ch'an School," trans. John R. McRae, in *Early Ch'an in China and Tibet*, ed. Lewis Lancaster and Whalen Lai (Berkeley, CA: Lancaster-Miller Press, 1983), 185–205, esp.192 and 204 n.25, where the first compound (for "encounter") is defined.
2. See the introduction to Hori, *Zen Sand*, which draws much of the material from the *Collection of Sayings from the Zen Forest* (*Zenrin Kūshū*).
3. There are different ways of organizing the cases or dialogues more generally into types or genres. For two recent examples see Lin Ming-yü, *Chan Ji* (Taipei: Lianya chubanshe, 1979) for a five-part typology based on the notion of dynamic activity in the moment (*ji*); and for a different approach based on various kinds of Chan encounters see Ishii Seijun, *Zen Mondō Nyūmon* (Tokyo: Kadokawa sensho 463, 2010).

4. See Albert Welter, *Monks, Rulers, and Literati: The Political Ascendancy of Chan Buddhism* (New York: Oxford University Press, 2006).

5. Yunmen's record consists of about one-quarter "responses to situation" 對機 and another quarter talks "in the [abbot's] chamber" 入室 or 室中.

6. Shaw, *The Blue Cliff Records*, 17–18.

7. Xiangyan's saying, "When hungry I eat, when tired I sleep" is cited in the commentary on the verse to case 88 but is attributed to "an ancient."

8. T47:580b21–22; see John Gill, Susan Tidwell, John Balcom, trans., *After Many Autumns: A Collection of Chinese Buddhist Literature* (Hacienda Heights, CA: Buddha's Light, 2011), 30.

9. T47:580c2.

10. T47:768a25–26. In a related story a stern-faced Ciming said to Huanglong, "If hearing the sound [that a master should have delivered] of three blows [means that the student, Deshan] deserves to be hit, then you deserve to be hit, from dusk till dawn, whenever you hear the sound of the crow crowing, the magpie singing, and the bell, drum, and fish-shaped board being struck," cited in Juhn Ahn, "Who Has the Last Word in Chan? Transmission, Secrecy and Reading During the Northern Song Dynasty," *Journal of Chinese Religions* 37 (2009), 12.

11. Xuedou's comment literally means, "A single hand does not make any sound" 雪竇著語云.獨掌不浪鳴; T48:157c27. Also in a dialogue Yunmen is asked paradoxically, "How is it that striking air makes a noise but hitting wood makes no sound?," so he strikes the air with his staff and says, "Ah hah!" Then he strikes a board and asks, "Does it make a sound?" The monk says, "It makes a sound." The master replies, "You ordinary fellow!" Again he strikes it and asks, "What is making the sound?"; T47:557c26–29.

12. See Ben Brose, "Crossing Thousands of Li of Waves: The Return of China's Lost Tiantai Texts," *Journal of the International Association of Buddhist Studies* 29/1 (2008), 21–42.

13. Steven Heine, *Like Cats and Dogs: Contesting the Mu Kōan in Zen Buddhism* (New York: Oxford University Press, 2014), 132–142.

14. Fenyang also draws upon the five positions of guest and host 五位偏正 (*wuwei pianzheng*) expounded by Caodong school founder, Dongshan Liangjie (807–869). According to Yuanwu, Xuedou uses this schema in his verse to case 87 on a dialogue attributed to Yunmen, which "is highly effective with its meaning in terms of host and guest, as you can see for yourself" 雪竇後面頌得最有工夫.他意亦在賓亦在主.自可見也; begins at T48:212b12–13.

15. See Hsieh, "Yuan-wu K'o-ch'in's (1063–1135) Teaching of Ch'an *Kung-an* Practice."

16. As cited in Pan, *Painting Faith*, 26 (altered); see X68:405a15–16.

17. Robert H. Sharf, "How to Think with Chan Gong'an," in *Thinking with Cases: Specialist Knowledge in Chinese Cultural History*, ed. Charlotte Further, Judith T. Zeitlin, and Ping-chen Hsiung (Honolulu: University of Hawaii Press,

2007), 208–210; in citing the Yuan dynasty explications by Sanjiao Laoren and Zhongfeng Mingben, Sharf discusses the role of public and private record-keeping and commenting on dialogues in light of the pattern of legal precedents. See also Y. W. Ma, "Themes and Characterization in the Lung-T'u Kung-An," *T'oung Pa* LIX (1973), 179–202; according to this, "the judge always appears in sharp focus and bold line against a canvas of tiresome puppets," 201, which seems partly true for Chan masters as well.

18. T48:153a14.

19. T48:153a15; the legal metaphor is used extensively in Sanjiao Laoren's preface from 1304, especially T48:139b29–c14.

20. Earlier scholarship dated this relatively obscure yet crucial text from 1133, but now the date of 1093 is generally accepted for its original composition and circulation; see Ishii Shūdō, "*Shūmon Tōyōshū* to *Hekiganroku*," *Indogaku Bukkyōgaku Kenkyū* 46/1 (2001), 215–221.

21. See Keyworth, "Transmitting the Lamp of Learning in Classical Chan Buddhism."

22. Entry in *The Princeton Dictionary of Buddhism*, ed. Robert E. Buswell Jr. and Donald S. Lopez Jr. (Princeton, NJ: Princeton University Press, 2014); see 祖庭事苑, X64.1261.

23. X.64.1261. The text is now included in the supplemental canon.

24. X.67.1306.

25. T.48.2006.

26. X.67.1299.

27. See cases 7 (which criticizes Qing's view), 31 (which cites him two times), 42, 60, 64, 82, 91, and 100 (includes criticism). Qing was apparently a well-trained follower of a disciple of Xuedou whose opinions were highly valued by Yuanwu, who received some criticism from opponents during the twelfth century for relying on a non-monastic's view of the *One Hundred Odes*. The current version of the text, however, hardly indicates a slavish devotion to this library prefect.

28. T48:158c28–159c2.

29. T48:159a2.

30. T48:201b5.

31. T48:201a24–26.

32. T48:224a02–4.

33. See Huang Jing-Jia, "A Study on Imitating Activities of Hanshan Poems by Chan Buddhist Monks in Song Dynasty," *Journal of Literature and Art Studies* 3/4 (2013), 204–212.

34. T48:224a6–24.

35. Cleary and Cleary note, "According to the recommendation of Tenkei Denson, this pointer has been exchanged with that of the hundredth case, but either is suitable for both," *The Blue Cliff Record*, 545.

36. T48:221a18–20.

37. This comment reads, 此集自大慧一炬之後.而又重罹兵燹.世鮮善刻
.今得蜀本.校正頗完.猶恐中間亥豕魯魚不無一二.四方具眼高人為一
是正之抄錄.見教當復改竄.俾成金美.禪宗幸甚.峒中書隱白; T48:185c12-17.

38. "Floating Yuanwu" 流れ圜悟 (*Nagare Engo*) is a hanging scroll 43.9 cm × 52.4 cm
(17.3 in × 20.6 in) that represents the first half of a certificate of Buddhist spiritual achievement 印可状 (*inkajō*) from 1124 given to Yuawwu's disciple Huqiu
Shaolong. This, the oldest extant document written by a Chan master written
in what the Japanese refer to as the *bokuseki* 墨跡 style of calligraphy using
bold strokes to reflect a mental state of deep concentration (samadhi), supposedly floated to Japan in a container and has been held at Daitokuji temple in
Kyoto and been on display at the Tokyo National Museum; see Gregory P. A.
Levine, *Daitokuji: The Visual Cultures of a Zen monastery* (Seattle: University of
Washington Press, 2005).

39. The Boat Monk makes an interesting comparison with Daolin, the so-called
Bird's Nest Monk who resided in seated meditation in the branches of a tree and
occasionally gave Dharma teaching to passersby, such as in a famous conversation held with poet Bai Juyi.

40. X85:127a6-7. In another verse, "A thousand-foot-long fishing line drops straight
down./ One wave no sooner rises than it is followed by tens of thousands./ The
night is quiet, water is cold, the fish won't take the bait,/ The boat returns, empty
of fish but full of moonlight." 千尺絲綸直下垂.一波才動萬波隨.夜靜水寒魚不
食.滿船空載月明歸. The second line is used in a Yuanwu correspondence with
a Chan disciple; see T47:782c1.

41. In *Five Lamps Meeting at the Source* 五燈會元 (*Wudeng Huiyuan*); see X80:115a.

42. T51:324b21; this was used as a capping phrase in a lecture by Faxiu 法秀 (1027—
1090); X78:778a17-18. On a stele at the temple today is inscribed a four-line
verse called "Receiving the Buddhist Precepts" 受佛戒 attributed to a Tang poet-
monk named Huiting Chuanzi 華庭傳子 that includes as the opening two lines,
"The sun is setting slowly in the west/ And the moon rises in a darkening sky
to the east/" 金烏漸漸墜西偏.玉兔東生挂碧天. The inscription indicates that
Shanhui included this in his journal, "Musings on Faith from a Vegetable Patch"
素園信, but I have not been able to find it in the canon.

43. Bret W. Davis, trans., "Nishitani Keiji's 'The Standpoint of Zen: Directly Pointing
to the Mind" in *Buddhist Philosophy: Essential Readings*, ed. William Edelglass and
Jay L. Garfield (New York: Oxford University Press, 2009), 100.

44. The full passage from *Empty Hall Collection* (*Xutangji*): 舉僧問夾山會禪師.如
何是夾山境(春日花開秋時葉落).山云.猿抱子歸青嶂後.鳥銜花落碧巖前(莫
向言中取則.直須句外明宗); X67:329c5-7.

45. This passage reads: 圜悟老師.在成都時.予與諸人請益其說.師後住夾山道林
.復為學徒扣之.凡三提宗綱.語雖不同.其旨一也.門人掇而錄之.既二十年矣;
T48:224b11-14.

46. The cases include 4, 18, 23, 31, 33, 36, 42, 48, 55, 61, 74, 81, 84, 85, and 91.

47. Kawamura Kōdo et. al. eds., *Dōgen Zenji Zenshū* (Tokyo: Shunjūsha, 1988–1993), vol. 5:208.

48. According to an oft-cited Dongshan passage, "Drumming and singing arise together" 敲唱双挙 (敲唱双び挙ぐ), which suggests instantaneous, unmediated inquiry and response in which there is no separation or impediment to expressions manifested and comprehended in the present situation. It is interesting to note the words of modern author Haruki Murakami in his essay "Jazz Messenger," *New York Times* (July 8, 2007), who says his writing was inspired more by music than examples of fiction in establishing rhythm, melody, and harmony allowing for free improvisation. Influenced by jazz interpreters such as Charlie Parker and Thelonious Monk, Murakami notes, "There aren't any new words. Our job is to give new meanings and special overtones to absolutely ordinary words. . . . I find the thought reassuring. It means that vast, unknown stretches still lie before us, fertile territories just waiting for us to cultivate them. . . . And if all goes well, you get to share that sense of elevation with your readers (your audience). That is a marvelous culmination that can be achieved in no other way."

49. The verse reads, "Mounting the bull slowly I return homeward./ The voice of my flute intones through the evening./ Measuring with hand-beats the pulsating harmony I direct the endless rhythm./ Whoever hears this melody will surely join me"; X64:774b10–11. An earlier version by Puming that culminates in the empty circle as the tenth image reads, "On the verdant field the beast contentedly lies idling his time away,/ No whip is needed now, nor any kind of restraint;/ The boy too sits leisurely under the pine tree, / Playing a tune of peace, overflowing with joy."

50. Pan, *Painting the Faith*, 28–29.

51. T48:213b12.

52. T48:213b10–12.

53. T48:192c12–21; note that "Mixed-Up Confusion" was the title of Bob Dylan's first officially released single, an electric rock tune that came out in 1963 before he became a star known initially for his acoustic folk songs.

54. T48:152a25–29.

55. T48:175b14.

56. T48:199b2.

57. T48:199b11.

58. T48:142c28-a3.

59. T48:182a04–5.

60. See Ogawa, *Zoku: Goroku no Kotoba*.

61. See Jeffrey Broughton, trans. with Elise Yoko Watanabe, *The Chan Whip Anthology: A Companion to Zen Practice* (New York: Oxford University Press, 2014).

62. Zhu, "The Hermeneutics of Chan," 387.

63. T48:150b23.

64. T48:149c18.

65. Katsuki Sekida notes several levels, negative and positive, implied by the term blindness, including willful heresy, subconscious ignorance, the ego-bound realization of a board-carrying fellow, justice that has no preference or bias, and the true maturity of Buddha that is flexible and beyond discrimination or non-discrimination; in *Two Zen Classics*, 176.

66. T48:182b4–5.

67. T48:152a25.

68. T48:152b6.

69. T48:196a17; the comment about thunder lacking rain is also used as a capping phrase regarding a monk's phony shouts that are dismissed by Muzhou in case 10.

70. T48:161c12.

71. Alok Jha, "What Is Heisenberg's Uncertainty Principle?," *Science*, November 10, 2013, http://www.theguardian.com/science/2013/nov/10/what-is-heisenbergs-uncertainty-principle (accessed December 6, 2014).

72. "I really feel like part of my mission is to be the person who says, 'It's OK. Be uncertain. Everybody's uncertain. Don't feel inadequate. Embrace it. Go with it. Let that lead you to the interesting stuff,'" cited by Dave Zeitlin, "Shell's Odyssey," *The Pennsylvania Gazette*, Sept.–Oct. 2013, 46–51.

73. Roberto Unger, *False Necessity: Anti-Necessitarian Social Theory in the Service of Radical Democracy*, rev. ed. (London: Verso, 2004), 279–280.

74. Caleb Crain, "The Red and the Scarlet: The Hectic Career of Stephen Crane," *New Yorker*, June 30, 2014.

75. Edward Said, *On Late Style: Music and Literature Against the Grain* (New York: Vintage, rpt. 2007).

76. "Joyce's Revisions of 'The Sisters': From Epicleti to Modern Fiction," *James Joyce Quarterly* 24/1 (1986), as cited by Brenda Maddox, "Introduction," in *Dubliners* (New York: Bantam, rpt. 1990, from 1914), xvii.

77. Jake Wallis Simons, "James Joyce's *Ulysses*: The Beginning of an Epiphany," *The Independent*, January 25, 2012, http://blogs.independent.co.uk/2012/01/25/james-joyces-ulysses-the-beginning-of-an-epiphany/ (accessed February 3, 2015).

78. Ibid. Note that in 361 CE the Roman historian Ammianus Marcellinus used the word for the first time to refer to a Christian feast (*epiphanion*). In the centuries that followed it was mainly used in connection to a variety of Christian festivals, which were celebrated differently, and at various times, by the different churches.

79. T48:178c17–18.

80. *Zhongguo Chanzong Dianji Congkan: Biyanlu* (Henan Zhengzhou: Zhongzhou guji chubanshe, 2013), 222.

81. See Ilaria Natali, "A Portrait of James Joyce's Epiphanies as a Source Text," *Humanicus* 6 (2011), 1–25.

82. Joyce, *Dubliners*, 192.

83. To comment briefly on another Chan parallel, Joyce's allusive literature can be compared to Yuanwu's approach, and his main disciple, Samuel Beckett, who assisted with research for writing *Finnegan's Wake*, is similar to Dahui in his postwar turn to minimalism based on his own epiphany while mourning for his mother's death that nobody could ever equal his mentor.

CHAPTER 3

1. Jacques Gernet, *Daily Life in China on the Eve of the Mongol Invasion 1250–1276* (Stanford, CA: Stanford University Press, 1962), 239.

2. See Yi-hsun Huang, "Chan Master Xuedou and His Remarks on Old Cases."

3. In a similar vein Richard Brody says of jazz pianist and composer Thelonius Monk, "Monk was the master of the single note, perfectly selected, timed, and struck so that it would have a symphonic amplitude; "The Best of Thelonius Monk," *The New Yorker*, May 20, 2015.

4. See Tony Barnstone and Chou Ping, trans., *The Art of Writing: Teaching of the Chinese Masters* (Boston: Shambhala, 1996).

5. John Allen Tucker pointed this out in a conversation; see also Weixiang Ding, "Zhu Xi's Choice, Historical Criticism and Influence—An Analysis of Zhu Xi's Relationship with Confucianism and Buddhism," *Frontiers in Philosophy of China* 6/4 (2011), 521–548.

6. Iriya Yoshitaka, "Chinese Poetry and Zen," *The Eastern Buddhist* 6/1 (1973), 59, as cited in Beata Grant, *Mount Lu Revisited: Buddhism in the Life and Writings of Su Shih* (Honolulu: University of Hawaii Press, 1994), 188.

7. "Zijue" 自覺 or "Self-awakening" verse in *Touzi Yiqing Chanshi Yulu*, and "one of three poems from a mountain hermitage"; X71:742a13.

8. T48:165c5.

9. T48:165c27–28.

10. T48:208b11–15.

11. T48:200b23–24.

12. Ma Tianxiang, "Yuanwu Keqin de *Biyanlu* Wenzi Chan de Fanlin," *Xinan Minzu Daxue Xuebao* 1 (2011), 57; see T48:153a3–4.

13. Keyworth, "Transmitting the Lamp of Learning in Classical Chan Buddhism," 156.

14. T48:175b12–13.

15. T48:175b14.

16. *Yuanwu Chanshi Yulu* 圓悟禪師語録, or *Yuanwulu* 圓悟録, is a compendium of the sermons, informal talks, verse, and prose of Yuanwu Keqin compiled by the master's foremost disciple, Huqiu Shaolong 虎丘紹隆 (1077–1136), and first published in 1134 with prefaces by the government officials Geng Yanxi 耿延禧

(n.d.) and Zhang Jun 張浚 (1086–1154), both lay disciples of the master. It contains formal sermons 上堂 (*shangtang*) in fascicles 1–7 ½; informal sermons 小参 (*xiaocan*) in 7½–13); public lectures for lay believers 普説 (*pushou*) in 13; informal talks on practice for monastic and lay disciples 法語 (*fayu*) in 14–16½; prose comments on gongan 拈古 (*niangu*) in 16½–18½; verse comments on gongan 頌古 (*songgu*) in 18½–19; and miscellaneous poems, essays and prose writings, verses for seekers, funeral sermons, and private correspondences (but only one letter) in 20.

17. *Mingzhou Xuedoushan Zishengsi Diliuzu Mingjue Dashi Taming* 明州雪竇山資聖寺第六祖明覺大師塔銘; T47:712a3–713b18. This funerary inscription was composed by literatus Lu Xiaqing 呂夏卿 (active 1025–1077) in 1065, thirteen years after Xuedou's death, according to the final passage. The other two sources—a brief biography of Xuedou in the *Zuting Shiyuan* (X64:322c14–20), and a longer biography in the *Chanlin Sengbao Zhuan* compiled by Juefan Huihong—are based on another funerary inscription (X79:514c8–515b15), with the latter adding more encounter dialogues between Xuedou and other monks to the biography.

18. T48:215a25.

19. T47:712b18–21.

20. T:674b1.

21. T48:218c15–16.

22. Yuanwu says of Xuedou's verse, "He has extra rhymes so he completes the teaching in literary style" 他有餘韻.教成文理, and he also argues that, with the case dialogue being ambiguous, Changqing does make it through the gate; T48:218c27–28.

23. T47:700c23.

24. T48:143a02–4; the legend of the dragon cave is mentioned in *The Dharma-Seal Sutra Spoken by the Buddha for the Naga King Sagara* 海龍王說法印經, T.15.599.

25. T48:143a26.

26. T47:710b29-c1; cited by Dōgen in *Tenzokyōkun*, in which the chief cook (*tenzo*) in response to a question comments, "One, two, three, four, five," which he says, "match one another."

27. T48:142a10.

28. Ibid.

29. T48:142a11.

30. T48:142b21.

31. T48:161b5–10.

32. T48:218c13.

33. T48:223a23.

34. T48:223a24–25.

35. T48:142a13.

36. T48:208b29–c1.

37. T47:524c12–13 (also T51:322b23). In another use of the term, Dongshan evokes a phrase that appears frequently in Yuanwu's capping phrases, "Overturn the meditation seat" 倒禪床; T47:523a11. In a related example of reversal a student asks Dongshan the meaning of Bodhidharma's coming from the west and the master turns the question back on the disciple by asking how he would respond when he becomes a teacher, and in another instance he replies that "he will answer only when Dong Creek flows backwards" 待洞水逆; T47:522c20; see Natasha Heller, "Why Has the Rhinoceros Come from the West? An Excursus into the Religious, Literary, and Environmental History of the Tang Dynasty," *Journal of the American Oriental Society* 131/3 (2011), 356.

38. T48:183c24.

39. T48:184b18.

40. Thomas Yuhō Kirchner, trans., *Entangling Vines: A Classic Collection of Zen Koans* (Boston: Wisdom, 2013), 45 (altered).

41. T48:212b15–18.

42. T48:212b17–18.

43. See http://www.sanbo-zen.org/Heko87.pdf (accessed January 8, 2015).

44. T48:208a7.

45. X67:244a3–4.

46. T48:193b7–8.

47. See cases 36, 42, 48, 61, 81, 84, 85, and 91.

48. T48:210b25–26.

49. T48:215c12.

50. T48:157c27.

51. T48:201b10–11.

52. T48:179b24.

53. T48:179c20.

54. Hsieh lists and analyzes various traditional historical sources in the section, "Biographical Sources and Problems of the Sources," of her dissertation, "A Study of the Evolution of *k'an-hua* Ch'an in Sung China," 29–32.

55. Keyworth says, "Yuanwu Keqin is more famous because of his student Dahui Zonggao than for of his reliance on the 'raising the precedent' [舉古] or 'praising the precedent' teaching methods," in "Transmitting the Lamp of Learning in Classical Chan Buddhism," 223.

56. Bells, pottery, hides, silk strings, wood, gourds, bamboo, and sounding stones were being used in orchestral performances at the time.

57. T47:956c7–9; and T51:643a11–15.

58. X80:396b5–6; see John Gill et al., *After Many Autumns*, 169.

59. Hsieh, "A Study of the Evolution of *k'an-hua* Ch'an in Sung China," 34–37.

60. Kirchner, *Entangling Vines*, 82.

61. Ibid.

62. See Miriam Levering, "Dahui Zonggao and Zhang Shangying: The Importance of a Scholar in the Education of a Song Chan Master," *Journal of Song-Yuan Studies* 30 (2000), 115–139; Robert M. Gimello, "Chang Shang-ying on Wu-t'ai Shan," in *Pilgrims and Sacred Sites in China*, eds. Susan Naquin and Chün-fang Yü (Berkeley: University of California Press, 1992), 89–149; and Robert M. Gimello, "Marga and Culture: Learning, Letters, and Liberation in Northern Sung Ch'an," in *Paths to Liberation: The Marga and Its Transformations in Buddhist Thought*, eds. Robert E. Buswell and Robert M. Gimello (Honolulu: University of Hawaii Press, 1992), 371–437.

63. In the *Yuanwu Foguo Chanshi Yulu*; T47.801b4–6.

64. See Yanagida Seizan, *Zen no Yuige* (Tokyo: Chōbunsha, 1973).

65. T49:686b21, and X79:570c11–12; note the AABA rhyme with gong, song, zhong.

66. Of these, 38 of the 145 correspondences were intended for lay followers.

67. This image is attributed to Tang dynasty master, Daolin, also known as "Bird's Nest Monk."

68. T47:738a25–27.

69. See Martin Collcutt, *Five Mountains: The Rinzai Zen Monastic Institution in Medieval Japan* (Cambridge, MA: Harvard University Press, 1981).

70. T48:331c6–9.

71. X69:457c3–4. Korean Zen master Taego Pou (1301–1382) added capping phrases to each line along with prose in addition to a final verse comment; see J. C. Cleary, *A Buddha from Korea: The Zen Teachings of Taego* (Boston, Shambhala, 1988), 85–86.

72. T48:293c18.

73. T48:164a25–28.

74. Xuedou composed seven texts in his record with prose comments on about 300 cases, and in most instances is parsimonious in that they are often limited to just one sentence. One of these texts composed later in his life became the basis of Yuanwu's additional prose commentary in *Record of Keeping the Beat* (*Jijielu*).

75. Hsieh, "Yuan-wu K'o-ch'in's (1063–1135) Teaching of Ch'an *Kung-an* Practice," 77.

76. Hsieh, "Yuan-wu K'o-ch'in's (1063–1135) Teaching of Ch'an *Kung-an* Practice," 79.

77. T48:139a6–11.

78. T48:141a11–12, 13–16. The last phrase refers to being held in the stocks 枷. Another version reads, "He whose eye is opened, can see how Setchō [Xuedou] sometimes picks and sometimes gathers, sometimes praises and sometimes blames, and with only four lines he measures the kōan." Generally speaking, the "commendatory verse" (J. *juko*, C. *sung-ku*) on a kōan demonstrates Zen in a roundabout manner, while its "critical comment" (J. *nenko*, C. *nien-ku*) takes up the significant points and gives critical remarks. Setchō at the outset makes this challenging gesture," in Daisetz T. Suzuki, trans., "The *Hekigan-roku* (*Pi-yen Lu*)," 16.

79. Huang, "Chan Master Xuedou and His Remarks on Old Cases," 87.

80. Ibid. Keyworth suggests a distinction between "raising the precedent (or main case)" and "praising the precedent," in "Transmitting the Lamp of Learning in Classical Chan Buddhism," 155, but this tends to ignore the additional role of "raising" 舉 (*ju*) the case used to introduce the dialogue in opening sections prior to the main case for 79 of the 100 fascicles in the *Blue Cliff Record*.

81. Cleary and Cleary, *The Blue Cliff Record*, 7. A 1998 version by Thomas Cleary is "Usually verses on ancient stories just explain Chan in a roundabout way; the general rule for presenting old stories is just to settle the case on the basis of the facts. Xuedou confronts him . . ." 17.

82. T48:144b16–20.

83. T48:165b10–12.

84. T48:165b14–21.

85. T48:188b5.

86. T48:188b15.

87. T48:182a17.

88. T48:189c18–21.

89. T48:142a23–b3.

90. T48:181c11–12.

91. T48:181b18–19.

92. T48:162b10–11.

93. T48:201b10–11.

94. T48:161b28.

95. T48:163c13–14.

96. T48:219a2–12.

97. T48:220a11.

98. Juhn Y. Ahn, trans. and John Jorgenson, ed., *Collected Works of Korean Buddhism*, vol. 7-2 (Seoul: Jogye Order of Korean Buddhism, 2012) [hereafter *Gongan Collections* II], 33 (altered).

99. Juhn Y. Ahn, trans. and John Jorgenson, ed., *Collected Works of Korean Buddhism*, vol. 7-1 (Seoul: Jogye Order of Korean Buddhism, 2012) [hereafter *Gongan Collections* I], 81–82 (altered). This verse is traditionally attributed to Xuedou Chongxian and can also be found in the *Mingjue Chanshi Yulu*; T47.679c14–16.

100. *Gongan Collections* II, 41; T47.672a25.

101. *Gongan Collections* II, 221.

102. *Gongan Collections* II, 224–225.

103. For this case, see *Gongan Collections* II, 594–600; case 55 in *The Iron Flute: 100 Zen Kōan with Commentary by Genrō, Fūgai and Nyogen*, trans. and eds. Nyogen Senzaki and Ruth Strout McCandless (Rutland, VT: C. E. Tuttle, 1961). The original title *Tetteki Tōsui* 鐵笛倒吹 literally means "the Iron Flute Played Upside Down." A different version is in the *Jingde Chuandenglu*: "When

he (Muzhou) saw a lecturer monk, he would call his chief seat. If the (lecturer) monk responded, the master would say, 'Narrow-minded 擔板 fellow";
T51:291b3–4.

104. X66:111b12–14; and X79:79b5–8.

105. *Gongan Collections* I, 597.

106. Ibid.

CHAPTER 4

1. T48:52c19–20. The *Blue Cliff Record* version says, "A monk asks Dongshan"
僧問洞山, but in *Wumen's Barrier* it says, "When a monk asks Priest Dongshan"
洞山和尚.因僧問. Adding 初 seems to have been introduced later as in, "When
a monk first asked Dongshan" 洞山初因僧問 in *Five Lamps Merged into One
Source (Wudeng huiyuan)*, vol. 15 and elsewhere, such as X65:700a17.

2. See Kawamura Kōdō et al., *Dōgen Zenji Zenshū* (Tokyo: Chikuma shobō, 1988–
1993), vol. 5: 212, but this version does not appear in Dōgen's *Eihei Kōroku*, vol.
9.68, which includes a verse comment. Also in *Tenzokyōkun* Dōgen remarks that
Dongshan was chief cook when he said this, so a possible rendering is "sesame"
instead of "flax."

3. Natasha Heller, *Illusory Abiding: The Cultural Construction of the Chan Monk
Zhongfeng Mingben* (Cambridge, MA: Harvard University Press, 2014),
242–243.

4. Hirota Sōgen, "Daie Sōkō no *Hekiganroku* Shōkyaku no Mondai," *Zengaku
Kenkyū* 82 (2004), 107–128.

5. See Thomas Cleary, trans., *Zen Lessons: The Art of Leadership* (Boston: Shambhala,
1989), "Translator's Introduction."

6. See T48:1036b21–c3 for this and the above citations of the same passage.

7. T48:1024c07–13.

8. See "Introduction to the History of Zen Practice," in Yamada Kōun, *The Gateless
Gate: The Classic Book of Zen Koans* (Boston: Wisdom, rpt. 2004), 259–260.

9. T48:185c12–17.

10. T48:224c17–225a1.

11. T48:139c22–25.

12. Jiang Wu, *Enlightenment in Dispute: The Reinvention of Chan Buddhism in
Seventeenth-Century China* (New York: Oxford University Press, 2008), 85.

13. Jih-chang Lin, "A Critique and Discussion of the View That Shi Miyuan Proposed
the Five-Mountain, Ten-Monastery System," *Journal of Cultural Interaction in
East Asia* 5 (2014), 45–65.

14. My recent book, *Like Cats and Dogs: Contesting the Mu Kōan in Zen Buddhism*
(New York; Oxford University Press, 2014), 49, highlights in detail the timeline
of Dahui's life and career as it affected the origins and implications of the keyword method.

15. Hsieh, "Yuan-wu K'o-ch'in's (1063–1135) Teaching of Ch'an Kung-an Practice," 76 n.30, notes based on the research on lineages by Abe Chōichi in *Chūgoku Zenshū no Kenkyū* (Tokyo: Seishin shobō, 1963) that Yuanwu had six disciples from Sichuan, the highest portion in the group, but Dahui from Anhui like most of the rest was very active in Zhejiang (when he was not in exile to the south).

16. Ahn, "Who Has the Last Word in Chan?," 37–38.

17. Thomas Cleary, trans., *The Undying Lamp of Zen: The Testament of Zen Master Torei* (Boston: Shambhala, 2010), 35–36.

18. The *huangyang* is a plant in the boxwood family that allegedly grows only an inch a year. Here it is an image for being stuck in a partial awakening with nothing at work in you to move you further along. Miriam Levering notes that *Zengaku Daijiten*, 145b; *Zen Gojiten*, 473a contains references in "Dahui Zonggao (1089–1163): The Image Created about Himself and His Teaching Style," in *Zen Masters*, ed. Steven Heine and Dale S. Wright (New York: Oxford University Press, 2010), 91–116. Alternatively, it could be "seat of thorns."

19. T47:883b2–5.

20. Another translation is, "They both come down together." This appears in *Record of Serenity* case 87; see Thomas Cleary, trans., *Book of Serenity: One Hundred Zen Dialogues* (Hudson, NY: Lindisfarne Press, 1990), 372.

21. T47:883b9–12.

22. T47.883a–b; Dahui discusses his postawakening conversations with Yuanwu in T47:883b–c.

23. T47:883b8–13. The version of the narrative in the *Entangling Vines Collection* indicates that Yuanwu "then conferred upon Dahui the *Record of the True School of Linji*, designated him his scribe, and had him give a lecture to the other monks," in Kirchner, *Entangling Vines*, 56. The transfer of this obscure lineal text that was supposedly compiled by Yuanwu himself to stress the pure heritage of the Linji school symbolized that at the age of forty Dahui had received genuine and full transmission in the lineage.

24. Levering, "Dahui Zonggao (1089–1163), 104; and J. C. Cleary, trans., *Swampland Flowers: The Letters and Lectures of Zen Master Ta-hui* (Boston: Shambhala, 1977), xiv. Another version is in Juhn Young Ahn, "Malady of Meditation: A Prolegomenon to the Study of Illness and Zen" (PhD diss. University of California at Berkeley, 2007), 159: "The old master then raised at will a series of public cases, which were cut down by me with two or three turning [words]." In a later version in the *Entangling Vines Collection*, there is a much tamer version of this part of the dialogue: "Yuanwu brought up [some cases] and Dahui spoke without hesitation" 圜悟連舉.師出語無滯; see Kirchner, *Entangling Vines*, 20–22.

25. This text (X.67.1309) from 1146 consists of 661 cases with capping phrase and brief prose comments and may have inspired Dōgen to use this title for his collections of 300 cases and 75 vernacular sermons. The *Zongmen Liandeng Huiyao* 宗門聯燈會要 was compiled in 1183 by Huiweng Wuming 晦翁悟明

(n.d.), three generations after Dahui in the same line. See Ishii Shūdō, "Daie Goroku no Kisōteki Kenkyū—*Shōbōgenzō* no Shuten to *Rentōeyō* to sono kankei," *Komazawa Daigaku Bukkyō Gakubu Kenkyū Kiyō* 32 (1974), 215–262.

26. See Robert E. Buswell Jr., trans., *The Korean Approach to Zen: The Collected Works of Chinul* (Honolulu: University of Hawaii Press, 1983).

27. See Morten Schlütter, *How Zen Became Zen: The Dispute Over Enlightenment and the Formation of Chan Buddhism* (Honolulu: University of Hawaii Press, 2009).

28. T48:292c22–293a14.

29. See Robert E. Buswell Jr., "The Transformation of Doubt (*Yiqing*) into a Positive Emotion in Chinese Buddhist Meditation," in *Love and Emotions in Traditional Chinese Literature*, ed. Halvor Eifring (Leiden: E. J. Brill, 2004), 225–236. The Yuan dynasty (1279–1368) monk Zhiche 智徹 wrote a work titled *A Collection on Resolving Doubt in the Chan Lineage* 禪宗決疑集 (*Chanzong Jueyiji*), in which he stresses the importance of doubt as a unique Chan approach to meditation and enlightenment.

30. I thank Andy Ferguson for pointing this out in a conversation in Berkeley, CA on January 30, 2015; his remarks were supported during my visit to Mount Jiashan in July 2015.

31. Dumoulin, *Zen Buddhism*, 249.

32. Buswell, "The Short-cut Approach of K'an-hua Meditation"; and Ahn, "Who Has the Last Word in Chan?," 35.

33. Senzaki and McCandless, *The Iron Flute*.

34. Anderl, "Chan Rhetoric," 42; he also says, "It is quite clear that according to Yuanwu's opinion the transmitted phrases and teaching methods of the famous Tang masters have themselves turned into 'dead words/phrases' and have assumed a status not different from the written words found in canonical Buddhist literature," 43. "Live words" 活句 (C. *huoju*, J. *katsuku*, K. *kogu*) reflects the dynamism of awakening in contrast to the mechanical quality of "dead words" 死句 (C. *siju*, J. *shiku*, K. *sagu*). See also Morten Schlütter, "Silent Illumination, Kung-an Introspection, and the Competition for Lay Patronage in Sung Dynasty Ch'an," in *Buddhism in the Sung*, ed. Peter N. Gregory and Daniel A. Getz Jr. (Honolulu: University of Hawaii Press, 1999), 145 n.85 and n.86, citing Robert Buswell and Ding-hwa Hsieh.

35. Hsieh, "Yuan-wu K'o-ch'in's (1063–1135) Teaching of Kung-an Ch'an Practice," 67, 89, and 90; note that she does not refer to the important role of the Huqiu lineage.

36. See Robert Sharf, "How to Think with Chan *Gongans*," in *Thinking with Cases: Specialized Knowledge in Chinese Cultural History*, ed. Charlotte Furth, Judith Zeitlin, Hsiung Ping-chen (Honolulu: University of Hawaii Press, 2007), 205–243.

37. Steffen Döll, *Im Osten des Meeres. Chinesische Emigrantenmönche und die frühen Institutionen des japanischen Zen-Buddhismus* (Stuttgart: Franz Steiner Verlag, 2010), 60–63, with a paraphrase, 63–64.

38. This recalls the method of "allusive variation" 本歌取り (*honkadori*), which is one of the main rhetorical devices used in the Japanese waka tradition.

39. X69:457b23–c2.

40. Ahn, "Who Has the Last Word in Chan?," 36.

41. Ahn, "Who Has the Last Word in Chan?," 40.

42. T.47.1998B.

43. Ahn, "Who Has the Last Word in Chan?," points out that in a letter by one of his followers Yunyo Xiaoying (12th c.) a harsh critique was launched against the otherwise comprehensive *Annual Chronology* (*Nianpu*) of Dahui for not mentioning the *Arsenal* and goes on to explain the provenance of its name. *Arsenal* was chosen as a title by a fellow disciple to playfully allude to the weapon storehouse mentioned in the biography of third-century scholar Du Yu (228–294). Also the *Annual Chronology* has no mention of Dahui destroying the *Blue Cliff Record*.

44. T47:837b26–c15.

45. T48:152c14–18.

46. See Alan Fox, "Self-reflection in the Sanlun Tradition: Madhyamika as the 'Deconstructive Conscience' of Buddhism," *Journal of Chinese Philosophy* 5/19 (1992), 1–24.

47. William M. Bodiford shows in several tables listing the number of citations of Chinese Chan and Japanese Zen masters for using key terms associated with various kinds of gongan interpretation that both Yuanwu and Dōgen along with Nampo Shōmyō 南浦紹明 (1235–1309), aka Daiō Kokushi 大應国師—in contrast to Dahui along with Mugaku Sogen 無覚祖元 (1226–1286), aka Bukko Kokushi 仏光国師, who fled Mongol rule in China to become the founding priest of Engakuji temple in Kamakura in 1282 at the behest of Hōjō Tokimune—have a strong affinity in using the term *xianzheng gongan* (J. *genjōkōan*); in "Keyword Meditation and Detailed Investigation in Medieval Japan," *Ganhwa Seon: Illuminating the World*, Conference Proceedings (Seoul: Dongguk University Press, 2010), 118ff.

48. Dōgen's saying is literally, "There is no remedy that satisfies hunger other than the painting of a rice cake" 畫餅にあらざれば充飢の藥なし.

49. Natasha Heller, "The Chan Master as Illusionist: Zhongfeng Mingben's *Huanshu Jiaxun*," *Harvard Journal of Asiatic Studies* 69/2 (2009), 300.

50. Buswell, "The Short-cut Approach of *K'an-hua* Meditation," 322.

51. Ibid.

52. T48:152c21.

53. T48:153a13. The image of the turtle draws from a *Lotus Sutra* parable in which the amphibian happens to lodge into a floating piece of wood and goes to land safely, representing the select few who attain enlightenment, thus making an interesting counterpoint with the image of determined fish as seekers navigating the Dragon Gate.

54. T48:153a12.

55. T48:152c21–25.
56. T48:152c25–29.
57. T48:152c26–153a1.
58. T48:153a2–7.
59. T48:153b29; Yuanwu uses the term *huatou* in the general sense of dialogue but not in a technical sense of keyword.
60. T48:153a18.
61. T48:152c20.
62. T48:153a26–27.
63. The "board-carrying fellow" as a typical Chan epithet for someone who is trapped by his or her own sense of tunnel vision functions as disingenuous insult-cum-praise for Dongshan.
64. T48:153a7–9.
65. T48:153a10.
66. T48:153a14–15.
67. T48:153a28.
68. T48:153a22.
69. T48:153a24–25.
70. T48:153b24.
71. T48:153c4–6.
72. Cleary, *Secrets of the Blue Cliff Record*, 42–43.
73. T48:153a17.
74. X67:565c7–9.
75. T47:802b21–25.
76. X65:700b12–13.
77. Baiyun (1025–1072) was a famous mentor of Wuzu, Yuanwu's teacher; X65:700b21–22.
78. X65:701a3–4.
79. T48:153c2–3.
80. He is known for saying, "Great doubt, great enlightenment; small doubt, small enlightenment; no doubt, no enlightenment," which was also used by Weilin.
81. Jeff Shore, *Zen Classics for the Modern World: Translations of Chinese Zen Poems & Prose with Contemporary Commentary* (n.p.: Diane Publishing, 2011), 47ff.
82. Hsieh, "Yuan-wu K'o-ch'in's (1063–1135) Teaching of Ch'an *Kung-an* Practice," p. 87.
83. Hsieh, "Yuan-wu K'o-ch'in's (1063–1135) Teaching of Ch'an *Kung-an* Practice," p. 91.
84. T47:879c11–23; this passage is cited with numerous alterations from Chün-Fang Yü, "Ta-hui Tsung-kao and Kung-an Ch'an," *Journal of Chinese Philosophy* 5/6 (1979), 211–235 (227).
85. T48:294a9–10.
86. T47:930a13–17.
87. T48:162b8.
88. T48:162b10.

89. T48:162b10–11; Xuedou is metaphorically doing the slapping in this passage, and is at once compared to the deceptive fox and cast in the role of its exorcist.

90. T48:162b24–26.

91. Ding-hwa Hsieh, "Poetry and Chan 'Gong'an': From Xuedou Chongxian (980–1052) to Wumen Huikai (1183–1260)," *Journal of Song-Yuan Studies* 40 (2010), 48–70 (65). A drawback in Hsieh's analysis is that she highlights Xuedou's allusions to the Chinese literary and mythological traditions and contrasts that with *Wumen's Barrier* but does not comment on the way Wumen uses this approach in the verses she cites, including cases 1 and 3. See also Grimstone, who notes that Xuedou's poems "are literary productions in their own right, often of great beauty, and their translation cannot be simply a matter of providing a literal rendering of their content," in "Introduction," 20. An example where Wumen uses *Blue Cliff Record*–style legal imagery is the ode to case 19 in which the Sixth Patriarch tells two monks it is neither the wind nor the flag that is moving but the mind: "Wind, flag, mind are moving,/ Their replies will all be listed in the same indictment./ Only knowing how to open his mouth/ [Huineng] was unaware of his crime." 風幡心動. 一狀領過.只知開口.不覺話墮; T48:296c25–26.

92. Despite Dahui's emphasis on lay practitioners seeking a spiritual breakthrough in their daily lives, his method has been primarily for monks in China (Wumen, Gaofeng), Korea (Jinul, Hyesim, Taego), and Japan (Musō, Hakuin), although with global spread encompassing Chan/Seon/Zen via current worldwide evangelical approaches the distinction between monastic and lay practice, which was a gray area in Southern Song's quasi-modernist society, is now once again increasingly breaking down.

93. See Zong-qi Cai, ed., *How to Read Chinese Poetry: A Guided Anthology* (New York: Columbia University Press, 2008).

94. T48:162a12–16. Another relevant passage is from case 1, T48:140b20–22: My late master Wuzu once explained, "If only you can penetrate 'empty, nothing sacred,' then you can return home and sit in peace." For some, this is a matter of striking at tangled vines. ... So, it is said, "If you can penetrate a single phrase, at the same time you penetrate a thousand phrases." 五祖先師嘗說.只這廓然無聖.若人透得.歸家穩坐.一等是打葛藤.不妨與他打破漆桶. ... 參得一句透.千句萬句一時透.

95. Keyworth, "Transmitting the Lamp of Learning in Classical Chan Buddhism," 321.

96. John C. H. Wu, *The Golden Age of Zen* (Taipei: United Publishing Center, 1975), 274–275. Wu adds, "It was not for nothing that the Lin-chi Zen after Ta-hui began to decay, just as the Fa-yen Zen began to fade after Yen-shou"; this is hardly the kind of estimation that Dahui's followers would endorse.

97. Kirchner, *Entangling Vines*, 142 (altered).

98. Kirchner, *Dialogues in a Dream*, 169.

99. Kirchner, *Dialogues in a Dream*, 170.

CHAPTER 5

1. For example the *Jianghu Fengyueji* 江湖風月全集, a text consisting of Chan poetry selections mainly from the Northern Song that was created by a Southern Song editor and was first published in 1288, later becoming very important among the Zen Five Mountains in medieval Japan, covers seventy-two lineages in 261 verses.

2. Ahn, "Who Has the Last Word in Chan?," 32–33; the characterization can be cast in a negative light if it seems to represent a distraction or obsession.

3. Ahn, "Who Has the Last Word In Chan?," 4, referring to Susan Cherniack, "Book Culture and Textual Transmission in Sung China," *Harvard Journal of Asiatic Studies* 54/1 (1994), 5–125.

4. Chün-fang Yü, "Chung-fen Ming-pen and Ch'an Buddhism in the Yüan," *Yüan Thought: Chinese Thought and Religion Under the Mongols*, ed. Hok-lam Chan and Wm. Theodore de Bary (New York: Columbia University Press, 1982), 448–455 (439).

5. Ibid.

6. X67:243c17–24a3.

7. X67:243c17–a1.

8. X67:244a4–9.

9. Kawamura et. al., *Dōgen Zenji Zenshū*, vol. 3: 78; see also Taigen Dan Leighton and Shohaku Okumura, trans. *Dōgen's Extensive Record: A Translation of the Eihei Koroku* (Boston: Wisdom, 2010), 159–160.

10. T48:171a28–b1.

11. The first version is in Cleary and Cleary, *The Blue Cliff Record*, 199, and the second is in Sekida, *Two Zen Classics*, 228. Yuanwu's prose comment seems to support Cleary and Cleary, "If you are an adept, even when you have no illness, still you should go ahead and take some medicine as a preventative measure" 任是作者.無病時.也須是先討些藥喫始得; T48:171b1.

12. T48:189a16.

13. See Thomas Yuhō Kirchner, ed., *The Record of Linji*, translation and commentary by Ruth Fuller Sasaki (Honolulu: University of Press, 2009); Albert Welter, *The Linji Lu and the Creation of Chan Orthodoxy: The Development of Chan's Records of Sayings Literature* (New York: Oxford University Press, 2008); and Jeffrey L. Broughton and With Elise Yoko Watanabe, trans., *The Record of Linji: A New Translation of the Linjilu in the Light of Ten Japanese Zen Commentaries* (New York: Oxford University Press, 2012).

14. Kirchner, *The Record of Linji*, 295–296.

15. Ahn, "Who Has the Last Word in Chan?," 28.

16. Zhu, "Hermeneutics of Chan," 383.

17. Ahn, "Who Has the Last Word in Chan?," 24–25.

18. T48:295c11.

19. T48:165c14.

20. T48:293c18.

21. Kirchner, *The Record of Linji*, 232.

22. Kirchner, *The Record of Linji*, 233.

23. T48:173b23–24.

24. T48:172c24.

25. T48:173b13.

26. See the dialogue in Kirchner, *The Record of Linji*, 304: The master asked Lepu, "Up to now it has been the custom for some people to use the stick and others to give a shout. Which comes closer [to the heart of the recipient]?" "Neither," replied Lepu. "What does come close?" asked the master. Lepu shouted. The master hit him. 師問樂普云.從上來.一人行棒.一人行喝.阿那箇親.普云.總不親.師云.親處作麼生.普便喝.師乃打.

27. T48:210b15–16.

28. T48:152c14.

29. Case 81 refers to an arrow that kills and gives life.

30. T48:139a24–27.

31. T48:178b15.

32. T48:147b9; see cases 66 and 100 for specific references to the sword.

33. T48:144c19.

34. See Ahn, "Who Has the Last Word in Chan?," 50; T47:951c19–22.

35. T48:177b5–6; the seven items of a teacher are (1) great capacity and great function, (2) swiftness of intellect, (3) wondrous spirituality of speech, (4) the active edge to kill or give life, (5) wide learning and broad experience, (6) clarity of mirroring awareness, and (7) freedom to appear and disappear. Also the seven accessories of a monk are three garments, bowl, censer, fly-whisk, stool (*nisidana*), paper, and material for washing 七事隨身常持者.三衣.鉢.香合.拂子.尼師檀.紙被.浴具也.

36. T48:177b7.

37. T48:177b9.

38. Urs Erwin App, "Facets of the life and teaching of Chan Master Yunmen Wenyan (864–949). (Volumes 1 and 11)" (PhD. diss., Temple University, 1989), 126.

39. T48:146b20–22.

40. See Ma Tianxiang, "Yuanwu Keqin de *Biyanlu* yu Wenzi Chan de Fanlan."

41. T48:177c15–16.

42. T48:216b14.

43. T48:216b20.

44. T48:175b12–13.

45. Tsuchiya Taisuke, "Shinsei Kokubun no Wuji Zen Hihan," *Indogaku Bukkyōgaku Kenkyū* 51/1 (2003), 206–208.

46. T48:163b6–7.

47. T48:167b29–c1.

48. T48:167c4.

49. This is in the *Precious Mirror Samadhi* (*Baojing Sanmei*), T47:515a26, or T47:526a6; see also the chapter on "Expedient Means" in the *Lotus Sutra*.

50. *Tetteki Tōsui* is in the *Sōtōshū Zensho* 曹洞宗全書 by Genrō Ōryū 玄樓奧龍 (1720–1813) with capping phrases added by his main disciple Fūgai Honkō 風外本光 (1779–1847). Both monks are from the Tenkei Denson 天柱傳尊 (1648–1736) lineage, rather than the dominant Manzan Dōhaku-Menzan Zuihō lineage; see Michel Mohr, "Japanese Zen Schools and the Transition to Meiji: A Plurality of Responses in the Nineteenth Century," *Japanese Journal of Religious Studies* 25/ 1–2 (1998), 167–213.

51. The term "iron flute" or "flute without holes" 無孔笛子, which appears in *Blue Cliff Record* cases 41, 51, and 82, probably was expressed at an early stage of Chan discourse and was used twice by Dōgen in the *Extensive Record* (*Eihei Kōroku*), in vols. 5.258 and 5.329, but the full term including "upside down" may have been first created by Wuyi Yuanlai 無異元來 (1575–1630): 親磕著得便宜.敢問.皮囊知不知.倒吹鐵笛音聲別; X72:294a07. Another example by Kaishan Qian 開善謙 is 樓頭浪蕩無拘檢.鐵笛橫吹過洞庭; X65:525c15.

52. T47:703a28–b1. According to the Senzaki version, "The moon floats above the pines,/ And the night veranda is cold/ As the ancient, clear sound comes from your finger tips./ The old melody usually makes the listeners weep,/ But Chan music is beyond sentiment./ Do not play again unless the great sound of Laozi accompanies you." Also, Lao-tsu (Laozi) said, "Great utensils take a long time to make. Great characters never were built in a few years. Great sound is the sound which transcends ordinary sound."

53. T48:165c17–19.

54. T48:186c12.

55. T48:186c13–15; see also case 13 in *Wumen's Barrier*.

56. T48:171a26.

57. T48:156c11.

58. T48:156c5–10. Another version in Yuanwu's record ends with the "teacher saying he will smash fox dens for thousands of years" 上堂.僧問鏡清.諸方只具啐啄同時眼.不具啐啄同時用.如何是啐啄同時眼.師云.打破千年野狐窟; T47:743c16–18.

59. T48:156c25–26.

60. T48:151c15.

61. T48:195a16; in many other collections the cat gongan takes one rather than two cases, as in case 14 of *Wumen's Barrier* or case 9 of *Record of Serenity*.

62. T48:195b2.

63. T48:195b1.

64. T48:195a23–24.

65. Ahn, "Who Has the Last Word of Chan?," 26–27 (altered).

66. See Chün-fang Yü, "Chung-feng Ming-pen and Ch'an Buddhism in the Yüan."

67. Ibid.
68. Kirchner, *Entangling Vines*, 92.
69. T48:331a14–331b.
70. T48:146a17.
71. T48:146b8–9.
72. In case 14, T48:154c10; sometimes the order of the second and third phrases is reversed.
73. T48:146b10–11.
74. Guishan calls her a cow and also refers to himself as a buffalo.
75. See Robert M. Gimello, "Chang Shang-ying on Wu-t'ai Shan," in *Pilgrims and Sacred Sites in China*, eds. Susan Naquin and Chün-fang Yü (Berkeley, CA: University of California Press, 1992), 89–149; and Steven Heine, "Visions, Divisions, Revisions: The Encounter Between Iconoclasm and Supernaturalism in Kōan Cases about Mount Wu-t'ai," in *The Kōan*, ed. Steven Heine and Dale S. Wright (New York: Oxford University Press, 2000), 137–167.
76. T48:165a23–25.
77. T48:165b7–8.
78. T48:165a29-b3; yet Wuzu also says, "Do not take having concerns as not having concerns; time and time again concern is born of unconcern" 莫將有事為無事.往往事從無事生.
79. See *Record of Serenity* case 77, which involves the drawing of a circle and a swastika.
80. T48:172a21.
81. T48:172b22.
82. T48:172b20.
83. T48:180b25.
84. Kirchner, *The Record of Linji*, 40.
85. T48:160b1.
86. T48:160a28.
87. T48:160b14.
88. Cleary and Cleary, *The Blue Cliff Record*, 138: "In Sung times some Lin Chi masters criticized the Ts'ao-Tung masters for being too fond of quiescence, abiding in extinction, absorbed by the vastness of the universe; the fifth rank of the Ts'ao-Tung's five ranks was symbolized by a solid black circle, which the Lin Chi masters often took to mean nirvana as extinction."
89. T48:161a12.
90. T48:161a21–24.
91. T48:207b20–21.
92. T48:157b18.
93. T48:166a7.
94. T48:147b27.
95. T48:203a25.

96. T48:197a26–27; and T48:197c3.
97. T48:197a14.
98. T48:197a1.
99. T48:197a15.
100. T48:143a1.
101. Zhou Yukai, *Chanzong Yuyan*, as cited by Caifeng Zhu, "The Hermeneutics of Chan Buddhism," 378.
102. T48:197a5.
103. Mario Poceski notes, "On the surface, stories of this kind usually seem to involve spontaneous interactions, grounded in actual circumstances, perhaps echoing the mental states of the main protagonists. At the same time, there are basic verbal and behavioral patterns that tend to be repeated over and over again. That includes the asking of formulaic questions and the performance of seemingly peculiar but oft-repeated symbolic or nonverbal acts, such as beating and shouting. In essence, elocutions or behaviors that at first sight might look eccentric, unconventional, or extemporaneous are turned into fairly conventional and predictable tropes, as they are reiterated time and again, with some variations," in *The Records of Mazu and the Making of Classical Chan Literature* (New York: Oxford University Press, 2015), 51. I disagree with this skeptical assessment of the genre.
104. T48:160a16–18.
105. T48:148c20–21.
106. Cleary and Cleary, *The Blue Cliff Record*, 16–17.
107. T48:205c7.
108. T48:206a10–11.
109. See McRae, *Seeing Through Zen*; and Steven Heine, *Zen Skin, Zen Marrow* (New York: Oxford University Press, 2008).
110. T48:216a18–21.
111. T48:152a27–28.
112. T48:208a20–22.
113. T48:169c12; this expression is used in case 30 and also in 47, 64, 78, and 86, see Ogawa, *Zoku: Zen no Goroku*.
114. T48:156c9.
115. This phrase, best known as the title of a fascicle in Dōgen's *Treasury of the True Dharma-Eye*, was also used by Linji/Rinzai school thinkers Zhongfeng Mingben and Musō Soseki.
116. Lin Mingyu, *Chan Ji* (Taipei: Lianya chubanshe, 1979).
117. *Gongan Collections* I, 62; see also Urs App trans., *Master Yunmen: From the Record of the Chan Teacher "Gate of the Clouds"* (Tokyo: Kodansha, 1994), 83 n.2; in the Zhuangzi chapter on "The Way of Heaven" 天道, a wheelwright tells the ruler that his natural skill "cannot be taught or learned," but it surpasses the "dregs" of dead ancients.

118. T51:296b15–16.

119. Kirchner, *The Record of Linji*, 166.

120. For example, Chün-fang Yü points out ecumenism in that, even though he was known for supporting the keyword and disputing other styles of Chan in a fair-minded and evenhanded way, in "Chung-feng Ming-pen and Ch'an Buddhism in the Yüan," 432. Furthermore, Yü notes, because differences among the five schools were mainly due to the different personalities of their founders, the language and techniques each school employed also differed.

121. See the lengthy note on uses of this term in Cleary and Cleary, *The Blue Cliff Record*, 16–17.

122. The theme of travels or visiting a master or temple is featured in cases 1, 4, 7, 10, 21, 24, 26, 28, 31, 33, 34, 35, 36, 55, 69, 98—note that this list includes a sequence of four cases in a row, unusual in the collection.

123. T48:158c16–17.

124. Other devices include the bamboo stick 竹篦, whip 策, and wooden stick carried in meditation 香板 (*xiangban*, literally, "incense board"), or 警策 (J. *kyōsaku* in Rinzai, and *keisaku* in Sōtō).

125. T48:198a21–22.

126. T48:159c21–24.

127. T48.160a11–12; in *Lotus Sutra* chapter 27, recalling a passage in the *Samyutta Nikaya*.

128. T47.550c21. Similarly, in regard to a reference to the *Nirvana Sutra* chapter 25, when someone asks Yunmen, "What is it like when the tree has withered and the leaves fallen?," the master says, "It is completely manifest as golden wind"; 問樹凋葉落時如何.師云.體露金風; T47.550c19–20.

129. T48:185b19.

130. T48.172b4–19.

131. These are usually read as constituting a pair of sequential dialogues belonging together in a grouping that is rare in gongan collections, in which cases usually seem to represent stand-alone discourses without necessarily evoking any sense of progression from one to the next (there is a similar sequence in cases 57, 58 and 59 on Zhaozhou's "arriving at the Dao is not difficult, just avoid picking and choosing," and in 70, 71 and 72 on the incapacity of both language and silence); see n.122 above on the sequence of travel cases.

132. This saying is also mentioned in cases 83 and 95.

133. T48.154c2, and T48.155a21–22; Yunmen's dialogues are, respectively, also in T47.550b24–25 (no difference from the *Blue Cliff Record* version) and T47.545c7–8 (with a difference).

134. T47:550b25; note that Yunmen's reply is used as a capping phrase to the case 2 verse.

135. Cleary and Cleary, *The Blue Cliff Record*, 97.

136. It is interesting that the term "topsy-turvy" is most closely associated with the musical style of Gilbert and Sullivan, including their deliberate misrepresentation of Japan in the *Mikado*.

137. T48.155b24.

138. T48.154c13–16; the line about "single truth" alludes to a passage in the *Dhammapada*. In commentary on case 15 Yuanwu notes, "Since there is only one word different [between the two cases], why are there thousands and tens of thousands of distinctions?" 只爭一字.為什麼卻有千差萬別; T48.155b7–8.

139. T48.152c17.

140. See Taigen Dan Leighton, *Visions of Awakening in Space and Time: Dōgen and the Lotus Sutra* (New York: Oxford University Press, 2007).

141. T48:183bl2–15.

142. Nikkyō Niwano, *Buddhism for Today: A Modern Interpretation of the Threefold Lotus Sutra* (Tokyo: Hosei, 1971), 194–195; see T17.723c13–21 for the source dialogue.

143. T47:805a2–4.

144. X65:680b6–7.

145. X65:680b8–9.

146. T47:805a7–9.

147. X65:680b19–20.

148. X65:680b21–22.

149. T48:208a27–28.

150. T48:208b25–27.

151. T48:208c29–a2.

152. T48:182b19–25.

153. The last sentence could be interpreted as meaning, "Experiencing subjectivity [through perception of an object] is rather easy, but realizing (or expressing) a de-objectification [beyond the subject-object dichotomy] must be quite difficult." In other words while "coming out of one's body" to hear the sounds is an internal release the ultimate experience of becoming one with external phenomena (raindrop sound) is much more difficult to achieve and explain. Consider Dōgen's waka on this topic: "Just at the moment/ Ear and sound/ Do not interfere—/ There is no voice/ There is no speaker"; Koe zu kara/ Mimi no kikoyuru/ Toki sareba/ Waga tomo naran/ Katarai zo naki. A literal rendering: "Because when the sound enters the ear naturally on its own, there is no conversation between friends." In some versions line four is a negation indicating, "There is no conversation and no friends," in Steven Heine, *The Zen Poetry of Dōgen: Verses from the Mountain of Eternal Peace* (Boston: Tuttle, 1997), 112 and 176.

154. T48:182c6.

155. T48:182c6–9.

156. T48:182c28–29; note that the grammar indicates mountains are the subject for the verb "driving," which highlights an all-encompassing quality in contrast to the monk's specific mention of "raindrops."

157. T48:209a6–7.

158. T48:209a16–18.

159. T48:177c14.

160. T48:209b1; these words are an ironic allusion to Chanyue's poem that is cited by Yuanwu called, "Traveling the Path is Difficult" 行路難.

161. In a capping phrase on Xuedou's verse on case 30 Yuanwu makes this accusation of the poet.

162. T48:147a26–27.

163. Ogawa, *Zoku: Goroku no Kotoba*, 107–158; the dialogue appears in vol. 25 of *Jingde Record*.

164. T48:147b9.

165. T48:147c7–8; some versions indicate not Fayan's approval but simply his "listening to" the verse.

166. T48:229a04–5.

167. "The bond forged between Deshao and Zhongyi became the pillar of the Wuyue state"; Albert Welter, *Monks, Rulers, and Literati: The Political Ascendency of Chan Buddhism* (New York: Oxford University Press, 2006), 146.

168. T48:147c17–20; Gundert, in *Bi-Yän-Lu* vol. 1, 170, rhymes the first two lines: "Im Land am Stron der Frühlingswind will un will nicht weh'n./ Ein Rebhun ruft tief in Versteck wo Blütenbüsche stehn'n." The verse recalls—but purposefully falls short of matching—an ancient poem cited in case 24 of the *Gateless Gate*: "I always recall springtime south of the river/ Where the partridges sing/ And the hundreds of flowers are so fragrant." 長憶江南三月裏、鷓鴣啼處百花香; T48:296a14.

169. T48:147c26.

170. T48:147b26.

171. T48:147c10–12.

172. Cleary, *Secrets of the Blue Cliff Record*, 26.

173. T48:150a27.

174. T48:198c4–6.

175. T48:148a19.

## CHAPTER 6

1. Mario Poceski, *The Records of Mazu and the Making of Classical Chan Literature*, 56. The references to the Bodhidharma account, for a total of five, are in case 17, T48.157a19–20; case 26 comment, T48.167b6–7; case 43 comment, T48.180b18–19; case 73, T48.200c15–24; and case 98 comment, T48.221c6. In the Chan

gongan tradition there are dozens of dialogues, as shown by D. T. Suzuki and others, that evoke this meme with all kinds of different responses, which in a way confirms Poceski's point but also shows nuance and complexity he does not take into account. One scholar has found more than 2,000 such references in the *Jingde Record* and related Chan works; see Christian Wittern, "Some Preliminary Remarks to a Study, Rhetorical Devices in Chan Yulu Encounter Dialogues," in *Zen Buddhist Rhetoric in China, Korea, and Japan,* ed. Christoph Anderl (Leiden: Brill, 2012), 267.

2. Poceski, *The Records of Mazu,* 126.

3. Cleary, *Book of Serenity,* xxxv.

4. See T47:743c16–44a2 for the full passage; see also a similar discussion from a Dharma hall sermon by Xueyan Zuqin 雪巖祖欽 (1215–1287); X70:623a19–b22.

5. Ongoing impact is also found with another Chan expression from the twelfth century attributed to a Dharma-nephew of Yuanwu that derived in large part from diverse precedent works but came to be considered seminal and with long-lasting significance for a wide variety of successors: Guoan's *Ten Oxherding Pictures* with poetic comments regarding the taming of a bull symbolizing the attainment of awakening. The Guoan version includes the empty circle as the eighth picture with the return to the marketplace as the final image, whereas an earlier version by Puming concludes with the empty circle. Both versions have been translated, redrawn, and commented on dozens of times. On the other hand, there is a degree of superficiality in regard to many kinds of claims for "number one" status that are commonly being made these days in China, including some assertions about Jiashan whereby traditional legends are often conflated or misrepresented to trumpet the temple's history.

6. See Jan Yün-hua, "Chinese Buddhism in Ta-Tu: The New Situation and New Problems," *Yüan Thought: Chinese Thought and Religion Under the Mongols,* eds. Hok-lam Chan and Wm. Theodore de Bary (New York: Columbia University Press, 1982). 375–417.

7. Because Wansong and his corpus was not so well known at the time, on some lineage charts his name was eventually inserted several generations after Dōgen's mentor Rujing, even though their lives overlapped.

8. For example see Nishioka Shuji, "*Shōyōroku* ni okeru Shō nitsuite: *Hekiganroku* to no Hikaku tōshite," *Indogaku Bukkyōgaku Kenkyū* 54/1 (2006), 155–158; and Shibe Ken'ichi, "Tenkei Denson to *Hekiganroku* nitsuite," *Indogaku Bukkyōgaku Kenkyū* 41/1 (1993), 277–280.

9. I agree in large part with Thomas Cleary who writes, "The large number of identifications of classical and literary allusions and expressions to be found in the *Book of Serenity* may be connected with the circumstances of its composition and reconstruction. Wansong himself writes that he did it not only to show he had not invented the interpretations himself but also to reveal the depths of Tiantong Hongzhi's own classical learning. This was not an idle exhibition of

literary erudition, but was part of a strategy of the time to outwardly protect Chan from the charge of being a haven for anti-intellectual illiterates and dropouts from the orthodox," *Book of Serenity*, xxxviii.

10. Xuedou citations are in cases 1, 7, 16, 18, 19, 21, 22, 23, 24, 25, 26, 29, 20, 33, 34, 35, 39, 48, 50, 55, 59, 62, 71, 74, 80, 85, 86, 88, 89, 93, 95, 97, and 99.

11. T48:247a2–3.

12. T48:267c8.

13. Cleary, *Book of Serenity*, xxxiv.

14. T48:250a16–b1.

15. T48:259a17–18.

16. T48:261a12–14.

17. T48:277b24.

18. T48:291b17.

19. X.67.1307.

20. X.67.1312, and X.67.1313; together these two collections are known as the *Two Hundred Questions of Tongxuan and Qingzhou* 通玄青州二百問 (*Tongxuan Qingzhou Erbaiwen*).

21. X67:701b12–14.

22. See Thomas Cleary, trans., *Timeless Spring: A Soto Zen Anthology* (New York: Weatherhill, 1980), 72–90.

23. T47:744a7–9; the first phrase is used frequently in Yuanwu's sayings.

24. X67:317b3–13.

25. X67:257a8–12.

26. Kraft, *Eloquent Zen*, 148–149.

27. Kraft, *Eloquent Zen*, 68; T48:183a18.

28. Kraft, *Eloquent Zen*, 149.

29. See Peter Haskel, "Bankei and His World," *Zen Notes* 56/4 (2009), 12–18, which is part of a series of articles about kōan study in medieval Japan in which Haskel notes that monks from China who were part of the new Ōbaku sect severely criticized some of these practices as inauthentic and a fraud; see also Andō Yoshinori, *Chūsei Zenshū Bunseki no Kenkyū* (Tokyo: Kokusho inkōkai, 1999), for an in-depth study of *shōmono* literature from the era.

30. See Musō Soseki, *Dialogues in a Dream*, trans. Thomas Yūhō Kirchner (Kyoto: Tenryu-ji Institute for Philosophy and Religion, 2010).

31. Sawada Tenzui, "A Study on the Japanese Gardens Viewed from the Rinzai Zen Buddhism (XIV)—A Case Study on the Tenryuji Garden Kyoto" (in Japanese), *The Journal of the Japanese Institute of Landscape Architecture* 43/2 (1979), 3–11.

32. Heinrich Dumoulin, *Zen Buddhism: A History, Japan* (New York: Macmillan, 1990), 227.

33. Sonja Arntzen, "The Poetry of the *Kyōunshū*," 70.

34. Matsuzaki Kakuhon, ed., *Hekiganroku Kōgi: Tenkei Denson Teishō*, 10 vols. (Tokyo: Kōyūkan, 1903).

35. Hakuin, *Hekiganroku Hisshō* (Tokyo: Nagata shunyū, 1915).

36. Thomas Cleary, trans., *The Undying Lamp of Zen: The Testament of Zen Master Tōrei* (Boston: Shambhala, 2010), 67–68; this was published posthumously in 1800 but is included in the Taishō canon, T.48.2575.

37. T47:685b25–c2.

38. X67:228b5.

39. T47:798b21.

40. T48:134b29; and T48:170a23.

41. According to the full case, "A monk asks Dalong, 'The physical body rots away: what is the steadfast Dharmakaya?,' and the master says, "Mountain flowers bloom like brocade as the valley streams are brimming blue as indigo." 僧問大龍.色身敗壞.如何是堅固法身.龍云.山花開似錦.澗水湛如藍; T48:208a26–27.

42. Anthony Lane, "Go Ask Alice What Really Went on in Wonderland," *The New Yorker*, June 8, 2015.

43. Natsume Soseki, *The Gate*, trans. William F. Silby (New York: New York Review Books Classics, 2012), 186–187 (altered).

44. Therese Sollien, "Sermons by Xu Yun—A Special Transmission Within the Scriptures," in *Zen Buddhist Rhetoric in China, Korea, and Japan*, ed. Christoph Anderl (Leiden: Brill, 2012), 417–437.

45. Yamada Mumon, *Hekiganroku Zen Teishō*, 10 vols. (Kyoto: Zen bunka kenkyūjo, 1985).

46. See Ishii, *Chūgoku Zenshūshi Wa*.

47. Kazuaki Tanahashi and John Daido Loori, trans. and eds., *The True Dharma Eye: Zen Master Dōgen's Three Hundred Kōans*, with Commentary and Verse by John Daido Loori (Boston: Shamhhala, 2005), 346; Dan Leighton told me he is planning to undertake a similar project for the entire *Verse Comments* text, which he has already cotranslated. Dōgen also writes a verse for case 84 (case 7 in the *Blue Cliff Record*) in the *Verse Comments*: "Reprimanding Huichao heralds spring on New Year's Eve,/ When Huichao turned his head there was no dust on the mirror./ How splendid was Fayan's ability to function./ By the time a single word was uttered [Huichao] had become a Buddha." 喚作惠超窮臘春.惠超廻首鏡無塵.良哉法眼拈来用.一語未終仏变神; in Kawamura Kōdō et al., ed., *Dōgen Zenji Zenshū*, 7 vols. (Tokyo: Shunjūsha, 1988–1993), vol. 4: 240; see also Taigen Dan Leighton and Shohaku Okumura, trans., *Dōgen's Extensive Record: A Translation of the Eihei Kōroku* (Boston: Wisdom Publications, 2004), 594.

48. Gundert, trans., *Bi-Yän-Lu*, vol. 1: 25; Gundert does not provide an explanation for this.

49. See https://www.pref.ishikawa.lg.jp/kyoiku/bunkazai/syoseki/2.html (accessed July 29, 2014).

50. Itō, *Hekiganshū Teihon*.

51. See the index and reference materials in Leighton and Okumura, *Dōgen's Extensive Record*.

52. Takeuchi Michio, "Dōgen Zenji *Hekiganroku* Shōrai nitsuite," *Indogaku Bukkyōgaku Kenkyū* 4/2 (1956), 476–477.

53. An exception may be case 31, which corresponds to case 299 in the *300 Cases* and may have been culled from the prose commentary on case 20 in the *Blue Cliff Record* but more likely stems from vol. 13 of Yuanwu's *Record*; cases in both texts include 24 in *300 Cases* (29 in *Verse Comments*), 26 (99), 46 (9), 52 (49), 81 (86), 95 (14/15), 105 (89), 108 (73), 127 (35), 136 (41), 141 (29), 158 (50), 159 (99), 182 (53), 186 (44), 202 (11), 203 (88), 205 (20), 214 (61), 225 (43), 245 (19), 249 (28), 252 (7), 284 (88), 286 (46), 289 (55), 295 (62), 298 (93).

54. The notion that the Daijōji version has authenticity related to the legend of the *One Night Blue Cliff*, while disregarded or disputed by some, tends to find its way into many contemporary and otherwise reliable Japanese records of Dōgen's life as well as chronological lists of yearly activities that are appended to scholarly works (other legends also regularly appear); however, noted Dōgen biographical researcher Nakaseko Shōdō does not deal with the topic, whereas biographer Takeuchi Michio explores it in detail and He Yansheng, among others, discusses its complexity.

55. Some of these reflections are based on my visit to Jiashan temple in June 2015 and on discussions with representatives there as well as consideration of a series of illustrations regarding temple history (or, rather, hagiography) painted on a structure located near the Blue Cliff Spring.

56. See William Bodiford, *Sōtō Zen in Medieval Japan* (Honolulu: University of Hawaii Press, 1993), 143–162; John Daido Loori, "Dogen and Koans," in *Sitting With Kōans: Essential Writings on the Practice of Zen Koan Introspection*, ed. John Daido Loori (Boston: Wisdom, 2006), 151–162; and Steven Heine, *Dōgen and the Kōan Tradition: A Tale of Two Shōbōgenzō Texts* (Albany: State University of New York Press, 1994).

57. Kagamishima Genryū, *Dōgen In'yō Goroku no Kenkyū* (Tokyo: Sōtōshūgaku kenkyūjo, 1995).

58. Kawamura, *Dōgen Zenji Zenshū*, vol. 3: 132–134; and Leighton and Okumura, *Dōgen's Extensive Record*, 212–213.

59. Kawamura, *Dōgen Zenji Zenshū*, vol. 3: 118; and Leighton and Okumura, *Dōgen's Extensive Record*, 198–199. Additional comments on Yuanwu by Dōgen include from the *Extensive Record* 1.74, 2.167 (similar to 6.469), 4.259, and 4.324 (quite positive); and from the *Treasury of the True Dharma-Eye* passages in the fascicles, "Shisho," "Gyōbutsuigi," "Kobusshin," "Shohō Jissō," Jishō Zammai," and "Jinshin Inga" (quite critical).

60. T47:793c6; Yuanwu refers to the expression as a "gongan."

61. T47:804a29–b1; see Kazuaki Tanahashi, ed., *Treasury of the True Dharma Eye: Zen Master Dogen's Shobo Genzo* (Boston: Shambhala, 2010), xxx–xxxi.

62. Kawamura, *Dōgen Zenji Zenshū*, vol. 1: 412.

63. Kawamura, *Dōgen Zenji Zenshū*, vol. 1: 413.

64. T48:213c11–12.
65. Kawamura, *Dōgen Zenji Zenshū*, vol. 3: 154; and Leighton and Okumura, *Dōgen's Extensive Record*, 234. Dōgen's use of the staff as a kind of rhetorical device is found in many examples throughout the *Extensive Record*.
66. Kawamura, *Dōgen Zenji Zenshū*, vol. 4: 86; and Leighton and Okumura, *Dōgen's Extensive Record*, 449.

# Sino-Japanese Glossary

Baiyun Shouduan　白雲守端
*Baize Songgu*　百則頌古集
Baizhang　百丈
Bankei　盤珪
Baofu　保福
*Baojing Sanmei*　寶鏡三昧
Baoshou　包綏
bayin she　八音社
benze　本則
bieyu　別語
biji　筆記
*Biyanji/Hekiganshū*　碧嚴集
*Biyanlu/Hekiganroku*　碧嚴錄
Boshan　博山
*Bukka Hekigan Hakan Gekisetsu*　仏果碧厳破関撃節
buqueding　不確定
Buson　蕪村
Caodong/Sōtō　曹洞
Caoshan　曹山
*Chanlin baoxun*　禪林寶訓
Chanmen Sandaqijing　禪門三大奇景
Chanmen diyishu [Zongmen diyishu]　禪門第一書/宗門第一書
*Chan Songgu Lianzhu Tongji*　禪宗聯珠通集
chang　唱
Changqing Lan'an　長慶懶安
Changsha　長沙
*Changuan Cejin/Zenkan Sakushin*　禪関策進
Chanlin Leiju 禪林類聚

*Chanyuan Qinggui* 禪苑清規

Chanyue 禪月

cheng 承

chuandenglu 傳燈錄

chuanyu 転語

chuishi 垂示

*Congronglu/Shōyoroku* 從容録

Cuifeng 翠峯寺

Cuiwei 翠微

Cuiyan Sizong 翠嵓宗枯

Dacisi 大慈寺

*Dahui Chanshi Wuku* 大慧禪師武庫

*Dahui Pujue Chanshi Nianpu* 大慧普覺禪師年譜

*Dahui Shu* 大慧書

Dahui Zonggao 大慧宗杲

Daijōji 大乗寺

Daitō Kokushi 大燈国師

daiyu 代語

Dajue Huailian 大覺懷璉

Danxia Tianran 丹霞天然

Danxia Zichun 丹霞子淳

Danyuan 耽源

dao 倒

*Daodejing* 道德經

Daolin 道森

Daoqian 道虔

Daoyuan 道原

Daquanxiuli Pusa/Daigenshūri Bosatsu 大權修理菩薩

dasi 大死

Dayu 大禹

densetsu 伝説

Deshan 德山

Deyun 德雲

Dongchansi 東禪寺

Dongshan Liangjie 洞山良价

Dongshan Shouchu 洞山守初

Dongting 洞庭

*Dongting Yulu* 洞庭語錄

Dufeng Benshan 毒峰本善

dui 對

duo 咄

Eihei Dōgen 永平道元

Fanghui Wanli　方回萬里
Fayan Wenyi　法眼文益
Fengxue　風穴
Fenyang Shanzao　汾陽善昭
*Fenyang Wude Chanshi Songgu Daibei*　汾陽無德禪師頌古代別
Fenyang　汾陽
Foguo Chanshi　佛果禪師
Fojian Huiqin　佛鑑慧懃
Fori　佛日
Foyan Qingyuan　佛眼清遠
Foyin Liaoyuan　佛印了元
Fu Daishi　傅大士
Fūgai Honkō　風外本光
Furong Daokai　芙蓉道楷
Gag'un　覺雲
Gānshǐjué/Kanshiketsu　乾屎橛
Gaofeng Yuanmiao　高峰原妙
Gaozong　高宗
ge　合
Genrō Ōryū　玄樓奧龍
geteng/kattō　葛藤
gongan/kōan　公案
guan/kan　關
Guanyu Wudeng　關友無黨
Guishan Lingyou　溈山靈祐
Guiyang　溈仰
Guizong　歸宗
guren　古人
guze　古則
Haiyin Xin　海印信
hakanai　儚い
Hakuin Ekaku　白隱慧鶴
Hakusan Myōri Gongen　白山妙理権現
Hanlin　翰林院
Hanshan　寒山
he　和
he　結
*Hekigan Agyō*　碧巖下語
*Hekigan Hyakusokuben*　碧巖百則辨
*Hekiganroku Hisshō*　碧巖録秘抄
*Hekiganroku Kōgi*　碧巖録講義
Heshan　禾山

Hongzhi Zhengjue　宏智正覺
Hongzhou　洪州
honmatsu wo tentō suru na　本末を転倒するな
hua　話
Huangbo Xiyun　黃檗希運
Huangchao　黃巢
Huanglong　橫龍
huatou/watō　話頭
Huichang　會昌
Huichao　慧超
Huineng　惠能
Huishi　慧思
Huitang Zuxin　晦堂祖心
Huiyan Zhizhao　晦巖智昭
Huizong　宋徽宗
Huqiu Shaolong　虎丘紹隆
*Hyakunijūsoku*　百二十則
Hyesim　慧諶
hyōgen sayō　表現作用
*Ichiya Hekigan*　一夜碧岩
Ikkyū　一休
Iriya Yoshitaka　入矢義高
(Iron Grindstone) Liu　鐵磨劉
ji/ki　機
jianchen gongan　見成公案
Jiangshansi　江山寺
jianxing/kenshō　見性
jiaochi　交馳
jiaowai biezhuan, buli wenzi　教外別傳, 不立文字
Jiashan　夾山
jifeng　機鋒
jijie tanshang　擊節嘆賞
*Jijielu*　擊節錄
jijing　機境
*Jingde Chuandenglu*　景德傳燈錄
Jingqing　鏡清
Jingshan　徑山
Jinshin Inga　深信因果
Jinul　智訥
jiyi　機宜
jiyuan wenda　機緣問答
Jizang　吉藏

Jogye　曹溪

Juefan Huihong　覺範慧洪

jueju　絕句

jugu/kyoko　舉古

Kaishan Qian　開善謙

Kajitani Sōnin　梶谷宗忍

Kamakura　鎌倉

kanbun　漢文

kanhua Chan　看話禪

Keizan Jōkin　瑩山紹瑾

*Kenzeiki*　建撕記

kirigami　切り紙

koke teien　苔庭園

*Kongguji*　空谷集

kyōsaku/keisaku　警策

*Kyōunshū*　狂雲集

Lanqi Daolong/Rankei Dōryū　蘭溪道隆

(Layman) Pang　龐居士

(Librarian) Qing　慶藏主

Lingyuan Weiqing　靈源惟清

*Linji Zhengzongji*　臨濟正宗記

Linji/Rinzai　臨濟

*Linjianlu*　林間錄

Linji-Huanglong　臨濟橫龍

*Linjilu*　臨濟錄

Linji-Yangqi　臨濟楊岐

Linquan Conglun　林泉從倫

Longmian　龍眠

Longmen　龍門

Longya　龍牙

*Lunyu*　論語

Magu　麻谷

*Mana Shōbōgenzō*　真字正法眼蔵

Manzan Dōhaku　卍山道白

Masanjin　麻三斤

Mazu　馬祖

Menren Wenzhen　門人文軫

Menzan Zuihō　面山瑞方

Miaofeng Shan　妙峰善

Miaoxi　妙喜

Mingjue　明覺

Mingzhao　明招

Missan　密參

mozhao Chan　默照禪

Muan Shanqing　睦庵善卿

*Muchū Mondō*　夢中問答

Mujaku Dōchū　無著道忠

mushō　無生

Musō Soseki　夢窓疎石

Muzhou　睦州

Nanquan　南泉

Nianfo　念佛

niangu　拈古

*Nianguji*　拈古集

Niutou　牛頭

Nyogen Senzaki　如幻千崎

Ogawa Takashi　小川隆

Peixiu　裴秀

ping　評

pingchang/hyōshō　評唱

pingshi Chan　平事禅

Puanyuan Renxi　普安仁銑

Puhua　普化

*Puquanji*　瀑泉集

pushou　普說

Puzhao　普照

qingqui　清規

qingtan　清談

*Qingyilu*　請益錄

*Qingzhou Baiwen*　青州百問

quanji/zenki　全機

*Rentian Yanmu*　人天眼目

Rinka　林下

Rujing　如淨

rulai Chan　如来禅

Ruyu　如玉

Ryūgin　龍吟

Sanbyōkyōdan　三宝教団

Sanjiao Laoren　三教老人

sanju　三句

Sansheng　三聖

*Sanshō Goyō*　參詳要語

sanxuan　三玄

sanyao　三要

satori e, satori kara　悟りえ, 悟りから

satori　悟り

satoru　悟る

*Seonmun Yeomsong Seolhwa*　禪門拈頌説話

*Seonmun Yeomsongjip*　禪門拈頌集

Shandao　善導

shangtang　上堂

Shenzong　神宗

shidafu　士大夫

shihua　詩話

*Shimen Linjianlu*　石門林間録

*Shimen Yuncong*　石門蘊聰

Shinchi Kakushin　心地覺心

Shishuang　石霜

Shitou　石頭

shizhong　示衆

*Shōbōgenzō Sanbyakusoku*　正法眼蔵三百則

shōmono　抄物

Shōmonosha　抄物者

shu　書

*Shūmon Kattōshū*　宗門葛藤集

*Shūmon Mujintōron*　宗門無盡燈論

Shushan Guangren　疎山光仁

*Sijia Pingchanglu*　四家評唱

Sixin Wuxin　死心悟新

Song Chan　宋禪

songgu/juko　頌古

*Songguji*　頌古集

Sōtō Zen　曹洞禪

*Sōtōshū Zensho*　曹洞宗全書

sottaku dōji　啐啄同時

Su Shi [Su Dongpo]　蘇軾/蘇東坡

Sueki Fumihiko　末木文美士

Suzong　肅宗

taming　塔銘

Taiping Xingguosi　太平興國寺

Taizong　太宗

Taizu　太祖

Tang　唐

Tanying　曇穎

Tao Qian/Tao Yuanming　陶謙/陶淵明

*Teiho Kenzeiki Zue*　訂補建撕記圖會

Tenkei Denson　天柱傳尊

*Tetteki Tōsui*　鐵笛倒吹

ti/tei　提

Tianning Wanshousi　天寧萬壽寺

Tianqi Benrui　天奇本瑞

*Tiansheng Guangdenglu*　天聖広燈錄

Tiantai Deshao　天台德韶

Tiantong　天童

tichang/teishō　提唱

*Tongxuan Baiwen*　通玄百問

*Tongxuan Qingzhou Erbaiwen*　通玄青州二百問

Tōrei Enji　東嶺圓慈

Touzi Yiqing　投子義青

Tōyō Eichō　東陽英朝

tutishen/dojishin　土地神

Uji　有時

Wan'an Daoyan　卍庵道顏

Wannian　萬年

Wansong Xingxiu　萬松行秀

Weilin Daopei　為霖道霈

wen　文

wenming　文明

wenzi Chan　文字禪

wu/mu　無

*Wudeng Huiyuan*　五燈會元

*Wujia Zongpai*　五家宗派

*Wujia Zongyao*　五家宗要

wujia　五家

Wumen　無門

*Wumenguan*　無門關

Wushan/Gozan　五山

wushi　無事

wuwei pianzheng　五位偏正

wuxin　無心

Wuyi Yuanlai　無異元來

wuzi Chan　無字禪

Wuzong　武宗

Wuzu Fayan　五祖法演

Xi Ling　希陵

xiancheng gongan/genjōkōan　現成公案

xiangban　香板

Xiangyan Zhixian　香嚴智閑

xiaocan　小參

Xiaoliangzhou　小梁州

Xiaozong　孝宗

*Xin Yao*　心要

Xinwen Tanben　心聞曇賁

Xu Yun　虛云

xuanji　對機

Xuansha　玄沙

Xuanzong　宣宗

Xuedou Chongxian　雪竇重顯

*Xuedou Heshang Nianguji*　雪竇和尚拈古集

*Xuedou Houlu*　雪竇後錄

*Xuedou Kaitanglu*　雪竇開堂錄

*Xuedou Qibuji*　雪竇七部集

*Xuedou Songgu*　雪竇頌古

Xuedoushan　雪竇山

Xuefeng　雪峰

Xuetang　雪堂

Xueyan Zuqin　雪巖祖欽

Xutang　虛堂

*Xutangji*　虛堂集

Yamada Kōun　山田耕雲

Yamada Mumon　山田無文

Yanagida Seizan　柳田聖山

Yangqi　楊岐

Yangshan Huiji　仰山慧寂

Yantou　巖頭

Yaoshan Weiyan　藥山惟儼

Yelü Chucai　耶律楚材

yiji yijing　一機一境

Yinzhi　隱之

yiqing　疑情

Yishan Yining　一山一寧

Yongming Yanshou　永明延壽

Yuanwu Chanshi　圓悟禪師

*Yuanwu Foguo Chanshi Yulu*　圓悟佛果禪師語錄

Yuanwu Keqin/Foguo Yuanwu　圓悟克勤

*Yuanwu Xinyao*　圓悟心要

*Yuanwu Yulu*　圓悟語錄

Yuanying　元瑩

Yucen Xiuxiu　玉岑休休

Yue'an　月庵

yulu/goroku 語録
Yunjushan 雲居山
Yunmen 雲門
Yunmen Wenyan 雲門文偃
*Yunmen Yulu* 雲門語録
Yunqi 雲隠
Ze/soku 則
Zeami 世阿弥
Zeng Hui 曾会
*Zengaku Tenseki Sōkan* 禅学典籍叢刊
*Zengo Jiten* 禪語辭典
*Zenrin Kushū* 禪林句集
Zhang Dian 張顛
Zhang Shangying 張商英
Zhanghui Mingyuan 張明遠
Zhantang Wenzhun 湛堂文準
Zhaojue 昭覺寺
zhaoyu 著語
Zhaozhou Congshen 趙州從諗
Zhaozhou 趙州
zheng 證
*Zhengfayanzang/Shōbōgenzō* 正法眼藏
Zhenjing Kewen 真淨克文
Zhenjue Chanshi 真覺禪師
Zhenru 真如
Zhenzong 宋真宗
Zhimen Guangzuo 智門光祚
Zhimen 智門
Zhongfeng Mingben 中峰明本
zhongwen qingwu 重文輕武
Zhou Chi 周墀
Zhu Xi 朱熹
zhuan 轉
Zhuangzi 莊子
zhuoyu 着語
zhuoyu/jakugo 著語
Zifu Rubao 資福如寶
ziji 自己
Zisheng 資聖寺
zishouyong sanmei 自受用三昧
*Zongmen Shigui Lun* 宗門十規論
*Zongmen Tongyaoji* 宗門統要集

Zongmi　宗密
zuojia　作家
zushi Chan　祖師禪
Zutangji　祖堂集
*Zuting Shiyuan*　祖庭事苑
*Zuyingji*　祖英集

# Bibliography

## Abbreviations

CBETA  Chinese   Buddhist   Electronic   Text   Association   (cbeta. org)  中華電子佛典協會

  T *Taishō Shinshū Daizōkyō*  大正新脩大藏經, 100 vols.

  X *Xu Zangjing*  續藏經, 150 vols.

### CHINESE BUDDHIST TEXTS (IN CBETA)

[*Xuedou*] *Baize Songgu*  [雪竇]百則頌古 [in Iriya, Kajitani, and Yanagida, 1981]

  *Baojing Sanmei*  寶鏡三昧 T.47.1986A

  *Biyanlu*  碧巖錄 T.48.2003

  *Changuan Cejin*  禪關策進 T.48.2024

  *Chanlin Baoxun*  禪林寶訓 T.48.2022

  *Chanlin Sengbao Zhuan*  禪林僧宝傳 X.79.1560

  *Chanlin Leiju*  禪林類聚 X.67.1299

  *Chanyuan Qinggui*  禪苑清規 X.63.1245

  *Chanzong Jueyiji*  禪宗決疑集 T.48.2021

  *Chanzong Songgu Lianzhu Tongji*  禪宗頌古聯珠通集 X.65.1295

  *Chuanxin Fayao*  傳心法要 T.48.2012A

  *Congronglu*  從容錄 T.48.2004

  *Dahui Pujue Chanshi Nianpu*  大慧普覺禪師年譜 J.01.A42 [Japan collection]

  *Dahui Shu*  大慧書 X.73.1456

  *Dahui Wuku*  大慧武庫 T.47.1998B

  *Dahui Yulu*  大慧語錄 T.47.1998A

  *Fayan Chanshi Yulu*  法演禪師語錄 T.47.1995

  *Fenyang Wude Chanshi Yulu*  汾陽無德禪師語錄 T.47.1992

  *Guzunsulu*  古尊宿語錄 X.68.1315

  *Hongzhilu*  宏智錄 T.48.2001

  *Jiatai Pudenglu*  嘉泰普燈錄 X.79.1559

  *Jijuelu*  擊節錄 X.67.1301

*Jingde Chuandenglu* 景德傳燈 T.51.2076

*Kongguiji* 空谷集 X.67.1303

*Liandeng Huiyao* 聯燈會要 X.79.1557

*Mingjue Chanshi Yulu* 明覺禪師語錄 T.47.1996

*Qingyilu* 請益錄 X.67.1307

*Qingzhou Baiwen* 青州百問 X.67.1313

*Rentian Yanmu* 人天眼目 T.48.2006

*Shanfang Yehua* 山房夜話 T.47.1524

*Shimen Wenzi Chan* 石門文字禪 X.73.1452

*Song Gaosengzhuan* 宋高僧傳 T.50.2061

*Tianqi Zhizhu Hongzhi Songgu* 天奇直註天童頌古 X.67.1306

*Tianqi Zhizhu Xuedou Songgu* 天奇直註雪竇頌古 X.67.1302

*Tiansheng Guangdenglu* 天聖廣燈錄 X.78.1553

*Tongxuan Baiwen* 通玄百問 X.67.1312

*Wudeng Huiyuan* 五燈會元 X.80.1565

*Wumen Heshang Yulu* 無門和尚語錄 X.69.1355

*Wumenguan* 無門關 T.48.2005

*Xu Guzunsu Yuyao* 續古尊宿語要 X.68.1318

*Xutang ji* 虛堂集 X.67.1304

*Yuanwu Foguo Chanshi Yulu* 佛果圜悟禪師碧巖錄 T.48.2003

*Yuanwu Keqin Xhanshi Yuyao* 圓悟佛果禪師語錄 T.47.1997

*Yunmen Kuangzhen Xhanshi Guanglu* 雲門匡真禪師廣錄 T.47.1988

*Zhaozhoulu* 趙州錄 X.68.1314

*Zhengfayanzang* 正法眼藏 X.67.1309

*Zhiyuelu* 指月錄 X.83.1578

*Zongjinglu* 宗鏡錄 T.48.2016

*Zongmen Liandeng Huiyao* 宗門聯燈會要 X.79.1557

*Zongmen Niangu Huiji* 宗門拈古彙集 X.66.1296

*Zongmen Tongyaoji* 宗門統要集 [in Komazawa U archive]

### DICTIONARIES

Morohashi Tetsuji. *Dai Kan-Wa Jiten*. 13 vols. Tokyo: Taishūkan shoten, 1955–1960.

Soothill, William Edward and Lewis Hodous. *A Dictionary of Chinese Buddhist Terms*. London: Kegan Paul, Trench, Trubner, 1937; rpt, Taipei: Buddhist Culture Service, 1962.

Zengaku Daijiten Hensansho, ed. *Zengaku Daijiten*. 3 vols. Tokyo: Taishūkan shoten, 1985.

### SELECTED SOURCES

Abe Chōichi. *Chūgoku Zenshū no Kenkyū*. Tokyo: Seishin shobō, 1963.

Ahn, Juhn Young, trans. *Collected Works of Korean Buddhism*, vol. 7–1, *Gongan Collections I*, ed. John Jorgensen. Seoul: Jogye Order of Korean Buddhism, 2012.

———, trans. *Collected Works of Korean Buddhism*, vol. 7–2. *Gongan Collections II*, ed. John Jorgensen. Seoul: Jogye Order of Korean Buddhism, 2012.

———. "Malady of Meditation: A Prolegomenon to the Study of Illness and Zen." PhD diss., University of California at Berkeley, 2007.

———. "Who Has the Last Word in Chan? Transmission, Secrecy and Reading During the Northern Song Dynasty." *Journal of Chinese Religions* 37 (2009), 1–71.

Anderl, Christoph. "Chan Rhetoric: An Introduction." In *Zen Buddhist Rhetoric in China, Korea, and Japan*, ed. Christoph Anderl. Leiden: Brill, 2012, 1–94.

Andō Yoshinori. *Chūsei Zenshū Bunseki no Kenkyū*. Tokyo: Kokusho inkōkai, 2000.

App, Urs. "Facets of the Life and Teaching of Chan Master Yunmen Wenyan (864–949). (Volumes 1 and 11)." PhD diss., Temple University, 1989.

———. *The Making of a Chan Record: Reflections on the History of the Records of Yunmen, Zen Bunka Kenkyūjo Kiyō* 17 (1991), 1–90.

———. *Master Yunmen: From the Record of the Chan Teacher "Gate of the Clouds."* New York: Kodansha, 1994.

Arntzen, Sonja. *The Poetry of the Kyōunshū "Crazy Cloud Anthology" of Ikkyū Sōjun*. Vancouver: University of British Columbia, 1979.

Balcom, John, John Gill, and Susan Tidwell, trans. *After Many Autumns: A Collection of Chinese Buddhist Literature*. Hacienda Heights, CA: Buddha's Light, 2011.

Barnstone, Tony, and Chou Ping, trans. *The Art of Writing: Teaching of the Chinese Masters*. Boston: Shambhala, 1996.

Bodiford, William. *Sōtō Zen in Medieval Japan*. Honolulu: University of Hawaii Press, 1993.

———. "Keyword Meditation and Detailed Investigation in Medieval Japan." In *Ganhwa Seon: Illuminating the World, Conference Proceedings*. Seoul: Dongguk University Press, 2010, 59–121.

———. "The Rhetoric of Chinese Language in Japanese Zen." In *Zen Buddhist Rhetoric in China, Korea, and Japan*, ed. Christoph Anderl. Leiden: Brill, 2012, 285–314.

Bol, Peter K. *"This Culture of Ours": Intellectual Transitions in T'ang and Sung China*. Stanford, CA: Stanford University Press, 1992.

Brody, Richard. "The Best of Thelonius Monk." *The New Yorker*, May 20, 2015.

Brose, Ben. "Crossing Thousands of Li of Waves: The Return of China's Lost Tiantai Texts." *Journal of the International Association of Buddhist Studies* 29/1 (2008), 21–62.

Broughton, Jeffrey L., trans. with Elise Yoko Watanabe. *The Chan Whip Anthology: A Companion to Zen Practice*. New York: Oxford University Press, 2014.

———, trans. with Elise Yoko Watanabe. *The Record of Linji: A New Translation of the Linjilu in the Light of Ten Japanese Zen Commentaries*. New York: Oxford University Press, 2012.

Buswell, Jr., Robert E. *The Korean Approach to Zen: The Collected Works of Chinul.* Honolulu: University of Hawaii Press, 1983.

———. "The 'Short-cut' Approach of K'an-hua Meditation: The Evolution of a Practical Subitism in Chinese Ch'an Buddhism." In *Sudden and Gradual: Approaches to Enlightenment in Chinese Thought,* ed. Peter N. Gregory. Honolulu: University of Hawaii Press, 1987, 321–377.

———. "The Transformation of Doubt (*Yiqing*) into a Positive Emotion in Chinese Buddhist Meditation." In *Love and Emotions in Traditional Chinese Literature,* ed. Halvor Eifring, Leiden: E. J. Brill, 2004, 225–236.

———, and Donald S. Lopez, Jr., eds. *The Princeton Dictionary of Buddhism.* Princeton: Princeton University Press, 2014.

Cai, Zong-qi. *How to Read Chinese Poetry: A Guided Anthology.* New York: Columbia University Press, 2008.

Cassirer, Ernst. *Language and Myth.* New York: Dover, 1953.

Chaffee, John W. *The Thorny Gates of Learning in Sung China.* Cambridge: Cambridge University Press, 1985.

Chan, Chung-yuan. *Original Teachings of Ch'an Buddhism: Selected from the Transmission of the Lamp.* New York: Grove Press, 1969.

Changjiu Liu. *Zhongguo Chanzong.* Beijing: Guangxi Shifan Daxue chubanshe, 2005.

Chappell, David W., ed. *Buddhist and Taoist Practice in Medieval Chinese Society: Buddhist and Taoist Studies II.* Honolulu: University of Hawaii Press, 1987.

Cherniack, Susan. "Book Culture and Textual Transmission in Sung China." *Harvard Journal of Asiatic Studies* 54/1 (1994), 5–125.

Cleary, J. C. trans. *A Buddha From Korea: The Zen Teachings of Taego.* Boston: Shambhala, 1988.

———, trans. *Swampland Flowers: The Letters and Lectures of Zen Master Ta-Hui.* Boston: Shambhala, rpt. 2006 (1978).

Cleary, Thomas. *The Blue Cliff Record.* Berkeley, CA: Numata, 1998.

———, trans. *Book of Serenity: One Hundred Zen Dialogues.* Hudson, NY: Lindisfarne Press, 1990.

———, trans. "Introduction to the History of Zen Practice." In *The Gateless Gate.* trans. Kōun Yamada. Boston: Wisdom, 2004, 247–263.

———, trans. *Secrets of the Blue Cliff Record: Zen Comments by Hakuin and Tenkei.* Boston: Shambhala, 2000.

———, trans. *Timeless Spring: A Soto Zen Anthology.* New York: Weatherhill, 1980.

———, trans. "Translator's Introduction." *Zen Lessons: The Art of Leadership.* Boston: Shambhala, 1989.

———, trans. *The Undying Lamp of Zen: The Testament of Zen Master Torei.* Boston: Shambhala, 2010.

Cleary, Thomas and J. C. Cleary, trans. *The Blue Cliff Record,* 3 vols. Boston: Shambhala, 1977.

Collcutt, Martin. "The Early Ch'an Monasic Rule: *Ch'ing-kuei* and the Shaping of Ch'an Community Life." In *Early Ch'an in China and Tibet*, ed. Whalen Lai and Lewis Lancaster. Berkeley, CA: Berkeley Buddhist Studies Series, 1983, 165–84.

———. *Five Mountains: The Rinzai Zen Monastic Institution in Medieval Japan.* Cambridge, MA: Harvard University Press, 1981.

Crain, Caleb. "The Red and the Scarlet: The Hectic Career of Stephen Crane." *The New Yorker*, June 30, 2014.

Davis, Bret W., trans. "Nishitani Keiji's 'The Standpoint of Zen: Directly Pointing to the Mind." In *Buddhist Philosophy: Essential Readings*, ed. William Edelglass and Jay L. Garfield. New York: Oxford University Press, 2009, 93–102.

Ding, Weixiang, "Zhu Xi's Choice, Historical Criticism and Influence—An Analysis of Zhu Xi's Relationship with Confucianism and Buddhism." *Frontiers in Philosophy of China* 6/4 (2011), 521–548.

Döll, Steffen. *Im Osten des Meeres. Chinesische Emigrantenmönche unddie frühen Institutionen des japanischen Zen-Buddhismus.* Stuttgart: Franz Steiner Verlag, 2010.

Duan Yuming and Yanfa Shi, et al. *Yuanwu Keqin Zhuan.* Beijing: Zongjiao wenhua chubanshe, 2012.

Dumoulin, Heinrich. *Zen Buddhism: A History, India and China*, trans. James W. Heisig and Paul Knitter. New York: Macmillan, 1988.

———. *Zen Buddhism: A History, Japan*, trans. James W. Heisig and Paul Knitter. New York: Macmillan, 1990.

Eberhard, Wolfram. *A History of China.* Berkeley: University of California Press, 1977.

Edson, Howard. *What Color Is Your Paradigm: Thinking for Shaping Life and Results.* N.p.: The Management Advantage, 2003.

Egan, Charles. *Clouds Thick, Whereabouts Unknown: Poems by Zen Monks of China.* New York: Columbia University Press, 2010.

Ferguson, Andy. *Zen's Chinese Teachings: The Masters and Their Heritage.* Boston: Wisdom, rpt. 2011.

Foulk, Theodore Griffith. "The 'Ch'an School' and Its Place in the Buddhist Monastic Tradition." PhD diss., University of Michigan, 1987.

Fox, Alan. "Self-reflection in the Sanlun Tradition: Madhyamika as the 'Deconstructive Conscience' of Buddhism." *Journal of Chinese Philosophy* 19 (1992), 1–24.

Fu, Charles Wei-hsun. "Chu Hsi on Buddhism." In *Chu Hsi and Neo-Confucianism*, ed. Wing-tsit Chan. Honolulu: University of Hawaii Press, 1986, 377–407.

Genro, Fugai and Nyogen Senzaki. *The Iron Flute: 100 Zen Kōans.* Ed. Ruth Strauss McCandless and Nyogen Senzaki. Rutland, VT: Tuttle, 1961.

Gernet, Jacques. *Daily Life in China on the Eve of the Mongol Invasion 1250–1276.* Stanford, CA: Stanford University Press, 1962.

Gimello, Robert M. "Chang Shang-ying on Wu-t'ai Shan." In *Pilgrims and Sacred Sites in China*, ed. Susan Naquin and Chün-fang Yü. Berkeley: University of California Press, 1992, 89–149.

———. "Marga and Culture: Learning, Letters, and Liberation in Northern Sung Ch'an." In *Paths to Liberation: The Mārga and Its Transformations in Buddhist Thought*, ed. Robert E. Buswell, Jr. and Robert M. Gimello. Honolulu: University of Hawaii Press, 1992, 371–437.

Grant, Beata. *Mount Lu Revisited: Buddhism in the Life and Writings of Su Shih.* Honolulu: University of Hawaii Press, 1994.

Grimstone, A. V. "Introduction," *Two Zen Classics: Hekiganroku, Mumonkan.* New York: Weatherhill, 1977.

Gundert, Wilhelm, trans. *Bi-Yän-Lu Meister Yüan-wu's Niederschrift von der Smaragdenen Felswand, verfasst auf dem Djia-schan bei Li in Hunan zwischen 1111 und 1115 im Druck erschienen in Sïtschuan um 1300.* Munich: Karl Hauser, 1954, 1965, 1973.

Guo-Jing. "Realization through Hearing in Chan Literature," trans. Jeffrey Kotyk. *Journal of Chinese Buddhist Studies* 27 (2014), 129–179.

Hakuin, *Hekiganroku Hisshō.* Tokyo: Nagata shunyū, 1915.

Hartwell, Robert M. "Demographic, Political and Social Transformations of China, 750–1550." *Harvard Journal of Asiatic Studies* 42 (1982), 365–442.

Haskel, Peter. "Bankei and His World." *Zen Notes* 56/4 (2009), 12–18.

Heine, Steven. *Dōgen and the Kōan Tradition: A Tale of Two Shōbōgenzō Texts.* Albany: State University of New York Press, 1994.

———. "Introduction: Fourth-Wave Studies of Chan/Zen Buddhist Discourse." *Frontiers History China* 8/3 (2013), 309–315.

———. *Like Cats and Dogs: Contesting the Mu Kōan in Zen Buddhism.* New York: Oxford University Press, 2014.

———. "Visions, Divisions, Revisions: The Encounter Between Iconoclasm and Supernaturalism in Kōan Cases about Mount Wu-t'ai." In *The Kōan*, ed. Steven Heine and Dale S. Wright. New York: Oxford University Press, 2000, 137–167.

———. *The Zen Poetry of Dōgen: Verses from the Mountain of Eternal Peace.* Mt. Tremper, NY: Dharma Communications, 2004.

———. *Zen Skin, Zen Marrow: Will the Real Zen Buddhism Please Stand Up?* New York: Oxford University Press, 2008.

Heller, Natasha. "The Chan Master as Illusionist: Zhongfeng Mingben's *Huanshu Jiaxun.*" *Harvard Journal of Asiatic Studies* 69/2 (2009), 271–308.

———. *Illusory Abiding: The Cultural Construction of the Chan Monk Zhongfeng Mingben.* Cambridge, MA: Harvard University Press, 2014.

———. "Why Has the Rhinoceros Come from the West? An Excursus into the Religious, Literary, and Environmental History of the Tang Dynasty." *Journal of the American Oriental Society* 131/3 (2011), 353–370.

Hirota Sōgen. "Daie Sōkō no *Hekiganroku* Shōkyaku no Mondai." *Zengaku Kenkyū* 82 (2004), 107–128.

Hori, Victor Sogen. *Zen Sand: The Book of Capping Phrases for Kōan Practice.* Honolulu: University of Hawaii Press, 2003.

Hsieh, Ding-hwa Evelyn. "Poetry and Chan 'Gong'an': From Xuedou Chongxian (980–1052) to Wumen Huikai (1183–1260)." *Journal of Song-Yuan Studies* 40 (2010), 39–70.

———. "A Study of the Evolution of *k'an-hua* Ch'an in Sung China: Yüan-wu K'o-ch'in (1063–1135) and the Function of *kung-an* in Ch'an Pedagogy and Praxis." PhD diss., University of California, Los Angeles, 1993.

———. "Yuan-wu K'o-ch'in's (1063–1135) Teaching of Ch'an *Kung-an* Practice: A Transition from the Literary Study of Ch'an *Kung-an* to the Practice *K'an-hua* Ch'an." *Journal of the International Association of Buddhist Studies* 17/1 (1994), 66–95.

Huang, Chi-chiang. "Elite and Clergy in Northern Sung Hang-chou: A Convergence of Interest." In *Buddhism in the Sung*, ed. Peter N. Gregory and Daniel A. Getz, Jr. Honolulu: University of Hawaii Press, 1999, 295–339.

———. "Experiment in Syncretism: Ch'i-sung (1007–1072) an 11th Century Chinese Buddhism." PhD diss., University of Arizona, 1986.

Huang, Jing-Jia. "A Study on Imitating Activities of Hanshan Poems by Chan Buddhist Monks in Song Dynasty." *Journal of Literature and Art Studies* 3/4 (2013), 204–212.

Huang Xianian, and Cengwen Yang, eds. *Biyanlu*. Zhengzhou: Zhongzhou guji chubanshe, 2011.

Huang, Yi-hsun. "Chan Master Xuedou and His Remarks on Old Cases in the *Record of Master Xuedou at Dongting*: A Preliminary Study." *Chung-Hwa Buddhist Journal* 22 (2009), 69–96.

Huang Yun-chung, *Chanzong Gongan Tixiangyong Sixiang Zhi Yanjiu*. Taipei: Taiwan zuesheng shuju yinxing, 2002.

Inoue Shūten. *Hekiganroku Shin Kōwa*. Tokyo: Kyōbun shoten, 1931.

Iriya Yoshitaka. "Chinese Poetry and Zen." *The Eastern Buddhist* 6/1 (1973), 54–67.

——— et al., eds. *Hekiganroku*, 3 vols. Tokyo: Iwanami bunko, 1994–96.

Iriya Yoshitaka, Kajitani Sōnin, and Yanagida Seizan, eds. *Setchō Hyakusoku Juko*, Zen no Goroku 15. Tokyo: Chikuma shobō, 1981.

Ishii Seijun, *Zen Mondō Nyūmon*. Tokyo: Kadokawa sensho 463, 2010.

Ishii Shūdō. "Chinese Chan and Dōgen Zen: Regarding Their Continuities and Discontinuities." Saishū Kōgi: Chūgoku Zen to Dōgen Zen—Sono Renzoku to Hirenzoku to nitsuite. Farewell Lecture at Komazawa University, Tokyo, January 24, 2014.

———. *Chūgoku Zenshūshi Wa: "Mana Shōbōgenzō" ni Manabu*. Kyoto: Zen bunka kenkyūjo, 1988.

———. "*Daie Fukaku Zenji Nenpu Kenkyū*." *Komazawa Daigaku Bukkyōgakubu Kenkyūkiyō*, 37 (1979), 110–143; 38 (1980), 97–133; 40 (1982), 129–175.

———. "Daie Goroku no Kisōteki Kenkyū—*Shōbōgenzō* no Shuten to *Rentōeyō* to no Kankei." *Komazawa Daigaku Bukkyōgakubu Kenkyūkiyō* 32 (1974), 215–262.

————. "*Shūmon Tōyōshū* to *Hekiganroku.*" *Indogaku Bukkyōgaku Kenkyū* 46/1 (2001), 215–221.

Itō Yuten. *Hekiganshū Teihon.* Tokyo: Kabushiki kaisha, Risōsha, 1963.

Jan, Yün-hua. "Buddhist Historiography in Sung China." *Zeitschrift der deutschen morgenländischen Gesellschaft* 114 (1969), 360–81.

————, "Chinese Buddhism in Ta-tu." In *Yüan Thought: Chinese Thought and Religion Under the Mongols,* ed. Hok-lam Chan and Wm. Theodore de Bary. New York: Columbia, 1982.

Jha, Alok. "What Is Heisenberg's Uncertainty Principle?" *Science,* November 10, 2013. http://www.theguardian.com/science/2013/nov/10/what-is-heisenbergs-uncertainty-principle. Accessed December 6, 2014.

Johnson, Norris Brock. "Mountain, Temple, and the Design of Movement: Thirteenth-Century Japanese Zen Buddhist Landscapes." In *Landscape Design and the Experience of Motion,* ed. Michael Conan. Washington, DC: Dumbarton Oaks Research Library, 2003, 157–185.

————. *Tenryū-ji: Life and Spirit of a Kyoto Garden.* Albany, CA: Stone Bridge Press, 2012.

Joskovich, Erez. "'Playing the Patriarch': The Zen Master Sermon as a Ritual Performance." Lecture at Tel Aviv University, Tel Aviv, June 16, 2014.

Joyce, James. *Dubliners.* Clayton, DE: Prestwick House Literary Touchstone Classics, 2006.

Kabanoff, Alexander. "Man and Nature in Gozan Poetry." *Petersburg Journal of Cultural Studies* 1/2 (1994), 73–88.

Kagamishima Genryū, ed. *Dōgen no In'yō Goroku no Kenkyū.* Tokyo: Sōtōshū shūgaku kenkyūjo, 1995.

Katō Totsudō. *Hekiganroku Daikōwa,* 15 vols. Tokyo: Heibonsha, 1939–40.

Kawamura Kōdō et al., eds. *Dōgen Zenji Zenshū,* 7 vols. Tokyo: Shunjūsha, 1988–1993.

————. *Eihei Dōgen Zenji Gyōjō: Kenzeiki.* Tokyo: Taishūkan, 1975.

Keyworth, George Albert, "Transmitting the Lamp of Learning in Classical Chan Buddhism: Juefan Huihong (1071–1128) and Literary Chan." PhD diss., University of California, Los Angeles, 2001.

Kirchner, Thomas Yuhō, trans. *Dialogues in a Dream.* Kyoto: Tenryū-ji Institution for Philosophy and Religion, 2010.

————, trans. *Entangling Vines: A Classic Collection of Zen Koans.* Boston: Wisdom, 2013.

————, ed. *The Record of Linji,* trans. Ruth Fuller Sasaki. Honolulu: University of Hawaii Press, 2008.

Kraft, Kenneth. *Eloquent Zen: Daitō and Early Japanese Zen.* Honolulu: University of Hawaii Press, 1992.

Lan Jifu. "Dahui Zonggao Fenshao *Biyanlu* Shijian de Lishi Pingshu—Fojiao Lunli Yu Shisu Lunli de Duili Jiqi Xiaojie." Tainan: n.p., 2014.

Lane, Anthony. "Go Ask Alice What Really Went on in Wonderland," *The New Yorker,* June 8, 2015.

Leighton, Taigen Dan. *Visions of Awakening in Space and Time: Dōgen and the Lotus Sutra.* New York: Oxford University Press, 2007.

Leighton, Taigen Dan, and Shohaku Okumura, trans. *Dōgen's Extensive Record: A Translation of the Eihei Kōroku.* Boston: Wisdom, 2004.

Levering, Miriam. "Ch'an Enlightenment for Laymen: Ta-hui and the New Religious Culture of the Sung." PhD diss., Harvard University, 1978.

———. "Dahui Zonggao (1089–1163): The Image Created by His Stories about Himself and His Teaching Style." In *Zen Masters,* ed. Steven Heine and Dale S. Wright. New York: Oxford University Press 2010, 91–116.

Levine, Gregory P. A. *Daitokuji: The Visual Cultures of a Zen Monastery.* Seattle: University of Washington Press, 2005.

Lewis, Zenrin R., trans. *The Blue Cliff Record Coming through Hakuin: The First Twenty Cases.* Jacksonville, FL: Zen Sangha Press, 2013.

Lin, Jih-chang. "A Critique and Discussion of the View That Shi Miyuan Proposed the Five-Mountain, Ten-Monastery System." *Journal of Cultural Interaction in East Asia* 5 (2014), 45–66.

Lin Ming-yü. *Chan Ji.* Taipei: Lianya chubanshe, 1979.

Loori, John Daido, "Dogen and Koans." In *Sitting With Kōans: Essential Writings on the Practice of Zen Koan Introspection,* ed. John Daido Loori. Boston: Wisdom, 2006, 151–162.

Lu, Wei-Yu. "The Performance Practice of Buddhist Baiqi in Contemporary Taiwan." PhD diss., University of Maryland, 2012.

Ma Tianxiang. "Yuanwu Keqin de *Biyanlu* Wenzi Chan de Fanlin" ("Yuanwu Keqin's *Blue Cliff Record* and the Output of Textual Chan"). *Xinan Minzu Daxue Xuebao* 1 (2011), 57–60.

Ma, Y. W. "Themes and Characterization in the Lung-T'u Kung-An." *T'oung Pao* LIX (1973), 179–202.

Maddox, Brenda. "Introduction," *Dubliners.* New York: Bantam, rpt. 1990 (1914).

Matsuzaki Kakuhon, ed. *Hekiganroku Kōgi: Tenkei Denson Teishō,* 10 vols. Tokyo: Kōyūkan, 1903.

McRae, John R. *The Northern School and the Formation of Early Ch'an Buddhism.* Honolulu: University of Hawaii Press, 1986.

———. *Seeing through Zen: Encounter, Transformation, and Genealogy in Chinese Chan Buddhism.* Berkeley: University of California Press, 2003.

Michel Mohr. "Japanese Zen Schools and the Transition to Meiji: A Plurality of Responses in the Nineteenth Century Japanese." *Journal of Religious Studies* 25/ 1–2 (1998), 167–213.

Murakami, Haruki. "Jazz Messenger." *New York Times,* July 8, 2007.

Nagai Masashi. "Xuedou no Goroku no Seiritsu ni Kansuru Ikkosatsu (part 2)." *Bukkyōgaku Kenkyū Nenpō* 7 (1973): 11–20.

Natali, Ilaria. "A Portrait of James Joyce's Epiphanies as a Source Text." *Humanicus* 6 (2011), 1–25.

Natsume Soseki. *The Gate*, trans. William F. Silby. New York: New York Review Books Classics, 2012.

Nishioka Shūji. "Shōyō ni okeru Akashi nitsuite—*Hekiganroku* to no Hikaku wo tōshite." *Indogaku Bukkyōgaku Kenkyū* 54/1 (2005), 155–158.

Niwano, Nikkyō. *Buddhism for Today: A Modern Interpretation of the Threefold Lotus Sutra.* Tokyo: Hosei, 1971.

Nukariya Kaiten. *Zengaku Shisōshi*, 2 vols. Tokyo: Meisho kankōsha, rpt. 1963.

Ogawa Takashi. *Goroku no Shisōshi: Chūgoku Zen no Kenkyū.* Tokyo: Iwanami shoten, 2011.

Pan, An-yi. *Painting Faith: Li Gonglin and Northern Song Buddhist Culture.* Leiden: Brill, 2007.

Poceski, Mario. *The Records of Mazu and the Making of Classical Chan Literature.* New York: Oxford University Press, 2015.

Protass, Jason. "Vegetables and Bamboo: Medieval Poetic Criticism of Buddhist Monastic Poetry." Unpublished paper presented in Kyoto and accessed by permission of the author in June 2012.

Rothenberg, David. *The Blue Cliff Record: Zen Echoes.* Albany: State University of New York Press, rpt. 2001.

Said, Edward. *On Late Style: Music and Literature Against the Grain.* New York: Vintage, rpt. 2007.

Sasaki, Ruth Fuller, and Isshū Miura. *The Zen Kōan: Its History and Use in Rinzai Zen.* New York: Harcourt, Brace & World, 1965.

Sasaki, Ruth Fuller, and Isshū Miura. *Zen Dust: The History of the Koan Study in Rinzai (Lin-chi) Zen.* New York: Harcourt, Brace, Jovanovich, 1966.

Sawada Tenzui. "Teien no Haigo Shisō to Kōsei ni kansuru Kenkyū (XIV)—Musō Kokushi to Tenryūji Teien no Kōsei nitsuite" (A Study on the Japanese Gardens Viewed from the Rinzai Zen Buddhism (XIV)—A Case Study on the Tenryuji Garden Kyoto)." *Zōen Zasshi (The Journal of the Japanese Institute of Landscape Architecture)* 43/2 (1979): 3–11.

Schlütter, Morten. *How Zen Became Zen: The Dispute Over Enlightenment and the Formation of Chan Buddhism in Song-Dynasty China.* Honolulu: University of Hawaii Press, 2009.

Sekida, Katsuki. *Two Zen Classics: Mumonkan and Hekiganroku*, ed. A. V. Grimstone. New York: Weatherhill, 1977.

Sharf, Robert H. "How to Think with Chan *Gong'an*." In *Thinking with Cases: Specialist Knowledge in Chinese Cultural History*, ed. Charlotte Further, Judith T. Zeitlin, and Ping-chen Hsiung. Honolulu: University of Hawaii Press, 2007, 205–243.

Shaw, R. D. M., trans. and ed. *The Blue Cliff Records: The Hekigan Roku, Containing One Hundred Stories of Zen Masters of Ancient China.* London: Michael Joseph, 1961.

Shibayama Zenkei and Jikihara Gyokusei. *Gōkōfūgetsushū.* Ōsaka: Sōgensha, 1991.

Shibe Ken'ichi, "Tenkei Denson to *Hekiganroku* nitsuite." *Indogaku Bukkyōgaku Kenkyū* 41/1 (1993), 277–280.

Shore, Jeff. *Zen Classics for the Modern World: Translations of Chinese Zen Poems & Prose with Contemporary Commentary.* N.p.: Diane Publishing, 2011.

Simons, Jake Wallis. "James Joyce's *Ulysses*: The Beginning of an Epiphany." *The Independent* January 25, 2012. http://blogs.independent.co.uk/2012/01/25/james-joyces-ulysses-the-beginning-of-an-epiphany/. Accessed February 3, 2015.

Sollien, Therese. "Sermons by Xu Yun—A Special Transmission within the Scriptures." In *Zen Buddhist Rhetoric in China, Korea, and Japan*, ed. Christoph Anderl. Leiden: Brill, 2012, 417–437.

Sueki Fumihiko. *Gendaigoyaku Heikiganroku*, 2 vols. Tokyo: Iwanami shoten, 2001–03.

———. *Hekiganroku o Yomu.* Tokyo: Iwanami seminaabukks 73, 1998.

———. "Sōdai Zenseki no Bunkenteki Kenkyū: *Hekiganroku* wo toshite." *Kaken Kenkyū Deetabeesu* (1989–1991), https://kaken.nii.ac.jp/d/p/01450002.ja.html. Accessed May 29, 2015.

Suzuki Daisetz T., *Bukka Hekigan Hakan Gekisetsu.* Tokyo: Iwanami shoten, 1942.

———, trans. "The *Hekigan-roku (Pi-yen Lu).*" *The Annual Report of Researches of the Matsugaoka Bunko* 26 (2012).

Takashi Ogawa. *Zoku: Goroku no Kotoba, Hekiganroku to Sōdai no Zen.* Kyoto: Zen bunka kenkyūjo, 2010.

Takeuchi Michio. "Dōgen Zenji *Hekiganroku* Shōrai nitsuite." *Indogaku Bukkyōgaku Kenkyū* 4/2 (1956), 476–477.

Tanahashi, Kazuaki, ed., *Treasury of the True Dharma Eye: Zen Master Dogen's Shobo Genzo.* Boston: Shambhala, 2010.

Tanahashi, Kazuaki, and John Daido Loori, trans. and eds. *The True Dharma Eye: Zen Master Dōgen's Three Hundred Kōans*, with Commentary and Verse by John Daido Loori. Boston: Shamhhala, 2005.

Tsuchiya Taisuke. "Shinsei Kokubun no Wuji Zen Hihan." *Indogaku Bukkyōgaoku* 51/1 (2003): 206–208.

Unger, Roberto. *False Necessity: Anti-Necessitarian Social Theory in the Service of Radical Democracy*, rev. ed. London: Verso, 2004, 279–280.

Wang, Youru. "The Pragmatics of 'Never Tell Too Plainly': Indirect Communication in Chan Buddhism." *Asian Philosophy* 10/1 (2000), 7–31.

Watson, Burton, trans. *The Complete Works of Chuang-tzu.* New York: Columba University Press, 1968.

Welter, Albert. *The Linji Lu and the Creation of Chan Orthodoxy: The Development of Chan's Records of Sayings Literature.* New York: Oxford University Press, 2008.

———. *Monks, Rulers, and Literati: The Political Ascendancy of Chan Buddhism.* New York: Oxford University Press, 2006.

Wittern, Christian. "Some Preliminary Remarks to a Study, Rhetorical Devices in Chan Yulu Encounter Dialogues." In *Zen Buddhist Rhetoric in China, Korea, and Japan*, ed. Christoph Anderl. Leiden: Brill, 2012, 265–284.

Wright, Dale S., *Philosophical Meditations on Zen Buddhism*. New York: Cambridge University Press, 2000.

Wu, Jiang. *Enlightenment in Dispute: The Reinvention of Chan Buddhism in Seventeenth-Century China*. New York: Oxford University Press, 2008.

Wu, John C. H. *The Golden Age of Zen*. Taipei: United Publishing Center, 1975.

Yamada, Kōun, trans. "Case 54: Unmon Stretches Out His Hands." *Hekiganroku (Blue Cliff Record)*. http://www.sanbo-zen.org/Heko54.pdf. Accessed January 26, 2015.

———, trans. "Case 87: Unmon's Medicine and Sickness." *Hekiganroku (Blue Cliff Record)*. http://www.sanbo-zen.org/Heko87.pdf. Accessed January 8, 2015.

Yamada Mumon. *Hekiganroku Zen Teishō*, 10 vols. Kyoto: Zen bunka kenkyūjo, 1985.

Yampolsky, Phillip, trans. *The Platform Sūtra of the Sixth Patriarch*. New York: Columbia University Press, 1967.

Yanagida Seizan. "The Development of the 'Recorded Sayings' Texts of the Chinese Ch'an School," trans. John R. McRae. In *Early Ch'an in China and Tibet*, ed. Lewis Lancaster and Whalen Lai. Berkeley, CA: Lancaster-Miller Press, 1983, 185–205.

———. "Kaisetsu." In *Setchō juko*, Zen no goroku 15. Tokyo: Chikuma shobō, 1981.

———. *Zen no Yuige*. Tokyo: Chōbunsha, 1973.

Yinshun. *Zhongguo Chanzong Shi*. Taipei: Zhengwen chubanshe, 1971.

Yizhang Ouyang. "'Biyanji' dian jiao 'shuoshi lunwen fulu.'" Taipei: n.p., 1994.

Yü, Chün-fang. "Ch'an Education in the Sung: Ideals and Procedures." In *Neo-Confucian Education; The Formative Stage*, ed. Wm. Theodore de Bary and John W. Chaffee. Berkeley: University of California Press, 1989. 57–104.

———. "Chung-fen Ming-pen and Ch'an Buddhism in the Yüan." In *Yüan Thought: Chinese Thought and Religion Under the Mongols*, ed. Hok-lam Chan and Wm. Theodore de Bary. New York: Columbia University Press, 1982, 432–455.

———. "Ta-hui Tsung-kao and *Kung-an* Ch'an." *Journal of Chinese Philosophy* 5/6 (1979): 20, 211–235.

Zeitlin, Dave. "Shell's Odyssey." *The Pennsylvania Gazette*, Sept.–Oct. 2013, 46–51.

*Zhongguo Chanzong Dianji Congkan: Biyanlu*. Zhengzhou: Zhongzhou guji chubanshe, 2013.

Zhou Yukai, *Chanzong Yuyan*. Taipei: Zongbo chubanshe, 2002.

Zhu, Caifang. "The Hermeneutics of Chan Buddhism: Reading Koans from *The Blue Cliff Record*." *Asian Philosophy* 21/4 (2011), 373–393.

Zong, Desheng. "Three Language-Related Methods in Early Chinese Chan Buddhism." *Philosophy East and West* 55/4 (2005), 584–602.

Zürcher, Erik. *The Buddhist Conquest of China: The Spread and Adaptation of Buddhism in Early Medieval China*, 2 vols. Leiden: E. J. Brill, 1959.

# Index